BUSINESS

ALWAYS LEARNING

PEARSON

Published by Pearson Education Limited, Edinburgh Gate, Harlow, Essex, CM20 2JE.

www.pearsonschoolsandfecolleges.co.uk

Text © Pearson Education Limited 2012, 2013
Typeset by Phoenix Photosetting, Chatham, Kent, UK
Original illustrations © Pearson Education Limited 2012, 2013
Illustrated by Adrian Barclay/KJA-artists.com and Phoenix Photosetting
Cover design by Pearson Education Limited and Andrew Magee Design
Front cover photos: Plainpicture Ltd: Scanpix
Indexing by Indexing Specialists (UK) Ltd. and Sophia Clapham

The rights of Carol Carysforth, Paul Bentley, Lisa Chandler-Corris, Mike Neild and Karen Glencross to
be identified as authors of this work have been asserted by them in accordance with the Copyright,
Designs and Patents Act 1988.

Units 1–8 first published 2012.
This full edition published 2013.

17 16 15 14
10 9 8 7 6 5 4 3

British Library Cataloguing in Publication Data
A catalogue record for this book is available from the British Library

ISBN 978 1 446901 36 6

Printed in Slovakia by Neografia

Websites
There are links to relevant websites in this book. In order to ensure that the links are up to date,
that the links works, and that the sites aren't inadvertently links to sites that could be considered
offensive, we have made the links available on our website at www.pearsonhotlinks.co.uk. Search for
the title BTEC First Business Student Book or
ISBN 978 1 446901 36 6.

Copies of official specifications for all Pearson qualifications may be found on the website:
www.edexcel.com

A NOTE FROM THE PUBLISHER

In order to ensure that this resource offers high-quality support for the associated BTEC
qualification, it has been through a review process by the awarding organisation to confirm that
it fully covers the teaching and learning content of the specification or part of a specification at
which it is aimed, and demonstrates an appropriate balance between the development of subject
skills, knowledge and understanding, in addition to preparation for assessment.

While the publishers have made every attempt to ensure that advice on the qualification and its
assessment is accurate, the official specification and associated assessment guidance materials
are the only authoritative source of information and should always be referred to for definitive
guidance.

No material from an endorsed book will be used verbatim in any assessment set by BTEC.

Endorsement of a book does not mean that the book is required to achieve this BTEC qualification,
nor does it mean that it is the only suitable material available to support the qualification, and
any resource lists produced by the awarding organisation shall include this and other appropriate
resources.

Contents

Acknowledgements

The publisher would like to thank the following for their kind permission to reproduce their photographs:

(Key: b-bottom; c-centre; l-left; r-right; t-top)

Alamy Images: 57stock 302, AlexSegre 13, Alvey & Towers Picture Library 331, Art Directors & TRIP 116, CF Images 238, Corbis Bridge 190, Directphoto.org 78, Elizabeth Leyden 109, Eric Nathan 71, Geoffrey Robinson 271, GeoPhotos 79, Gregory Wrona 205, Janine Wiedel Photolibrary 111, Jeff Gilbert 24, Jeff Grimberg 417, Jeremy Sutton-Hibbert 90, Juice images 125, Justin Kase zsixz 148, Londonstills.com 152, Mars Photographics 284, Martyn Goddard 112, Nathan King 20, Paul KIngsley 26, Per Andersen 231, Peter Phipp / Travelshots.com 200, Peter Titmus 426c, Philippe Hays 270, PSL Images 377, Robert Johns 128, Robert Stainforth 81, 87, Simon Hawkins 229, Stephen Barnes 411, THINGX 357; **Bananastock:** 370; **Ben Moss:** 131; **Booka Bookshop:** 429t, 429b; **Brand X Pictures:** Burke Triolo Productions 336t; **Caroline Gooder:** 193; **Catherine Carysforth:** 355; **Chris Reid:** 61; **Copyright (c) The LEGO Group:** 76; **Corbis:** David Madison 292, Drew Myers 156, Helen King 142, Jason Stang 335, Kelly Redinger / Design Pics 311, Mark Chivers 305b, Mika 100, Moodboard 263, 347, Phil Boorman / Cultura 228, Randy Faris 40, Ren Zhenglai / Xinhua Press 110, Roy McMahon 217, Simon Kimber / Demotix 89, Zero Creatives / Cultura 390; **Courtesy of John Lewis PLC:** 396; **Courtesy of Shelf Logic Software Projects:** 419; **Courtesy of SurveyMonkey:** 391t; **Croft Mill UK Ltd:** 393; **Daniel Chang:** 14; **Fotolia.com:** Adam Borkowski 383, Adam Radosavljevic 380, 394, Adisa 385b, Bikeworldtravel 315, Comugnero Silvana 359, foto ARts 230, Joe Gough 387, NAN Des-Tree/Conl, Patrick 402l, 402r, PicciaNeri 412, Pressmaster 386, Racamani 413, Ruth Black 397, Simonkr 304, TanTan_117 426r, Vladimir Gerasimov Banner-U10; **FT.com:** 379; **Big Funky Pictures Ltd:** Jason Gilliat 17; **Getty Images:** AFP 203, Chris Ryan / OJO Images 35, Colorblind / Stone 97, Erik Dreyer / Stone 104, Helen Ashford / Workbook Stock 167, Herve Bruhat / Gamma-Rapho 420, Inti St. Clair / Digital Vision 121, Sturti / E+ 232; **innocent ltd:** 92; **Lowri Roberts:** 165; **Pearson Education Ltd:** Clark Wiseman / Studio 8 144, Studio 8 224, Sophie Bluy 406, Gareth Boden 120, 288, 336b, 346, Rob Judges 6, Jules Selmes 96, Richard Smith 362; **Philip Johnson:** 305t; **Photolibrary.com:** Imagesource 343, Masterfile 339; **Plain English Campaign:** 275; **Red Bull Content Pool:** Jay Nemeth 233; **Revolver World:** 95; **Rex Features:** ITV 318, Jonathan Hordle 376, Ray Tang 246, Tony Kyriacou 391b; **Sam Clayton:** 273; **Science Photo Library Ltd:** Victor De Schwanberg 160; **Shelagh Brownlow:** 365; **Shutterstock.com:** AISPIX by Image Source 58, Andresr 22, Andrew Bassett 137, Andrey Popov 208, Banner-U8, Boris Djuranovic 38, Chad Kawalec Studios 404, Claus Mikosch 289, corgarashu Banner-U12, Dmitrijs Dmitrijevs Banner-U3, Dmitriy Shironosov 187, Emran Mohd Tamil 213, erobanks 194, Fleming Photography 180, Hydbzxy 426l, Jennifer Stone Banner-U9, Kamira 11, Konstantin Chagin Banner-U11, Kurhan 83, leungchopan 166, Losevsky Pavel 127, Martin Haas 107, Max Earey 75, Maxisport 300, Maxx-Studio 77, Monkey Business Images 2, 51, moshimochi 57, Netrun78 3, Norman Pogson 176, Otna Ydur Banner-U2, pcruciatti 84, Portokalis 29, PT Images 70, R. Nagy Banner-U1, Rido 74, Roberto Chicano Banner-U17, Serge64 175, Sergey Furtaev 34, Serhiy Shullye 47, StockLite 184, 195, Takeshi Nishio 225, Toria 371, Banner-U14, Vladm 407, wavebreakmedia ltd 119, Yuri Arcurs 138, 170, Banner-U4, Banner-U5, Banner-U7; **Sonya Clarkson:** 219; **SuperStock:** Cultura Limited 135; **The Gro Company:** 23; **Veer/Corbis:** Artem Mykhailichenko 388, jirkaejc 243, Monkey Business images 310, Piotr Pawinski 385t, rodho 344, ronfromyork Banner-U13, Rui Vale de Sousa 333, ruigsantos 328, Timur Arbaev 242, Yuri Arcurs 321; **www.etsy.com/shop/whildthingsdresses:** 255; **www.imagesource.com:** 237, Nigel RIches 262

Cover image: *Front:* **Plainpicture Ltd:** Scanpix

All other images © Pearson Education

In some instances we have been unable to trace the owners of copyright material, and we would appreciate any information that would enable us to do so.

Authors' acknowledgements

The authors would like to thank all the people and organisations who have helped us by providing information on their business activities. This has enabled us to produce a book which accurately reflects current business practice and is appropriate for today's BTEC First learners.

For agreeing to be featured in WorkSpace features and help with other case studies we are hugely indebted to: Sam Clayton, a talented self-employed photographer; Daniel Chang, the creator of the Dream Sheep app; Ben Fox, whose vision led to On your Bike (Recycle) Ltd; James Plant and James Moss, who own and run Plant and Moss Ltd, Birmingham; Chris Reid, the brains and energy behind Connect Technology Group; Steve Wells and Eric Metcalf at Brook Food Processing Equipment for their help with bakery costings; Paul Birch, the MD of Revolver World; Ben Moss, manager at R A Bennett & Partners, estate agents; Janet McGregor, Customer Service Representative for a major phone company; Lowri Roberts, the owner of Siop Cwlwm in Oswestry; Caroline Gooder, Engineering Administrator at Cummins Turbo Technologies; Sonya Clarkson, Head of Employment Services at East Lancashire Hospitals NHS Trust; Carrie and Tim Morris, joint owners of Booka Bookshop and Karen and Roger Neild, joint owners of J A McNulty Ltd; Caroline Boardwell Reid, the enterprising MD of Croft Mill Ltd; Kirsty Hartley, the creative genius behind Wild Things Dresses; Philip Johnson, Architect and Shelagh Brownlow of Brownlow's Accountants for her sound financial advice for new entrepreneurs; Paul and Antony Carysforth, for their online marketing and programming expertise, Jeffrey Young, MD of Allegra Strategies and Anya Marco, Director of Insight and Catherine Carysforth LLB and Peter Gold LLB for their advice and guidance on legal issues.

As always, thanks are also due to the team at Pearson who worked so hard to produce this book, especially Lewis Birchon, our publisher, for his constant help and support, Laura Bland our original editor, for her patience and calm efficiency and Rachael Harrison, our conscientious and adept project editor, for being such a pleasure to work with.

We hope this book will help teachers and tutors to deliver the new BTEC First with ease and confidence and provide a useful and inspirational resource for their students.

About this book

This book is designed to help you through your BTEC First Business qualification and is divided into 15 units from the qualification.

About your BTEC First Business

Choosing to study for a BTEC First Business qualification is a great decision to make for lots of reasons. This qualification will prepare you for virtually any career by equipping you with financial skills, organisational ability, marketing knowledge and the ability to present your ideas clearly. The principles of business underpin every shop, office and organisation in the UK economy, meaning that you will have skills and knowledge that will be valued by employers in every sector. In addition, a BTEC First Business qualification can help you to progress to the next level of study.

About the authors

Paul Bentley worked in retail management before training as a teacher. He currently works at St Edmunds Catholic School in Wolverhampton where he is a lead practitioner and the coordinator of vocational education. Paul is a doctoral research student at a Russell Group university and is also an experienced author, having written and co-written tutor support materials, delivery guidance, and journal articles.

Carol Carysforth has enjoyed a varied business career. In addition to being involved with two family businesses, she has worked in HR, travel and tourism, manufacturing and sales and marketing. She has worked both for private industry and in the public sector. During her teaching career she specialised in teaching business studies and administration to FE and HE students and became Deputy Dean of Faculty of Business and Management at Blackburn College. She has worked as a consultant on several curriculum development projects at national level.

Lisa Chandler-Corris taught BTEC in school and college for many years before working as a Training Consultant. In this role, she produces teaching and training materials, reviews educational resources and gives advice on teaching and training.

Karen Glencross was an IT trainer in a multinational engineering company in the North East of England before working in the Further Education sector. She moved to Redcar and Cleveland College and during that time held the post of Head of Faculty for Business Information and Technology. She is now self-employed working as a Qualifications Manager for a training provider.

Mike Neild started his post-graduate career as a research scientist at GCHQ in Cheltenham. A move north resulted in a complete change of career to production manager for a large international company. After studying for higher level management qualifications, Mike's interest in teaching was aroused and he started his teaching career at Blackburn College, specialising in business and management. Mike became Senior Tutor at the College and headed two different departments before deciding to focus on writing full-time.

How to use this book

This book contains many features that will help you use your skills and knowledge in work-related situations, and assist you in getting the most from your course.

These introductions give you a snapshot of what to expect from each unit – and what you should be aiming for by the time you finish it.

How this unit is assessed

Learning aims describe what you will be doing in the unit.

A learner shares how working through the unit has helped them.

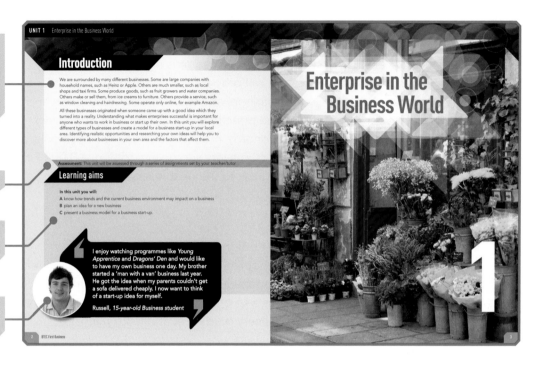

Features of this book

There are lots of features in this book to help you learn about the topics in each unit, and to have fun while learning! These pages show some of the features that you will come across when using the book.

Topic references show which parts of the BTEC you are covering on these pages.

Getting started with a short activity or discussion about the topic.

Key terms boxes give definitions of important words and phrases that you will come across.

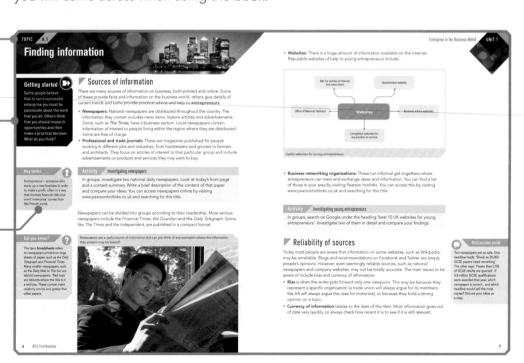

Activity — Researching ethical trading

Research ethical trading and then find out which businesses you know are members of the Ethical Trading Initiative.

Activities will help you learn about the topic. These will be done in pairs or groups, or sometimes on your own.

Question 1

Ashraf has started his own car valeting business. Divide the following items into start up costs and running costs. [4]

(a) Pressure washer

(b) Car shampoo and polish

(c) Promotional leaflet

(d) Telephone bill

A chance to practise answering the types of test questions that you may come across in your test. (For Unit 2 and Unit 9 only.)

Assessment activity 1.1 — *Maths* — 2A.P1 | 2A.P2 | 2A.M1 | 2A.M2 | 2A.D1

You have been asked to produce your own booklet for young entrepreneurs in your area. This will describe the local business environment and identify trends and changes that may affect a start-up business. Your booklet should be divided into three sections:

1 The first section should focus on the current business environment that exists in your own area. You should also be aware of changes that can take place and explain how these can affect a start-up business.

2 The next section should focus on trends you have researched. If you wish, you can focus on trends and that could affect your own idea for a start-up business. You need to compare how two trends have impacted on a start-up business.

3 The final section should focus on the current risks, opportunities and trends in the current business environment for a start-up business. Your assessment should be based on the data you have researched and you should focus on appropriate guidance for an entrepreneur.

Tip

You **assess** information by carefully considering all the factors or events that apply and identifying which are the most important or relevant. Use your research to provide evidence for your conclusions.

You **compare** by identifying the main factors in two or more situations. Point out the similarities and differences and, if appropriate, say which is best and why. Or explain the effects these factors have had.

Activities that relate to the unit's assessment critera. These activities will help you prepare for your assignments and contain tips to help you achieve your best results. (For all units **except** Unit 2 and Unit 9.)

Just checking

1 What is inflation and why is high inflation bad for businesses?

2 Why do the government and business entrepreneurs both want employment levels to be high?

3 List four types of taxes paid in the UK.

Use these to check your knowledge and understanding of the topic you have just covered.

Someone who works in the business industry explains how this unit of the BTEC First applies to the day-to-day work they do as part of their job.

Enterprise in the Business World   **UNIT 1**

WorkSpace

Sam Clayton

Photographer

Many would-be entrepreneurs struggle to start their own enterprise because they don't have the skills or cannot raise the money required. In that case, they could do worse than to follow Sam Clayton's example. Sam successfully runs one of the millions of one-person businesses in the UK.

After leaving school, Sam trained to become a nursery nurse and spent several years working with children. Working in a nursery and watching a photographer take photos of the children, she remembered her previous interest in photography. Her father was a keen photographer. Sam decided to take a course in photography and borrowed her father's camera to create her own photos. She created her own darkroom at home and persuaded the nursery managers to let her become the official nursery photographer.

It wasn't until Sam photographed her manager's wedding that she realised she wanted to start a photographic business.

Sam continued to work full-time to finance her growing business. She carried out research, attended training courses and looked for photographers and images which inspired her. She made some mistakes, spending money on advertising that wasn't effective and buying unnecessary equipment, and she struggled to price her skills when people asked her to quote for a job. An online American forum for wedding and portrait photographers was a great help to Sam. Exchanging views with like-minded photographers on Facebook and Twitter helped, too.

In April 2006, five years after starting her business, Sam took the plunge and set out as a fully self-employed photographer. She has never looked back.

Think about it

1 How did Sam overcome the problem of raising finance to run her business?

2 In what way did Sam's previous experience come in useful? How do you think it helps her now?

3 How can Facebook and Twitter help Sam to promote her business?

4 To be successful, businesses need a USP (unique selling point) that makes them stand out. Look at Sam's website by visiting Pearson hotlinks. Identify her USP and suggest why she receives so many referrals by word of mouth from clients.

17

This section also gives you the chance to think more about the role that this person does, and whether you would want to follow in their footsteps once you've completed your BTEC.

BTEC Assessment Zone

You will be assessed in two different ways for your BTEC First in Business. For most units, your teacher/tutor will set assignments for you to complete. These may take the form of projects where you research, plan, prepare, and evaluate a piece of work or activity. The table in this BTEC Assessment Zone explains what you must do in order to achieve each of the assessment criteria. Each unit of this book contains a number of assessment activities to help you with these assessment criteria.

The table in the BTEC Assessment Zone explains what you must do in order to achieve each of the assessment criteria, and signposts assessment activities in this book to help you to prepare for your assignments.

Assessment criteria

Level 1	Level 2 **Pass**	Level 2 **Merit**
Learning aim A: Know how trends and the current business environment may impact on a business		
1A.1	**2A.P1**	**2A.M1**
Identify factors of the business environment that can impact on a start-up business	Outline how the business environment can impact on a start-up business **See Assessment activity 1.1, page 19**	Explain how changes in the current business environment are likely to impact upon a start-up business **See Assessment activity 1.1, page 19**

Activities in this book will show you the kinds of task you might be asked to do to meet these criteria when your tutor sets an assignment.

Question 1

Which two of these items are fixed costs for a florist? [2]

Click on **two** of these boxes:

Staff wages	[X]
Flowers	[ ]
Monthly rent	[X]
Ribbons and wrapping paper	[ ]

For Unit 2 of your BTEC, you will be assessed by an onscreen test. For Unit 9 you will be assessed by a paper-based test. The BTEC Assessment Zones in Unit 2 and Unit 9 help you to prepare for your tests by showing you some of the different types of questions you will need to answer.

Planning and getting organised

The first step in managing your time is to plan ahead and be well organised. Some people are naturally good at this. They think ahead, write down commitments in a diary or planner and store their notes and handouts neatly and carefully so they can find them quickly.

How good are your working habits?

Improving your planning and organisational skills

1 Use a diary to schedule working times into your weekdays and weekends.
2 Also use the diary to write down exactly what work you have to do. You could use this as a 'to do' list and tick off each task as you go.
3 Divide up long or complex tasks into manageable chunks and put each 'chunk' in your diary with a deadline of its own.
4 Always allow more time than you think you need for a task.

Sources of information

You will need to use research to complete your BTEC First assignments, so it's important to know what sources of information are available to you. These are likely to include the following:

Textbooks
These cover the units of your qualification and provide activities and ideas for further research.

Internet
A vast source of information, but not all sites are accurate and information and opinions can often be **biased** – you should always double-check facts you find online.

Sources of information

Newspapers and magazines
These often cover business topics in either dedicated business sections or through articles about businesses.

People
People you know can be a great source of opinion and experience – particularly if you want feedback on an idea.

Television
Programmes such as *The Apprentice* and *Dragons' Den* can give you an insight into the world of business. The news also regularly shows how business affects the wider world.

Take it further

If you become distracted by social networking sites or texts when you're working, set yourself a time limit of 10 minutes or so to indulge yourself. You could even use this as a reward for completing a certain amount of work.

Key terms

Bias – People often have strong opinions about certain topics. This is called 'bias'. Newspaper or magazine articles, or information found on the internet, may be biased to present a specific point of view.

Remember!

Store relevant information when you find it – keep a folder on your computer specifically for research – so you don't have to worry about finding it again at a later date.

Organising and selecting information

Organising your information

Once you have used a range of sources of information for research, you will need to organise the information so it's easy to use.

- Make sure your written notes are neat and have a clear heading – it's often useful to date them, too.
- Always keep a note of where the information came from (the title of a book, the title and date of a newspaper or magazine and the web address of a website) and, if relevant, which pages.
- Work out the results of any questionnaires you've used.

Selecting your information

Once you have completed your research, re-read the assignment brief or instructions you were given to remind yourself of the exact wording of the question(s) and divide your information into three groups:

1 Information that is totally relevant.

2 Information that is not as good, but which could come in useful.

3 Information that doesn't match the questions or assignment brief very much, but that you kept because you couldn't find anything better!

Check that there are no obvious gaps in your information against the questions or assignment brief. If there are, make a note of them so that you know exactly what you still have to find.

◤ Presenting your work

Before handing in any assignments, make sure:

- you have addressed each part of the question and that your work is as complete as possible
- all spelling and grammar is correct
- you have referenced all sources of information you used for your research
- all work is your own – otherwise you could be committing **plagiarism**
- you have saved a copy of your work.

 Key terms

Plagiarism – If you are including other people's views, comments or opinions, or copying a diagram or table from another publication, you must state the source by including the name of the author or publication, or the web address. Failure to do this (when you are really pretending other people's work is your own) is known as plagiarism. Check your school's policy on plagiarism and copying.

Introduction

We are surrounded by many different businesses. Some are large companies with household names, such as Heinz or Apple. Others are much smaller, such as local shops and taxi firms. Some produce goods, such as fruit growers and water companies. Others make or sell them, from ice creams to furniture. Others provide a service, such as window cleaning and hairdressing. Some operate only online, for example Amazon.

All these businesses originated when someone came up with a good idea which they turned into a reality. Understanding what makes enterprises successful is important for anyone who wants to work in business or start up their own. In this unit you will explore different types of businesses and create a model for a business start-up in your local area. Identifying realistic opportunities and researching your own ideas will help you to discover more about businesses in your own area and the factors that affect them.

Assessment: This unit will be assessed through a series of assignments set by your teacher/tutor.

Learning aims

In this unit you will:

A know how trends and the current business environment may impact on a business

B plan an idea for a new business

C present a business model for a business start-up.

I enjoy watching programmes like *Young Apprentice* and *Dragons' Den* and would like to have my own business one day. My brother started a 'man with a van' business last year. He got the idea when my parents couldn't get a sofa delivered cheaply. I now want to think of a start-up idea for myself.

Russell, *15-year-old Business student*

Enterprise in the Business World

1

Assessment Zone

This table shows you what you must do in order to achieve a **Pass**, **Merit** or **Distinction** grade, and where you can find activities in this book to help you.

Assessment criteria			
Level 1	**Level 2 Pass**	**Level 2 Merit**	**Level 2 Distinction**
Learning aim A: Know how trends and the current business environment may impact on a business			
1A.1 Identify factors of the business environment that can impact on a start-up business	**2A.P1** Outline how the business environment can impact on a start-up business **See Assessment activity 1.1, page 19**	**2A.M1** Explain how changes in the current business environment are likely to impact upon a start-up business **See Assessment activity 1.1, page 19**	**2A.D1** Maths Assess the current risks, opportunities and trends in the business environment for a start-up business **See Assessment activity 1.1, page 19**
1A.2 Identify current trends that may impact on a start-up business	**2A.P2** Maths Explain how current trends will impact on a start-up business **See Assessment activity 1.1, page 19**	**2A.M2** Maths Compare how two trends have impacted on a start-up business **See Assessment activity 1.1, page 19**	
Learning aim B: Plan an idea for a new business			
1B.3 Identify the features of successful businesses	**2B.P3** Describe, using relevant examples, the features of successful businesses **See Assessment activity 1.2, page 27**	**2B.M3** Compare the features, strengths and weaknesses of two successful businesses **See Assessment activity 1.2, page 27**	**2B.D2** Maths Justify how the initial plan for a business idea has potential for success in relation to existing local businesses **See Assessment activity 1.2, page 27**
1B.4 English Maths Prepare an initial plan for a business idea for the local area	**2B.P4** English Maths Prepare a realistic initial plan for a business idea suitable for the local area **See Assessment activity 1.2, page 27**	**2B.M4** Maths Explain how the initial plan for a business idea has the potential to respond to market needs **See Assessment activity 1.2, page 27**	
Learning aim C: Present a business model for a business start-up			
1C.5 Outline the choice of format selected for a business start-up	**2C.P5** Explain the reasons for the choice of format selected for a business start-up **See Assessment activity 1.3, page 33**	**2C.M5** English Present a realistic business model for a business, explaining how the format and business model will enable it to carry out its activities successfully **See Assessment activity 1.3, page 33**	**2C.D3** English Present a realistic business model for a business, explaining how the format and supporting evidence justifies the initial business idea **See Assessment activity 1.3, page 33**
1C.6 English Present, with guidance, a business model for a business start-up	**2C.P6** English Present a realistic business model for a business start-up **See Assessment activity 1.3, page 33**		

English Opportunity to practise English skills

Maths Opportunity to practise mathematical skills

How you will be assessed

The unit will be assessed by a series of internally assessed tasks. You will research your own ideas for a start-up business and prepare an initial plan which shows that you have considered current trends and the needs of your local business environment. You will then plan your business model, deciding which would be the best format for your own business and giving reasons for your choice. You will need to prepare explanatory notes to support your model before you present it.

Your evidence for this unit will be collected and prepared throughout your course and stored in a portfolio, together with any observation records or witness statements.

Your assessment could be in the form of:

- a business model with explanatory notes
- a presentation in which you put forward your ideas and/or business model and answer questions about it

More about your portfolio

Your portfolio must contain the information you have researched, your notes and other evidence that led you to make certain decisions about your proposed business.

This should be divided into the following sections:

- Ideas for your start-up business
- Research for the start-up business
- Initial plan for a business idea
- Format of business start-up and reasons for choice
- Business model
- Presentation
- Observation records/witness statements. These may be from your teacher/tutor, other learners in your group or other contacts you have made as part of your investigations or research.

You will find activities to help you to assemble your research materials as well as assessment activities that cover all the criteria as you progress through the unit.

Remember

As you work through this unit, date all your reference and research notes and keep them safely in a folder or your portfolio, so that you don't lose anything.

Finding information

Sources of information

There are many sources of information on business, both printed and online. Some of these provide facts and information on the business world, others give details of current trends and some provide practical advice and help to **entrepreneurs**.

- **Newspapers:** National newspapers are distributed throughout the country. The information they contain includes news items, feature articles and advertisements. Some, such as *The Times*, have a business section. Local newspapers contain information of interest to people living within the region where they are distributed. Some are free of charge.
- **Professional and trade journals:** These are magazines published for people working in different jobs and industries, from hairdressers and grocers to farmers and architects. They focus on articles of interest to that particular group and include advertisements on products and services they may want to buy.

Activity   Investigating newspapers

In groups, investigate two national daily newspapers. Look at today's front page and a content summary. Write a brief description of the content of that paper and compare your ideas. You can access newspapers online by visiting www.pearsonhotlinks.co.uk and searching for this title.

Newspapers can be divided into groups according to their readership. More serious newspapers include the *Financial Times*, *the Guardian* and the *Daily Telegraph*. Some, like *The Times* and the *Independent*, are published in a compact format.

Newspapers are a useful source of information but can you think of any examples where the information they present may be biased?

- **Websites:** There is a huge amount of information available on the internet. Reputable websites of help to young entrepreneurs include:

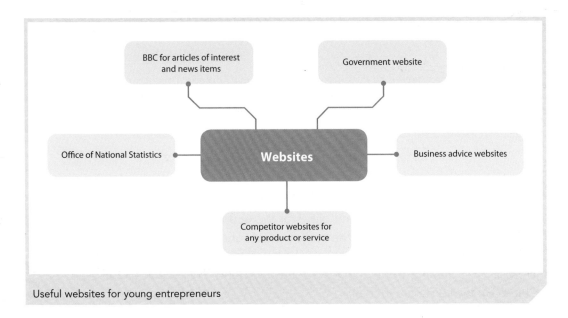

Useful websites for young entrepreneurs

- **Business networking organisations:** These run informal get-togethers where entrepreneurs can meet and exchange ideas and information. You can find a list of those in your area by visiting Pearson hotlinks. You can access this by visiting www.pearsonhotlinks.co.uk and searching for this title.

> **Activity**   Investigating young entrepreneurs
>
> In groups, search on Google under the heading 'best 10 UK websites for young entrepreneurs'. Investigate two of them in detail and compare your findings.

Reliability of sources

Today most people are aware that information on some websites, such as Wikipedia, may be unreliable. Blogs and recommendations on Facebook and Twitter are simply people's opinions. However, even seemingly reliable sources, such as national newspapers and company websites, may not be totally accurate. The main issues to be aware of include bias and currency of information.

- **Bias** is when the writer puts forward only one viewpoint. This may be because they represent a specific organisation (a trade union will always argue for its members; the AA will always argue the case for motorists), or because they hold a strong opinion on a topic.

- **Currency of information** relates to the date of the item. Most information goes out of date very quickly, so always check how recent it is to see if it is still relevant.

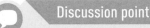
Discussion point

Two newspapers are on sale. One headline reads: 'Shock as 20,000 GCSE papers need remarking'. The other says: 'Fewer than 0.5% of GCSE results are queried'. If 5.8 million GCSE qualifications were awarded that year, which newspaper is correct, and which headline would sell the most copies? Discuss your ideas as a class.

Factors to consider in the current business environment

Getting started

What is the business environment like in your area? Which types of business are thriving and which are not? Compare your ideas as a class.

Introduction

All businesses are affected by the current business environment. This means the local and national factors that will affect it. They include the location of the business and its customers and the political and economic situation that prevails at the time.

▼ National factors

Some people are not interested in politics or the **economy** unless something bad happens to them, such as losing their job. In 2011, unemployment rose, especially among young people. Few people received pay rises, but fuel and energy prices increased. This meant people had less money to spend. This affects all business because sales and profits then fall.

It is important that anyone thinking of starting a business understands the national factors that can affect them.

Political issues

There are three main political parties in the UK – Conservative, Labour, and Liberal Democrat (Lib Dem). In 2010, a coalition government was formed between the Conservatives and the Lib Dems because no single party gained an outright majority share of the vote. The coalition will govern the country until the next General Election.

Key terms

Economy – the system by which a country's money and goods are produced and used.

Exchange rates – the value of an individual currency against other currencies.

Interest rates – the cost of borrowing money.

Activity   Finding out about voting

The date of the next General Election is given on the Government website. There are two reasons why a General Election might be held sooner. Go to Pearson hotlinks to find out about what these are and to learn more about voting.

Did you know?

The government gets its money through taxation and by borrowing money. The government uses this money to provide public services in Britain, such as education, the NHS and road networks.

Type and level of government support for business

All political parties want businesses in the UK to thrive and more overseas firms to operate here. The reasons are simple:

- If jobs are available and people are working, then they pay tax and fewer people need benefits. This means the government receives more money and pays out less and therefore has more money to spend.

- If people feel positive about the future and think the government is doing a good job, they are more likely to re-elect that political party next time.

To help businesses, governments aim to have a stable and growing economy. They may also offer assistance by providing loans or grants. The government has introduced a National Loan Guarantee scheme to make it easier for small firms to borrow money and entrepreneurs to raise funds to start up a business. It provides online help for businesses at Business Link and on the BIS (Department for Business Innovation and Skills).

Taxation

The main taxes collected by Her Majesty's Revenue and Customs (HMRC) are:

- **Income tax** – paid by employees on a PAYE (pay as you earn) basis
- **National Insurance** – paid by both employers and employees
- **Value added tax (VAT)** – added to many sales transactions. VAT-registered businesses can reclaim the VAT they pay on most purchases
- **Corporation tax** – paid by limited companies and based upon the profit made.

The economy

The 'economy' refers to a country's wealth and resources and how much money it earns by producing goods and services. This determines the standard of living of the people who live there. It is much better to live in a country with a stable and growing economy.

Figure 1.1 is a simple description of how the economy operates. Consumers buy goods from firms which use this money to hire workers and pay wages. These workers then buy more goods, and so on. The more this happens, the greater the number of people employed and the richer they can become.

Indicators that show how well the economy is working include:

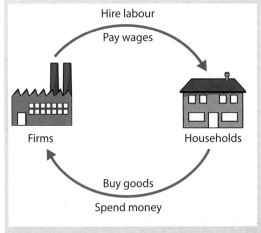

Figure 1.1   How the economy operates

- **Level of employment:** If this is high, people have more money to spend so the economy is likely to grow.
- **Inflation:** Low inflation means that prices and wages only increase a small amount each year. This is better for businesses as the costs involved in running the enterprise should remain about the same.
- **Exchange rates:** These determine whether British goods and services are cheap or expensive to overseas buyers. The more we sell overseas the more money Britain earns. However, when UK residents buy foreign goods, money leaves the country. Ideally we want to earn more on exports than we spend on imports.
- **Interest rates:** These are also referred to as the cost of loans. If these are low, businesses are more likely to borrow money to invest in better machinery, equipment or buildings. This enables UK businesses to stay up to date and competitive.

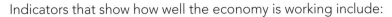

Activity   Susie's cuddly toys

Susie's cuddly toys sell well in America. To meet a new order Susie needs to borrow £5,000 to buy more equipment. The order is worth US$30,000.

1   If interest rates are 7.5% and she borrows the money for a year, how much will she repay?

2a   If one pound sterling is currently worth $1.5, how much is the order worth in sterling?

2b   If, by the time the goods are sent, £1 = $1.6, will she make more money or less?

Give a reason for your answer.

CONTINUED ▸▸

◤ Local factors

The type of enterprise will influence the premises that are needed and where they should be situated. Many small businesses are run from home. The advantages are that there is no rent to pay, no travelling costs and no commuting time, but you need to be self-disciplined as there are often distractions at home!

Location

The best location is the cheapest place which provides enough space and easy access to customers and suppliers. If you start an eBay business, you can work from home easily. If you open a retail outlet you need to be near shoppers – whether on a high street, in a market or in a mall. If you start a sandwich shop, you need passing trade, so a busy main road (with parking) is better than a side street or housing estate.

Requirements for resources

All businesses need resources. The main aspects to consider are summarised in Table 1.1.

Table 1.1   Resource factors to consider

Resources	Factors to consider
Premises	These may be a shop, office, workshop or small industrial unit. The appearance is important if customers visit you, and so is nearby parking. Small business and enterprise centres provide accommodation at reasonable rates with many services, such as electricity and wi-fi, included.
Staff	Any staff you employ must be able to reach you easily. If unemployment is high in the area, labour costs may also be lower.
Equipment and other supplies	A dog walker needs little equipment, whereas a DJ needs equipment plus transport. A car valeting firm needs a supply of water, cleaning materials and a forecourt. Allow enough space to store and use any necessary items.
Stocks of goods and raw materials	How large are these items, how many will you need to store? If they are valuable, you may need a safe. If they are perishable, such as flowers or ice cream, you will need a cold room or freezer.
Location of suppliers	If you are dependent on regular supplies of materials or fresh food, then you will save money on travel or delivery costs if you are near to a major outlet or producer. You will also need less storage space if you replenish stocks regularly.
Customers	Customers are essential to your business survival. If you visit customers, aim to keep travel time and costs down. If they come to you, then location and 'your image' is more important. Will they book an appointment or do you want to attract passers-by? Where are your main competitors, and why? Should you be near them?

What factors should you consider when choosing premises for your business?

Many local councils support new business start-ups and also offer accommodation in specially built units and centres. Search online to find those available in your local area.

Impact of factors

When you decide which factors are relevant to your own business idea, you must consider how any decision you make would affect a target group of customers.

Ideally, your target group will consist of people who would use your services or buy your products and whom you can ask for feedback. You can then find out if you are on the right track by testing out your ideas. If the feedback is generally negative, you might have to consider swapping your business proposition for an alternative!

Just checking

1 What is inflation and why is high inflation bad for businesses?
2 Why do the government and business entrepreneurs both want employment levels to be high?
3 List four types of taxes paid in the UK.

Activity Factors affecting your business

Factors that will influence the location of a coffee shop are: the proximity of other shops and businesses; plenty of space for customers; good wi-fi access; easy access for suppliers to deliver; passing trade; nearby parking and availability of staff. Produce your own list of factors that will influence the location of a different type of enterprise. Now add any other factors that may affect your idea for a business. Keep your notes safely in your folder.

Trends affecting business

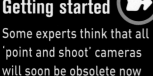

Getting started

Some experts think that all 'point and shoot' cameras will soon be obsolete now that everyone can take photos with their mobile phones. Do you agree?

All businesses are affected by changes in the world around them. These can provide new opportunities but they can also threaten the survival of organisations that fail to adapt. In 1888 Kodak made its name by producing the first cameras and rolls of film that people could easily use. In 2011 it filed for bankruptcy. The company had failed to adapt quickly enough to new developments in digital photography.

The types of trends that affect business are shown in Figure 1.2:

Figure 1.2 Trends affecting business

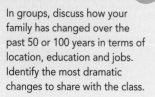

Discussion point

In groups, discuss how your family has changed over the past 50 or 100 years in terms of location, education and jobs. Identify the most dramatic changes to share with the class.

Social trends

These involve the way we live and behave. Sixty years ago fewer people owned a car or went abroad on holiday and borrowing money was considered shameful. Today driving to the airport to catch a plane and paying by credit card is considered normal. Society has changed a lot in a short time. So how does this affect business?

- **Population changes** – the population of Great Britain increased by over 20 million people between 1911 and 2011, according to ONS Census figures, and there are more elderly people because life expectancy has increased as a result of improved diet and healthcare. This presents opportunities for organisations like Saga who target 'silver spenders'. A more culturally diverse population has provided opportunities for ethnic speciality shops, from kosher butchers to Asian wedding planners.

- **Households and families** now often consist of a 'blended' family where parents, step-parents, children and step children live together. Couples may opt to cohabit rather than marry. In the UK, civil partnerships between same-sex couples are now legal and accepted by society.

- **Education** has improved with more young people achieving good GCSE and A-level grades and attending university. Some students now choose to study near their home to keep their living costs down.

- **Labour market** changes have seen more women working and more families reliant on good quality childcare. Employment laws have given workers more protection and have allowed employees to request flexible working. Many people work from home, and some have more than one part-time job. There is more temporary work available and people expect to have several different jobs during their working life.

- **Increasing travel for work** – many people endure long commutes to their workplace, often to avoid the high cost of housing in city centres. In some families, one person may work away during the week, or work abroad on a short-term contract, while their partner and children remain at home. Some people emigrate to improve their career prospects.

Why do you think so many people commute to work?

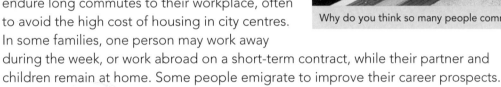

Activity Brainstorming business opportunities

Today most people are far more aware of health and fitness. In groups, brainstorm the business opportunities that have occurred as a result. Then choose one other social or lifestyle trend and make a similar list. Compare your ideas as a class.

Technology trends

These not only affect what people buy and how they work and spend their leisure time, but also mean that some products rapidly become obsolete. Videotapes gave way to DVDs, now there are internet-ready Blu-ray players and high definition TVs. 3D and Smart televisions are now on sale and an integrated iTV from Apple is a possibility, too. As Internet connection speeds increase, DVDs and Blu-ray disks may take second place to movie streaming on demand.

Today most people have a computer. For personal use, laptops, smartphones and tablets now outrank PCs and provide almost continuous access to the internet. Banking and shopping, communicating, researching information, social networking and sharing photos are common online activities and a fundamental part of many people's lives. Cloud computing will mean that in the future, programs and data are stored remotely, rather than on computers themselves.

CONTINUED ▶▶

Case study

Two new technology trends have been the rise in online buying by mobile phone (300% higher at the end of 2012 than 2011) and the massive increase in application or 'app' downloads.

This has led to increased income for app stores and for developers, and has tempted many people to try their hand at creating an app. As over 50% of downloaded apps in the UK are games, this is probably the best place to start.

Certainly Daniel Chang thought so. Daniel already worked for a well-known animation studio but spent much of his spare time over eight months developing 'Dream Sheep', an addictive game involving floating sheep, lethal stars and fluffy clouds. The basic game is free from the iTunes Store.

Daniel honed his skills designing the game, writing the music and carrying out the programming. However, basic guidance is given at many sites online, so all you need is a very good idea, money to pay a developer and friends who will spread the word on Facebook and Twitter!

Dream Sheep

1 What has caused the surge in demand by consumers for downloaded apps?

2 Suggest two reasons why writing a game app is a good idea, especially if you have the skills?

3 Given the number of apps available, what do you think Daniel's biggest challenge is now?

4 Find out more about 'Dream Sheep' by visiting Pearson hotlinks. If you have an iPhone, iPod Touch or iPad, try it out yourself and tell your friends if you like it!

Did you know?

Many businesses have made a feature out of being 'green', such as Ecover products and The Natural Nursery. The Green Oil business was started in a garden shed by Simon Nash. Use the internet to find out more about these businesses.

Environmental trends

Most people are aware of the negative effects of some consumer and commercial actions on the environment. They know that the planet's resources will not last for ever, that sustainability is important and that pollution of any type is a bad thing.

- **Renewable energy** comes from natural sources, such as the sun or wind. Therefore solar power and wind power are renewable, whereas oil, gas and coal are not.

- **Recycling** means that items are reused instead of being thrown away. People now expect suppliers to incorporate recyclable materials in their products and packaging.

Ethical trends

Ethics relates to principles and standards of behaviour. Consumers now expect businesses to behave ethically and to give something back to the community. What does this actually mean? Ethical issues are often closely linked to environmental concerns and include:

- **Carbon footprint,** which is calculated by the amount of emissions produced by an activity. The aim is to become 'carbon neutral' by using less energy and compensating for unavoidable use, such as by tree planting or investing in schemes to provide renewable energy in developing countries.
- **Responsible sourcing** of all types of supplies. Although timber has had the most publicity, because of the global effects of destroying the rainforests, ethical companies also look at many other aspects relating to their suppliers. These include a ban on child labour, and insisting on fair pay rates, reasonable working hours and good working conditions.
- **Animal welfare** in the UK is now covered by the Animal Welfare Act which governs the way animals must be treated by breeders, those who keep working animals and pet owners.

> **Activity**   Researching ethical trading
>
> Research ethical trading and then find out which businesses you know are members of the Ethical Trading Initiative.

Business and the community

Responsible businesses do not wait for the law to tell them what to do. They identify their own values and write an ethical code which states the actions they will and will not take.

Many businesses also have charitable trusts or foundations which enable them to contribute to the welfare of their suppliers, the local community or other needy causes.

Business in the Community is a charity which promotes responsible business practice and gives awards to outstanding organisations and projects.

> **Activity**   Research trends and changes
>
> Research the main trends and changes that could affect your ideas for a start-up business. Divide these into risks that would threaten your business and opportunities from which you would benefit. Keep your notes safely in your folder.

Size of business and type

Introduction

Businesses come in all shapes and sizes. In 2012, there were about 4.8 million business enterprises in the UK. Over 60% of these were owned by one person, often working without any other staff.

Types of business

Most businesses in the UK are small and are known as **SMEs** (small and medium enterprises). **Microbusinesses** are even smaller. Each category is defined by the number of people they employ, as shown in Table 1.2.

Table 1.2   Types of business enterprise

Type of enterprise	Number of employees	Number of enterprises in the UK at start of 2012	Total number of people employed (thousands)
Microbusiness	Up to 9	1,022,695	3,848
Small enterprise	10–49	177,950	3,471
Medium enterprise	50–249	29,751	2,909
Large business	250 or more	6,455	9,763

(Source: Department for Business, Innovation and Skills)

Activity   Calculating SMEs

Use Table 1.2 to calculate the total number of SMEs in the UK and the number of people they employ.

Start-ups and existing businesses

Start-ups are new businesses, whereas existing businesses are those that are already open and trading. Over 200,000 new enterprises were set up during 2011 but unfortunately not all of them were successful. The Office of National Statistics figures show that about 20,000 businesses close down every year. Many of these are small enterprises.

The government is trying to encourage more new start-ups because successful businesses help everyone and some will grow. They provide an income for the entrepreneur, provide employment for staff, give customers more choice and help to keep prices low because there is more competition for goods and services.

Discussion point

Why do some businesses fail while others survive? Is it because the owner is poor at running the enterprise or for some other reason? Discuss this in groups and see how many reasons you can suggest.

Activity   Researching a website

Russell's brother has a 'man with a van' business. Visit Pearson hotlinks to visit the AnyVan site. You can access this by going to www.pearsonhotlinks.co.uk and searching for this title. Customers can list jobs and ask for quotes. Can you suggest two benefits of the website for customers and for small business enterprises?

WorkSpace

▶ ## Sam Clayton

Photographer

Many would-be entrepreneurs struggle to start their own enterprise because they don't have the skills or cannot raise the money required. In that case, they could do worse than to follow Sam Clayton's example. Sam successfully runs one of the millions of one-person businesses in the UK.

After leaving school, Sam trained to become a nursery nurse and spent several years working with children. Working in a nursery and watching a photographer take photos of the children, she remembered her previous interest in photography. Her father was a keen photographer. Sam decided to take a course in photography and borrowed her father's camera to create her own photos. She created her own darkroom at home and persuaded the nursery managers to let her become the official nursery photographer.

It wasn't until Sam photographed her manager's wedding that she realised she wanted to start a photographic business.

Sam continued to work full-time to finance her growing business. She carried out research, attended training courses and looked for photographers and images which inspired her. She made some mistakes, spending money on advertising that wasn't effective and buying unnecessary equipment, and she struggled to price her skills when people asked her to quote for a job. An online American forum for wedding and portrait photographers was a great help to Sam. Exchanging views with like-minded photographers on Facebook and Twitter helped, too.

In April 2006, five years after starting her business, Sam took the plunge and set out as a fully self-employed photographer. She has never looked back.

Think about it

1 How did Sam overcome the problem of raising finance to run her business?

2 In what way did Sam's previous experience come in useful? How do you think it helps her now?

3 How can Facebook and Twitter help Sam to promote her business?

4 To be successful, businesses need a USP (unique selling point) that makes them stand out. Look at Sam's website by visiting Pearson hotlinks. Identify her USP and suggest why she receives so many referrals by word of mouth from clients.

How business ideas can be successful

Getting started

All entrepreneurs spend time and risk their savings to make their idea a reality. They also risk failure. What skills and abilities are needed to be an entrepreneur? Discuss your ideas as a class.

Introduction

Some businesses are very successful, others are not. Why is this? Can you guarantee success if you have a good idea? In this topic, you can find out.

Successful business ideas

There are usually good reasons why some business ideas are successful and others are a disaster.

These are the main reasons why some ideas are so successful:

- **Finding innovative solutions:** Solving a problem by thinking of something new is always a good idea. Recent innovations include the SkyBox (which can pause live programmes) and the electric car. James Dyson built his business on innovative solutions such as the bagless vacuum cleaner and bladeless fan.

- **Meeting customer needs:** This means selling products or services that people want to buy at the right price. Clever businesses offer additional services to beat their competitors, such as free delivery and a personal service. If you do all this *and* offer something different, you should have a recipe for success.

- **Identifying new needs:** Focusing on a new and growing area is always a good idea.
  - Mentoring and coaching are techniques used to help people to develop their full potential in many areas, from work or communication skills to sports and fitness.
  - Using digital media, such as social media websites, to target customers more effectively is now the aim of many businesses.

- **Continuing to meet established customer needs:** Some customer needs, such as transport, food, toiletries and clothes are standard, but there are still opportunities in these areas. Look at what is on offer, identify any gaps and then review and improve your idea. For example, many taxi firms now offer stretch limos or minibuses (for hen or stag parties) and airport services. Speciality foods cater for different tastes, and luxury toiletries and fashionable accessories are also in demand.

- **Being entrepreneurial** means taking risks, having good ideas and being persistent. Find examples of inspirational entrepreneurs such as Tanya Budd, who designed the HypoHoist; Rose Grimond, the business woman behind Orkney Rose, Mark Zuckerberg who founded Facebook, or someone else.

- **Importance of having a strong vision and seeing it through:** The late Steve Jobs, the co-founder of Apple, always had faith in his own belief, even when things went wrong. The key is to learn from a problem and not give up.

- **Measures of success:** These relate to methods of checking the success of a business, for example:
  - Financial – by looking at sales and revenue figures
  - Social – by checking out how many people like the business on Facebook or are following it on Twitter
  - Customer satisfaction – by obtaining feedback from customers who use the product or service.

Assessment activity 1.1   *Maths* | 2A.P1 | 2A.P2 | 2A.M1 | 2A.M2 | 2A.D1 |

You have been asked to produce your own booklet for young entrepreneurs in your area. This will describe the local business environment and identify trends and changes that may affect a start-up business. Your booklet should be divided into three sections:

1 The first section should focus on the current business environment that exists in your own area. You should also be aware of changes that can take place and explain how these can affect a start-up business.

2 The next section should focus on trends you have researched. If you wish, you can focus on trends and that could affect your own idea for a start-up business. You need to compare how two trends have impacted on a start-up business.

3 The final section should focus on the current risks, opportunities and trends in the current business environment for a start-up business. Your assessment should be based on the data you have researched and you should focus on appropriate guidance for an entrepreneur.

Tip

You **assess** information by carefully considering all the factors or events that apply and identifying which are the most important or relevant. Use your research to provide evidence for your conclusions.

You **compare** by identifying the main factors in two or more situations. Point out the similarities and differences and, if appropriate, say which is best and why. Or explain the effects these factors have had.

Link

You can read more about sales and revenue figures in *Unit 2: Finance for business*.

Business ideas

Introduction

Some people think that brilliant ideas come unexpectedly – they call these a 'light bulb' moment. Others believe they come through research and experience. What do you think?

Key term

Unique Selling Point (USP) – a special feature of a product (or service) that makes it easy to promote and sell.

Discussion point 💬

Twitter was the result of a brainstorming session. Brainstorming is a short, focused discussion where you suggest ideas. The trick is to be open to all suggestions and see where they lead. Work in groups to identify 'the best business idea for a lifetime' and see what happens.

In the last topic you saw examples of how business ideas can be successful and you may have already thought of some good ideas yourself. If not, then this topic will help.

What is the **Unique Selling Point (USP)** of Cirque du Soleil?

Activity   Identifying your skills

Guy Laliberté built on his talents as a street performer. A teenage Tommy Hilfiger started his business because he kept being asked where he bought his clothes. List your skills, abilities, interests and hobbies to see if they trigger any good business ideas.

▶ Researching the market

You often hear people ask why a certain product is not made or why they cannot buy something. **Market research** aims to find out what potential customers think or want. This can identify gaps in the market and potential opportunities to provide what people want.

A successful example of market research is Moonpig®. The website was launched to satisfy the demand for greetings cards that could be individually customised.

There are two methods of research you can use:

- **Primary research** is the collection of original data. This is the way to get new ideas, to find out about people's individual buying habits and establish individual customer needs.

- **Secondary research** is desk-based and means researching online and in books and newspapers. Use this to check whether the **market** is growing or declining, how large it is, the range of goods or services provided, who sells them and the prices they charge.

Key terms

Market – the customers for a particular product or service

Market research – finding out customer views and opinions

Activity   Carrying out research

1 Work in small groups to find out what ideas your friends and family have for new or updated products or services that would meet their needs. Design a short questionnaire to find out. Talk to people, send emails and texts, use Facebook. Try to find answers from 10 people to compare with your group.

2 Go online to find out what types of enterprises other people are setting up at Enterprise Nation. List any that appeal to you.

3 Mintel is a large market research agency. Check its blog to find current trends.

4 Investigate your own ideas further. Remember that some useful sources were given at the start of this unit.

Keep all your notes safely as you will need them for your next assessment activity.

Selecting a product or service

Do you make or sell a product or offer a service? What is the difference?

- **A product** is an item that is produced to satisfy the needs of the market. You can make a product yourself or buy items ready-made and then sell them to customers.

  Making products like clothes or jewellery means you need suitable equipment or facilities. Producing any type of food means you must check out the regulations that apply (see next topic). All products must be good quality and value for money if you want repeat sales.

- **A service is** a task you perform – such as valeting a car or walking a dog. Some services, such as mowing lawns and DJ-ing, mean you will need transport and some basic equipment.

  To get a good reputation your work must be of high quality and you must be totally reliable.

Remember

Offering a quality product or professional service is essential if you want repeat business and your customers to recommend you to others.

CONTINUED ▶▶

Targeting customers

Your target customer is the person who will benefit most from your product or service. Small enterprises usually do better by specialising in supplying items or services to a certain group, known as the **niche market.** This is smaller than the **mass market** which is a term used to describe goods that everyone buys, such as shampoo or chocolate. It makes it easier for you to set a competitive price but it is vital that you target your customers accurately. For example, if you plan to sell children's mittens, you will have an entirely different target customer than if you sell gardening gloves.

Activity — Finding a niche

Check out some niche markets yourself on Amazon. Simply click on a major category, such as accessories, then pick an item, such as gloves and see how many different types you are offered!

The main ways in which customers can be targeted are shown in the table below.

Table 1.3 Categories of target customers

Category	Focus on	Examples
By age	Babies, toddlers, pre-school, teenagers, young adults, older or retired customers	Children's party entertainers, face painting, many types of books, magazines, music, films and TV programmes
By gender	Male or female	Many toys, toiletries and clothing shops
By location	The local community, national market or selling internationally	Local sandwich shop or market stall, eBay store, website with e-commerce facilities
By interests concerns	Culture, lifestyle, hobbies, health or needs	Henna tattoos, juice bars, computer games, exercise classes, mobility aids, pet services.

Meet the needs of your target customer

You will only meet the needs of your **target customer** if you understand what they want and why they want it. This means finding out how they think, where they buy, how often they shop and how much they spend.

Put this information into a **customer profile**. This is a snapshot of your customer that summarises:

- their age and lifestyle
- where they live
- what they like and dislike, worry about and value
- how much they would be prepared to pay
- their shopping and spending habits.

Create a profile for this customer. What products and services do you think she's interested in?

Creating a customer profile

Create a customer profile that represents your own class. Compare your ideas. Then think about how it would change for a different age group or by location.

Benefits versus features

Your target customer will buy your product or service because of the benefits they obtain. The features are less important. For example, the benefit of a microwave oven is that you can heat and defrost food quickly and have some meals ready in minutes. Features (such as pre-programmable settings) are useful but less relevant.

Remember

Lulu is a grandmother and Alan Sugar is a grandfather – both are fit, lively and intelligent! Avoid making assumptions about different groups of people and research your target customer properly.

Case study

Providing a major benefit can guarantee success. The Gro-clock enables parents to pre-programme a sun icon to appear to indicate when it's time to get up. This helps the early-waking tot to learn to stay in bed longer – which benefits the parents, too! For most buyers this is their reason for purchase.

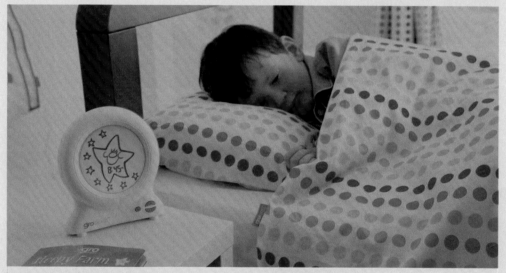
What are the benefits of the Gro-clock?

The Gro Company started with a Grobag Baby Sleep Bag – a smaller size sleeping bag designed by two parents when they needed to keep their own baby warm at night. Read their success story online by accessing their website via Pearson hotlinks and see what other products they make.

1 Who is the target customer for the Gro-clock? Give a reason for your answer.

2 Why was the Grobag Baby Sleep Bag so popular?

3 Suggest two reasons why The Gro Company itself has been so successful.

Key terms

Mass market – all the consumers in one market

Niche market – a small group of customers for a specialised item

Target customer – the customer that a business aims to supply

Customer profile – the main features of a particular group of customers.

Activity Thinking about benefits

List the benefits of your planned product or service. Remember, these must meet the needs of your target customer.

Assessing the suitability of a business idea

Introduction
Once you have come up with your business ideas, you need to assess them to find out which are the most suitable. This means putting your enthusiasm to one side for a while, and thinking carefully about the prospects of success.

Did you know? ❓

Many church halls and community centres rent out their premises for short periods during the week. They can be used by anyone who wants to offer aerobics, yoga or Zumba dance classes, for example.

The resources required

Although you might dream of starting an airline business or competing with Facebook, you are unlikely to do so, given the resources required. It is easy to get carried away with an idea without considering the resources you would need.

- **Time and skills:** How much **time** is needed to develop the idea? Do you need help from other people? Do you have all the necessary **skills** and expertise? If not, who has? How much would it cost you to hire them?

- **Personal commitment:** How much energy and **personal commitment** are you prepared to invest? Would you be happy to neglect your social life for several months to work on it? What are your other commitments and how high would this project rank on your list of priorities?

- **Finance, premises, materials and equipment:** Some start-up businesses need all of these, others need very few. If you aim to work from home, then your life is easier. Even if you rent premises to save money, you will have to pay a deposit equivalent to several months' rent. If all you need is a desk and a computer (and you already have both), then you will need to buy less than if you plan to offer a gardening service.

Selecting the most appropriate idea

The most appropriate idea is not necessarily the one that requires the least resources, but is unlikely to be the one that needs the most. At this stage you should be able to eliminate any non-starters and should be left with some ideas that are still feasible.

What resources would you need to run a dance class?

List the resources required for each of your business ideas. Estimate the likely cost of each one in terms of time, skills, commitment, finance, premises, materials and equipment. Rank each idea according to how appropriate and feasible you think it is. Keep your notes safely in your folder.

Likelihood of success or failure

You now need to decide which one of your remaining ideas is most likely to be a success. You can do this by:

- identifying your prospective customers and deciding how easy it would be to contact them and tell them about your business
- looking at existing demand for your product or service to find out whether it is growing or declining in your area
- estimating how profitable your idea would be – for example, for each item you make or each service you offer, how much money could you make?

Identification of major barriers to entry

'Barriers to entry' is the term used when it is difficult to start a new business because there are many problems and requirements to consider. These could include:

- **large start-up costs** because of the type of premises or amount of equipment needed
- **cash flow issues** because you have to spend money on start-up costs but would not be paid by customers for some time (see Unit 2: Finance for Business)
- **licences** to operate, insurance and other regulations to consider, such as food handling requirements. If you aim to work from home, you need to check that the type of enterprise you plan would be allowed by your local authority.
- **competitors** who are already well established in the area.

Remember

It is essential to come up with a good business name that people will remember. It should summarise what the business is all about. You must not copy competitors' names, although it is helpful to bear them in mind when coming up with ideas yourself.

Assess your own business ideas by carrying out the following activities.

1 Review the business ideas you have come up with so far. Identify the ones that are most likely to be successful by considering which are innovative and will meet new needs or established customer needs.

2 Provide evidence for your views by researching your market and identify gaps or opportunities.

3 Create a profile for your target customer.

4 Assess how easily you will be able to access these customers and the problems or barriers that you might face setting up the business.

Keep your notes safely in your folder.

Producing an initial plan for a business idea

Introduction

You should now have enough information to select the most suitable business idea and produce an initial business plan.

 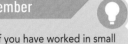
What is a rationale?

Your rationale explains why you think your idea is realistic and is worth pursuing further. It must include the following:

- **Your vision**: How do you see your enterprise at the start? What problem will it solve or what customer needs will it fulfil? How will your product or service do this? What will make it different from products and services offered by existing competitors? (For an example of a vision, see the 'On your Bike' case study later in this unit.)

- **The concept**: Provide a clear description of your business idea and how the business will operate, that is, how the business will make money.

Supporting evidence

This is all the information you have researched and collected throughout this unit. As well as providing this, you need to list the evidence you have obtained and explain why this supports your vision and business concept, for example:

- **Possible customers**: By now you should have prepared a customer profile. It is helpful if you also know the potential size of the market and trends that are affecting it.

Who is the target customer for your product or service?

- **Possible routes to market:** How do you plan to supply your goods or service or deliver them to your customers? What alternatives are there?
- **Your strategy (plan) for dealing with competitors:** Do you intend to offer a different product or service, operate in a different location or have a different pricing strategy? Do you have a USP like Sam Clayton (see the WorkSpace feature earlier in this unit)? How is your idea better than the competition?
- **Ideas for financing:** This should be linked to the resources that you have identified will be needed.
- **Ideas for implementation:** How do you see your plan becoming a reality? How would you put it into practice and over what timeframe? How would you cope until the business started making a profit? Do you have all the necessary skills and, if not, what are your plans for acquiring these or getting someone else to help you?

Assessment activity 1.2   *Maths*   *English*   2B.P3 | 2B.P4 | 2B.M3 | 2B.M4 | 2B.D2

Prepare a presentation in which you will outline your own initial plan for a business idea in your local area and explain why it will succeed against others. You will also summarise the research that you have carried out, and the information you have obtained to support this idea. This must include:

1 Your own description of the features of successful businesses you have personally identified and a comparison of the features, strengths and weaknesses of two successful businesses.

2 Your own realistic plan for a business together with a rationale including your vision and concept. Your plan should include the resources you would require and any barriers you have identified as well as your ideas for financing and implementation. You should also refer to the research you have carried out to explain why your plan is suitable for your own area and how your business idea has the potential to respond to market needs. This means showing that you have researched gaps in the market, created a customer profile and identified the best routes to market.

3 Your own justification for how your idea has the potential for success in relation to existing local businesses.

Tip

Justify your views by giving evidence to support your conclusions, for example by explaining your USP and how you will deal with competitors. You should also demonstrate that you have considered the factors that have made other local businesses successful.

Choice of business format

Introduction

The **business format** relates to the way a business is legally owned and operated. All entrepreneurs must choose the format that they think is the most appropriate for their business at the time. The format options are described in the table below.

Did you know?

Some well-known businesses are franchises, such as Body Shop, KFC and Subway. The owner (franchisor) allows other people (franchisees) to use the name and set up an identical business in their own area in return for a fee and, often, a share of the profits.

Table 1.4 Different business formats

Business format	Description/comments	Benefits	Issues
Sole trader – the smallest and most popular type of business in the UK	The business is owned by one person with or without employees. The owner is personally responsible for every aspect of the business, from keeping the premises clean to doing the accounts.	• Easy to set up – just register with HMRC (the tax office). • After paying tax, all the profits are yours. • Record keeping is simple. • You can trade under your own name without needing permission.	• Illness or holidays may mean there is no income. • You need business skills. • You are personally responsible for paying all debts, otherwise you could be declared bankrupt. This is called **unlimited liability**.
Partnership – owned by two or more people who share responsibility for running the business	Drawing up a Partnership Agreement stating each person's role and share of profits helps to prevent disputes.	• Partners can share skills and ideas. • Problems can be discussed and different views taken into account. • The business will still operate if one partner is ill or on holiday.	• Partners may disagree or not contribute equally. • Profits must be shared. • Decision-making is slower. • Partners still have unlimited liability unless they form a Limited Liability Partnership (LLP).
Private limited company – many family firms have this format. The name always ends with 'Ltd'	The business is registered at Companies House as a limited company. Each person invests money in the business and receives shares in return. The company now pays corporation tax on its profits.	• The owners have **limited liability** for debts. If the business fails, they are only liable up to the amount they invested in the business. • Banks are more willing to lend money.	• Shares in a private company cannot be sold to the public. • Limited companies must comply with more laws and send their accounts to Companies House each year. • All directors and company officers have certain legal duties and obligations.
Public limited company – the largest type of privately owned enterprise in the UK. The business name always ends 'plc'	Many started as private limited companies and were then **floated** on the Stock Exchange. This is the term used when a public limited company is launched. Now anyone can buy shares in the company.	• The business receives far more capital which can be used to grow the company. • If the business is successful, the value of the shares will increase, which will increase the overall value of the company. • Some of the profit, after tax, can be paid to the shareholders as dividends.	• The company must comply with more rules and its accounts are reported in the press. • An Annual General Meeting must be held each year and all shareholders are invited. • If the shares fall in value, many shareholders may sell which lowers the value of the company.

Activity ⟩ Starting a limited company

Find out more about starting and registering a limited company at the Companies House website.

Social enterprises

A **social enterprise** is a business formed with the aim of using any profit or surplus to fulfil social objectives. It may be run as a sole trader, a partnership or a limited company. The format will depend on the type of business, its operations and its objectives.

Case study

On your Bike (Recycle) Ltd is a charitable social enterprise and was started by Ben Fox in July 2010. Ben loves bikes, is passionate about sustainability and detests the fact that the UK dumps over 2000 used bikes into landfill every day. His charity works with schools, hospitals and businesses to obtain and recycle bikes that have been donated or dumped. All the bikes are checked and repaired before being sold to new owners.

Can you think of any other social enterprises that support sustainability?

Ben's vision goes beyond repairing and recycling bikes. He wants to teach students how to check and repair bikes, provide training for the unemployed, promote cycling for health and train people to cycle safely. He also wants to set up a cycle hire with his local authority.

You can find out more about Ben's business by visiting www.pearsonhotlinks.co.uk. If you are a cyclist living in Somerset, do pass on any old bikes to him!

1 Explain Ben's vision in your own words.
2 Explain the difference between a limited company that is not a social enterprise and one that is.

Key terms

Social enterprise – a business which uses its profits or surplus to fulfil social objectives, such as helping others.

Business format – the way a business is legally owned and operated.

Unlimited liability – the owners are personally responsible for all debts, even if this means selling personal possessions.

Limited liability – the owners are only responsible for debts up to the amount they have invested in the business.

Floating – launching a public limited company on the Stock Exchange.

Activity ⟩ Assess business formats

Assess the advantages and disadvantages of each type of business format for your own business idea. Keep your notes safely in your folder.

Sources of help and support in developing a new business

Getting started

Megan argued there was so much to do before she started her enterprise that she couldn't afford the time to ask for advice or support. Her father replied that she couldn't afford not to. What did he mean? And who is right?

Introduction

There are many sources of help and support available to new entrepreneurs which offer advice and help to prevent unnecessary mistakes.

Sources of help

You may need help in various ways, for example:

- **finance:** Most high street banks employ advisers who will provide entrepreneurs with help and guidance. They also give advice on their websites, run free online courses and publish guides and case studies.

- **start-up capital:** This is the money needed to pay for your initial requirements before you receive any revenue. Options for raising this money include:
  - a loan from family, a bank or specialist organisation (such as The Prince's Trust)
  - selling shares to friends and family
  - an overdraft – arranging with the bank to let you spend more than is in your account, on a temporary basis.

- **further research on your chosen idea:** Your best sources are other similar enterprises. If they are located in a different area which means you would not be a direct competitor, they may be willing to provide information and advice. Otherwise, check their website and investigate case studies online and in newspapers and magazines.

- **independent advice:** This is available, free of charge, from the Business Link website. The portal StartUp Britain was also set up by the government to help entrepreneurs. You can visit this website and search the National Enterprise Network at Pearson hotlinks to find your nearest centre. The StartUp website also offers useful advice on many topics.

Activity   Researching business support

In small groups, divide up and share out the research tasks below.

- Identify five major banks and investigate each one to find the help and services it provides.
- Find out about The Prince's Trust, how it works and what it can offer young entrepreneurs.
- For a business idea your group has come up with, investigate what your competitors have to offer.
- Check out three different sources of independent advice.
- Search on Google under the heading 'Sources of Business Advice' to see what else you can find!

Each group should give a short presentation to summarise its findings as well as provide a brief handout.

Support networks

Talking to people about business worries or problems is a useful way of obtaining advice. Several support networks exist to promote contact between business people:

Why is it helpful to talk over your ideas with someone else?

- **Chambers of Commerce** are a network of organisations that offers support and advice to their members who run local businesses. Find your local branch by visiting Pearson hotlinks. You can access this by going to www.pearsonhotlinks.co.uk and searching for this title.
- **Trade associations** provide specific help and guidance to their members who work in a particular trade, from aromatherapists to builders. Check the list by visiting Pearson hotlinks.
- **Professional bodies** represent professionals, such as doctors, lawyers and architects. Many also set and mark professional examinations.
- **Friends and family** can be an invaluable support, particularly if you know people who run a business or are experienced in finance or accounts.
- **Charities and voluntary organisations** include The Prince's Trust and UnLtd which supports social entrepreneurs. ADP (Association of Disabled Professionals) provides help and support to anyone who is disabled and wants to set up a business.

 Did you know?

The government has set up a mentoring programme to enable entrepreneurs to receive advice and guidance from experienced professionals. Visit Pearson hotlinks to find a link to their website.

Activity   Researching two organisations

The Federation of Small Businesses represents thousands of small businesses and provides advice on its website. Shell LiveWIRE, funded by Shell UK limited, provides free information to young people on running a business and enables them to network with other entrepreneurs and talk to online mentors. It also runs an annual competition.

Find out more about both organisations on their websites.

 Remember

Keep all your research materials safely in your folder. You will need them when you prepare your business model.

Business model

Did you know?

Many business models are a variation on other similar businesses. For example, a restaurant, a fast-food outlet, a sandwich bar and a party caterer are all in the food trade, but their business models are very different.

Introduction

A business model is a description of a business which explains exactly how it will operate. Your task now is to use all your research to create your own description, based on your own realistic idea for a business start-up.

Your business model must include all the components and functions of your business and state the revenues it will generate, the expenses it will incur and show how you will make a profit. A more detailed list is given in the table below.

Table 1.5   Components of a business model

Component	Explanation
Research results	The results of researching your chosen market. This must include: • a description of your potential customers (and whether these are businesses or individual consumers) • information about your main competitors.
Goods or services	What you intend to produce or offer for sale. If you are selling goods, you must state whether you intend to make these yourself, or buy them and resell them.
Means of delivering to the customer	How do you intend to sell your good(s) or service(s) – over the internet or by making direct sales? Or both? Would you consider taking on a franchise or not. Why?
Business aims	These are your long-term goals, i.e. what you want to achieve over the next three to five years.
Business objectives	These are short-term targets you want to achieve in the first few months or year. The most effective objectives are SMART, for example someone who makes jewellery may aim to create 15 individual items a week. • This is **Specific**, because it focuses on one target • This is **Measurable** because they can check how many are made • This must be **Achievable** with the resources they have if they work hard • This must be **Realistic** in the time available • This is **Time-related** because 'a week' has been specified.
Stakeholders and their influence	Stakeholders are those people directly affected by your business. They include: • the owners, including any business partners who will have views on what you should do • employees who have opinions and also legal rights • customers who will have opinions about what they want to buy, the quality they expect, the price they think is reasonable and associated services, such as delivery • financiers, i.e. anyone who lends you money such as a bank, charitable organisation or your shareholders. If they fear their money is at risk, they could ask for it back! • suppliers who will rely on you for orders but will also influence your profits, especially if their prices increase. They will want to be paid promptly or may refuse to supply you • the local community who may object if you want to set up a noisy business or one from home with constant visitors, but otherwise will support you and may become customers.

Table 1.5 Components of a business model

Component	Explanation
Finances and start-up costs	You need to list all the start-up costs that you have identified and how you intend to obtain the finances needed to open your business.
Evidence to justify why the idea will succeed	This must be more than wishful thinking! It should include projected sales figures and sales income, based on your chosen pricing policy. You need to estimate your running costs and forecast your potential profit and when this will be achieved. You can also include details of similar successful businesses and how your business model is an improvement on those.

Assessment activity 1.3 — *English*   2C.P5 | 2C.P6 | 2C.M5 | 2C.D3

You are to meet a local group of business financiers who may be interested in supporting a realistic and original business idea that has the potential to be successful. Your task is to prepare a presentation to illustrate your idea and business model and to give a short sales pitch to explain it. To support your arguments, you should ensure that your portfolio is up to date and includes all the relevant evidence. Be prepared to discuss your presentation, explain how your idea has developed and the components of your model, and to answer any questions.

Your presentation should include the following information:

- an outline of the format you have chosen for your business start-up with an explanation of the reasons that made you choose this particular format rather than any other
- your business model together with all the essential components, such as your aims and objectives, method of operation, projected revenues and expenses
- a definition of what success is, using your business plan and comparisons to existing businesses to show how likely it is that your business will be successful.

Provide evidence to show why your model is realistic.

In your sales pitch, you should:

- explain how the format and model will enable the business to carry out its activities successfully. This must be based on its potential for success in relation to existing local businesses. You will need to identify and explain how it has the necessary features to respond to market needs by giving reasons for its suitability and explaining why you rejected other ideas
- explain how the format and supporting evidence justifies your initial idea. You could illustrate this by tracing the steps you have taken from your original business ideas to your final vision. This should include how you evaluated the different ideas you had using the sources of information you had obtained, and why you continued to develop this particular one.

Tip

Use your presentation as an opportunity to demonstrate the alternatives you considered, the timeline over which you have been working and your creativity in responding to market needs. Practise explaining your ideas and use the materials in your presentation to prompt you.

Introduction

Every business must be financially healthy to survive. In this unit, you will learn that to achieve this, the amount of money a business spends (its costs) must be less than the money it receives (its revenue). When this happens, the difference between these two figures is known as profit.

This does not happen by accident; it requires careful planning and there are several 'tools', or techniques, that help businesses to do this. These include predicting when a profit will be made by preparing a break-even analysis, and budgeting to ensure that revenue is as predicted and spending is within planned limits. It also means monitoring the money the business has in the bank and can be expected to receive and pay out in the future.

Preparing key financial documents also enables the business to measure its success and identify areas where improvements are needed. You will learn how to prepare these documents as well as the main techniques used by businesses to plan and monitor their financial situation.

This unit provides the basis for you to go on to study *Unit 13: Financial Planning and Forecasting*.

Assessment: You will be assessed using an onscreen test lasting one hour.

Learning aims

In this unit you will:

A understand the costs involved in business and how businesses make a profit

B understand how businesses plan for success

C understand how businesses measure success and identify areas for improvement.

> My sister is a really good hairdresser but struggled when she started up her own business. Luckily her friend was good at finance and showed her what to do. She says understanding cash flow has been crucial to her survival – so I'm looking forward to learning about business finances.
>
> Tom, *16-year-old Business student*

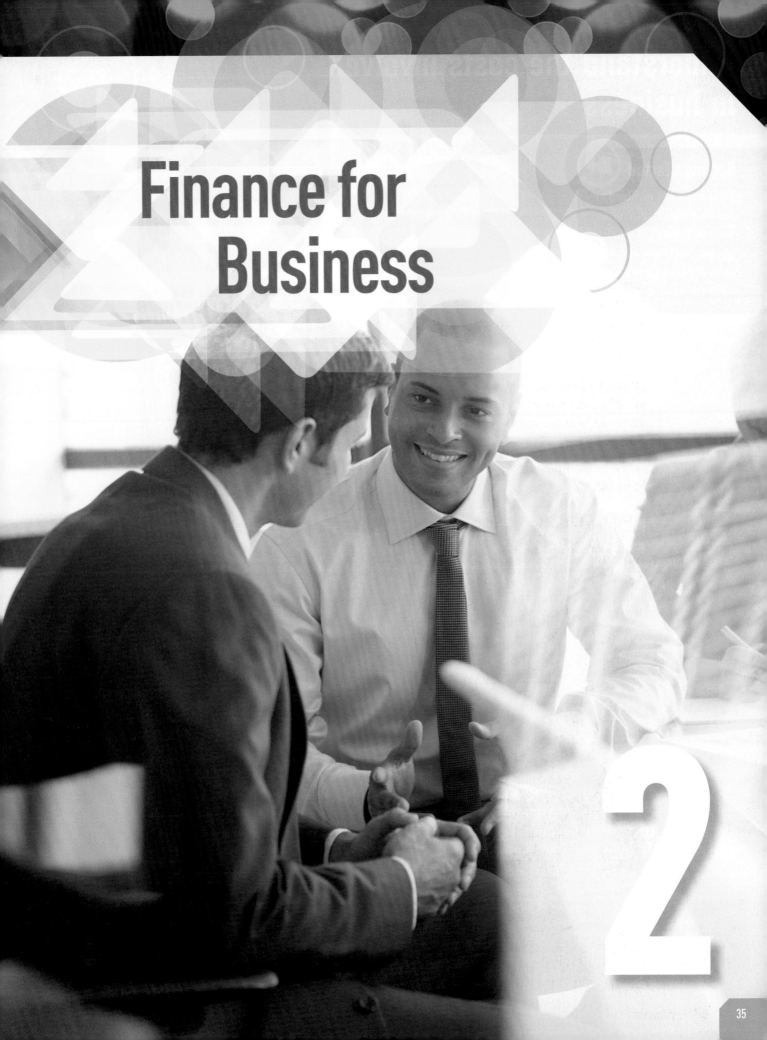

Finance for Business

2

Understand the costs involved in business

Getting started

What costs are involved in setting up and running a sandwich shop? In small groups, list these and then compare your list with other groups.

Introduction

Even the smallest business has various costs. For example, a local newsagent has to buy stock items of newspapers, magazines, confectionery and crisps, pay staff wages (including people delivering newspapers), pay rent and business rates for the property as well as bills for gas, electricity and telephone.

How much will it cost Sam to start up his business?

Key terms

Start-up costs – the amount of money spent setting up a business before it starts trading.

Operating costs (or running costs) – money spent on a regular basis to keep a business running.

Income – money which is paid into a business.

Understand and identify the costs of a business

The costs incurred in running a business can be split into two main categories:

- **start-up costs**
- **operating costs** (or running costs).

Start-up costs

When people start a new business from scratch, there are various items that are required before they can start trading. A driving instructor needs a car; a print shop needs a computer and a copier. Both will need to advertise their business to attract customers. The main point about start-up costs is that these are incurred *before* any **income** is received and the owner has to find this money. It may come from savings but often is obtained as a loan, perhaps from family or from a bank.

Running costs

These are the day-to-day costs incurred in the running of a business. A driving instructor must buy fuel for the vehicle, and a print shop has to buy paper and pay for electricity.

Did you know?

The total amount of money required to start a new business is known as start-up capital.

Activity   Separating your costs

Divide your list of costs for a sandwich shop into start-up costs and running costs.

Understand, define and identify different types of running costs

The running costs of a business can also be split into two types:

- **fixed costs** (or **indirect costs**)
- **variable costs** (or **direct costs**).

Fixed costs

These have to be paid no matter how many products the business makes or sells or how many customers it has. Driving instructors must tax and insure their cars, whether they have one client or fifty. The print shop must pay for heating and lighting. These are often called **indirect** costs because there is no direct link between these costs and the amount sold.

Variable costs

These costs *are* directly related to the number of items sold or produced. Driving instructors use more fuel if they have more clients, because they are on the road more. Print shops use more paper and ink if they are producing more posters or documents. These are also called **direct** costs because they relate directly to the amount produced or sold.

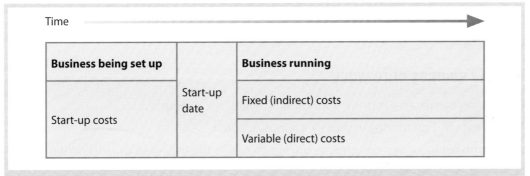

Figure 2.1 Types of business costs

<aside>
Key terms

Fixed costs (or indirect costs) – expenditure on items which does not change with the number of items sold or produced.

Variable costs (or direct costs) – costs which vary according to the number of items sold or produced.

Total costs – the total amount of money spent running a business over a certain period of time (e.g. a month).
</aside>

Calculate total costs

The **total costs** of running a business are found by adding the fixed and variable costs. This is shown in the formula below.

total costs = fixed costs + variable costs

<aside>

Remember

You must know the difference between fixed and variable costs and remember this formula in the assessment.
</aside>

Activity Calculating your costs

1 Divide your list of running costs for the sandwich shop into fixed costs and variable costs.

2 Use the formula to calculate the total costs of the business for a year if the fixed costs per month are £1000 and the total variable cost per month is £2000.

3 In the print shop, the price of ink suddenly increases considerably. Suggest two actions the owner might take.

Understand how businesses make a profit

Introduction

Businesses make a profit by generating revenue through selling their products or services. If this revenue is greater than the cost of making or obtaining the items, and running the business, then the owner(s) makes a profit. After paying tax, the owner(s) can choose what to do with the profit they have made.

In this topic, you will learn more about revenue, different types of expenditure and how to calculate profit.

Understanding revenue

Usually businesses make their revenue by selling goods and/or services to customers. There are thousands of different products on sale, ranging from chocolate bars costing less than a pound, to passenger aircraft costing millions of pounds.

Some businesses sell a service, such as hairdressers, window cleaners and fitness clubs. Some businesses sell both products and services, for example, many car dealerships operate vehicle workshops for services and repairs.

When customers pay for products and services, this produces revenue (or income) for the business.

Identify sources of revenue

Businesses can receive money from other sources, for example:

- **interest** paid on money in a bank savings account
- **investment** income from people buying shares in the business or lending it money (a bank loan, for example)
- **leasing or rental income** by renting out property or equipment that is not currently required to another business.

Guide Dogs for the Blind generates income in a variety of ways.

Calculate revenue

The formula used to calculate the revenue earned for each type of item sold by a business is:

revenue = number of sales × price per unit

For example, if a business sells 1000 small boxes of chocolates at £4.00 each, the revenue will be 1000 × £4.00 = £4000

If a business sells several types of products or services, this formula is applied to each one and the totals are then added together to give the overall revenue figure.

Understanding expenditure

All businesses must spend money to succeed. They have to pay the bills involved in running the enterprise on a day-to-day basis, in the same way that a family must pay the bills at home. A business needs to buy stock or pay for raw materials to produce goods, for example bread and fillings to make sandwiches, or denim, thread and fasteners to make jeans. They may want to spend money on advertising or promoting the business to increase sales and will want to employ staff who can provide excellent customer service.

Identify types of expenditure

There are many different types of business expenditure. Some examples are given in Table 2.1.

Remember

• You must learn the formula to calculate total revenue. It will not be provided in the assessment.

• Consumable items are not the same as raw materials. Raw materials are used to make a product. Consumable items are not.

Table 2.1 Types of business expenditure and their purpose

Type of business expenditure	Purpose
Rent and business rates	To use and operate business premises
Staff wages	To pay for staff who carry out the activities needed to run the business, such as sales and office staff
Raw materials/components/packaging	To make, assemble and pack the finished products
Stock items for resale	Items purchased by retailers to sell to customers
Utility bills (gas, electric and water)	To use power, energy and water on the premises
Telecommunications links and website maintenance	To communicate and provide information to customers and potential customers
Vehicles and fuel	To obtain stock and deliver goods to customers
Consumable items	To be used and replaced regularly by the business, e.g. paper and printer cartridges in the office and soap in the washrooms
Advertising and printing costs	To promote the business to potential customers

CONTINUED ▶▶

Expenditure and overheads

The term **expenditure** relates to all the money the business pays out. Some of these will be fixed costs and some will be variable costs.

You already know that fixed costs have to be paid whether the business is busy or quiet. A newsagent near a school or college would be busier in term time than during the holidays; however, it has fixed costs to pay at all times. Another name for these is **overheads**.

Understanding profit

Revenue and expenditure

All business owners need to be constantly aware of how much revenue is being received and how much money is being paid out. You cannot run a successful business without this information because you will not know whether you have:

- made a **profit**, or
- made a **loss**.

This is obviously important as no business can make a loss for any length of time without having to close down.

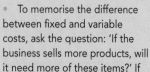

Key terms

Expenditure – money that a business spends.

Overheads – the everyday running costs of the business.

Profit – occurs when revenue is more than expenditure.

Loss – occurs when expenditure is more than revenue.

Remember

- To memorise the difference between fixed and variable costs, ask the question: 'If the business sells more products, will it need more of these items?' If the answer is 'yes', the cost is variable. Otherwise it is fixed.

- Some businesses have many fixed costs, others do not. For each flight an airline has to pay airport landing fees, salaries to the crew, and fuel, maintenance and cleaning costs. The fixed costs for a painter and decorator will mainly relate to the van that is used.

What would be the overheads in a car showroom?

Definitions of profit and loss

- Profit means that revenue is more than expenditure.
- Loss means that expenditure is more than revenue.

Calculate profit

Profit or loss is calculated by using the following formula:

Profit/loss = revenue – expenditure

If the revenue of a business is £3000 and it spends £2500 in the same period, the formula gives:

Profit/loss = £3000 – £2500 = +£500

As the figure is positive, the business has made a profit of £500.

However, if the business has the same income but its expenditure is £3500, then the formula gives:

Profit/loss = £3000 – £3500 = (£500)

As the figure is negative, the business has made a loss of £500.

So the rule is: if the result of applying the formula is a positive figure, then the business is in **profit**. If the figure is negative, it is making a **loss**.

Remember

You must learn the formula to calculate profit. It will not be provided in the assessment.

Did you know?

A negative figure may be shown with a minus sign, i.e. –£500, but is often shown in brackets in business documents, i.e. (£500).

Activity   Calculating costs, revenue and profit

Write down the answers to the following questions, then check them with your teacher/tutor.

1 Which one of the following items is a source of revenue for a hairdressing business?
a) advertising, b) selling shampoo and conditioning products, c) staff wages, d) electricity bill

2 Asiya's expenditure in her first three months of trading was £5000 and her revenue £6250. Use the appropriate formula to calculate her profit or loss.

3 Tom runs a small business selling costume jewellery online. He estimates that he will sell 200 items next month which will cost him an average of £20 each. He thinks that his overheads will amount to £2000.

a) Copy the table below and complete it to calculate his total costs for the month.

Variable costs	200 × _____ =
Fixed costs	
Total costs	

b) Tom has two bills to pay. The first is for 40 small jewellery boxes. The second is for his internet connection. Which of these is a variable cost and which is a fixed cost?

Understand the planning tools businesses use to predict when they will start making a profit

Introduction

You have learned that when revenue is greater than expenditure, the business makes a profit, but if revenue is less than expenditure it makes a loss. Between these two situations, there is a point called breakeven where income and expenditure are equal.

Often, when a business starts up, it makes a loss for a short time before it starts to make a profit. The point at which this occurs (the break-even point) is an important milestone in the progress of the business.

Defining breakeven

Breakeven occurs when a business has made enough money through product sales to cover the cost of making them. There is no profit and no loss.

There are two ways of calculating the break-even point. The first is using a formula and the second is creating a chart.

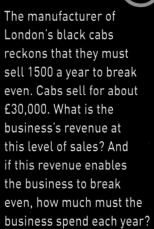

Figure 2.2 Loss, breakeven and profit

Calculating break-even point using a formula

The formula used to calculate the break-even point is:

$$\text{break-even point} = \frac{\text{fixed costs}}{\text{selling price per unit} - \text{variable cost per unit}}$$

You can see how the formula works in this example.

Tom is considering starting a mobile hot dog van business. He reckons that his fixed costs (for example, insurance and tax for the van) would average at £100 per week and the variable cost for each hot dog would be 80p. He aims to sell the hot dogs for £1.30 and wants to find out how many he would need to sell in a week before he would start to make a profit. He therefore applies the formula:

$$\text{break-even point} = \frac{£100}{£1.30 - 80p} = \frac{£100}{50p} = 200 \text{ hot dogs}$$

Activity Calculating break-even point

If a product sells for £5, the variable cost is £3 and the fixed cost is £300, what is the break-even point? Use the formula to calculate it.

Break-even charts

The break-even point can be identified by drawing a chart. Carry out the next activity so that you understand how the chart has been created.

Activity   Working through the chart

Study the break-even chart in Figure 2.3 and read through the list of features in the table below. Do this several times if necessary. Ask your teacher/tutor if there is anything you do not understand.

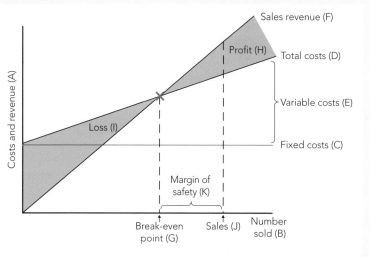

Figure 2.3 A break-even chart where 'X' marks the break-even point

Table 2.2 Features of a break-even chart

Feature	Explanation
A – Costs and revenue	The vertical axis shows the amount of money spent as costs and received as revenue.
B – Number sold	The horizontal axis shows the number of products which could be sold.
C – Fixed costs	This line is horizontal because the fixed costs never change no matter how many products are sold.
D – Total costs	This line shows the fixed costs plus the variable costs. It starts at the left-hand side where the fixed cost line meets the vertical axis. At this point, there are no sales so the variable costs are zero. The line is then drawn to show how variable costs increase in direct proportion to the number of items sold. It then shows the total cost for each level of sales.
E – Variable costs	The difference between the fixed costs line and the total costs line is the variable costs. This gap widens as the level of sales increases.
F – Sales revenue	This line starts at the zero point since no sales means that no income is being earned. The sales revenue is calculated by multiplying the price charged by the number of items sold.
G – Break-even point	This is the point where the sales revenue line crosses the total cost line and shows the number of sales needed for the business to break even.
H – Profit	To the right of the break-even line sales revenue is greater than total costs, so the business is making a profit. The distance between the two lines shows the amount of profit for each level of sales.
I – Loss	To the left of the break-even line sales revenue is less than expenditure and the business is making a loss. The distance between the lines shows the amount of loss at each level of sales.
J – Sales	This shows that sales are higher than the number required to break even.
K – Margin of safety	This is the amount by which sales would have to fall before the break-even point is reached.

Just checking

1 Why is the fixed cost line horizontal on a break-even chart?

2 Which two figures must be equal for the business to break even?

Present break-even information graphically

The following case study shows how a break-even chart is created. Use graph paper to draw one yourself by following the step-by-step instructions. Although you will not have to do this in the assessment, this will help you to better understand break-even charts. Use the illustrations to help you if necessary.

Case study

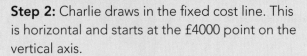

Charlie has a three-week Christmas break from college and wants to make some money. He has been talking to a man who sells Christmas trees to different outlets and wonders if he could sell enough to make a profit.

He knows of an empty car showroom for rent and has also noted the rental terms for a van he could hire for collection and delivery. He would also need to pay two friends to help him. He jots down some figures on a notepad:

> **Christmas tree project**
>
> Fixed costs — van hire, staff wages, showroom rental etc = £4000
>
> Variable cost — price of trees, £30 each
>
> Selling price £50

Charlie's workings

Charlie draws a break-even chart by following these steps.

Step 1: Charlie decides that the most trees he can sell is 400, so he labels his vertical axis to the maximum possible income, i.e. 400 × £50 = £20,000. The bottom (horizontal) axis shows the number of trees sold, so he labels this from 0 to 400.

Step 2: Charlie draws in the fixed cost line. This is horizontal and starts at the £4000 point on the vertical axis.

Step 3: Charlie adds the total cost line to the chart. He calculates that if he sells 400 trees, his variable costs would be £30 × 400 = £12,000. He adds this to his fixed costs of £4000 to give a total cost figure of £16,000. These would be his maximum costs if he sold all the trees.

Charlie plots this mark at the right side of his chart, above the '400' mark on the horizontal axis. He then joins this to the start of the fixed cost line on the vertical axis. This is the line he drew in step 2.

Step 4: Charlie draws the sales income line by starting at 0 (no sales, no income) and ending at the point which shows the maximum possible income if he sells 400 trees (£50 × 400 = £20,000).

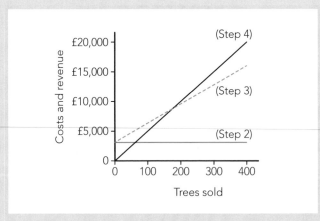

Figure 2.4 Charlie's break-even chart

Show your finished chart to your teacher/tutor. If you have done it properly, the break-even point should read 200 on the horizontal scale and £10,000 on the vertical scale.

Now label all of the following features: costs and revenue axis; number sold axis; fixed cost line; total cost line; variable cost area; sales revenue line; break-even point; sales of 300 and the margin of safety for this amount; profit area; loss area.

Analyse the effect on the break-even point if the figures change

The break-even point changes if sales or costs change. For example, if Charlie has to pay more for his trees, his costs will increase. He will either have to increase his selling price (which could mean he sells fewer) or earn less money on each tree. This means he will have to sell more to break even.

Table 2.3 summarises the likely impact of different changes on the break-even point.

Table 2.3 Summary of changes in sales or costs on the break-even point

Type of change	Effect on break-even point
Increase in sales	The margin of safety increases.
Decrease in sales	The margin of safety decreases. If sales fall below the break-even level, the business could make a loss.
Increase in costs	The number of sales required to break even increases so the profit level would fall or even become a loss.
Decrease in costs	Break-even point is lower so the business makes more profit.

You can see from the table that increased sales and decreased costs are good. However, if sales fall or costs increase, then action must be taken before the business makes a loss. For example, if raw material costs increase, the business could look for a cheaper substitute or try to get the same material cheaper from another supplier.

?   **Did you know?**

In retail, the difference between the buying and selling price of goods is called the 'margin'. The higher the margin, the more potential profit, providing the goods are still priced competitively.

Discussion point

Discuss the actions a business might take if sales started to fall – ideally without adding too much to costs!

CONTINUED ▸▸

The importance of break-even analysis and risks of ignoring it

Business people need to plan to be successful. Someone starting out in business must understand the costs involved in selling a product as well as be able to predict future sales. Without knowing these, the business could stock too many items or try to sell them at too high or too low a price.

The value and importance of break-even analysis is that it could show that some business propositions would not be sensible, because the costs are too high and a profit would never be made.

A summary of the benefits of carrying out a break-even analysis, and the risks of not doing so, are summarised in Table 2.4.

Table 2.4 Benefits and risks of break-even analysis

Benefits of break-even analysis	Risks of not completing a break-even analysis
Both the fixed and variable costs are known.	Costs are unknown and/or too high.
Projected sales revenue is calculated.	The selling price is too low or too high.
The owner knows how many items must be sold to make a profit.	The owner has no idea how many items must be sold to make a profit.
The owner can make adjustments to try to make a profit sooner, e.g. reduce costs by obtaining cheaper materials or increase selling price.	The business makes a loss over a long period of time without any action being taken.
The margin of safety is known.	The margin of safety is unknown.
The best goods are stocked and sold at the optimum price so the business is successful.	Stock costs too much, is sold at the wrong price (maybe at less than cost price!) and the business fails.

Remember

Break-even analysis is one of several financial planning tools that businesses use.

Just checking

1 What costs are combined to make the total cost line on a break-even chart?
2 What is represented by the space between the total cost line and the sales income line above the break-even point?
3 Identify three benefits Charlie gains by carrying out break-even analysis.

Case study

Bridget's Bread

When Bridget Kelly left school she decided to make her own speciality bread, using an old family recipe. To keep costs down, Bridget registered her mother's kitchen so she could produce food there. Her father bought her a little second-hand car so she decided to sell at farmers' markets and to charge £1.50 a loaf. She wrote down her daily costs:

Rent for stall: £20 + travelling expenses: £10 = £30

Cost of making each loaf: = 50p

Three months later Bridget was worried. The markets were quiet due to poor weather and one week she sold only 10 loaves. Unless she made a profit, she earned no money.

Then she had a lucky break. A customer recommended her bread to the buyer at Foodies, a speciality food chain. He visited her and offered her a deal. He is prepared to buy 2000 loaves every week and pay £1 for each one.

Bridget knows that to produce 2,000 loaves a week she would need different premises and more equipment. She already knows the cost of making each loaf but needs to find out what her new fixed costs would be. This is her list.

Rent and rates: £10,000 a year

New kitchen equipment: £15,000 per year (on a 3 year credit scheme)

Van running costs: £2,000 per year

Electricity and miscellaneous office costs: £3,000

Bridget doesn't know what to do. Use your knowledge of break-even analysis to give her advice.

1. Define the term break-even for Bridget. Then calculate her break-even point, using the formula, to show why she made a loss when she only sold 10 loaves at the farmers' markets.

2. The chart below illustrates Bridget's possible new venture.
   a) Identify the meaning of each of the areas marked A – F.
   b) Identify how many loaves she must sell to break-even. Use this information to decide whether this is sensible proposition or not.

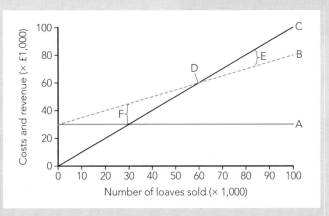

Figure 2.5 Bridget's break-even chart

3. Explain the effect on Bridget's break-even point if:
   a) she employs an assistant to help her
   b) she buys second hand kitchen equipment which is much cheaper
   c) Foodies reduce their offer to 90p a loaf
   d) she finds a cheaper flour supplier.

4. Write a brief summary of the benefits Bridget will gain by doing break-even analysis as she plans for her new business.

Understand the tools businesses use to plan for success

The purpose of budgeting

Budgeting helps people (and businesses) to get what they want by planning. If Donna ran a business in the way she runs her private life, it would soon be in trouble.

Budgeting is a process of setting targets for spending and revenue over a future period of time. They are used in many business situations, such as:

- forecasting start-up costs for a new business
- introducing a new product or building an extension to a factory
- forecasting sales revenue.

The main purpose of budgeting is to ensure that the business is in control of its revenue and expenditure so that it makes a profit.

The budget should be set carefully, ideally using financial information from the previous year as guidance. Then any future predictions about revenue or costs must be considered, based on market trends. Ideally the budget should be realistic, achievable and challenge all the staff to do their best.

Did you know?

- In large organisations, each department has its own budget for expenditure and must keep to this. The target for sales revenue is different because the more sales a business makes, the better!
- The process of measuring performance and taking corrective action is called 'control'. A simple example is driving a car. The driver knows the speed limit (standard of performance), reads the speedometer (measuring actual performance) and uses the brakes or accelerator to adjust the speed (corrective action).

Activity   Talking about budget holders

The person in charge of monitoring the budget is the budget holder. Your school or college will have a budget. Ask your teacher/tutor who is the budget holder and why this person's job is so important.

Budgeting and budgetary control

Setting the budget is only the first stage. Once set, there must be a system to ensure that the targets are met. This is **budgetary control** and can be achieved by:

1 measuring actual performance regularly – normally at least once a month
2 giving this information to the budget holder who checks for any differences between the planned target and actual performance. If expenditure has been too high or sales targets have not been met, the budget holder will take action to correct this
3 if this action works, then next month the performance should be better and match the targets set.

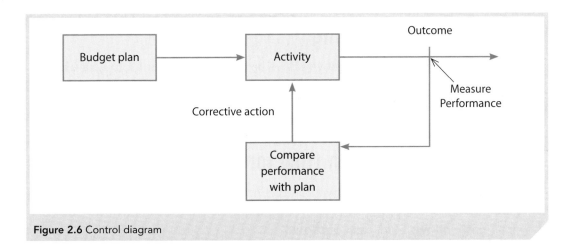

Figure 2.6 Control diagram

Activity   Thinking about budgets

1 In groups, identify two benefits of budgeting as a planning tool and two risks of not doing so. Use the information in the case study below to help you. Then compare your ideas.

2 Budgeting is usually harder for new business owners. Why do you think this is the case?

Remember

Make sure that you can explain the difference between budgeting and budgetary control.

Case study

James Plant and James Moss design and produce small batches of high-quality domestic furniture, lighting and other products at their business in Birmingham. To ensure it is successful, they need to keep a close eye on costs.

When they produce their budget, they forecast the cost of making and selling an item. This includes production materials (for example, wood, metal, concrete and components such as cable), manufacturing costs, labour time and overheads. Their biggest problem is a sudden increase in costs, such as the 65 per cent price rise of stainless steel between 2009 and 2012.

James Plant says they try to minimise the problem by negotiating with other suppliers to see if they can save by ordering larger quantities and looking for different materials. However, they sometimes have to pass on the increase to customers.

Their overheads are all the costs involved in running the business, from employee salaries, to office and marketing costs. These must be paid regardless of the number of items produced, but fortunately are more predictable!

Find out more about Plant and Moss by visiting their website. You can access this by going to www.pearsonhotlinks.co.uk and searching for this title.

1 a) Explain the difference between variable costs and overheads.
   b) Give two examples of variable costs at Plant and Moss and suggest two examples of **i)** office costs and **ii)** marketing costs.

2 What actions do they take to try to minimise the problem of rising costs?

3 Explain why it is important that costs are monitored and controlled at Plant and Moss.

CONTINUED ▶▶

Cash flow forecasting

Have you ever suddenly realised that you have an important present to buy at a time when you are really short of money? Maybe you can borrow money from a relative and repay it later. In business terms, you have a cash flow problem. Businesses try to avoid this happening because they have to pay interest on any money they borrow.

The purpose of cash flow forecasting

Cash flow forecasting is concerned with predicting all the money that is expected to enter and leave a business's bank account over a given period of time. This money is known as 'cash inflows' and 'cash outflows'.

The purpose of doing this is to identify how much money will be left in the bank account. If this figure is positive, then the business can afford to pay its bills. However, if the cash flow forecast predicts a negative figure for the bank balance, the business could be in trouble, especially if the trend continues.

Cash inflows and outflows

Cash inflows

For most businesses, the main type of cash inflow is payment by customers for goods or services they have bought. However, there are other possible sources of income such as:

- **capital from investors:** larger companies are funded by investors who buy shares in the business. In return they receive dividends. As well as providing capital to set up a business, shareholders can also be asked to buy more shares if extra capital is needed, for example to buy another business or more efficient equipment.
- **loan from a bank:** many businesses borrow money from a bank either at business start-up and/or to expand a business which is doing well
- **property rental:** sometimes businesses rent out part of their building to other businesses to provide extra income.

Cash outflows

Businesses can have many forms of cash outflows. The following are the most common types:

- **staff wages:** this is probably the main form of expenditure for most businesses
- **utilities (gas, electricity, telephone):** most businesses use all three
- **materials for manufacturing:** these depend on the nature of the business. At Plant and Moss they include wood and stainless steel, whereas a jeans factory requires cloth and thread
- **insurance:** businesses insure against fire, damage to property and injury to staff or visitors
- **interest on loan:** this is charged when a business borrows money from a bank
- **dividends:** these are paid to shareholders if the business makes a profit
- **rental:** a business may rent its premises from a landlord.

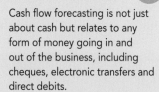

Did you know?

Cash flow forecasting is not just about cash but relates to any form of money going in and out of the business, including cheques, electronic transfers and direct debits.

Key terms

Cash inflows – the amounts of money entering a business's bank account.

Cash outflows – the amounts of money leaving a business's bank account.

Net cash flow – the difference between the cash inflow and outflow figures over a particular time period.

Cash balance – the amount of money forecast to be in the bank account after the net cash flow figure has been added or subtracted from the existing bank balance.

Activity   Identifying cash inflows and outflows

Below is a list of cash inflows and outflows for a manufacturing business. Separate these into two columns, headed 'Cash inflows' and 'Cash outflows'.

Staff wages; consumables; sales income; utility bills (gas, electricity, etc.); window cleaning; rental on a sub-let office; production materials; loan from bank; telephone bills; ingredients for the coffee machine; cash from the coffee machine; interest on bank loan; selling shares.

The purpose of a cash flow forecast

The aim of a cash flow forecast is to identify the possible inflows and outflows, to add them together in each category and to work out the difference, which is known as the '**net cash flow**'. When the net cash flow figure is added or subtracted from the money already in the bank, the resulting figure is the '**cash balance**'.

Activity   Thinking about Sophie's calculations

Sophie runs a small florist's business. On 1 June she decides to carry out a cash flow forecast for the month ahead. She does some calculations and notes the following figures:

Cash inflow £2400

Cash outflow £2100

Opening bank balance £1200

She then does the following calculations:

Net cash flow = £2400 – £2100 = £300

Closing cash balance in bank = £1200 + £300 = £1500

Study Sophie's calculations and then work out what would happen if the outflow figure was £2600 and all of the other figures remained the same.

CONTINUED ▶▶

▶▶ CONTINUED

Key term

Overdraft – this occurs if a business pays more out of its bank account than it has in credit. The bank may allow this but will make an extra charge.

Impact of timings of inflows and outflows

The actual times when money enters and leaves a business's bank account can be critical. For example, if a large payment from a customer is overdue, the bank balance could be negative and **overdraft** charges would apply.

The table below shows some of the effects of the timing of inflow and outflow payments on different types of businesses. You will learn later in this unit how varying the timing of payments can affect a business.

Table 2.5 The effects of the timing of inflow and outflow payments on different types of businesses

Type of business	Effect on cash inflow	Effect on cash outflow
Retail shop where customers pay cash, shopkeeper gets one month's credit from suppliers	Payment is received immediately goods are bought, so there are no delays receiving revenue.	Business only needs to settle bills once a month, which helps if trade is quiet during that month.
Manufacturer which supplies goods to other businesses on credit (e.g. Heinz to Tesco)	Depends on how quickly payment is received. Some customers may need chasing for payment.	Manufacturer needs to pay for raw materials but may delay payment, too. They cannot delay other payments such as staff wages.
Seasonal business, e.g. crop farm or seaside hotel	Revenue is received over a short period, e.g. when the crop is harvested or when the hotel is open or busy.	Some expenses, such as utility bills must be paid all year. Extra money may be needed for expenses out of season, e.g. the cost of seeds for planting or the cost of decorating when the hotel is closed.
Business undertaking large projects, e.g. house and road builders	Payment may only be received in one large sum when the project is complete.	Money for materials and labour is needed regularly throughout the time the project is being undertaken.

Discussion point

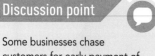

Some businesses chase customers for early payment of their debts, but pay their own bills from suppliers as late as possible. Can you think why? Is this good for business or bad?

The benefits of cash flow forecasts and risks of not completing them

Cash flow forecast information is another important planning tool. Creating the forecast enables the business to plan for success because if things are going well, it can ensure there are finances available to produce new goods or services, expand its activities or invest in new resources. If there is less money available, then other actions may need to be taken to save money, such as negotiating with suppliers to change payment dates or spread payments, or reducing activities. You will learn more about this when you read the WorkSpace case study at the end of the unit.

Table 2.6 shows the main benefits of using and risks of not using a cash flow forecast.

Table 2.6 Benefits and risks related to cash flow analysis

Benefits of cash flow analysis	Risks of not using cash flow analysis
The timing of all expected revenue is known (cash inflows) and reminders are sent if any is overdue.	Revenue may be received late or not at all.
The timing of all expenditure is known (cash outflows) and payment dates can be renegotiated if there is a temporary problem.	Payments are delayed and suppliers become alarmed and may refuse to trade with the business.
If there is likely to be a deficit, the owner has time to take action to delay payments or obtain a temporary loan if necessary.	The business may have to pay high interest charges on an unauthorised overdraft or emergency loan.
The owner has warning if there is a long-term problem because costs will need to be reduced or revenue increased for the business to survive.	The business cannot afford to pay its bills and eventually has to cease trading.

Completing and analysing a cash flow forecast

A cash flow forecast is completed by entering the inflows and outflows for a month, calculating the net cash flow and then working out what the closing bank balance will be at the end of that month. This is then the opening balance for the following month.

When you analyse a cash flow forecast, the most important figure is the **closing bank balance**.

- A small but positive figure means that the business can pay its bills and has little danger of going bankrupt.
- A large positive figure means that there is money available for investment or expansion, for example in new products or activities, updated equipment to improve efficiency, energy conservation.
- A small negative figure means that money may have to be borrowed, at least for a short while, so more money has to be paid out next month.
- A large negative closing balance means that the business cannot pay its way and may go bankrupt unless action is taken to increase inflows and/or reduce outflows.

Activity　　Completing Eleanor's cash flow forecast

Copy out and complete the cash flow forecast for Eleanor, who runs a pet ambulance service. She discovers that her van is in need of repair and will be off the road for two weeks in July.

How do you think Eleanor will react to this information? What would you advise her to do?

Eleanor's cash flow forecast			
	June (£)	July (£)	August (£)
Total receipts (inflows)	1000	400	1200
Total payments (outflows)	500	1200	1500
Net cash flow			
Opening balance	200		
Closing balance			

Understand how businesses measure success

Introduction

Businesses always plan to succeed. Break-even analysis and cash flow forecasting are two ways in which businesses can plan to be successful. However, no plan ever works perfectly and, when events have taken place, business managers need to know exactly what has happened. When they know this, they can make plans to improve performance in the future if necessary.

The two main financial analysis documents which are produced to help managers assess how successful the business has been are:

- **the income statement** (also known as the **profit and loss account**)
- **the statement of financial position** (also known as **the balance sheet**).

The income statement lists all of the business's actual income and expenditure for a year. Hopefully, the income is greater than the expenditure and the business has made a profit. The balance sheet shows how the money invested in the business (its **capital**) has been spent.

Making a profit

Cost of sales

It costs money to make any product and this amount is called the **cost of sales**. If you were making teddy bears and the raw materials for each one cost £15, this is your cost of sales. You would have to deduct this amount from the sales revenue you received to work out your **gross profit**.

The items that comprise cost of sales will vary from one business to another, depending upon what they produce. For example, the cost of sales for a building firm would include all of the components and materials used in making a house, such as bricks, sand, cement, wood for the roof supports and roof tiles.

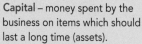

Key terms

Capital – money spent by the business on items which should last a long time (assets).

Cost of sales – the cost of producing a product.

Gross profit – the money made from selling a product (the sales revenue) after the cost of producing that product (cost of sales) has been deducted.

Net profit – the money made from selling a product after all costs (expenditure) have been deducted from the gross profit.

Activity Identifying cost of sale items

You sing with a band in your spare time and you decide to produce a CD to sell at the gigs where you play. In small groups, write a list of your cost of sale items. Compare your list with other groups.

Gross profit

The formula for calculating gross profit is:

> gross profit = revenue – cost of sales

Example:

A business sells £20,000 worth of goods and the total cost of sales is £4000.

> Gross profit = £20,000 – £4000 = £16,000

Net profit

Net profit is the amount of money left when all the expenses other than cost of sales are deducted from the gross profit figure, for example rent, business rates, electricity and gas, telephone and wages of office staff. The formula for calculating net profit is:

> net profit = gross profit – expenditure

Activity Calculating net profit

If the gross profit of a business is £15,000 and all expenses except cost of sales amount to £11,000, what is the net profit?

The impact of positive and negative profit figures

All businesses want to have a positive profit figure because a negative profit amounts to a loss.

Table 2.7 The impact of gross profit and net profit

Gross profit and its impact	Net profit and its impact
If gross profit is positive, this means that revenue is greater than cost of sales.	If net profit is positive, this means that gross profit is also positive and expenditure is within budgeted levels.
If gross profit is low or negative, action to take is: • increase sales revenue (e.g. by increasing sales volumes or prices) • reduce cost of sales (e.g. using cheaper raw materials, bulk buying, changing supplier or negotiating better discounts).	If net profit is low or negative, this may be because gross profit is too low and/or expenses are too high. Action to take is: • increase gross profit • reduce expenses by checking overheads to see where savings can be made.
See Plant and Moss case study.	See WorkSpace case study.

Remember

You must know and be able to use both these formulas in the assessment.

Did you know?

The total assets less current liabilities figure is equal to the shareholders' funds figure (£2500). This is the 'balance' on the balance sheet, the two items being the same.

Discussion point

• Businesses can try to sell more products by reducing the price, or aim to increase income by inc reasing the selling price. What are the dangers of both methods, and which one would you choose to increase income? Discuss both options as a group.

• Some people argue that you will never become rich if you don't take a few risks. They borrow as much as possible and pay their bills as late as they can. Do you agree with this approach? What are the dangers?

CONTINUED ▶▶

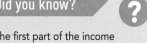
Looking at financial statements

Financial statements summarise the financial activities of a business and provide an immediate indication of its financial position. They are studied by a number of people because they show how well the business is being managed. The types of people who are interested in the accounts of a business are shown in Table 2.8.

Table 2.8 People who are interested in financial statements

Category of person	Reason for interest in financial statements
Shareholders	Is the money they invested safe? Will a good dividend be paid?
Managers	Is the business being managed well? Is it expanding or contracting?
Employees	Are their jobs safe? Can a wage rise be afforded?
Suppliers	Has the business enough money to pay what it owes?
Customers	Is the business sound enough to ensure that it can meet orders?
The government (HMRC)	How much corporation tax is owed?
Competitors	Are we making more or less profit than our main competitors?

Income statement (profit and loss account)

This statement shows how a business has performed financially over a period of time, usually a year. It shows how much revenue was received from sales of products and/or services, how much of this money was spent and how it was spent. An example is shown in Table 2.9 .

Table 2.9 Income statement (profit and loss account)

	£	£
Income from sales		50,000
Cost of sales	15,000	
Gross profit		35,000
Expenses/overheads		
Wages	25,000	
Utilities	5000	
Net profit		5000

The top three lines are the trading account.

The lower section lists the expenses.

This figure is found by subtracting the total expenses from the gross profit.

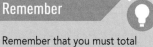
Activity　Checking the income statement

Work through the income statement carefully and make sure that you understand all the calculations. Ask your teacher/tutor for help if you are unsure.

Statement of financial position (balance sheet)

The purpose of a statement of financial position

All businesses have money invested in them – even a window cleaner must have a bucket and a ladder. Balance sheets show how much money is invested in the business and what it has been spent on.

Businesses normally produce a statement of financial position once a year on the last day of their **financial year**. This statement is a snapshot of the business's financial situation on that particular day. (Remember that an income statement summarises activities for the whole of the year).

What does the statement of financial position show?

The statement shows three different types of items.

- The **assets** of the business. These are all the items that the business owns, the money it has in the bank and the money it is owed by other people, for example customers who have bought on credit. These are called **debtors** (or **trade receivables**).

  Assets are divided into two types:

  - **fixed assets** are items that the business must keep to be able to trade, such as a van or a computer. They are called 'fixed' because they are here to stay

  - **current assets** are items that are changing with every transaction, such as stock, debtors and cash in the bank. Current assets can be turned into cash quickly, if necessary.

- The **liabilities** of the business. These include all the money the business owes to others, for example to suppliers or to the bank.

  Liabilities are also divided into two types:

  - **current liabilities** are money that must be paid back within a year, such as to suppliers and a bank overdraft

  - **long-term liabilities** include loans that can be repaid over a longer period.

- The capital that is put into the business. This may include:

  - **money invested** by the owner or shareholders (called **share capital**)

  - **retained profits** from previous years.

Remember

The business can be funded from internal sources, e.g. share capital and profits kept back to reinvest in the business, and from external sources, e.g. bank loans. This money enables the business to buy assets.

What is the purpose of a statement of financial position?

Did you know?

All the assets added together must always equal all the liabilities plus the capital invested in the business. This is why the statement is often referred to as a balance sheet.

CONTINUED ▶▶

Preparing a statement of financial position

Case study

Imran set up his business last month with £2500 he saved and a £500 bank overdraft. He spent £1000 on a van and £500 on a computer. He currently has £800 of stock which he has bought on credit from Tom, a friend, and has £1100 in the bank. He has sold goods worth £400 to another friend, Ashraf, who promises to settle up with him soon. What will his balance sheet look like at this point?

1 **Fixed assets:** Imran's fixed assets are his van and computer. He cannot run his business without them.

2 **Current assets:** Imran's current assets are his stock and the money in the bank. Ashraf is also an asset because he is a debtor – he owes money for the goods he bought.

3 **Current liabilities:** Tom is a creditor. He is a current liability because Imran must pay him soon. He must also repay his overdraft within a year.

4 **Working capital (or net current assets):** This figure represents the amount of money Imran has available to run the business every day, so it is very important. If it is too low, or becomes negative, he may not be able to pay his debts when they are due.

5 **Total assets less current liabilities:** This figure always equals the shareholders' funds if the calculations are correct.

6 **Capital:** This is the money Imran put into the business. There are no retained profits because it is Imran's first year of trading.

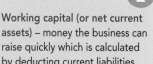

Key term

Working capital (or net current assets) – money the business can raise quickly which is calculated by deducting current liabilities (all current debts owed by the business) from current assets (all money owed to the business at the current time).

Table 2.10 Imran's statement of financial position (balance sheet)

Assets	£	£
Fixed assets		
Van	1000	
Computer	500	1500
Current assets		
Stock	800	
Debtors (trade receivables)	400	
Cash in bank	1100	2300
Total assets		3800
Liabilities		
Current liabilities		
Creditors (trade payables)	800	
Overdraft	500	1300
Working capital (current assets minus current liabilities)		1000
Total assets less current liabilities		**2500**
Shareholders' funds		
Share capital	**2500**	
Retained profit	0	

Activity Preparing a statement of financial position

1 Work through Imran's statement of financial position with your teacher/tutor. Make sure you understand each entry and each calculation.

2 Imran continues trading for some time, but he is rather worried. His sister suggests that he reworks his balance sheet to see what it says now.

Imran buys a camera for £500 for taking photographs of stock for his website, and more stock for £2000. Although he sells most items for cash, he is owed £1100 by his debtors. He has increased his overdraft to £1500 and owes his creditors £1400. He has £300 in the bank.

Copy out the balance sheet format above, enter the figures and calculate Imran's working capital. Keep your work safely as you will need it for the next activity.

Did you know?

• It is a legal requirement for many businesses to produce a balance sheet and profit and loss account each year.

• It is normally the net profit figure that tells you how well a business is being run, because the cost of overheads is more under the control of managers than raw material prices. Plant and Moss had few options when stainless steel prices dramatically increased.

Remember

When a figure in a financial report is presented in brackets, (£5000), this means that the figure is negative.

Understand how businesses can be more successful

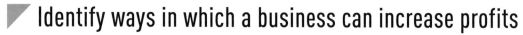

◤ Identify ways in which a business can increase profits

There are two main ways in which businesses can increase profits:

- by increasing income
- by reducing expenditure.

Income can be increased, for example by selling more products, increasing the selling price of products, increasing the range of products sold and encouraging customers to pay bills on time or earlier.

Expenditure can be reduced, for example by negotiating a better price for materials and utilities, looking for cheaper materials to use, reducing staffing levels, moving to cheaper premises, running machines more quickly to speed up production and delaying paying suppliers for as long as possible.

◤ Analyse financial statements and suggest actions to take

Income statements and statements of financial position provide useful information about the financial health of a business. The main points to look for are as follows.

Income statement

- Has the firm made a healthy net profit? Has anything changed/improved since the report a year ago?
- If the business is making a loss, what can be done to improve the situation?

Statement of financial position

- Is there enough working capital to cover the amount owed to creditors? If there is not, and suppliers are not paid, they may refuse to provide goods to the business.
- Is there enough cash at the bank to cover immediate debts or emergencies?
- Is there money saved as **reserves** to increase the shareholders' funds?
- If working capital is low, this needs to be increased. The first step is to ensure there is enough money in the bank to pay suppliers and cover emergencies. Cash can be increased by selling stock and/or chasing debtors to pay their bills.
- The money raised must be used wisely. It is no use spending it all on stock again! If current liabilities are high, these should be reduced so there is less chance of the business being unable to pay its immediate debts.

Remember

Gross profit is improved by increasing sales revenue and reducing the cost of sales. Net profit is improved by increasing gross profit and reducing expenses.

Key term

Reserves – money that has been saved from previous profitable years.

Just checking

1   Which two of the following would be included in the cost of sales figure for a small printing business? Electricity; staff wages; paper; printing ink; fuel for delivery van.

2   What figure is produced when the total expenses are subtracted from the gross profit figure?

3   Which two of the following would appear as current assets on a balance sheet? Stock; trade payables; share capital; trade receivables.

WorkSpace

▶ ## Chris Reid

Managing Director, Connect Technology Group

Connect Technology Group develops and produces specialist software and hardware designed to meet the needs of childcare and security firms. Managing Director Chris Reid set up the business in 2004. His company has gone from strength to strength and now employs 14 staff.

Chris always wanted to be his own boss, but says that his main challenges have often been linked to cash flow. He says that it 'often feels that more money is going out of the business than is coming in!'

The reason for this is that many of his suppliers insist on payment within 21 days, whereas some of his customers will only pay their bills 60 or 90 days after receiving the goods. Fortunately he has a good relationship with one supplier, who allows him up to 60 days credit.

To keep costs down, the business has recently moved to cheaper premises. These are 'managed' which means Chris only has to pay one monthly bill covering rent, utilities, heating, security and maintenance. As the office equipment he uses is normally only cheap, he prefers to buy this rather than pay a monthly leasing bill.

December and January are quiet months, but Chris still has to find the money for his staff wages and overheads. To help provide a steady source of income, the company has now set up maintenance contracts on equipment it supplies that brings in a regular income every month.

Think about it

1 Why does Chris Reid prefer to operate from 'managed' premises?

2 Why is it important that Chris negotiates the longest credit terms he can with his suppliers?

3 What effect do the two quiet months a year have on Chris's cash flow, and why?

4 Why has setting up maintenance contracts been a good idea?

5 **a)** What terms would be used for i) the suppliers to whom Chris owes money and ii) the customers who still owe Chris money?
b) Which of these is a current asset and which is a current liability?

Assessment Zone

This section has been written to help you to do your best when you take the assessment test. Read through it carefully and ask your tutor if there is anything that you are still not sure about.

Hints and tips

Before the test

You will improve your chances if you make sure that you have revised all the key areas that are likely to be covered. A list of these is given below. Use this as a checklist to make sure that you haven't forgotten anything!

Arrive in good time for the test, so you are not in a panic.

Listen carefully when the invigilator gives you instructions.

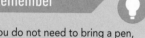

Remember

You do not need to bring a pen, paper or calculator.

> **Key revision topics** (your tutor may add to these)
> * Identify start-up and running costs and state the difference between these.
> * Identify fixed and variable costs and explain the difference between these.
> * Define and give examples of overheads.
> * List sources of revenue for a business and types of expenditure.
> * Calculate revenue and calculate profit.
> * Define breakeven and calculate break-even point using a given formula.
> * Identify different components on a break-even chart.
> * Explain the difference between budgeting and budgetary control.
> * Explain the purpose of cash flow and complete a cash flow forecast.
> * Explain the benefits of using different planning tools, i.e. breakeven analysis, budgeting and cash flow forecasting and explain the risks of not doing so.
> * Analyse a break-even chart and a cash flow forecast.
> * Calculate gross profit and net profit and explain how both can be improved.
> * Identify the components of a trading account and explain its use.
> * Complete and analyse an income statement (profit and loss account).
> * Identify and give examples of assets (fixed and short-term), liabilities (current and long-term) and capital.
> * Calculate working capital.
> * Complete and analyse a statement of financial position (balance sheet).

During the test

Take a deep breath when you are told you can begin. If you have a tendency to panic, look through a few questions before you start. You can answer the questions in any order, so you might want to start with one that you find easy, to give you confidence.

Read each question carefully before you attempt an answer. Check that you are clear about what you have to do.

Remember that the number of marks relates to the number of answers you are expected to give. If you are asked to identify two variable costs, you cannot gain full marks if you only select one!

You will not lose any marks for a wrong answer, so if you are not sure, you are better to guess than to leave a blank.

On some questions you will see a 'working box' that you are invited to use. Use it! If you get part of an answer wrong, the examiner will check this box. If your workings are correct, then you may gain a mark.

Check the time regularly and use it wisely. If you complete the test early, use the rest of the time to review your answers and check that they are correct.

Most questions ask you to click a box to select an option or type your answer in a box. Others are more 'open-ended'. In this case, you may be asked to discuss or explain something and given a scrollable box in which to type your answer. These questions are worth more marks, so you need to think carefully about your response. Try to include one point for each of the allocated marks for that question.

Sample questions

On the next few pages you will find five sample questions with answers. Read these carefully and note the hints and tips that are given. Then answer the remaining six questions yourself and check your answers with your tutor.

Remember

If any question baffles you, you can 'flag' it and come back to it later.

This question is checking if you know the difference between fixed and variable costs. Variable costs are directly related to sales and you might find it easier to identify those first.

Question 1

Which two of these items are (fixed costs) for a florist? [2]

Click on **two** of these boxes:

Staff wages	X
Flowers	☐
Monthly rent	X
Ribbons and wrapping paper	☐

Question 2

(a) Joanne runs her own nail bar but is not sure how to calculate her net profit. In the box below, enter the formula she should use [1]

You may be asked to provide a formula in the assessment test.

Gross profit – expenses = net profit

(b) Joanne would like to increase her net profit next year. Give **three** actions she could take.

Joanne can increase her net profit in these ways:

1   By reducing her expenses, such as her telephone bill.

2   By reducing her cost of sales, such as the cost of her nail polish. This will increase her gross profit figure.

3   By increasing her sales revenue. She could do this by attracting more clients or increasing her prices. This would also increase her gross profit figure.

[3]

The examples show that the learner fully understands the components of gross and net profit. This answer would gain full marks.

Question 3

Seb works for a garden centre and his boss is thinking about building an extension to display lawnmowers for sale. The table below shows their predicted figures for the next year.

Selling price per lawnmower	£50
Variable cost per lawnmower	£20
Fixed costs	£5000

The formula to calculate break-even is

$$\text{Break even} = \frac{\text{fixed costs}}{\text{Selling price per unit} - \text{variable cost per unit}}$$

> You should expect a question on break-even in the assessment. If this involves using the formula, it will be provided.

(a) How many lawnmowers would the business need to sell to break-even? Put your answer in the box below. [2]

> 250

You may use the working box to show your calculations.

> WORKING BOX
>
> $$\frac{5000}{50 - 30} = \frac{5000}{20} = 250$$

> Using the working box shows the examiner that you know how to use the formula.

(b) Outline what is meant by the term 'break-even point'. [2]

> The break-even point is when a business has made enough money from product sales to cover the cost of making that item. There is no profit and no loss.

> Knowing this definition is useful.

Question 4

Jason runs a gardening business.

(a) *Insert the following items correctly into this extract from his statement of financial position (balance sheet) as at 31 March.* [8]

Stock £200	Equipment £700

Trade Payables £400	Trade Receivables £600

(b) *Complete the calculations.*

	£	£
Fixed assets		
Motor vehicle	2500	
Equipment	700	
		3200
Current assets		
Stock	200	
Trade receivables	600	
Cash	2300	
	3100	
Current liabilities		
Trade payables	400	
Overdraft	600	
	1000	
Working capital (net current assets)		2100

White spaces are left for you to complete the entries but you must know which items are fixed assets, current assets and liabilities to answer this question correctly.

Remember that working capital is current assets minus current liabilities.

(b) *Analyse the extract from Jason's balance sheet. Identify **two** ways in which he could improve his financial position.* [2]

He could pay his creditors and pay off his overdraft and still have money left in the bank. Two actions Jason could take are to pay off his overdraft, because then he will not have to pay bank charges. He could also get his debtors (trade receivables) to pay the money they owe him, particularly if some bills have been overdue for some time.

This answer shows the learner can interpret and analyse the figures correctly and can make sound business decisions based on this information.

Question 5

Alice is thinking about taking over an ice-cream kiosk in a busy shopping centre. She is concerned about possible cash-flow problems since the business is seasonal.

The examiner is looking for a reasoned argument here

Discuss the benefits for Alice of using cash-flow forecasting in her business and the steps she could take to improve her cash-flow through the year. [8]

A seasonal business is one where sales vary depending upon the time of year. Alice will probably sell more ice cream in summer than in winter because people are less likely to buy ice cream when it is cold weather. Her sales will fall at this time but she will still have her fixed costs to pay.

It is important to show you are thinking of the business example in the question. The fact the business is seasonal is important.

The forecast shows the projected inflows and outflows and when these are expected. This means Alice can plan ahead and see exactly what costs she will have to cover when sales are low. This way she can make plans to help the business survive.

This shows the learner understands the main purpose of cash flow forecasting.

Alice needs to find some way of increasing revenue during the winter months. She could find something else to offer for sale at the kiosk, such as hot drinks or umbrellas. She could close the kiosk in the winter and find a different job, for example over Christmas and during the January sales. This will lower her fixed costs. She could offer special promotions to encourage customers to return, such as giving a raffle ticket with each ice-cream purchased during the quiet period, with a weekly prize.

The learner has identified that the main action to take is to increase revenue. If this is not possible then reducing fixed costs is important. These are sensible suggestions but other realistic alternatives would be just as acceptable.

This box will keep scrolling until you have finished your answer.

Over to you!

Question 1

Ashraf has started his own car valeting business. Identify the following two running costs. [2]

(a) Pressure washer

(b) Car shampoo and polish

(c) Promotional leaflet

(d) Telephone bill

Question 2

Petra runs a small business making handmade photograph frames. The following figures list her projected income and expenditure for three months.

(a) Complete her cash-flow statement below by filling in the blank spaces. [3]

2012	April (£)	May (£)	June (£)
Total receipts	2000	1000	2100
Total payments	1700	1500	1600
Net cash flow			
Opening balance	1200		
Closing balance			

(b) Using the information in the cash flow, suggest one action Petra should take to manage her finances for these three months. [1]

Question 3

Misha makes children's T-shirts which she sells for £5.50 each. Last year she sold 7000 T-shirts.

(a) Calculate her total revenue. [1]

(b) Identify which one of the following expenditure items would count towards her cost of sales. [1]

Sewing machine

Cotton material

Advertising costs

Internet connection

Question 4

Jack is launching his own smoothie business and has prepared a breakeven chart.

(a) Read the chart below and label the following

   (i) The fixed costs line

   (ii) The total cost line

   (iii) The sales revenue line   [3]

(b) Identify the break-even point   [1]

(c) Outline **two** benefits of carrying out a break-even analysis: [2]

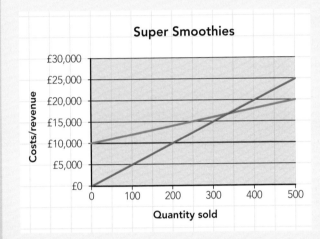

Question 5

Naseem has a sportswear shop and wants to complete his statement of financial position (balance sheet). He needs to identify which two items are short-term assets.   [2]

(a) Cash register

(b) Stock

(c) Shop fitments

(d) Cash in the bank

(e) Shop safe

Question 6

Marsha has been in business for one year as a mobile hairdresser and is preparing her income statement (profit and loss account). Explain how the information it provides can help her to improve her financial position.   [4]

Introduction

A brand is a way of communicating with customers. If it is done well, it makes a business unique and increases the value of a product. This unit explains how a business builds a brand and why this is important.

This unit looks at a number of promotional techniques that can be used to make people aware of your brand. You will have an opportunity to examine the differing ways that companies in business to business (B2B) and business to consumer (B2C) markets promote their brands.

You will look at the different elements that must be included in a promotional campaign, and examine ways of reviewing the success of a brand.

Finally, you will have an opportunity to use your creativity and imagination to create a unique brand for the products offered by a selected organisation.

Assessment: This unit will be assessed through a series of assignments set by your teacher/tutor.

Learning aims

In this unit you will:

A explore the use of branding and the promotional mix in business

B develop and promote a brand for a business.

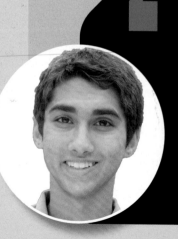

"My hobby is drawing so I enjoyed the creative aspect of this unit. Being able to create a brand for a product was really exciting because I got to use my imagination. It was interesting to do research into different media channels and find out how people respond to different types of promotion.

Jabez, *15-year-old Business student*

Promoting
a Brand

BTEC
Assessment Zone

This table shows you what you must do in order to achieve a **Pass**, **Merit** or **Distinction** grade, and where you can find activities in this book to help you.

Assessment criteria			
Level 1	**Level 2 Pass**	**Level 2 Merit**	**Level 2 Distinction**
Learning aim A: Explore the use of branding and the promotional mix in business			
1A.1 Describe the importance of branding for a business	**2A.P1** Explain how branding is used in two businesses **See Assessment activity 3.1, page 89**	**2A.M1** Compare the use of brand promotion in two businesses **See Assessment activity 3.1, page 89**	**2A.D1** Evaluate the effectiveness of the promotional mix for a selected branded product **See Assessment activity 3.1, page 89**
1A.2 Identify elements of the marketing mix for a selected branded product	**2A.P2** Assess the marketing mix for a selected branded product **See Assessment activity 3.1, page 89**	**2A.M2** Explain the importance of selecting an appropriate promotional mix for a selected branded product **See Assessment activity 3.1, page 89**	
1A.3 Identify elements of the promotional mix used for a selected branded product	**2A.P3** Describe the purpose of elements of the promotional mix used for a selected branded product **See Assessment activity 3.1, page 89**		
Learning aim B: Develop and promote a brand for a business			
1B.4 Outline an idea and select a target market for a brand	**2B.P4** Use branding methods and techniques to recommend a brand personality and a target market for a brand **See Assessment activity 3.2, page 94**	**2B.M3** Explain how branding methods and techniques were used to recommend a brand personality and a target market for a brand **See Assessment activity 3.2, page 94**	**2B.D2** Evaluate the effectiveness of a promotional campaign for a brand and recommend improvements **See Assessment activity 3.2, page 94**
1B.5 Outline elements of a promotional campaign for a brand	**2B.P5** English Plan a promotional campaign for a brand **See Assessment activity 3.2, page 94**	**2B.M4** Justify the choice of promotional mix for a brand **See Assessment activity 3.2, page 94**	

English Opportunity to practise English skills

How you will be assessed

This unit will be assessed by a series of internally assessed tasks. You will need to collect examples of promotional materials and label them to highlight different features. You will need to gather evidence of how well a brand has been promoted.

You will need to produce an original promotional campaign for a brand. You might produce a mail shot or a radio advert and then give a presentation on why it will appeal to a specific target market.

Your assessment could be in the form of:

- a presentation, pitching an idea for a brand to a local business
- a package of promotional materials
- a review of the use of promotion by different companies
- a podcast about the ways that different companies use branding
- a report on the appropriateness of different types of promotional material.

The importance of branding to businesses

What makes some mobile phones stand out from others?

What is a brand?

- **A strategy** – a long-term plan for the promotion of a company or a product.
- The **perception of a customer** – a brand is how the public sees a product or a business. It must represent everything the company stands for, for example, Innocent, the UK-based fruit drinks company, has a pure and natural brand image.
- **A logo** – part of a brand is the symbol that can be placed on a product so that people know it belongs to a particular company. The Nike 'swoosh' is a well-known example.
- **A legal instrument** – a brand is the exclusive property of its owner. This means that no one else can profit from it. Companies work hard to protect their brands.
- **A company** – for example, Virgin applies its brand to a range of different companies, each of which benefits from how well recognised the name is.
- **A personality** – customer perceptions of a brand include how they imagine a brand might behave; they see it as being almost like a person. For example, many people see Innocent as being quirky and imaginative.

- **A vision** – brands are often created with the intention of using them on a whole range of products, for example, the Easy brand was developed to include hotels, car rental and offices.
- **An identity** – a brand gives a company a unique identity that **differentiates** it from other companies. This might be because of the quality of the product or the way it makes the user feel. For example, Porsche drivers enjoy the luxury image of their cars.
- **An image** – each brand has its own unique associations. BMW has an image of reliability, whereas Porsche has an image of luxury.

Brands must be careful to protect their image.

Key terms

Perception – what a customer or consumer thinks about something.

Differentiate – make your business noticeably different from your competitors.

Activity   Creating an image

In a group, list 10 brands. For each brand, discuss how it has created a unique image. Consider the products that it represents and the types of advertising that you are aware of. Feed back your findings to your class.

Why businesses use branding

Branding is used by businesses to create a clear image that customers can recognise. A brand shows that something is the product of a particular company, giving customers a message about what they can expect from their purchase. For McDonald's this might be value and convenience. Topshop might want its brand to represent fashion and style.

Types of branding

Businesses use different types of branding.

- **Product branding** – this brand represents a specific product, for example Jaffa Cakes.
- **Service branding** – this brand represents a specific service, for example Visa.
- **Corporate branding** – this brand represents a company and can be applied to all of their products and services, for example Kellogg's.

Adding value

The purpose of a brand is to add value to products. A good brand will **differentiate** a company from its competitors by making its product seem more valuable than those of unbranded competitors.

CONTINUED ▶▶

Benefits of successful branding

These are shown in Table 3.1.

Table 3.1 Benefits of successful branding

Image	A brand creates an association in peoples' minds about the image of a product. For example, Costa Coffee has an image linked to excellent customer service.
Quality	A brand tells people how good a product is.
Recognition	The golden arches of the McDonald's logo are well known throughout the world. People know what it stands for regardless of the language they speak.
Long-lasting perceptions	A well-established brand creates a lasting impression on customers. For example, Coca-Cola's 'Holidays are coming' adverts are connected with the start of Christmas in many peoples' minds.
Trust	Customers know that a product with a familiar brand will meet a certain standard. For example, a Travelodge room will be warm and comfortable anywhere in the country.
Marketing multiple products	This is called brand extension. Once a brand is successful, it can be used to promote a range of products.

Lego have extended their brand to include theme parks and video games.

Unsuccessful branding

Branding can sometimes go wrong. Negative publicity caused by unethical business practices or disasters can damage the reputation of a brand. This damages the customer perception of the brand. For example, in 2012, horsemeat found in some ready meals threatened the reputation of several well-known companies.

Promotion in businesses

◤ Why businesses need to promote themselves

Promotion is a vital activity for all businesses. Effective promotional activity allows a business to stay ahead of its competition. This is because good promotional activity will inform customers about a company's products and persuade them that they should make a purchase from that company.

Businesses benefit from promotional activity by creating awareness of their brand. This should lead to increased sales and profits. Promotion is one of the four elements of the **marketing mix**. When it is well designed, promotion will support the other elements of the marketing mix.

◤ Activities used in the marketing mix

The marketing mix consists of product, price, place and promotion. These are the four elements of a good marketing campaign.

Product

This is what a business sells to its customers. A product is a combination of features and benefits.

- **Features** are what a product does or what it is made of.
- A customer **benefits** from using a product or service. For example, subscribers to LOVEFiLM have access to exclusive films that aren't available on other websites.

What are the features of a smartphone?

> **Key terms**
>
> Marketing mix – the combination of product, price, place and promotion. This is often referred to as the 4 Ps.

> **Link**
>
> This topic links to *Unit 9: Principles of Marketing*.

Activity	Identifying the 4 Ps

In pairs or small groups research how a local business uses the 4 Ps. Recommend four improvements.

CONTINUED ▸▸

Price

It is important to make the right decision about how much to charge your customers. If you charge too much, people might not want to buy your products. If you charge too little, you will not be able to make a profit.

The price that you charge will depend on the quality of your product. Better-quality products command a higher price. Demand from customers is also important. The more demand you have from potential customers, the more you can charge. It is also important to take into account your competitors. If your company charges £100 less than your rival, then customers will come to you.

Place

- It is important to think about where your products will be sold. It is no good offering luxury chocolates in a discount store. Businesses must decide how to offer their goods for sale in a way that will appeal to their target market. Are shops better than catalogues? Is the internet best or should you choose door-to-door selling?

- You must also decide if you will sell directly to the market yourself or if you will use a **wholesaler**. **Direct distribution** is more profitable because you keep all the revenue, but using a wholesaler might mean your products are offered in a wider range of outlets so more customers see your product.

- Websites such as Folksy and Etsy allow small businesses to sell directly to the public anywhere in the world. This means that designers keep their profits after paying a small fee.

- Food manufacturers might use a wholesaler such as 3663 to sell their goods to small shops and restaurants. This wholesaler provides a range of goods in bulk at a discount, delivering goods to their customers.

How would the promotion of luxury products be different to that of cheaper alternatives?

Promotion

This is how a business communicates with potential customers. Once the other elements of the marketing mix have been set, promotional activities are used to create awareness of your product. For example, to promote its orange juice, Tropicana took a giant orange ball to town centres during the winter. They hung this from a crane over rows of deckchairs and gave away bottles of their juice so that people could sit under the 'sun' and enjoy a drink. Each bottle came with a money-off voucher to encourage people to buy Tropicana.

Can you think of any inventive ideas to promote a business?

Benefits of promotion to businesses

Promotion is essential for businesses to communicate with customers about their goods and services. The different methods of promotion are covered in detail later in this unit.

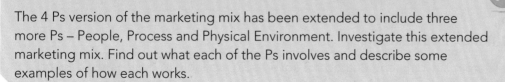

Take it futher

The 4 Ps version of the marketing mix has been extended to include three more Ps – People, Process and Physical Environment. Investigate this extended marketing mix. Find out what each of the Ps involves and describe some examples of how each works.

Elements of the promotional mix and their purposes

Introduction

The promotional mix refers to the different elements that a business can use to encourage customers to buy its products. Which promotional methods have you seen successful brands like Coca-Cola or Virgin use?

Advertising

Advertising is when a business pays for space in the prime media to communicate with the public about their products and services. This can be expensive and businesses must ensure that they spend their **advertising budget** carefully.

The purpose of advertising

There are two main purposes of advertising:

1 **To inform people.** You need to make potential customers aware of your product and its benefits. If you are advertising food, you might tell people about the nutrients it contains.

2 **To persuade people to make a purchase.** You might tell people about the great benefits that you offer or the low prices that you have set.

Different companies use adverts with one or both purposes. The NHS might use adverts to inform people about the dangers of obesity and persuade people to lose weight.

Message and medium

When you design an advert, you must think about what you want to tell people (the **message**) and how you will tell them (the **medium**).

Your message might be what you sell, where you sell it and how much it costs.

The medium that you use for your advertising depends on your advertising budget and the type of market that you are trying to reach. A large company such as McDonald's might use TV adverts because it has a lot of money and it wants to reach the whole country. A small independent cafe might use a local newspaper to reach its local community.

Methods of advertising

There are many different methods of advertising available to businesses, depending on the medium that they choose.

- **Moving image:** This type of advert, which is often shown on television or in cinemas, is useful where products have many features or moving parts. It allows dynamic demonstrations of products being used. These adverts can be put onto DVDs and given away at shop counters or videos can be uploaded to sites such as YouTube.

- **Print:** It is possible to pay for advertising space in newspapers and magazines. Alternatively, eye-catching billboards can be placed beside busy roads. Modern technology means that digital signs are used, allowing the advert to be changed at different times of day.
- **Ambient:** Adverts in public spaces such as the sides of buses can be effective at catching the eye of potential customers.
- **Digital:** Adverts can be placed on websites or sent to customers via a text message. Companies such as Google and Facebook have developed technology that makes adverts appear when people type in certain key words.
- **Audio:** Radio adverts provide an opportunity to talk to customers about your product. For a relatively low cost, you can tell people about the features of your product and where they can buy it. Sometimes these adverts feature famous voices to give them extra credibility.

Did you know?

Adverts printed on the odd-numbered pages (right-hand side) of a newspaper or magazine cost more than those printed on the even pages (left-hand side). This is because people see the right-hand side of the paper first when they are turning the pages.

Why is this type of advertising so effective?

Activity Choosing methods of advertising

The type of product or service that you are promoting will influence your choice of advertising method. For each of the following businesses, suggest a type of advert and explain why you think it is appropriate.

1 A local car dealer
2 An online retailer
3 A national chain of coffee shops
4 An office cleaning company.

CONTINUED ▶▶

Discussion point

Why do you think levels of demand return to normal once a sales promotion finishes? If demand only increases for a short period of time, is it worth using sales promotions? Discuss your ideas in your group.

Link

This topic links to *Unit 5: Sales and Personal Selling*.

◢ Sales promotion

Sales promotions are used to encourage customers to purchase your products or for distribution channels to stock your goods. This involves offering an incentive to make it more attractive to make a purchase.

Sales promotion methods include:

- **Price promotion:** This could be a simple discount on a product (e.g. 25p off), a multi-buy offer (e.g. buy one get one free) or a larger package for the same price (e.g. 25 per cent extra free). Price promotions are useful in **B2B markets** because they help businesses to negotiate with **distribution channels** by offering a lower price for a larger order.

- **Coupons:** This is a small paper or card token, offering customers a discount or free gift when they buy something.

- **Competitions:** This is when customers win a prize when they buy a product. This might include an 'instant win' offer where a prize is in a package.

- **Money refunds:** Some companies offer a cash back scheme. When a customer makes a purchase, a portion of the cost is refunded over a period of time such as a year. This is popular for products such as cars or mobile phones.

  Another type of refund promotion is offered by some supermarkets. If a customer is able to buy products cheaper in a competitor's store, the supermarket will refund the difference between its price and its competitor's price.

- **Loyalty incentives:** Loyalty schemes are offered by many companies. Caffè Nero uses a simple scheme where it gives customers a card on which they can collect stamps. When their card is full, they can exchange this card for a free drink.

◢ Personal selling

This is where a representative of a company interacts directly with a potential customer. The salesperson uses their **interpersonal skills** to try to persuade the potential customer to make a purchase. This is called 'closing a sale'.

This can be a much more appropriate method than advertising if products or services are complicated. The salesperson is able to explain the features to the customer and answer any questions that they might have.

Computer shops are a good example of personal selling in a business to consumer market (**B2C market**). Sales staff can explain technical information in terms that the customer understands.

Activity   Investigating trunk shows

Stella and Dot moved to the UK in 2011. They use a modern twist on direct selling called a trunk show. Visit their website to find out more about their business. You can access this by going to www.pearsonhotlinks.co.uk and searching for this title.

1 What is a trunk show?
2 Why do you think Stella and Dot employ stylists rather than salespeople?

There are a number of methods of personal selling.

- **Face to face:** The salesperson watches the customer's body language and listens to the tone of their voice to assess how interested they are in making a purchase. This allows them to adapt their sales **pitch**.
- **Telephone:** This method does not allow the salesperson to read the customer's body language. However, a good salesperson can still hear a lot from the tone of the customer's voice and the words that they use.
- **Email:** Deals can be discussed over a period of time. The salesperson can send their customer attachments containing details of their product or links to relevant websites.
- **Video or web conferencing:** The use of a webcam allows the salesperson to see the customer wherever they are in the world. They can demonstrate products on camera as well as sending the customer files or links to relevant websites.

Activity   Selling mobile phones

Imagine you are a salesperson for a mobile phone company.

1 Which method of personal selling would you choose? Why?
2 What steps would you take to make sure that your customer bought a phone?

The customer and the salesperson meet.

Did you know?

Energy companies and banks have been criticised because their salespeople have given customers misleading information to make sales. This is because their salespeople are paid money for each sale that they make.

CONTINUED ▸▸

◢ Public relations activities

Public relations are the activities a business carries out to place information in the media without paying for it directly. If this is successful, then the time gained on television or presence in the press can be worth thousands of pounds.

A potential problem is that the message you are trying to give the public might not be transmitted exactly as you intended. With television or print advertising, you have some control over what is published. When you send public relations material out to the press, you no longer have any control over it.

Public relations activities include:

- **Exhibitions:** An exhibition is when one or more companies present and display their products. These are often large events, such as 'Clothes Show Live' where many different stalls are set up to highlight the latest and most exciting new products on offer.
- **Sponsorship:** This is when you pay to display your brand at an event such as a music concert or on a television programme; for example, McCain Foods sponsor films on Channel 4. Some companies use sponsorship to create a positive image for their company. BP sponsors a number of art galleries in the UK. Unfortunately, this has attracted negative publicity for the art galleries, with climate change groups protesting outside some galleries.
- **Press releases:** Issuing a press release involves writing a statement which can be used by journalists as part of a news story. Journalists get many press releases each day, so it is important to highlight something interesting in your press release to get their attention.

Activity   Writing a press release

Think about a recent success at your school or college. It might be the triumph of a sports team or it might be a visit that you have made to a local business. Write a press release that could be sent to your local newspaper to promote this achievement.

Discussion point

Fast food companies often sponsor sporting events to try to improve their unhealthy image. Tobacco companies used to sponsor sports such as snooker and Formula One motor racing until a change in the law prevented this to protect public health. In your group, discuss whether there should be controls over which companies can be sponsors, or whether the public should be left to make its own decisions.

Link

This activity will be explored further in *Unit 10: Using Business Documentation*.

Did you know?

One of the biggest exhibitions held in the UK is called Spring Fair. Over 70,000 people visit the event over a week in February to see stalls set up by three thousand exhibitors. You can find out more by going to www.pearsonhotlinks.co.uk and searching for this title.

Why are exhibitions a good way of promoting new products?

Direct marketing

Direct marketing is when a business communicates directly with a customer, establishing an individual relationship between the business and the customer.

While adverts are shown to everyone in a specific area, direct marketing material is aimed at a specific customer and can be tailored according to the individual or group to whom it is sent. According to the mail preference survey, postal sales in the UK are worth £25 billion a year, but the public often call these mailshots 'junk mail'. Why do you think this is?

Direct marketing techniques include the following:

- **Direct mail:** Letters posted to customers give them information about new products or special offers.
- **Mail order catalogues:** Sending customers a catalogue containing photographs and details of different products allows them to look at your products in the comfort of their home. Sometimes these catalogues are distributed by agents who take and deliver orders, for example Avon.

Activity	Researching direct marketing

Customers sometimes find forms of direct marketing such as junkmail and cold calls unpleasant and frustrating.

You can find websites to learn more about the mail preference service and the telephone preference service by visiting www.pearsonhotlinks.co.uk and searching for this title.

Magazines: Some companies produce short magazines which can be sent out to the people on their mailing list. These often contain pictures and short descriptions to inform customers about new products.

Activity	Analysing magazines

Topman produces a monthly magazine called *Generation* about music, clothes and celebrities. Read a copy of this magazine online. You can access this by going to www.pearsonhotlinks.co.uk and searching for this title.

1 How does the magazine support Topman in promoting its brand?

2 Compare the features in the magazine to the products in a branch of Topman. Would reading the magazine make you more likely to make a purchase from the store? Explain your answer.

3 Find examples of magazines produced by five contrasting businesses. Compare the contents and features, suggesting reasons for any similarities or differences.

4 Rank the magazines in order from most effective to least effective at promoting that company's products. Explain your decisions.

- **Telemarketing:** This is when a phone call is made to a customer to tell them about your latest product and invite them to make a purchase. Telemarketers sometimes make uninvited calls to customers. This is called cold calling.

Promotional activities in business

Introduction

Promotional activity can be expensive so it is important to carefully plan how you will spend your budget. The first step is to consider what type of market you will target.

Types of market

To create an effective promotional campaign, businesses must identify which customers they want to target with their promotions.

Business to business (B2B) markets

When a company sells goods or services to other companies it is targeting a B2B market. Companies such as Heinz are part of these markets. Its customers are companies such as the supermarket chain Morrisons, which buys cans of beans and soup, for example.

Companies in B2B markets often use a 'push and pull' strategy when choosing their promotional mix; they use methods such as advertising to create demand from consumers and personal selling to sell their products to shops.

Business to consumer (B2C) markets

Consumers are the people who use goods and services. There is a range of products available in B2C markets, including phones, clothes, food, toys and many other items.

In a B2C market, the purpose of promotion is to gain sales from the public. A company might use loyalty cards to encourage people to come back to its store or adverts to create awareness of its latest product.

B2C companies also use 'push and pull' strategies. Companies might push their products to people on Facebook who have 'liked' them, and pull customers in by encouraging them to click a link with the promise of a discount.

Activity   Choosing promotional methods

For each of the following products, suggest which promotional methods you would use to sell it in a B2B market and a B2C market:

1 Laptop computer
2 Frozen chips
3 Flight to America
4 BTEC Business Student Book

Give a reason for each of your choices.

Market segmentation

Dividing a market up into groups of people allows money to be spent more efficiently. The process of identifying and targeting a group of people with similar interests is called segmentation. Markets can be **segmented** in a number of different ways.

How could a shopping centre segment its customers?

Age

People have different needs at different stages in their lives. Teenagers might be interested in mobile phones and the latest fashion. The elderly, those over the age of 80, might be more interested in excursions and theatre offers.

Family status

People have different needs depending on whether they are married or single and whether they have children. Walt Disney World® promote holidays for younger families with children.

Gender

Goods such as hair care and deodorant are promoted differently to men and women. Arcadia has different brands of clothes to appeal to men (Topman, Burton) and women (Topshop, Dorothy Perkins).

Income

Consumers can be divided up according to how much they earn. People with different incomes have different needs and wants. Supermarkets aim their premium products at wealthier customers while providing a value range for the less well off. For example, Sainsbury's has a 'Taste the Difference' range of premium goods and a 'Basics' range of simpler, more affordable items.

Attitudes

People buy different products according to how they see the world. Some people are interested in ethical products, such as **Fairtrade** goods. Newspapers such as *The Times* are targeted at people with conservative views, while *The Guardian* is aimed at those with more liberal ideas.

Lifestyle

Markets can be segmented according to people's hobbies, interests and the way that they live their lives. Some services appeal specifically to people who are busy with their career, such as shirt-ironing services.

Activity

Comparing promotional materials

Compare the promotional materials for Lynx, which is aimed at men, and Impulse, which is aimed at women.

How do the messages in the adverts differ to appeal to each group?

Activity

Explaining market segmentation

Car manufacturers often segment their markets according to the income of their customers. Companies such as Ford and Toyota produce a range of cars at different prices. Explain why you think it is important for these companies to appeal to customers with different incomes.

CONTINUED ▸▸

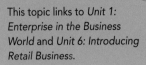

Link

This topic links to *Unit 1: Enterprise in the Business World* and *Unit 6: Introducing Retail Business*.

The use of promotional activities in business

Setting objectives

There is no point spending time designing your promotional mix if you don't know what you want to achieve. When you are planning promotional activity, it is important to set appropriate SMART objectives.

Table 3.2 SMART objectives

Specific	What do you want to gain from the promotional activity? More customers? Extra revenue?
Measurable	How many customers do you want to attract? How much market share do you want to gain?
Achievable	Is it possible to meet the objective? Are there enough customers in the market?
Realistic	Do you have the capacity to meet the objective? Can you manufacture enough products?
Time-related	When do you want to achieve the objective by? In a month? A year?

Activity   Setting objectives

Imagine you are the marketing director for a new soft drink brand. You are launching your new product in three months' time. Write three suitable SMART objectives for your new product.

How appropriate is your promotional mix?

The type of promotional activities that you select will depend on the type of product you sell and the market you are aiming at. If you want to sell to a B2B market, then cinema adverts might not be appropriate. If you wish to sell to a large consumer market, selecting an appropriate promotional mix based on personal selling might be far too expensive.

The appropriateness of your promotional mix will also depend on your target segment. For example, digital advertising might be more appropriate for younger consumers. Audio channels such as radio might be more appropriate for older age groups.

Benefits of selecting an appropriate promotional mix

Selecting an appropriate promotional mix means that money is spent efficiently. Otherwise money is wasted on activities that attract few customers. Well-planned promotional activities will also make a business more competitive. Staying ahead of competitors is an important business aim. If your competitors are more effective at promotion than your business is, they will win more customers than you.

The AIDA model

AIDA stands for awareness/attention, interest, desire, action. It describes the stages that a customer goes through when looking at well-designed promotional material. This model can be used to evaluate the quality of the different elements of your promotional mix.

Did you know?

Many firms targeting young people use social networking websites. Facebook has over 1 billion active users, 50 per cent of whom log in every day. Facebook's advertising revenue was over $5 billion in 2012.

Awareness/attention

Good promotional material attracts people's attention. Eye-catching slogans or striking images make people notice your message.

Interest

The features of your product should be communicated to your customer in a way that they will find interesting. It is important to understand the needs of your market segment. If you are selling a mobile phone, teenagers might want to know how many songs it can store. Their parents might be more interested in security features.

Desire

Having gained your customer's interest, you have to persuade them to buy from you. Highlighting the price and any special offers might be enough to achieve this.

What methods are being used to attract people's attention?

Action

Once you have created the desire for your product, you must give your customer an opportunity to buy it. This could mean telling them where they can make a purchase, for example by stating where it is for sale. If you are using a digital advert in an email or on a website you might provide a link to an online shop. Alternatively, you might provide a phone number so that your customer can call your telesales staff.

Assessment activity 3.1

2A.P1 | 2A.P2 | 2A.P3 | 2A.M1 | 2A.M2 | 2A.D1

Colin is leaving school next year and he wants to set up a bookshop. He has been advised that he should create a brand to make his business stand out from its competitors. He thinks that this will be an important part of the marketing mix for his business.

Colin thinks that his main competitors will be high street retailers such as Waterstones and online retailers such as Amazon. He is particularly interested in understanding how successful companies plan their marketing mix.

His own knowledge is limited to the work experience he did with the Red Cross whilst he was doing his BTEC and he is therefore interested in looking at some of the branded products of market leaders.

1 Investigate how branding is used by both Innocent Smoothies® and the Red Cross and why it is important for each company. Then find out more about Innocent by visiting a retailer selling their products and viewing the company website. Collect examples of the company's promotional material and other relevant evidence. Consider how well Innocent have designed their marketing mix before assessing how well they apply each of the 4 Ps of the marketing mix and how they have used each element of their promotional mix.

2 Write a report for Colin summarising your findings. Include a section which evaluates the promotional mix used by Innocent. Explain to Colin how important each element is and whether or not it is being used effectively.

Activity

Comparing adverts

Collect 10 adverts for different products. Compare the different features of the adverts. How do they gain attention or create interest and desire to buy? Which adverts are most effective? Explain your decisions.

Branding methods and techniques

Introduction

An effective brand combines a number of different elements to represent an appropriate image for a business. A successful brand may combine several elements:

- **Logos:** A logo is a symbol that represents a company, for example the golden arches of McDonald's. It can be used in adverts and on packaging to tell people that a product belongs to that company.
- **Straplines:** These are short phrases that make people think of a particular product. One of the most famous examples is Nike's 'Just Do It' slogan. While this does not refer directly to its products, it creates an active image for the company.

Discussion point

Tiger Woods and Wayne Rooney both endorsed a number of products until allegations about their private lives were reported in the press. In your group, discuss why it is important to carry out thorough research into a celebrity's background before asking them to endorse your products.

Activity   Designing a logo

Design a new logo and write a strapline that your school and college could use on its promotional materials. Explain why it is appropriate to the image of the institution.

- **Celebrity endorsements:** If a celebrity who appeals to your target market is seen to use your product, it can encourage people to use it themselves. Nintendo used a major advertising campaign featuring numerous celebrities such as Jamie Oliver and Louise Redknapp to promote their Wii™ and DS™ consoles.

Link

Learn more about celebrity endorsements in *Unit 9: Principles of Marketing*.

Have you ever been influenced by celebrity endorsements?

Planning ideas for a brand for a business

When you are planning a brand for a business, the first thing to consider is what type of brand you want to create.

- **Concept brands** – these are often used by charities or political parties to sell an idea to the public, for example 'New Labour' or 'Keep Britain Tidy'.
- **Commodity brands** – this is when a brand is placed on a company or a product. It creates a unique identity which differentiates the product from its competitors.

You must take a number of different factors into account to ensure that your brand is suitable for your target market. These are listed in Table 3.3.

Table 3.3 Factors you must consider to ensure your brand is suitable

Factor	Implications	Example
Race/nationality	The culture of different countries is important. Tastes vary in different areas.	Germans prefer to rent houses rather than buy them with a mortgage.
Religion	It is important not to offend any religious groups with your brand.	Tesco stores stock ranges of kosher foods in areas with a Jewish population.
Children	If your brand is appealing to children, it should not be used on products that are unsuitable for them.	Alcopop brands have been criticised for appealing to children.
Disabilities	Your brand should be sensitive to people with physical or mental disabilities.	Use a clear font in your logo so people with poor sight can see it clearly.
Environmental	Some brands benefit from being linked to environmentally friendly practices.	Ikea only uses wood from sustainable sources.

Did you know?

The term 'branding' comes from the practice of farmers stamping a symbol onto their animals to show who owns it. The purpose of a brand is to show that a product has come from a specific organisation.

The Red Cross is also known as the Red Crescent in countries that aren't traditionally Christian so that people do not think it is a religious organisation.

In groups, research two brands that appeal to different age groups. Each member of the group should interview six people of different ages about what they think of the brand. Discuss your findings and present them to your class.

Brand personality

Some businesses try to give their brand a personality to appeal to the target market. This helps customers relate to the product. It might be the language in the adverts or the type of images used on the packaging. Peperami is well known for being 'a bit of an animal', which is reinforced by eye-catching adverts featuring an animated sausage.

Discussion point

Find out which major company now owns Innocent. To what extent does this alter your perception of the brand? Discuss your ideas.

How have Innocent created a brand personality?

Brand objectives

It is important to decide what you want to achieve when you create your brand. Objectives might include brand awareness (how many people know about your brand) or brand value (how much your brand is worth to the public).

Target market

Your brand must meet the needs of your target market. You should ensure that the promotional methods you choose are relevant to your audience and that the brand personality is appropriate.

Promoting a brand

Promoting a brand image

The way that you promote your brand makes a big difference to how customers perceive it. The type of media that you use will influence their views. More people will see an advert on television because it has greater reach, but an advert in a magazine might be more relevant to your target market because a magazine is more specialised.

Activity | Investigating brand promotion

Different types of media influence the way people see a brand. For example, brands wanting to be seen as modern and innovative might use web-based media. If a brand wants to look cool, they might use guerrilla advertising methods. Investigate five brands with different images. Explain how they use different forms of promotion to create their brand image. Suggest why certain forms of promotion create a different image.

Planning a promotional campaign

When you plan a promotional campaign, there are several stages that you must go through:

1 **Setting promotional objectives**

Table 3.4 Types of promotional objective

Raise awareness	Make the public aware of the product or service that you are offering.
Remind	Jog the public's memory about the product or service that you are offering.
Differentiate	Create a unique image for your brand so you stand out from your competitors.
Persuade or inform	Do you want to let people know about the features and benefits of your product or convince them to buy it? Many promotions aim to achieve both.
Create market presence	To win sales, customers must be aware that your product is available.
Increase market share	You must persuade people to buy your product.

2 **Developing the most appropriate promotional mix**

Once you have set your objectives, you must choose promotional activities that will help you achieve them. For example, if you want to create brand awareness, you might choose a national television advert.

3 **Justifying the choice of promotional mix**

You must be able to explain why the promotional activities you choose are appropriate for your target market.

4 **Designing promotional activities**

This involves thinking about the message that you want to deliver and the purpose of your activities. Do you want to persuade or inform? Colours and images must be carefully selected to fit your brand personality.

Assessment activity 3.2   *English*   2B.P4 | 2B.P5 | 2B.M3 | 2B.M4 | 2B.D2

Colin is opening his bookshop next month. He has asked you to design a brand and to plan a campaign to promote it. You need to investigate the market for bookshops and prepare a presentation of an idea for a brand that is targeted at a specific target market.

Based on this you must produce suitable promotional materials and prepare a presentation in which you explain your choices to him. Your presentation should include:

- The brand personality and target market you recommend for Colin's bookshop. Support your recommendations by providing information about the branding methods and techniques you used.

- The promotional campaign you have planned for the bookshop, including examples of promotional materials and information about the promotional mix you consider would be best.

- Your own evaluation of the promotional campaign that you have created for Colin. Recommend improvements that could be made to your work before it is launched to the public.

WorkSpace

▶ Paul Birch

Managing Director, Revolver World

After running a record company for 30 years, Paul Birch wanted to put something back into the community. He became interested in the principles of fair trade, because he wanted to give a fair deal to farmers in poorer countries. This interest led him to extend his existing brand into a new market.

After carrying out some research, Paul found some suppliers of fair trade coffee in Africa and Colombia. The next step was to create a brand personality. He created characters to use on the packaging to represent the farmers who grow the coffee. Paul decided to make the packaging yellow because potential customers thought that this looked fresh and bright.

Paul uses personal selling to encourage stores to sell his coffee. When a store stocks his products, he sends his staff to run free tasting sessions to encourage people to buy the product. This creates sales for the retailer and helps Paul to create brand awareness. The other target market for the coffee is 18–35-year-olds. He uses discount vouchers to encourage them to try the coffee. Paul has a website to inform people about the brand and his other fair trade products.

Think about it

1 Which elements of the promotional mix does Paul use to sell his coffee?

2 Is Paul's promotional mix appropriate to his target market? What improvements would you recommend?

3 What objectives would you suggest that Paul should set for his brand? How will this help him to evaluate the success of his new brand?

Introduction

Customer service is one of the most important aspects of running a business, because customers are vital to the success of every business. Making sure customers come back to the business again and again helps the business to grow, and it costs less to keep existing customers than to find new ones.

Anticipating customer needs is a key factor in business, but so are meeting and exceeding customer expectations. If customers leave your business feeling satisfied (their experience of your business has been good), they are more likely to return and more likely to tell their friends about your product or service.

This unit introduces you to the different types of customers that businesses come into contact with, and how to deal with them to ensure that their expectations are met. You will demonstrate the interpersonal skills required in customer service situations and identify the key skills required to offer a professional and efficient service.

Assessment: This unit will be assessed through a series of assignments set by your teacher/tutor.

Learning aims

In this unit you will:

A understand how businesses provide customer service

B demonstrate appropriate customer service skills in different situations.

" I work part-time in a shop, so this unit really helps me to understand how what I do affects the business. When I help customers, they form an impression of the shop based on their impression of me. Fortunately customers come back time and again, so I must be doing something right!

Marcus, *16-year-old Business student*

Principles of Customer Service

4

BTEC
Assessment Zone

This table shows you what you must do in order to achieve a **Pass**, **Merit** or **Distinction** grade, and where you can find activities in this book to help you.

Assessment criteria			
Level 1	Level 2 Pass	Level 2 Merit	Level 2 Distinction
Learning aim A: Understand how businesses provide customer service			
1A.1 Define customer service, giving an example of a customer service role in a selected business	**2A.P1** Describe the different types of customer service provided by two selected businesses **See Assessment activity 4.1, page 109**	**2A.M1** Compare how two selected businesses satisfy customers **See Assessment activity 4.1, page 109**	**2A.D1** Assess the effect of providing consistent and reliable customer service on the reputation of a selected business **See Assessment activity 4.1, page 109**
1A.2 Identify features of consistent and reliable customer service	**2A.P2** Describe the characteristics of consistent and reliable customer service **See Assessment activity 4.1, page 109**	**2A.M2** Explain how a selected business attempts to exceed customer expectations **See Assessment activity 4.1, page 109**	
1A.3 Identify how organisational procedures contribute to consistent and reliable customer service	**2A.P3** Explain how organisational procedures and legislation contribute to consistent and reliable customer service **See Assessment activity 4.1, page 109**	**2A.M3** Compare the impact of legislative and regulatory requirements affecting customer service on a selected business **See Assessment activity 4.1, page 109**	
1A.4 Outline how legislative and regulatory requirements affect customer service in a selected business	**2A.P4** Explain how legislative and regulatory requirements affect customer service in a selected business **See Assessment activity 4.1, page 109**		

Assessment criteria			
Level 1	Level 2 Pass	Level 2 Merit	Level 2 Distinction
Learning aim B: Demonstrate appropriate customer service skills in different situations			
1B.5 Identify different types of internal and external customer in a selected business, giving an example for each type	**2B.P5** Describe how a selected business meets the needs and expectations of three different types of customer **See Assessment activity 4.2, page 118**	**2B.M4** English Demonstrate effective communication skills when responding to customer problems and complaints in three customer service situations **See Assessment activity 4.2, page 118**	**2B.D2** English Evaluate the effectiveness of own customer service skills, justifying areas for improvement **See Assessment activity 4.2, page 118**
1B.6 Identify when it is necessary to refer a customer service problem to someone in authority	**2B.P6** Describe, using examples, the limits of authority that would apply when delivering customer service **See Assessment activity 4.2, page 118**		
1B.7 English Demonstrate appropriate communication skills in three customer service situations	**2B.P7** English Demonstrate effective communication skills to meet customer needs when dealing with three different customer types in customer service situations **See Assessment activity 4.2, page 118**		

English / Opportunity to practise English skills

How you will be assessed

This unit will be assessed by a series of internally assessed tasks. You will be expected to research two different businesses to show that you understand how good customer service impacts on a business, and ways in which a business can exceed customer expectations. You will also demonstrate a range of different customer service skills in a real or simulated work environment.

Your assessment could be in the form of:

- a written account, display or presentation of your research
- video role-play evidence of customer service skills
- a personal statement reflecting on your demonstration of customer service skills
- observation records from your tutor.

Customer service in business

The meaning of customer service

Customer service can be defined as 'all the ways in which a business meets customer expectations to satisfy customers'. This may include:

- greeting customers
- having products in stock and available to buy
- providing information about products and services
- staff completing sales, wrapping goods, assisting customers using self-service checkouts, etc.
- after-sales support, such as a customer helpline.

Different customer service roles in a business

In business, employees can be involved in many different customer service roles. They can be involved directly with the customer, or indirectly:

- Roles that are *directly* involved with customers include receptionists, contact centre workers, shop assistants, delivery drivers, etc. These roles normally involve direct contact with customers.
- Roles that are *indirectly* involved with customers include cleaners, gardeners, engineers, etc. Although these staff are usually in the background, they contribute to the business by providing a good experience for its customers.

The different types of customer service businesses have

Businesses offer different types of customer service. This depends on the industry and the needs of the customers, so a vehicle repair garage may offer customers a courtesy car, whereas a retail store will help with packing or providing a gift-wrapping service.

Key terms

Service deliverer – a member of staff who delivers customer service.

Front-line customer service staff – those people who are a customer's first point of contact with the business.

Face-to-face customer service – when the customer receives service in front of a member of staff.

Remote customer service – when a business offers customer service by telephone or online.

Did you know?

- First impressions are very important because they stick in our memory and colour our judgement. Can you remember your first day at school or college? What other 'firsts' can you remember?

- It can cost around five times more to bring a new customer into a business than it costs to keep an existing customer.

Service deliverer

The person providing customer service is known as the **service deliverer**. They are often the first person a customer comes into contact with in a business. As service deliverers are the 'face' of the business, there are usually set standards and guidelines they must follow. This allows all **front-line customer service staff** to provide a consistent level of service.

Why are service deliverers so important?

Face-to-face customer service

Face-to-face customer service is delivered in many businesses, for example:

- in a hotel, face-to-face customer service is provided by the receptionist
- in a restaurant, face-to-face customer service is provided by the waiter
- in a leisure centre, face-to-face customer service is provided by personal trainers and pool attendants.

Activity	Identifying customer service roles

In groups, identify two staff at your school/college who are directly involved with the customer and two who are not. Then do the same for a hospital and a retail store. Compare your ideas.

Remote customer service

Many businesses provide **remote customer service** so that customers can contact them without visiting the premises. Remote customer service is essential for businesses that sell only online, such as Ticketmaster. This type of customer service includes:

- call centres, which may be based in the UK or overseas
- online options for contacting customer service staff, such as an online form, email, or 'call me' website button. Some international businesses, such as British Airways, use Skype so that customers can make video or voice calls over the internet.

Customer service teamwork

Providing good customer service requires teamwork. If a customer has a complaint or a complex query, it may be necessary to liaise with another member of the team or the team leader to find the answer and provide excellent customer service.

Table 4.1 shows when teamwork is essential.

Table 4.1 Customer service teamwork

Cooperation is essential between...	When...
Departments	… a receptionist in a business needs to direct customers, or visitors from other businesses, to different departments.
Individuals	… a customer has a query that you cannot answer, you may need to ask a colleague who will be able to tell you the answer.
Businesses	… a customer returns a faulty product or has a problem with a product, the business needs to contact the manufacturer (if the product was made by another business) to report the problem and suggest a solution.

Activity	Comparing customer service experiences

Think of a time when you received good customer service, and a time when you received bad customer service. What made the customer service good or bad? How did this affect the way you thought about the business? Compare your ideas.

Providing customer service

Customer satisfaction

Providing **consistent** and reliable customer service is vital in business. If customers are not satisfied, they do not return.

What is customer satisfaction?

Customers are satisfied when they receive the service they expect. Customer satisfaction may relate to:

- **Confidence in the service:** Customers know they can trust the business to keep its promises.
- **Value for money:** Customers feel that the quality, features and benefits they gain are worth paying for.
- **Repeat custom:** Satisfied customers are more likely to make future purchases.
- **Word-of-mouth reputation:** Satisfied customers often share their experiences with others, which enhances a company's reputation effectively and cheaply.
- **Loyalty:** When customers are loyal to a business, they are likely to buy more and spend more.

How businesses can satisfy customers

The techniques a business chooses need to be matched to the products and services that the company provides. Many popular techniques are shown in Figure 4.1.

Figure 4.1   How businesses can satisfy customers

Key terms

Consistent (customer service) – providing the same service over and over again to a high standard every time.

Value for money – belief that the price paid is fair.

Word of mouth reputation – customers tell their friends, family and colleagues about their experiences with an organisation.

Discussion point

What is the difference between 'cheap' and 'value for money'? Does this mean that all sale items must be a good deal? Discuss your ideas as a group.

Activity   Identifying examples of techniques

Look at the techniques for providing customer satisfaction in Figure 4.1. Can you identify an example of each technique in businesses in your area?

Consistent and reliable customer service

Consistent and reliable customer service means that customers can rely on good service no matter how or when they contact the business. This is achieved in the following ways.

- **Staff knowledge of products and services:** Customers may have several queries before they are ready to make a purchase. Businesses should provide regular training so staff product knowledge is up to date.

- **Staff knowledge of scope of their job role:** Staff should know the limits of their authority and when to refer a query or problem to their team leader or manager.

- **Staff attitude and behaviour:** Businesses may have procedures for how customer service staff should address and respond to customers. This may include answering phone calls within a set number of rings and making sure that someone is always available to help a customer.

- **Meeting specific customer needs:** Customers have different needs which affect the product, service or advice they need. They may have a technical query or want to report a fault. They may need help choosing accessories or seek advice on a personal issue. The aim should be to assist all customers, no matter what their needs.

- **Working under pressure:** Even when the business is busy, customer service staff must remain calm and deal with each customer as quickly as possible while keeping the same high standard of customer service.

- **Confirming service meets needs and expectations:** Customer-focused organisations may follow up a purchase with a short phone call or online questionnaire to check customers are happy with their purchase and the service provided.

- **Dealing with problems:** Businesses often have specific return periods (for example a 28-day money-back guarantee) and helplines so that customers can check what to do if they have a problem. Dealing with a problem promptly and effectively builds trust and restores a customer's faith in the business.

? Did you know?

- Portakabin, the company that provides high-quality permanent and temporary buildings, has the motto 'Quality this time, next time, every time' to ensure the customer service it delivers is consistently excellent.

- Fitness First promises that all its gym staff and personal trainers are fully qualified so that customers can have confidence in the knowledge and experience of the staff.

- Christmas Day is the busiest day of the year for Orange call centre workers. This is because many people receive mobile phones as presents and they don't know how to use them.

Activity   Providing consistent customer service

In groups, select one organisation from the following list:

- a) a leisure centre
- b) a call centre
- c) a large hotel
- d) a cafe.

Identify how each organisation can provide consistent customer service. Then exchange ideas with another group.

Just checking ✔

1 Suggest three ways in which an organisation can achieve consistent and reliable customer service.

2 Describe what is meant by a 'service deliverer'.

3 What is the difference between 'remote' and 'face-to-face' customer service?

Good customer service and customer expectations

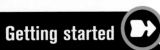
The effect of good customer service

There are many benefits to providing good customer service:

- **building a good reputation** by providing:
  - quality products – Dyson and Apple are renowned for these
  - value for money – John Lewis guarantees they are 'never knowingly undersold'. To keep this promise, they lower their price if a competitor is selling the same item more cheaply
  - consistency – Pizza Express guarantees to provide the same service, quality and menu at each restaurant
  - a reliable and trustworthy service
- **increased sales** through effective selling of related products and services, and attracting new customers through a strong reputation
- **increased profit** as the business may need to spend less on promotional activities and will gain through customer loyalty
- **retention of existing customers**, which means the business may need to spend less on advertising
- **new customers** who are attracted to the business when they hear about its reputation, possibly through word of mouth.
- **competitive advantage,** which means that customers consider the business offers the best value for money or provides a better service than its competitors
- **staff job satisfaction and motivation** because staff who feel they are giving customers a positive experience are more likely to be happy in their jobs. This helps to keep staff and reduces the costs involved in recruitment and training

Did you know?

Businesses use social media such as Facebook and Twitter to monitor what is said about their business. This means they can respond to problems quickly and try to ensure that customers recommend them to their friends or followers.

Activity   Identifying ways to save money

Excellent customer service can save businesses money. In groups, identify three ways in which businesses can gain these financial benefits.

What elements of customer service can you identify in this photo?

Different ways of exceeding customer expectations

Exceeding customer expectations improves the reputation of the business. The aim is to 'delight' customers, rather than merely 'satisfy' them.

Table 4.2 Exceeding customer expectations

Exceeding customer expectations by ...	How this exceeds expectations
... providing value for money	Value for money is important to most customers, so retailers may offer a price-matching service to build customers' trust, e.g. John Lewis.
... providing information and advice quickly	Some queries are easy to answer, but others may be complicated. Making the effort to find out additional information or to answer a difficult enquiry will impress a customer.
... providing additional help and assistance	Additional help may be helping a customer to their car with purchases, checking when an item will be in stock or pointing out discounts and special offers. Dealing promptly with problems, offering additional products or services and giving information about the company's returns policy are ways to provide extra assistance.
... providing exceptional help and assistance for customers with special requirements	Some customers may have special requirements, e.g. they may have physical disabilities or English may not be their first language. Exceptional help may be providing leaflets in relevant languages, a large print version, an accessible website (with a user-friendly design that takes into account colour blindness) and an induction loop system at customer service counters for anyone with hearing difficulties.

Assessment activity 4.1   *Introduction*

Your boss is training new business entrepreneurs in the importance of customer service. She asks you to produce a leaflet that summarises excellent customer service and gives examples of good practice. Choose two different businesses to investigate, such as a retailer, delivery firm, fitness centre or other service provider. Research the types of customer service both businesses provide, and the ways in which they aim to satisfy customers and exceed their expectations.

1 a) Start your leaflet with a clear definition of customer service, and describe the different types of customer service provided by each business.
   b) Describe the characteristics of consistent and reliable customer service, and compare how your two selected businesses satisfy their customers.
   c) Select one business and explain how it aims to exceed customer expectations.

2 Make notes for a report on the link between providing good, consistent and reliable customer service and the reputation of a business. Do this by identifying examples to illustrate how the reputation of your selected business has been affected by different aspects of its customer service. Keep your notes safely as you will complete this task in later in the unit.

Providing effective customer service

Introduction

Organisational procedures are instructions that tell staff how to carry out specific tasks, such as responding to a complaint or giving a refund. These help to ensure that all customers are dealt with fairly and correctly and according to their legal rights.

Key terms

Organisational procedures – step-by-step instructions issued to staff to ensure consistent standards.

Code of practice – a set of guidelines that set standards of service customers can expect.

Organisational procedures

Businesses can provide effective customer service by:

- monitoring customer service, often through customer feedback (from questionnaires or feedback forms) or through 'mystery shoppers'
- following **codes of practice** that set out certain standards:
  - Industry codes relate to a particular type of business, such as the mobile phone industry which has codes of practice about mobile phone content.
  - Organisational/business codes are set by the business itself. In the public sector these are often called customer charters – or student charters in a college or university.
  - Professional codes set out minimum standards for professionals such as doctors, solicitors and accountants, and are often drawn up by a professional body on behalf of its members.
- meeting legal and regulatory requirements, which is essential for all organisations.
- having ethical standards, which means having strong principles and, in business, not compromising these to make a profit: for example, never misleading customers or trying to withhold a valid refund.

Activity Investigating mystery shoppers

Many agencies advertise online for mystery shoppers to visit businesses and check the standards of service. Find out more about these jobs by searching online.

Ensuring that correct procedures are followed

It is important that all staff follow the correct procedures. These may include:

- when to refer to someone in authority – the procedures may tell you to do this if there is a serious complaint, if a decision is outside your area of authority or if you are asked a question that you cannot answer
- dealing with a refund, which may require a supervisor's approval if the item is damaged, was purchased some time ago or if the customer has lost the receipt
- treating customers equally, which is a legal requirement.

Did you know?

Once a customer query has been dealt with, your team leader may check to see if you have followed the correct procedure.

Minimising hazards and risks

All businesses have a legal responsibility to minimise hazards and risks. (See also the following topic). The first step is to identify where customers could be injured and then take steps to minimise the risk. Examples are given in Table 4.3.

Table 4.3 Minimising hazards and risks

Action to take	How the risk is minimised
Informing people about dangers	Display safety or warning signs if there is a danger. For example, if the floor has just been cleaned, a 'Wet floor' sign should be in place until it is dry.
Complying with fire regulations	Fire exits should be clearly indicated and staff should know the location of fire extinguishers. Fire drills should take place regularly so that staff know the evacuation procedure and meeting points.
Dealing with security alerts	During a security alert, all staff must react appropriately. Any messages received must be passed promptly to management, and the correct evacuation procedures followed.

The purpose of organisational procedures

Organisational procedures contribute to consistent and reliable customer service in several ways.

Meeting or exceeding customer service offered by rivals

Businesses offering similar products or services may compete on price, but many aim to offer a better service. If customers know they will get excellent service every time, this gives the business a competitive edge.

Following company mission/vision statements

A mission or vision statement explains the main purpose of the business and may define the brand for its customers. If the procedures are based on this statement, the business shows it is striving to achieve this aim.

Meeting external quality benchmarks

Benchmarks are set by independent organisations to denote a level of quality in an area. For example, the Crystal Mark, awarded by the Plain English Campaign to businesses, sets a standard for documents in clear everyday English. This gives customers confidence that they will understand the information provided by the business.

Remember

Procedures help to ensure that all customers are treated fairly and equally (see also next topic).

What other signs help to prevent accidents in the workplace?

Discussion point

McDonald's mission statement is: 'Our mission is to be our customers' favourite place and way to eat'. Discuss how excellent customer service can help McDonald's to achieve this aim.

Activity   Investigating procedures at your school or college

Find out how visitors to your school/college are dealt with when they come in for the first time. Do the reception staff follow a procedure? What information are visitors given on evacuation procedures in the case of an emergency?

Customer service requirements

Introduction

All businesses are subject to different forms of **legislation** and regulatory requirements. Customer service staff must know those that directly affect customers.

Complying with legislative and regulatory requirements

Health and safety

The Health and Safety at Work Act is the main law relating to health and safety. Additional **regulations** apply to areas such as noise and the use of work equipment. The aim is to ensure the safety of employees, customers, suppliers and anyone visiting a business premises.

To comply with the law, businesses carry out risk assessments to identify hazards. If these cannot be eliminated, then precautions must be taken, such as limiting access to hazardous areas, putting up safety signs and issuing protective equipment such as hard hats. All businesses must have an emergency evacuation procedure which is known to all staff.

> **Activity**   Researching health and safety
>
> 1 Find out more about the Health and Safety at Work Act by visiting the HSE website. You can access this by going to www.pearsonhotlinks.co.uk and searching for this title.
>
> 2 Find out how visitors to your school/college are warned about hazards. What procedures exist to ensure the safety of any wheelchair users in an emergency evacuation?

Sale of goods

The Sale of Goods Act is the main law that regulates sales transactions. It states that all goods, whether new or second-hand, must be:

- as described, e.g. leather shoes must be made of leather
- of satisfactory quality, given the price, description and age of the item
- fit for the purpose for which they are intended.

If these conditions are not met, then the buyer can reject the item and insist on a refund.

The Supply of Goods and Services Act covers buyers of services, such as dry cleaning, and states that these should be carried out for a reasonable charge, within a reasonable time, with reasonable care and skill and using satisfactory materials.

Data protection

The Data Protection Act covers personal information collected, stored, processed and distributed by business organisations. It includes information held on employees, customers, potential customers and suppliers. Anyone who has data held on them can formally request to see it to check that it is up to date and accurate. Breaching customer or employee confidence by selling or buying personal data is a serious offence, with an unlimited fine.

All staff who handle or have access to personal data, such as contact details, medical records or bank details, must store this securely and must never disclose it to any unauthorised person.

Discussion point

Discuss why police records are not covered by the Data Protection Act.

Equal opportunities

Many laws and regulations aim to ensure that employees and customers are treated fairly and equally. Discrimination (treating someone differently) is unlawful on many grounds, for example age, gender, race, sexual orientation, disability, gender reassignment, religion and belief. **The Equality Act** states that all disabled people must receive the same service as able-bodied customers. Unfavourable treatment may result in the business having to pay compensation.

Activity | Investigating equality

British banks have been criticised for ignoring the needs of disabled people. In the USA, blind users can plug headphones into a cash machine that 'talks' to them.

How good is a) your centre and b) your selected business at providing access to services for anyone with special requirements? Investigate both of these.

What other adaptations can be made to businesses to make them accessible to those with disabilities?

Assessment activity 4.1

2A.P1 | 2A.P2 | 2A.P3 | 2A.P4 | 2A.M1 | 2A.M2 | 2A.M3 | 2A.D1

For the training event for new entrepreneurs, you are asked to produce a display which shows the impact of organisational procedures and legislation/regulations on customer service.

1 Obtain specific examples of organisational procedures, such as how refunds are processed, and explain how these have contributed to consistent and reliable customer service. Remember to show a clear link between the procedures and their contribution to consistency and reliability.

2 For one of the businesses you selected in the introduction to this activity, explain how legislative and regulatory requirements have affected its customer service.

3 Compare the impact of the different legislative and regulatory requirements on your selected business by identifying the different effects each one has had and explaining the similarities and differences.

4 Add to the report notes you made in the introduction to this activity by identifying examples that show how the procedures in place at your selected business, and its response to its legislative and regulatory responsibilities, have contributed towards providing excellent and consistent customer service.

5 Then write a report in which you assess the effect of providing consistent and reliable customer service on the reputation of that business.

Tip

Ensure you evaluate how much each aspect of customer service has contributed towards the reputation of the business.

Who are your customers?

Customers

Types of customer

- **Internal customers** are those people who work in the same organisation, including managers, colleagues in your own team or other departments, supervisors and other staff.
- **External customers** are existing and new customers. They include individuals, groups, members of the public and other businesses who need the goods and services provided by your organisation.

Table 4.4 The main differences between internal and external customers

Internal customers	External customers
- They work in the same organisation as you.	- They are not part of the same business as you.
- They may need information about a customer or order you have dealt with.	- They may contact the business with an enquiry, to make a purchase or to return a faulty item.
- They may need your assistance to deal with their own external customers effectively.	- They can choose to go somewhere else if dissatisfied.
- They rely on you for prompt cooperation to do their job properly.	- They may complain or tell others if they are unhappy with the product or service provided.

Key terms

Internal customers – colleagues who work in the same organisation and need you to do something.

External customers – outside businesses and individuals who want to make a purchase.

Customers with special requirements include:

- **Non-English speaking:** You should talk relatively slowly and use simple words and short sentences. Writing something down may help. Know which colleagues speak other languages and ask for help.
- **Different ages:** Businesses that deal with various age groups often aim to meet their varying needs, for example by providing toys in a hospital waiting area and seating in a store for older customers. Elderly customers vary just as much as young ones but many dislike making quick decisions.
- **Different cultures:** Cultural differences affect what we wear, what we eat and drink and our expectations. You should know the main cultural differences of your usual customers. If you are uncertain, ask a more senior colleague for advice and remember what you are told.

Why is it important to recognize cultural differences and ask a colleague if you are unsure how to pronounce a name?

- **Gender:** Research shows that men and women shop very differently. Women like to browse and look at goods over a longer period of time, whereas men are usually more direct, tend to buy the targeted item as quickly as possible and then leave the shop.
- **Families:** Many businesses that deal with families offer group booking discounts and facilities for everyone, such as a soft-play area and teashop at a visitor attraction.
- **Customers with special needs:** Customers with visual, hearing or mobility disabilities may need extra support such as Braille leaflets, hearing aid induction loops, or ramps and lifts within the business.

Factors that impact on different customer service expectations

Factors that may affect a customer's expectations include:

- **The customer's age or culture:** These factors may affect the speed or type of service a customer expects. Young customers may want to browse for a while, whereas older customers may be less patient and want instant attention.
- **The public image of the business or owner:** Customers who are attracted to a business because it has a good reputation or because they are told the owner provides a high level of personal service will have high expectations.
- **The customer's disposable income:** A customer buying a premium product will expect a better level of service.

Activity Listing your expectations

You have won a competition and will stay in a luxury hotel in Paris for three days. In groups, list the ways in which you would expect the service and facilities to be better than in a standard hotel.

Assessment activity 4.2 *Introduction*

Your group will be helping with events at your school or college involving outside guests. These include parents' evenings, open evenings and social events. You will be involved in several different customer service situations as follows.

Before the event, you will assist prospective visitors who telephone or email asking for information.

During the event, you will greet guests, show them round if appropriate, run the enquiry desk, keep records and provide information and literature

Prepare for this by identifying the different types of internal and external customers that may visit the premises. Then find out how your school or college aims to meet the needs and expectation of three different types of customer. Write notes that will help you describe this to your tutor. Keep these safely because you will need them when you carry out the assessment activity later in the unit.

Tip

Remember that you must identify the needs and expectations of each of your three types of customer before you can describe how your school or college meets these.

AN INDUCTION LOOP IS PROVIDED FOR THE BENEFIT OF HEARING AID USERS. TO USE PLEASE SWITCH YOUR HEARING AID TO 'T'

Where can you find this type of information?

Customer service skills

Getting started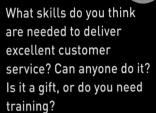

What skills do you think are needed to deliver excellent customer service? Can anyone do it? Is it a gift, or do you need training?

Discussion point

Most large retail stores issue an employee handbook that stresses the importance of personal appearance. How do you think a team leader should deal with a member of staff who disregards this?

◣ Skills required to deliver consistent and reliable customer service

Creating a good impression

Professional customer service staff have the skills required to create a good impression. These include the following.

- **Good manners:** Being polite to customers at all times is essential. Many organisations train staff to use a specific greeting.

- **Appropriate dress:** Many businesses require their employees to wear a uniform, e.g. airlines, travel agents. If there is no uniform available, there may be a dress code which sets specific rules about jewellery, hairstyles, makeup and style of clothes.

- **Using appropriate language:** When you are dealing with different customers, you may need to vary the language that you use. For example, it is not appropriate to use technical language to someone buying a computer unless you know they are computer literate.

- **Good posture/body language:** Greeting a customer with a smile and looking them in the eye (not staring) will create a much better impression than appearing bored and not making eye contact.

- **Tidy work area:** An untidy work area may give a customer the impression that you are disorganised. It is your duty as an employee to ensure that your work area is kept tidy and does not present a health and safety hazard to customers and colleagues.

How is this doorman creating a good impression?

Positive attitude

Having a positive attitude will give a good impression to customers and will also help develop relationships with your fellow colleagues. For example:

- **good timekeeping** – always being on time for work, or being in the right place at the agreed time, is important and shows that you care about your job and your customers

- **being conscientious** about your role gives customers confidence in your ability because they know you will take care to do your best

- **being motivated** means that you are keen to help a customer and enthusiastic about your business's products and services. This impresses a customer and inspires trust in the business.

Effective communication with customers

Communicating effectively is vital to customer service. This involves both **verbal communication** (what you say and how you say it) and **non-verbal communication** (what you do).

Table 4.5   Essential factors for effective communication with customers

Verbal communication	Non-verbal communication
Give an appropriate greeting, such as 'Good morning' or 'How may I help you?'	Smile at the customer and appear friendly and approachable.
Speak clearly using language that the customer will understand and try to avoid jargon.	Make eye contact with customers and look at them when you're talking to them.
Use an appropriate tone of voice.	Use open body language, i.e. don't cross your arms or put your hands in your pockets.
Make sure you don't speak too loudly, but also make sure you can be heard.	Your facial expression must make you approachable, and look as though you want to help the customer.
Adjust the language you use and the speed you speak at if customers do not speak English as their first language.	

Activity   Demonstrating body language

In small groups, research positive and negative body language online. Then devise a customer service role play that will demonstrate both. Two people should enact the roles of customer and employee. The rest of the group should observe and identify how body language affects the customer's experience.

Completing communication with the customer

The way you end a conversation is important. Make sure that you don't leave the customer wondering what will happen next.

- Thank the customer, whether they have bought anything or not.
- Use an appropriate tone of voice.
- Use positive body language.
- Use an appropriate form of address. If you are unsure of the customer's name, use 'Sir' or 'Madam'.
- Use the customer's name if you know it, but don't be overfamiliar (for example, use 'Mr Smith' not 'John').
- Offer further assistance by asking if there is anything else you can do such as packing goods, carrying items to their car or telling them when an item is in stock.
- Check the customer is happy with the service they received by following up with a telephone call or questionnaire.

Key terms

Verbal communication – what you say and how you say it.

Non-verbal communication – the process of communication through body language, facial expressions, gestures, eye contact and tone of voice.

Discussion point

In some stores, staff are trained to ask customers when they are paying for goods whether they have forgotten anything. Is this annoying or helpful? How would you feel if you were in a long queue and in a hurry?

Customer service skills

Getting started

How do customer service skills vary between people who work in a shop and a call centre? Or are they all the same?

Developing customer service skills

If you work in customer service, you have to respond to customers in different ways. The skills you need to communicate effectively are shown in Table 4.6.

Table 4.6 Effective customer service skills

Type of communication	Presentation skills	Personal skills	Communication skills
Face to face	Keep a professional appearance at all times. Your body language tells people your manner and attitude.	Greet customers appropriately, and be friendly and keen to meet their needs.	Speak clearly and use an appropriate tone of voice. Avoid jargon and slang.
Telephone	Smile during a conversation – your voice will let the caller know you are friendly.	Greet the caller. Show your concern by your response and tone of voice.	A clear voice and appropriate pace are essential as gestures cannot be seen.
Writing	Write neatly and use a clear layout. Check your spelling and grammar. Always proofread your work.	All written communications should be courteous and tactful, and the wording appropriate for the situation.	The degree of formality depends on who you are writing to, and why you are writing.
Email	The style and layout of your message must follow a business format.		Business emails must follow organisational rules and standards.

Remember

It is just as important to use the right tone when you are dealing with internal customers over the telephone as it is with external customers.

Dealing with customer queries

How you deal with customer queries will decide how they feel afterwards. You should always:

- **be polite** – no matter how difficult the customer may be
- **show empathy** – this means showing you really understand how the customer feels about a problem
- **keep customers informed** – if you are dealing with a query and arrange to contact the customer again later, make sure that you do this. Even if you still don't have the answer, contacting the customer gives them reassurance that you are still doing all you can to help them
- **don't disagree** – even if you think the customer is wrong. Being tactful is important. Focus on the topic rather than an opinion. If the situation becomes very difficult, ask for assistance. After all, the customer may be right!
- **use appropriate body language**, including making eye contact – this gives the customer positive signals that you are interested in helping them.

In small groups, select four difficult, but realistic, queries that you might receive in a store that sells beauty products and medicines, such as Boots or Superdrug. Pass your questions to another group to decide on appropriate answers. Then vote for the best responses. You can extend this and gain further practice by changing the store to one that sells stationery, toys, DVDs, or any other type of product you choose!

Dealing with customer problems and complaints

Customers usually complain for a reason. The first rule is to listen carefully so that you understand the problem and what the customer wants you to do to put it right. This will usually mean:

- offering an alternative if a product is currently unavailable
- offering an exchange or a refund if the original is faulty
- immediately telling your supervisor or manager if the customer problem or complaint is very serious or outside the limit of your authority (see below).

Customer types

You may come into contact with many different types of customers. Table 4.7 gives guidelines about how to deal with them.

> **?** **Did you know?**
>
> The 'grey pound' is worth over £100 billion a year. This is the amount spent by UK customers who are over 50 years of age. Remember this next time you are tempted to ignore or rush someone who is much older than you!

Table 4.7 Dealing with different customer types

Type of customer	Do ...	Do not ...
Difficult customers	<ul><li>be patient</li><li>listen to what the customer is saying</li><li>remain positive</li><li>seek help if required from a more senior colleague.</li></ul>	<ul><li>lose your temper</li><li>be impatient</li><li>argue or contradict them.</li></ul>
Abusive customers	<ul><li>stay calm</li><li>get help in a face-to-face situation if the customer does not calm down</li><li>inform the customer that if the abuse continues you will end the call (if on the telephone).</li></ul>	<ul><li>shout back at the customer or get angry</li><li>let the situation get out of hand</li><li>get upset or distressed.</li></ul>
Customers with disabilities	<ul><li>focus on the person, not the disability.</li></ul>	<ul><li>treat them any differently from any other customer.</li></ul>
Elderly customers	<ul><li>be patient</li><li>listen to their needs</li><li>speak clearly</li><li>show respect.</li></ul>	<ul><li>be impatient</li><li>dismiss their needs</li><li>try to get rid of them too quickly.</li></ul>
Customers needing technical information	<ul><li>be patient</li><li>explain clearly</li><li>seek help (if required) from a more experienced colleague.</li></ul>	<ul><li>use lots of jargon/technical language</li><li>assume that the customer knows what you are talking about</li><li>guess what they want.</li></ul>

CONTINUED ▶▶

Different customer service situations

Customer service staff may have to deal with a range of different situations:

- **providing information about products and/or services:** to do this competently you must be familiar with the range of items available, their features and prices. This means having any relevant information leaflets or catalogues to hand and being familiar with the content

- **promoting additional products and/or services that may meet the customer's needs,** for example underlay for a carpet or upholstery protection for a car or sofa

- **giving advice** to help the customer to make the best decision in their particular circumstances

- **taking and relaying messages,** which means being able to identify and record the key facts accurately, and ensuring the message is promptly passed to the correct person.

Activity   Identifying skills and knowledge

You need a new blind in your bedroom. You have no idea what types are available, how they are fitted or how much they cost. What skills and knowledge would the person who handles your enquiry need to help you?

Case study: Other customer service skills

Carl has a part-time job driving a van to deliver groceries ordered online. He must keep an accurate record of the deliveries he makes and any incidents that occur. For example, if a product has been substituted and is rejected by the customer, he can process a refund. If a product is damaged, he may be able to let the customer keep it without charge. If he is delayed for any reason, he must phone ahead to warn the customer that he might be late. If he breaks down, he must call the depot immediately.

Why does Carl need additional customer service skills?

As a service deliverer for the store, Carl is the 'face' of the business to online customers. In addition to being polite and helpful, he needs to demonstrate other skills.

CONTINUED ▶▶

Case study: Continued

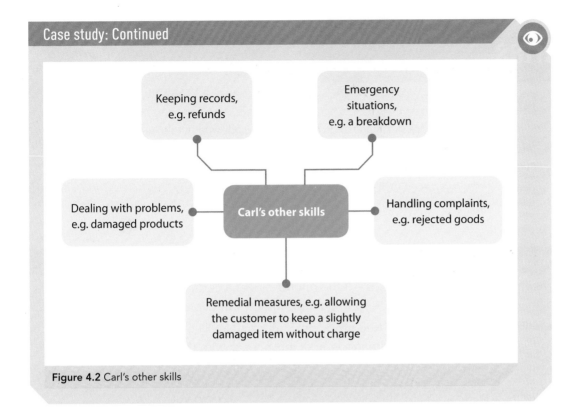

Figure 4.2 Carl's other skills

Complying with organisational procedures/policies

It is important to comply with the procedures and policies that are in place in a business. These may include:

- **A complaints procedure** which gives details about the information that must be obtained, the actions that can be taken by each level of staff and the senior person who is responsible for resolving serious problems.
- **A disclaimer**, which is a statement that denies responsibility. For example, many retail stores disclaim responsibility for damage to cars in their car park. Note that a business can never disclaim responsibility for personal injury to customers on its premises.
- **Service specification statements**, which are also known as service level agreements and tell customers the level of service they can expect to receive when they are dealing with the organisation.

 Discussion point

A shop owner decides he will put up a notice that disclaims all responsibility for any faulty products he sells. Can he do this? Discuss your ideas as a group.

 Key term

Service specification statement – issued by an organisation giving details of the level of service to be expected.

Just checking

1. What specific skills are needed to talk to customers on the telephone rather than face to face?

2. What is 'empathy' and how can you demonstrate it?

3. A customer is opinionated and argumentative. What skills are required to deal with this person?

4. Suggest two reasons for recording complaints that are received.

Limits of authority and customer queries

Introduction

In any job role there are decisions and actions you are allowed to take and those you must refer to someone more senior. This is good, because it prevents junior employees from making serious errors that could have major consequences. In customer service, the usual authority levels are as shown in Table 4.8.

Table 4.8 Limits of authority

Role	Limit of authority
Service deliverer, e.g. shop assistant, receptionist, call centre operator	• has limited authority on refunds – if the refund is over a certain amount or the item is damaged, a supervisor may need to authorise the transaction • has limited authority to offer free products. Staff can usually only do this if there is a special promotion. In other situations, staff must check with their line manager.
Line manager/ supervisor	• has greater authority to authorise refunds and may be able to authorise discounts or free goods. They must work within the organisational guidelines • has supervisory or line management responsibilities for junior members of staff • ensures that all policies and procedures are carried out by their staff.
Management	• may be a branch manager and have control of a branch • is able to authorise exceptional changes to policies and procedures, and make decisions where unusual or difficult issues arise.

Assessment activity 4.2

2B.P5 | 2B.P6 | 2B.P7 | 2B.M4 | 2B.D2

You will now be helping with events at your centre involving outside guests.

- Before each event, identify your own job role and the limits of your authority by preparing a summary sheet on which you list and describe actions you can take and situations where you must notify a tutor.

- On your own, discuss your summary sheet with your tutor and also describe how your school or college meets the needs and expectations of three different types of customer using the notes you made in the introduction to this assessment activity.

- In groups, discuss the request and enquiries you will receive, the types of customers you will meet and how to cope with any problems and complaints.

Practise your skills by role playing typical scenarios for your tutor.

- At each event, your tutor will conduct individual observations and record your performance to identify whether you were able to demonstrate effective communication skills when you were dealing with different customers in different situations and responding to problems and complaints.

- After each event, evaluate your own performance. Think about the skills where you would receive a high customer feedback score, and those areas where you would not. Take into account your tutor's feedback and write your own report in which you identify areas for improvement and justify each of your choices.

Tips

If you deal with customers on other occasions, such as when working in a school or college shop, in a part-time job or on work experience, then you can also use evidence in the form of witness statements to help you achieve this unit. Discuss with your teacher/tutor the evidence that you will need to produce.

WorkSpace

Janet McGregor

Customer Service Representative

Janet is a customer service representative for a large mobile phone company. She is a member of a team in the retentions section of a contact centre in the North East of England.

Janet's main role is to ensure that customers who call her section are retained. They may call because they have received a large bill or are unhappy with the coverage on their phone. Or they may have problems using their phone or be unhappy about roaming charges. Janet has to ensure that they remain with the company by resolving their issues.

She does this by often upgrading their phone and trying to get them the best deal on calls and texts. Janet can only upgrade to a certain level of cost to the company. Beyond that, she must involve her team leader.

Janet knows that excellent customer service is vital. She always makes sure that she keeps in regular contact with the customer if she has to put them on hold to investigate an issue. She wants them to know that she is still dealing with the problem and hasn't left them holding on.

After the call, the customer receives an automatic text message asking them to grade the service they have received. Each representative receives a grade between 1 and 10 (10 being brilliant) and these scores form part of the staff targets each month.

Janet is very busy at times, especially at Christmas, but really enjoys her job. She likes interacting with customers and helping to solve their problems, and gets a buzz when she hits targets!

Think about it

1 How can Janet ensure she makes a good impression when she receives a call?

2 Identify five additional skills that Janet needs to do her job successfully.

3 **a)** Why does Janet have to refer some phone upgrades to her team leader?
   b) Suggest two other occasions when she would involve her team leader.

4 Suggest two reasons why the phone company asks callers to grade the service they have just received.

Introduction

Can you think of a business that does not involve selling? Selling is a vital business skill and jobs in sales are vibrant and exciting with good promotion prospects. Nowadays many of us shop online, but most of us still prefer personal selling where we talk to a salesperson face to face or over the telephone. We like the personal attention and it is good to get a quick response to our questions and help finding the right product.

If you want to work in sales, your main job will be to promote and sell products. You need to be knowledgeable about the products and able to communicate well with customers. If you are ambitious, quick-thinking and able to create a positive first impression, you will go far.

This unit explores the role of sales staff and will help you to demonstrate personal selling skills and processes.

Assessment: This unit will be assessed through a series of assignments set by your teacher/tutor.

Learning aims

In this unit you will:

A explore the role of sales staff

B demonstrate personal selling skills and processes.

"Before studying this unit, it never occurred to me how important I was to the business and I didn't realise that there were so many things that I could do to increase sales. I now get quite a buzz from making a sale and keeping my customers happy.

Chloe, *16-year-old Business student and part-time sales assistant*"

Sales and Personal Selling

5

This table shows you what you must do in order to achieve a **Pass**, **Merit** or **Distinction** grade, and where you can find activities in this book to help you.

Assessment criteria			
Level 1	**Level 2 Pass**	**Level 2 Merit**	**Level 2 Distinction**
Learning aim A: Explore the role of sales staff			
1A.1 Identify two functions of sales staff in a selected business	**2A.P1** Describe, using examples, four functions of sales staff in a selected business **See Assessment activity 5.1, page 133**	**2A.M1** Compare the functions of the sales staff and the different sales skills used in two selected businesses **See Assessment activity 5.1, page 133**	**2A.D1** Assess the effectiveness of sales skills and knowledge used by sales staff in two selected businesses **See Assessment activity 5.1, page 133**
1A.2 Identify the sales skills used by sales staff in a selected business	**2A.P2** Describe the sales skills used by sales staff in three different selling situations **See Assessment activity 5.1, page 133**		
1A.3 Outline the importance of product knowledge when making sales	**2A.P3** Explain the knowledge and skills needed to sell two selected products **See Assessment activity 5.1, page 133**		
1A.4 Outline legislation which affects personal selling in a selected business	**2A.P4** Explain the legislation which affects personal selling in a selected business **See Assessment activity 5.1, page 133**	**2A.M2** Assess the importance of complying with the legal requirements for customer care and selling products in a selected business **See Assessment activity 5.1, page 133**	

Assessment criteria

Level 1	Level 2 Pass	Level 2 Merit	Level 2 Distinction
Learning aim B: Demonstrate personal selling skills and processes			
1B.5 Identify product knowledge required to make personal sales	**2B.P5** Prepare for the sales process for making personal sales to two different types of customer **See Assessment activity 5.2, page 143**	**2B.M3** English Demonstrate handling a customer problem or complaint **See Assessment activity 5.2, page 143**	**2B.D2** English Demonstrate the confident use of personal selling skills when making sales in at least three different personal sales situations **See Assessment activity 5.2, page 143**
1B.6 English Answer two routine customer enquiries in a personal sales situation	**2B.P6** English Demonstrate handling two different types of customer enquiry **See Assessment activity 5.2, page 143**	**2B.M4** Assess the effectiveness of the selling skills and processes used in two different situations **See Assessment activity 5.2, page 143**	**2B.D3** Evaluate the preparation, skills and processes used in two different personal sales situations and recommend improvements **See Assessment activity 5.2, page 143**
1B.7 English Use selling skills in two personal sales situations	**2B.P7** English Demonstrate effective customer care skills in two personal sales situations **See Assessment activity 5.2, page 143**		

English   Opportunity to practise English skills

How you will be assessed

The unit will be assessed by a series of internally assessed tasks. You will be expected to explore the role of sales staff by investigating selected businesses and selling situations. You will also complete tasks that require you to demonstrate and provide evidence of your own personal selling skills and processes in a simulated or real-work environment.

Your assessment could be in the form of:

- a written account or presentation detailing your investigations
- video role-play evidence of personal selling skills
- log or sales diary evidence of personal selling skills
- a personal statement reflecting your own selling skills.

The role of sales staff

Introduction

Sales staff work in a wide range of businesses. You often see sales staff at work on the high street or in out-of-town shopping centres, selling anything from clothes and beauty products to electrical goods and mobile phones. You may have been stopped in the street by a salesperson who has tried to sell you a raffle ticket for charity, and sales staff may have telephoned you at home to offer you a deal on your mobile phone contract.

The principal job of all sales staff is to make a sale. To be successful, a salesperson has to be knowledgeable about the product they are selling and skilful in the way they make a sale.

Sales staff are crucial to the success of many businesses. They are the public face of an organisation and are very influential in the customer's decision as to whether or not to make a purchase.

Selling

Selling is the most important part of the salesperson's job. Sales staff around the world sell millions of different things, but what they sell normally fits into the following categories:

- goods – physical products, e.g. clothes, food, cars, houses
- services, benefits or experiences offered by a business, e.g. cleaning, hairdressing and dog walking
- product surrounds – the features and benefits related to a product or service, e.g. brand name, company's reputation, reliability.

Table 5.1 Examples of products, services and product surrounds

Product	Service	Product surround
Xbox®	A subscription to their online gaming community	Microsoft's backing
Micro scooter®	A spares and repairs service	The reputation of the maker
Kindle™	Access to over 900,000 books, magazines and newspapers	The Amazon brand

As well as making a sale, the salesperson has a number of other roles.

Providing information

Sales staff give information to the customer about the product. They must communicate in a way that the customer will understand. A person selling laptops needs to be able to simplify the features of a laptop so that a customer with little knowledge of IT can understand what they are buying. They should be able to adapt their approach and use more technical language for the more IT-literate customer.

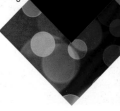

Dealing with routine enquiries

Customers may have many questions including questions about the product itself, the range of products offered, the shop's opening hours, the company's policy on exchanging goods and whether the company sells online.

Customers are not impressed if a salesperson is unable to answer their questions, as this gives a poor impression of the business.

Representing the organisation

Sales staff represent the business and the product. They are often the first person the customer comes into contact with when they see the product, and many customers judge the product on their impression of the sales staff. It is essential that sales staff make a good impression by dressing and behaving appropriately and by being informative.

How important is the appearance of sales staff?

Just checking

1 What is the primary objective of sales staff?

2 What are three other functions of sales staff?

3 What is the difference between goods and services?

4 What is a product surround?

? Did you know?

Holland and Barrett, the well-known retailer of vitamins, minerals and herbal supplements insist that all their sales staff complete a staff training programme to teach them about their products. This ongoing training programme enables their staff to recommend appropriate products based on the customer's requirements.

Remember

It only takes a few seconds for somebody to judge you when they first come into contact with you. People use your appearance, body language and mannerisms to form an impression of you and this happens every time you meet somebody new. Sales staff should aim to make great first impressions and never forget that they are the public face of the business.

Knowledge and skills

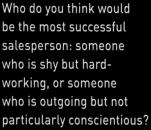

Getting started

Who do you think would be the most successful salesperson: someone who is shy but hard-working, or someone who is outgoing but not particularly conscientious?

The answer is probably neither of them. A shy person might struggle to deal with people, but the outgoing person who is not very hard-working might not be motivated enough to learn the additional knowledge and practise the necessary skills to become effective in their job.

What knowledge and skills do sales people need?

Product knowledge

Sales staff must know enough about a product and how it works to match the customer with the appropriate product. Sales staff should know the following:

- **Stock availability** – what is normally available and when out-of-stock items will become available
- **Price information** – the prices of the products and how these compare with other available products
- **Store information** – location of products in the shop and the delivery/collection arrangements
- **Product care** – how to look after the product and what after-sales service is available such as warranties, servicing and repair
- **Key information** – how to demonstrate how the product works. The main features, uses and what variations in colour, size etc. are available.

Activity	Demonstrating product knowledge

You have received two emails from friends who have job interviews next week for part-time sales jobs. One friend has an interview at a pet shop and the other has an interview at a mobile phone shop. Both of them are very excited, but worried that they do not know enough about what the shop sells. Choose one friend to help and send them an email giving them advice on what you think they should know about the products sold in the shop. Also, advise them about where they can find the information they need.

Sales motivation

Motivation is the driving force that enables people to achieve their goals. Successful sales staff are highly motivated individuals who are eager to make a sale. They are often seen using inventive techniques such as **cross-selling** and **up-selling** to increase sales.

Motivated sales staff are ambitious, hard-working and enthusiastic people who set themselves high targets. They appear to be passionate about the product they are selling, and their desire to succeed motivates them to try hard to match their products to their customer's needs.

Activity	Role-playing sales situations

In pairs, role-play a number of sales situations where a salesperson uses cross-selling to suggest a related item to the customer.

Understanding potential customers

Being able to identify potential customers and understand their requirements is vital to being able to recommend the right product to the customer. This also helps sales staff to communicate with customers appropriately.

Some people are naturally more intuitive and have better interpersonal skills, but salespeople who carefully listen and ask the right questions can learn more about the potential customer.

Sales preparation skills

The physical sales environment, that is the shop, the market stall, the car showroom or the exhibition hall, is very important in enticing customers to make purchases. The **sales environment** should be welcoming, clean and tidy and products should be clearly displayed and be accessible to everyone.

The design of the sales environment should reflect the business's image. Sales staff are often involved in the preparation of the sales environment, and depending on their position in the company and the size of the business, they may be involved in designing, setting up and maintaining displays and exhibition stands.

Some interesting tactics are used to increase sales:

- Fast music can be used to encourage customers to purchase more quickly. This is useful during busy periods in a fast food outlet. Slow music can be used to encourage customers to take their time when buying expensive products such as jewellery.
- Some supermarkets pump the smell of fresh bread near the entrance of their store to give the impression that bread is available all day. Some coffee shops do the same with fresh coffee.

Key terms

Cross-selling – suggesting a related product to a customer to increase the overall sale, for example a hairspray to go with a haircut.

Up-selling – promoting a more profitable alternative to increase the value of the sale.

Sales environment – the place where sales are made.

Did you know?

Businesses attempt to increase their sales staff's motivation by paying them a sum of money, known as commission, based on the value of what they sell. This means that top salespeople can earn a lot of money. However, some jobs are paid commission only, which means that the salesperson only earns money if they make a sale.

What is attractive about this **sales environment**?

CONTINUED ▶▶

Sales techniques

Here are some of the sales techniques used by businesses in personal selling:

- **Cold calling:** This sales technique involves contacting a stranger unexpectedly, usually by telephone. It is 'cold' because they have shown no prior interest in the product. You need to be patient and resilient to use this technique because you are likely to get many refusals and some hostility. Cold calling is sometimes used to sell double glazing and insurance.

- **Face to face:** This is when the salesperson talks to the customer in person, and this is usually the most effective way of selling a product. This technique is used by sales staff in shops, door-to-door salespeople and by street sellers.

- **Drop-in visits:** This is when salespeople visit potential customers, which are usually businesses rather than individuals. Drug companies employ sales representatives who make drop-in visits to doctors' surgeries to promote their products.

- **Telemarketing:** Also known as telesales, this technique involves contacting prospective customers usually by telephone and delivering a sales pitch. Calls are either pre-recorded messages or made from people in call centres.

This is different from cold calling because the people who have been called have been selected through a system that has identified them as being a potential customer. A holiday company selling clubbing holidays may use telemarketing by contacting young adults who have been identified as enjoying clubbing through having previously been on a clubbing holiday.

What are the advantages and disadvantages of telemarketing?

Discussion 💬

In a group, discuss your experiences of aggressive, high-pressure selling, known as hard selling. Do you think that it encourages people to buy? When can its use be criticised?

Activity   Evaluating sales techniques

Discuss the strengths and weaknesses of the different sales techniques. Include in your answer information about the effectiveness, the benefits and the likely problems with each of the methods.

Closing a sale

Sales staff can spend hours over many days carefully negotiating and persuading the customer to make a purchase. Knowing how and when to close the sale is a skill which many good salespeople find challenging.

Legislation and organisational policies

Table 5.2 demonstrates how legislation, aimed at protecting the customer, affects personal selling. Organisational policies offer additional benefits to the customer but do not affect the customer's legal rights.

Table 5.2 Legislation aimed at protecting the customer

Legislation	Effects on personal selling
Sale of Goods Act 1979 (amended in 1994, 1995 and 2002) Items purchased must be: • of satisfactory quality – given the price, description and age of item • fit for the purpose for which they are intended • as described – match the description on the packaging or the one given by the seller.	The after-sales service should provide a refund, repair or replacement for problems and complaints about a purchased item that does not meet these rights. Customers may be entitled to additional rights beyond that stated in the guarantee.
Supply of Goods and Services Act 1982 Services purchased must be carried out with reasonable care and skill, at a reasonable price that reflects the skills of the provider and within a reasonable time.	Poor workmanship is unacceptable. Businesses cannot charge excessively for services – a builder cannot charge a day's work for changing a light bulb.
The Consumer Protection from Unfair Trading Regulations 2008 (CPRs) It an offence to treat customers unfairly through misleading actions such as lying, exaggeration or making inaccurate claims/discounts/offers. This act also stops sellers missing out key information and behaving aggressively.	Shops cannot have closing down sales that last for months, they cannot have discounts and special offers, such as price-matching policies that do not exist, and they cannot be too forceful in their sales techniques.

Link

Learn more about this topic in *Unit 12: Introducing Law and Consumer Rights*.

Did you know?

• If you do not want to receive marketing and unsolicited sales calls you can register your telephone number with the Telephone Preference Service and companies will no longer be able to legally contact you.

• When you buy something from private sellers, for example on eBay, you have fewer rights. The goods only have to be as described and theirs to sell.

Discussion point

The television programme *Watchdog* has a feature called 'Rogue Traders' that investigates complaints from customers about services they have received. Read through some of the cases on their website and identify a trader that you think is particularly bad. Give reasons for your opinion.

Organisational policies

Many organisations have policies that offer the customer additional benefits beyond their legal requirements. These policies benefit the business because they encourage customers to make impulse buys even if some are returned at a later date.

Table 5.3 Organisational policies

Organisational policy	Features
Price matching	Some businesses offer to match the cheaper price of a competitor for the same product. This sometimes excludes online purchases.
Discounting	Discounts may be given to customers who make repeat purchases, who spend over a certain amount or who are trade customers.
Guarantees	Some businesses offer extended guarantees well beyond their legal requirements.
After-sales service	Some organisations offer additional services after the purchase of the product, such as free delivery, order tracking, spare parts and a repair service.
Customer care	Additional services and facilities are sometimes available to help the customer, for example gift-wrapping and children's play areas.
Dealing with problems and complaints	To help the customer, some organisations have special policies for handling problems and complaints, e.g. giving the customer the name and direct line of the person dealing with their complaint.

Did you know?

In 2011 the supermarket Asda introduced its own price guarantee policy that promises to refund the difference if they are not 10 per cent cheaper on comparable grocery shopping. Customers can check this themselves using Asda's website.

Reflective practice

Good sales staff think carefully about why they did not make a sale to improve their skills. This is known as reflective practice. Professor Graham Gibbs put together a method of reflecting on your performance called the cycle of reflection and this is illustrated in figure 5.1.

You can use Gibbs's cycle to reflect on your performance in the unsuccessful encounters you have with people. It will help you to learn from your mistakes by making sense of what happened.

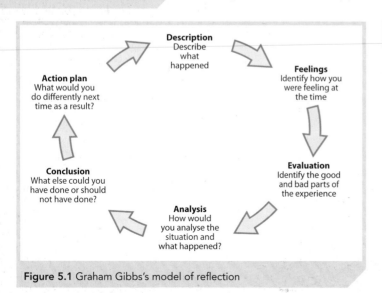

Figure 5.1 Graham Gibbs's model of reflection

Activity   Reflecting on your own performance

1 Think of an encounter you have had with someone that did not go well. If possible, use a selling situation.

2 Reflect on your own performance by using each element of Graham Gibbs's model of reflection.

WorkSpace

Ben Moss

Estate Agent – R A Bennett & Partners

Buying your own home may be the biggest purchase you will ever make and one that you will not enter into lightly. Therefore, estate agents need extensive knowledge and skills and the ability to communicate well.

Ben Moss is the manager of the Winchcombe branch of the estate agent R A Bennett & Partners. He built up his expertise from a sales career that started with door-to-door selling of gas and electricity and telemarketing of advertising space before quickly progressing up the career ladder as an estate agent.

Ben believes that when promoting a property it is important to highlight the features that match the buyer's needs. He reminds us that your views on what is a positive feature might not be the same as the customer's. After all, not everyone likes a big garden.

Ben emphasises the importance of knowing your product. Before promoting a house, Ben makes sure that he and his team have an in-depth knowledge of the property by making an initial visit.

To establish potential buyers' needs, Ben asks questions to discover more about their requirements and listens carefully to people's responses. For instance, if someone says that a double garage is a must-have, Ben will find out why. If it is for an artist's studio, a property with no garage but alternative space may still be an appropriate match.

Estate agents need to be able to solve problems and they must be skilful at negotiating to satisfy the different goals of both the buyer and the seller.

Ben thinks that the personality of a salesperson is important. Good estate agents have confidence both in the service that they are selling and in dealing with people from different backgrounds. They are persistent and do not give up easily. They are intuitive and understand that buying and selling property can be stressful.

Ben stresses that if someone is inviting you (a stranger) into their home it is important to look professional and he recommends wearing a traditional business suit.

Finally, Ben targets and evaluates every part of the selling process on a regular basis. Knowledge of what you have done and what you want to do leads to improvement and better results for customers.

Think about it

1 Why do you think it is important for estate agents to have a good knowledge of the properties they are selling?

2 Identify both the products and the service that estate agents sell.

3 What communication skills do you think have been important to Ben in his sales career?

4 Why does Ben think that reflective practice is important?

The process of personal selling

Introduction

Personal selling is important for most businesses and it offers a number of benefits.

Helping businesses remain competitive

There is likely to be fierce competition from other businesses, so you must be able to stand out from the crowd. This can be achieved through the following:

- providing special facilities, for example, toys to entertain children
- extra services, for example, gift-wrapping and free delivery
- excellent customer service
- sales promotions, for example, price reductions.

| Activity | Identifying how businesses compete |

In small groups, choose three shops that you are all familiar with and discuss what you think they are doing to remain competitive.

Establishing customer requirements

Effective sales staff identify their customers' requirements and match them to appropriate products.

Matching goods/services to customer requirements

All sales staff must listen carefully to the requirements of their customers or clients. For example, estate agents know that house buyers do not appreciate being contacted with details of properties that are in the wrong area, too expensive or not suitable.

Complying with the law

Sales staff must follow the law. See Table 5.2 for details about how the law governs products sold, pricing and customer care.

Developing customer care and building relationships

You must look after your customers from your very first encounter, throughout the whole buying process and in any aftercare you provide.

Customers want to be treated well. You must handle their queries efficiently and deal with complaints in a professional manner.

Gathering feedback

Feedback is important to businesses in order to make improvements. This is done through informal questions or questionnaires; for example, holidaymakers are often asked to complete questionnaires on their experience.

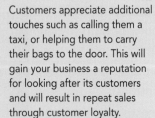

Remember

If you admit that you do not have a suitable product/service and advise the customer where to find it, you will create a good impression of the business and the customer may return in the future.

Did you know?

Customers appreciate additional touches such as calling them a taxi, or helping them to carry their bags to the door. This will gain your business a reputation for looking after its customers and will result in repeat sales through customer loyalty.

First point of contact

If a customer walks into your sales environment and sees a messy display or feels ignored, they may walk out and never return.

Activity   Observing first point of contact

Note which of the following happens next time you are shopping.

- The salesperson acknowledges your presence with a polite hello and a quick comment that they are available if you need them.
- They leave you alone to browse, but stay close enough to help if required.
- They approach you to see if you need assistance.

Promoting the product

Sales staff are trained to promote the product by:

- informing the customer of the features and benefits
- reminding and/or persuading them using the features and benefits.

To do this they have to appear passionate about the product.

Assessment activity 5.1   2A.P1 | 2A.P2 | 2A.P3 | 2A.P4 | 2A.M1 | 2A.M2 | 2A.D1

Your school/college is holding a careers fair and they have asked you to put together some information on jobs in retail. To do this, you can use your own observations as a customer and job descriptions that can be found online on relevant companies' websites.

1 Describe, using examples, four functions of sales staff working in a supermarket.

2 Now select a business selling bicycles as a comparison, and compare the functions of sales staff and the different sales skills used in the two selected businesses.

3 Describe the sales skills used by sales staff working in each of the following scenarios: a) an online bookshop, b) a call centre selling flights, c) a florist.

4 Explain the knowledge and skills needed to sell a pair of children's shoes and a laptop.

5 Explain the legislation which affects personal selling in a business selling double glazing.

6 Assess the importance of complying with the legal requirements for customer care and selling products in a car sales garage.

7 Visit two different shops. Observe the sales staff in order to assess the effectiveness of sales skills and the knowledge used by sales staff in two selected businesses.

Tips

- Think about how the sales skills needed would differ in each scenario because of the different selling methods used.
- Think about specialist knowledge that would be needed and whether any special skills would be needed for working with small children.
- Ensure you have to identify the sales skills used and knowledge demonstrated and then judge how effective they are in making a sale.

Remember

The features of a product/service are its attributes or its characteristics, whereas the benefits are why the feature is important to someone, for example it saves them time or money, is convenient, fun or has a good image.

Demonstrate personal selling skills

Introduction

If you want to become a top salesperson, ask yourself the following questions:

Personal selling skills: Are you ready to make a sale? Are your appearance and attitude right? Do you know how to communicate with the customer? Can you close a sale?

The selling process: Do you understand what you have to do to make a sale? Are you able to manage other sales-related tasks such as handling customer complaints?

Sales staff continually learn and improve their skills throughout their careers, but if you want to get ahead, preparation and practice are the key to success.

Preparing for the sales process

Before you meet any customers, you must make sure that you have the appropriate product information, that you can identify the features and the benefits of the product and that you know how to present this information to customers.

When you are new to a job, this can be more difficult and you may have to carry out extra research in your own time about the products you are selling. If you do this, you will feel more confident when meeting customers and you are much more likely to be able to answer their questions and help them to find what they are looking for.

Activity   Preparing for a sale

Try to persuade a friend to buy membership to a sports club/leisure centre. To do this, select a local club and if necessary look at their website, making sure that you are aware of the features and benefits of membership. Use this information to persuade your friend to join.

Maintaining an appropriate appearance

Sales personnel should be clean and tidy. Customers will be unimpressed if you have muddy shoes and scruffy hair.

- **Personal hygiene:** You need to be pleasant to be around, so you should be fussy about personal hygiene. Remember that body odour, stale breath and dirty fingernails are big turn-offs.

- **Dress:** You may be given a uniform to wear and it is important that you wear it correctly. Some businesses allow you to wear your own clothes, but have a dress code. You need to be disciplined about keeping to the dress code and ensure that you have enough appropriate clothes in your wardrobe. Where there is no dress code or uniform, you must dress appropriately according to the business and the product you are selling. It may be appropriate to wear a tracksuit if you work in a sports shop, but it will not be appropriate in a car showroom.

Maintaining an appropriate attitude

Do you prefer to deal with an enthusiastic person or a negative, resentful one? Employers and customers like dealing with people with a good attitude. In maintaining an appropriate attitude at work, you should be aware of the following:

- **Good manners** show respect and include saying please and thank you, holding the door open for customers, not swearing or using offensive language, not spreading gossip and not interrupting people when they are talking.
- **Courtesy and consideration** means putting other people first and being polite at all times. You should always appear interested in the customer and have excellent manners.
- **Language** is important. You need to speak in a more formal way than you are probably used to. Avoid starting sentences with 'um' or 'er', and instead of using the phrases 'like' or 'you know', you should say 'such as'. Addressing customers as 'Sir' or 'Madam' makes them feel valued and respected.
- **Positivity** is all about showing optimism and enthusiasm, which are both important in making sales. Avoid the negative, focus on the positive, smile and forget your own worries.

Just checking

1 What can you do to prepare for the selling process?
2 What is an appropriate appearance and attitude for a salesperson?
3 Why do sales staff need excellent communication skills?

? Did you know?

The popular high street retailer Topshop likes their staff to wear the clothes that they are selling, so they give their retail staff a clothing allowance of up to £1500 a year and a 25 per cent discount off all their merchandise.

💡 Remember

It is rude to use your mobile when talking to a customer, and if you really have to answer your mobile, you should apologise and walk away from the customer.

How is this sales assistant meeting the customers' expectations?

▸▸ CONTINUED

Link

This topic links to *Unit 4: Principles of Customer Service*.

Remember

Be aware of the limits to your authority – for example, most sales staff cannot make big price reductions.

Remember

• We send more messages to other people using non-verbal communication than verbal communication.

• Non-verbal communication often gives away our true feelings and is hard to fake.

Key terms

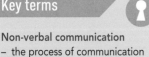

Non-verbal communication – the process of communication through body language, facial expressions, gestures, eye contact and tone of voice.

Body language – the messages communicated through facial expressions, gestures and posture.

Dealing with different types of customers

Sales staff must know how to help different types of customers, for example:

- Customers for whom English is not a first language – it may help to speak relatively slowly using simple words in short sentences.
- Customers with physical disabilities – inform them of appropriate special facilities.
- Families with young children – offer appropriate facilities such as toys, books to read or colouring pens and paper to keep children occupied.

Communicating with customers

In most selling situations, communications are face to face and your speaking, listening and **non-verbal communication** skills are crucial.

However, technology such as email and call-me buttons on websites mean that sales can be made remotely. Here a different set of skills are important. You need good listening skills to establish over the telephone what a customer wants and you need good written skills if you have to promote something on a website.

All salespeople have to answer customers' questions and this requires a range of good communication skills and product knowledge.

Table 5.4 Tips for communicating with customers

Type of communication	Tips
Spoken	Speak clearly, not too quickly or too loudly, and use words the customer will understand.
Written	Write clearly, use spell check and use words that the customer will understand.
Listening	Think about what the customer is saying and do not interrupt.
Non-verbal	Convey the right impression with a firm handshake, stand upright, avoid slouching and show you are interested by smiling and nodding.
Face to Face	Make sure your **body language** is right and that you are clean and tidy and dressed appropriately.
Eye contact	Show that you are interested in your customer by making regular eye contact, but do not hold their gaze for too long.
Remote	Speak clearly and slowly as connections are not always good. Sit near the microphone, ask for confirmation and speak one at a time. Be precise and concise as time/space may be limited.
Limits of authority	Never overstep your own job role and do not make promises you cannot keep. Ask colleagues for advice if you are unsure what to do.

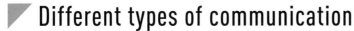

Different types of communication

- **Greeting:** It is disrespectful to shout 'Hiya!' across the shop, even if this is how you normally say hello. Instead, a polite and unthreatening 'Good morning, let me know if I can help you' is more suitable and creates a good impression.
- **Introductions:** Telling customers your name will help you to build a relationship with them.
- **Attracting customers' attention and interest:** Reassure the customer that you have what they are looking for, and give the impression that you are knowledgeable about the product range. Mentioning benefits that they might not be aware of heightens their interest in the product.
- **Identifying and meeting customers' needs:** Avoid talking too much. Instead, listen to the customer and ask the right questions to establish their requirements, and then use your extensive product knowledge to recommend the most suitable product/service.
- **Presenting products/product information:** Clearly and succinctly outline the main features of the product in appropriate language that your customer will understand.

Closing techniques

You will find out about closing techniques in Table 5.5.

Preparing the sales area

Sales staff must prepare the sales area so that it is a healthy and safe environment for customers and staff. Make sure that spilt liquids are correctly cleaned up, and walkways are kept clear by removing obstacles such as bags and boxes. The main legislation that protects people at work is the **Health and Safety at Work Act of 1974**. Sales staff must prepare the sales area so that it complies with this legislation, which states that those who create health and safety risks in the workplace are responsible for managing those risks as far as reasonably possible.

Awareness of personal space

Personal space is the area around a person's body that they feel belongs to them. You should be aware of this space and avoid overcrowding people by standing too close to them. Customers often want time alone to chat to each other or to browse.

 Remember

Think of your customer having an invisible bubble around them that you are not allowed to enter. Research has shown that if you get too close to people, they will feel uncomfortable and are likely to move away from you. This could mean that they walk out of your shop and you do not make a sale.

 Did you know?

The majority of major injuries in 2010–11 involved sales and retail assistants. Previous data has shown that most accidents occur from slips and trips and more than half involve people working in supermarkets and food stores.

In some retail jobs it may be necessary to enter the customer's personal space. What can you do to put the customer at ease?

Demonstrate personal selling processes

Introduction

The sales process can be split into three stages: initiate the sale, make the sale and close the sale.

| Greeting and introduction | ➤ | Attracting customers' attention and interest | ➤ | Presenting product information | ➤ | Persuading customers to buy. |

Figure 5.2 The sales process

Recording information

After you have closed the sale, it is good practice to record the following information:

- **customer information** – their name, title, address, telephone number and email address and, where relevant, the business's name, type of business, size of business and the buyer's name, title and position in the company
- **transaction information** – the name of the salesperson, item purchased, amount paid, method of payment, any discounts or offers and the date.

This information is useful for accurate marketing that targets the right people, and it can be helpful if a customer returns with a complaint or query.

Closing techniques

Table 5.5 Different types of closing technique

Closing technique	Method
Direct close	This is using a straightforward question to close a sale, e.g. 'How would you like to pay?' Beware – it can be risky if you get your timing wrong.
Silent close	Ask a closing question and then keep quiet. This can be awkward if the customer does not respond.
Alternative close	Offer the customer two choices as your closing question, e.g. 'Would you like it delivered or would you like to take it away now?'
Presumptive close	Close the sale by making a statement that shows that you have assumed that they have decided to buy, e.g. 'You are going to really enjoy this holiday.'

Is being able to close a sale the most important sales skill?

Activity   Closing a sale

Practise the following closing techniques through role-playing a selling scenario with a partner: direct close, silent close, alternative close and presumptive close. Then discuss how each closing technique felt. Finally, research alternative closing techniques online.

Customer care and after-sales services

- **Delivery:** Sales staff often arrange the delivery of the product. Delivery may be free of charge and may be made to alternative addresses.
- **Warranty:** Sales staff often try to sell customers a warranty once they have made a purchase.
- **Satisfaction:** Sales staff may check that customers are happy and they have received the service they expect. Only satisfied customers make repeat purchases and recommendations.
- **Follow up:** Sales staff sometimes check that individual customers are satisfied by contacting them a few days after they have received the product.
- **Feedback:** Sales staff occasionally gather feedback through questionnaires.

Dealing with enquiries

Customers often telephone or visit several businesses to ask questions about a product or service before they decide where to purchase the product.

If you get your response right, you are much more likely to see the customer return. Customers will expect you to be approachable and knowledgeable. Ideally, you should try to give the customer a quick but accurate response.

Before answering customers' questions, you need to work out exactly what they want by carefully listening to them and asking further questions.

Handling complaints or problems

It is inevitable that there will be situations where things go wrong from the customer's point of view. Handling complaints can be difficult especially when faced with angry or dissatisfied customers. You must:

- know the company's procedures for recording and reporting a complaint and follow these procedures correctly
- stay calm and establish the details of the complaint by sympathetically listening to the customer
- know which problems you can handle yourself and which you have to pass on to a manager/supervisor
- know the appropriate way to rectify the problem (refund, repair or replacement).

 Remember

Try to see complaints as an opportunity to improve things for future customers, and remember that if you handle the complaint well, you could build a rapport with the customer and increase your chances of repeat sales.

CONTINUED ▶▶

Overcoming barriers to closing the sale

If you can see that the customer is hesitating to close the sale, it is likely that they have some objections that you must overcome first. These objections are known as barriers to closing a sale. They can be overcome by reinforcing the features and benefits of what you are selling and by adapting behaviour to audience requirements. Showing respect for your customer and empathising with their views will also help.

Table 5.6 gives examples of different types of objections with suggestions of how to overcome these barriers.

Discussion point

How do you respond when a sales person tries to persuade you to buy?

What excuses do you give to justify a refusal? Compare your ideas as a class.

Table 5.6 Barriers to closing a sale

Type of objection	Example	How to overcome these barriers
Price	'It is too expensive.'	Reinforce the benefits of the product, e.g. 'This is cheap to run.'
Item	'I'm worried about parking a car of this size.'	Reinforce the features of the product, e.g. 'It has parking sensors.'
Competition	'I'm going to look online to see if I can find it cheaper elsewhere.'	Point out the benefits of buying the product from your business, e.g. 'All of our cars come with a one-year guarantee against any type of mechanical problem.'
Timing	'I don't need it yet.'	Adapt your behaviour to audience requirements by creating a sense of urgency, e.g. 'I can offer you a 10 per cent discount today.'
The brand	'I had one of these before and it kept breaking down.'	Empathise with their views, e.g. 'The products are much more reliable today than when they first appeared on the market.'

Activity   Closing a sale

Work with a partner to practice closing a sale. First identify an item to sell, such as a mobile phone or T-shirt. The 'buyer' should express interest and the 'seller' should then point out the main benefits and features of the item before trying to close the sale. It is the seller's task to overcome any (valid) objections raised by the 'buyer'. Then change places.

Repeat sales

If you have treated your customer well and kept them happy, they are much more likely to return and make a repeat purchase. For that reason it is sensible to maintain contact by email, phone and mail-shots so that you can point out new products or special offers that may be of interest.

Up-selling

Sales staff can increase overall sales by using up-selling. This is when you recommend your customer a more expensive, upgraded product. This can be done as part of the sales process, or at a later date you could contact the customer to alert them of a new upgrade that has just become available.

Did you know?

Many businesses make repeat sales through using social networking sites such as Facebook and Twitter to inform customers about their new products/offers and services.

Remember

Up-selling happens all the time and applies to cheap items as well as expensive ones. Cinemas make higher profits because they promote bargain buckets of popcorn and giant size drinks. Fast-food outlets will offer you 'large fries' or a 'family meal' rather than a smaller size. Because it costs very little to give you a larger portion, but the price is higher, profits are also higher.

Why is this an example of up-selling?

Activity   Researching upselling and cross-selling

As a class, research both upselling and cross-selling and find five examples of each. Then identify how many occasions you are 'upsold' in the next week and compare your findings. Identify how a small business of your choice could benefit from this strategy and share your ideas.

Just checking

1 Describe three barriers to closing a sale.
2 How could you overcome these barriers?

CONTINUED ▶▶

Liaison with other departments

Sales staff work as part of a team and they must liaise with other departments such as:

- **Customer collection:** Customer collection points are usually found in larger stores and they enable customers to collect their shopping at leisure. This is useful for customers who want to continue shopping without carrying heavy bags. The customer is given a receipt to hand over at the collection point to claim the goods.

- **Despatch:** The despatch department is responsible for getting the product to the customers. The customer either collects the product from the despatch department or the despatch department sends the customer the product. Sales staff need to liaise with the despatch department and the customer to organise this process.

- **Accounts:** This department stores information about money paid, received, borrowed or owed to the business. Sales staff liaise with accounts when dealing with financial matters such as setting up credit arrangements, or when they need information about a previous sale.

- **Service:** Technical services support both customers and sales staff in situations where specialist knowledge and skills are needed, such as engineering or IT. Customer services, however, are primarily concerned with customer welfare. Customers contact this department with a complaint and they may liaise with sales staff to help them to deal with that complaint.

Methods of recording

It is important to keep records of sales in an organised and concise manner. Some organisations rank customers by profile and spending patterns so that they can target customers who are most likely to make large repeat purchases. The Pareto effect means that 20 per cent of customers are likely to provide 80 per cent of sales income. A good ranking system will enable you to target this top 20 per cent so that you can invite/send them to special functions or send them brochures or emails to inform them of new products and discounts.

Why is the organisation of records so important in a despatch department?

Assessment activity 5.2   *English*   2B.P5 | 2B.P6 | 2B.P7 | 2B.M3 | 2B.M4 | 2B.D2 | 2B.D3

As a whole class activity, set up a college or school shop selling products and/or services that learners will find useful, for example second-hand uniform, books, stationery and snacks. It is important that everybody in the class takes part in the activity. Working in the shop will give you the opportunity to demonstrate your own personal selling skills and processes. You will need to provide evidence through keeping a personal log or sales diary detailing that you have completed a number of tasks, and your teacher/tutor will observe you and assess your individual performance and provide an individual written observation record.

You must complete the following:

1   Make necessary preparations to sell, including preparing the shop, self-preparation and ensuring you have the necessary product knowledge.

2   Demonstrate that you can process personal sales to two different types of customer and respond to two different types of customer enquiry.

3   Demonstrate good customer care skills in two different situations.

4   Demonstrate that you can show good customer care in handling a customer complaint or problem.

5   Assess the effectiveness of your selling skills and processes in two personal sales situations.

6   Demonstrate confidence in selling goods and services in at least three different situations.

7   Evaluate your own preparation skills and processes used in two different personal sales situations and recommend improvements.

Tips

- You need to help set up the sales environment, dress appropriately and conduct some research on what you are selling.

- If you do not get any complaints/problems, ask a friend to pretend to be a customer with a complaint so that you get the opportunity to demonstrate your response.

- You need to reflect on your own performance in a written statement.

If you find that you do not have the opportunity to demonstrate all of these skills and processes, you could ask your teacher/tutor to observe you role-playing these situations.

Introduction

The retail sector employs over three million people in the UK alone. Britain's biggest private sector employer is a retail business. London is one of the world's leading cities for retail sales. It has over 26,000 shops and an annual non-food turnover of more than £64.2 billion. This emphasises the importance of retail to the British economy.

This unit looks at the structure and organisation of the retail sector in the UK. You will learn about the different types of retail organisation in the UK and the type of employment opportunities they offer.

You will consider the place of retail within the economy and the wider community, looking at how developments such as retail parks can have a positive and negative impact. You will also think about online retail which is growing steadily.

Finally, you will look at the issues that retailers face when they expand abroad, and explore the issues faced by retail managers who want to operate in a foreign country.

Assessment: This unit will be assessed through a series of assignments set by your teacher/tutor.

Learning aims

In this unit you will:

A explore the structure and organisation of retail business

B investigate the relationship between retail business and the external environment.

I always wanted a job in retail, it seemed like an exciting environment where I could interact with a lot of different people. This unit helped me to learn about the different career paths that are available in this sector so that I could make an informed decision about which job to apply for.

Summa, *15-year-old Business student*

Introducing Retail Business

6

Assessment Zone

This table shows you what you must do in order to achieve a **Pass**, **Merit** or **Distinction** grade, and where you can find activities in this book to help you.

Assessment criteria

Level 1	Level 2 Pass	Level 2 Merit	Level 2 Distinction
Learning aim A: Explore the structure and organisation of retail business			
1A.1 Identify the sub-sector, channels, format, size and location of a retail business	**2A.P1** Describe the sub-sector, channels, format, size, ownership and location of two retail businesses operating in different sub-sectors **See Assessment activity 6.1, page 159**	**2A.M1** Assess two different types of ownership of selected retail businesses **See Assessment activity 6.1, page 159**	**2A.D1** Evaluate how two retail businesses operating in different sub-sectors measure their performance, with reference to Key Performance Indicators (KPIs) **See Assessment activity 6.1, page 159**
1A.2 Outline the functions of two job roles in store operations	**2A.P2** Describe the functions of two job roles in store operations and their progression routes **See Assessment activity 6.1, page 159**	**2A.M2** Explain how and why two retail businesses operating in different sub-sectors use aims and objectives **See Assessment activity 6.1, page 159**	
1A.3 Identify two types of business that support retail businesses	**2A.P3** Explain, using examples, the role of two businesses that support retail businesses **See Assessment activity 6.1, page 159**		
1A.4 Identify types of non-outlet retailing used by two retail businesses	**2A.P4** Describe how two retail businesses operating in different sub-sectors make use of non-outlet retailing **See Assessment activity 6.1, page 159**		
1A.5 Outline one aim and one objective of a retail business	**2A.P5** Describe the aims and objectives of two retail businesses operating in different sub-sectors **See Assessment activity 6.1, page 159**		

Assessment criteria

Level 1	Level 2 Pass	Level 2 Merit	Level 2 Distinction
Learning aim B: Investigate the relationship between retail business and the external environment			
1B.6 Outline two issues of concern and two benefits that can arise from two retail developments in the UK	**2B.P6** Explain, using examples, two issues of concern and two benefits that can arise from retail developments in the UK **See Assessment activity 6.2, page 164**	**2B.M3** Assess the benefits for the local community of a retail development in the UK **See Assessment activity 6.2, page 164**	**2B.D2** Evaluate the impact of a retail development in the UK on the local community **See Assessment activity 6.2, page 164**
1B.7 Identify three issues UK businesses must consider when they decide to operate in another country	**2B.P7** Explain, using examples, three issues facing UK retail businesses when they decide to operate in another country **See Assessment activity 6.2, page 164**		

How you will be assessed

This unit will be assessed by a series of internally assessed tasks and you will be expected to show an understanding of the retail business in your local area. The tasks will be based on a scenario where you provide advice to the owner of a local retail business or promote opportunities in the retail sector in your area.

Your assessment could be in the form of:

- a map, showing details of different retail outlets in your local area
- training materials for retail businesses such as leaflets and posters
- a website providing advice to the owners of retail businesses in your area.

The nature of retailing

What is retail?

We all participate in retail and go shopping for items such as food, clothes and magazines. Some of us shop using the internet to buy groceries, books, clothes and music downloads or apps for our mobile phones.

Retail can be defined as selling products to the public in small quantities. **Retailers** buy goods in bulk from **wholesalers** or **manufacturers** and then sell them in smaller quantities to the public.

Retail is the final stage in the **chain of production** where products are sold to the public. At every stage in the **supply chain** the amount of profit that can be made by the retailer is reduced because each business wants to earn some money.

Wholesalers and manufacturers

Small manufacturers make products and they need help to get them on the shelves in your local shop. A wholesaler will sell products to a retailer in bulk at a discount. Some large manufacturers deal directly with retailers so that they don't have to split their profits with anyone else.

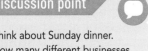
The supply chain

The supply chain is the series of stages that a product goes through to reach a customer, for example wholesaler to manufacturer to retailer.

Some large retailers have cut out the middlemen in the supply chain. This allows them to make more money on each sale.

Why does it benefit supermarkets such as Asda to buy directly from suppliers and transport goods to stores using their own lorries?

Retail channels

A retail channel is the method that a retailer chooses to sell their products or services to the market. A retailer might use only one channel or a number of channels; for example, Sainsbury's uses a number of different retail channels to reach the market including shops, e-tailing and catalogues. Table 6.1 shows the different types of retail channel.

Table 6.1 The different types of retail channel

Shops and stores	Shops and stores take a variety of forms. Corner shops have limited selling space, whereas hypermarkets have a very large selling space. In shops, customers handle and select products themselves, taking their purchases to counters or tills to pay for them.
Showrooms	A showroom is a large space where products can be set up, allowing customers to try out their features. An example is Euronics, an electronics retailer, where people can look at different items and measure goods such as fridges to make sure that they will fit in their houses.
E-tailing	A website contains details of the goods or services offered by a business, allowing customers to make a purchase using a credit card or a payment service such as PayPal.
Mobile technology	Devices such as e-book readers and smartphones can link to online shops via the internet, allowing people to buy content directly for their device. It is possible to buy books on your Kindle or music and film on your iPad. iPod, iPad and iPhone customers can buy apps from the App Store and other items from online stores on their device.
Catalogues	A catalogue can be a short booklet or a longer hardback book. Businesses produce catalogues of their products giving details such as sizes, colours and features. Customers can find out about products in the comfort of their own home and then place an order by phone or post.
Home shopping	This is where customers watch television channels such as QVC which broadcast information about products. Customers can then make purchases on the phone or the internet.
Market stalls	Market stalls can be indoors or outdoors. They tend to have a low rent which makes them popular with entrepreneurs who want to try out an idea for a new business with less risk than a shop.

Did you know?

- In 2010, there were 286,680 retail businesses in the UK with total sales of over £293 billion. More than a third of this was spent in shops.

- Apple and Amazon integrate their own e-tailing channel into their digital devices. iPod Touch, iPad and iPhone devices allow customers to buy content directly from iTunes. Kindle users can buy books and newspapers on the internet through their device. Therefore once a customer has bought a product, they continue to generate money for the company by passing sales through their store using that product.

Activity   Researching a retail chain

Research a major retail chain such as Sports Direct.

1 Which retail channels does your chosen retailer use?

2 Why do you think that it operates in these retail channels?

3 Suggest one way that it will benefit from operating in more than one retail channel.

Remember

Many retailers will operate in more than one retail channel so that they can make the most of their opportunities to sell products to the public.

Just checking

1 Can you name all of the retail channels used by HMV?

2 Produce a diagram of the supply chain for a corner shop.

3 Explain the difference between a wholesaler and a manufacturer.

Sub-sectors and ownership

Introduction

Retail is a broad sector of the economy, covering the sale of a very wide range of goods. Similarly, the businesses in the retail sector range from very small to very large, with different types of business ownership.

Retail sub-sectors

The retail sector can be divided up into a number of **sub-sectors** according to the types of products that they sell. Table 6.2 shows these sub-sectors.

Table 6.2 Retail sub-sectors

Sub-sector	Description	Example
Automotive	Sellers of vehicles and related products such as oil or stereo equipment	Halfords, Carcraft
Clothing	Sellers of clothes and related products such as sewing equipment	H&M, Topshop, Next
Food and grocery	Companies which specialise in a specific type of food (for example frozen or fresh) or sell a range of products	Iceland, Londis, The Co-operative
Footwear	Shops which sell shoes and provide related services such as repairing heels	Footlocker, Clarks
DIY	Shops which sell products such as tools and wood for people who wish to improve their homes	B&Q, Homebase
Electrical goods	Shops which sell a wide range of products from fridges to PCs, and MP3 players to ovens	Currys, PC World
Homeware	Retailers which focus on selling products for the home. This might include furniture, carpets or ornaments	Ikea, Utility
Music and video	Shops which sell music and films in physical formats such as CD and DVD or as downloads such as MP3 files	HMV, iTunes Store
Specialised stores	Stores which specialise in selling a specific type of product or service. These are often unique goods that are not sold in general retailers	Holland and Barrett, Hotel Chocolat
Personal care	Retailers which sell goods and services for personal hygiene. These stores might sell products such as soap or services such as manicures	Boots, Lush
Second-hand goods	Companies which sell products that have been owned by someone else previously	Cash Converters, CEX

Activity   Carrying out a survey

Carry out a survey of the different retail sub-sectors on a shopping street or retail park near your school or college. How many of the sub-sectors are represented?

Retail business ownership

The most appropriate type of business ownership for a retail business will vary according to the size of the business and the retail sub-sector in which it operates.

Sole trader

Small retail businesses such as local corner shops or food kiosks on busy high streets tend to operate as sole traders. Many market stalls are run by sole traders. An example is Richard Branson's first business which was a stall selling records.

Partnership

One of the most well-known partnerships is the John Lewis Partnership. Every member of staff owns a part of the business and receives a share in the profits. Some specialist retailers such as opticians set up as a partnership to share skills with people who have experience of customer service.

Private limited company (Ltd)

Family-run retailers often choose this form of ownership so that they can benefit from the security of limited liability but still have control of their business. Some retailers such as the Arcadia Group, owned by Philip Green, stay private as they want to operate without the pressure of having to satisfy shareholders.

Public limited company (plc)

Large retail chains such as Tesco raise money from selling shares to expand across the UK and the world. Expanding a public limited company (plc) is risky; if new stores fail, this can be expensive and therefore the protection of limited liability is important.

Franchise

When a retailer wants to expand quickly, they can sell franchises, allowing them to share the costs with potential investors. The cost of a franchise varies depending on the brand. A United Carpets franchise costs £30,000 compared with a Shell franchise at £100,000, but the franchisee will still have to pay the start-up costs for the business.

Activity   Starting up a franchise

If you choose to open a retail franchise, in addition to paying for the rights to use the brand name, you will have to pay all of the start-up costs and operating costs for the business.

1 What start-up costs would you have to pay to open a retail outlet? List as many as you can.

2 Considering all of the costs involved in setting up a new retail store, do you think it would be better to be a sole trader or a franchisee? Explain your answer.

Link

This topic links to *Unit 1: Enterprise in the Business World*.

Key terms

Economy – the system by which a country's money and goods are produced and used.

Retail sector – the section of the national economy made up of retail businesses.

Sub-sector – a specific category of products or services offered by a retailer.

Did you know?

Both public and private limited companies benefit from limited liability, which means that if the business fails, its owners will only lose what they have invested in the company.

Remember

A franchisee can be a sole trader, partnership or private limited company. The term 'franchise' actually refers to the legal contract between the franchisor and franchisee, not the type of ownership.

Retail outlets

Link

This topic links to *Unit 1: Enterprise in the Business World.*

Organising retailers by size

The size of a retail business depends on the number of staff they employ.

Table 6.3 The size of retail businesses

Size	Micro	Small	Medium	Large
Number of employees	Up to 9	10–49	50–249	250 +

As retail businesses get bigger, they gain a number of benefits. Larger retailers can buy goods in bulk for lower prices. This helps them to earn more profits. Larger retailers can also invest in hiring specialist staff such as accountants or marketing specialists.

Activity   Judging business size

The number of employees is not always the best way to assess the size of retail businesses. For example, a market stall and an art gallery might both employ five people, but their earnings might be significantly different. In groups, discuss other ways that you could judge the size of businesses.

How many different types of retail outlet can you see on this high street?

Types of retail outlet

Independent trader

These are small firms that are not part of a bigger company. They are often family businesses. They tend to be sole traders.

Convenience store

These are small shops, often located on busy streets. They normally sell a range of food and beverages, newspapers and magazines. Convenience stores account for over £30 million of sales in the UK each year.

Symbol group

This is where small retailers join an organisation that allows them to make purchases in bulk and to use a well-known brand name on their store. An example of a symbol group is SPAR. They provide advice and support to their network of independent grocers as well as specialist services like advertising. Other examples include Londis and Costcutter.

Specialist outlet

These outlets vary in size and ownership. They focus on selling a specific type of product or service. The Apple store is a specialist outlet.

Market stall

Market stalls can be indoors or outdoors. They often have low rents and short notice periods which allow entrepreneurs to try out new ideas with little risk. The goods and services offered can be varied, for example fruit and vegetables, clothes or electronics.

Kiosk

This is a small booth, often seen at bus or train stations. They do not normally have a large amount of space to display goods and a member of staff supplies goods to their customers over a counter.

Multiple/chain store

This is where one company has 10 or more stores which operate under the same brand. These stores can be any size and they normally operate as a plc with a high degree of centralised control. For example, Timpson is a small multiple while Currys and PC World are large chain stores.

Discount store

These retailers focus on selling goods at a reduced price. Companies like Poundland buy branded goods and sell them for one pound. In recent years, chains such as Home Bargains and 99p Stores were among the fastest growing chains on the high street, opening branches in stores once occupied by Woolworths.

Cooperative

A cooperative is a business owned by its customers, suppliers and/or workers. Many of these companies focus on ethical products such as fair trade products. Chains such as the Co-operative Group and Southern Co-ops account for over £10 billion of grocery sales in the UK each year.

Franchising

This could be a shop or store such as Costa Coffee or a concession in a larger store such as a branch of McDonald's within an Asda store. Selling franchises helps retailers to expand quickly at a lower cost.

Superstore

Normally, these stores are more than 20,000 square feet in size and sell a range of goods. These stores are owned by major chains such as Asda, but there are some independent supermarkets such as Stan's in St Martin's, Shropshire, which is run by the family of the original owner.

Hypermarket

These are some of the biggest retail outlets, normally over 100,000 square feet in size. They might sell a range of goods (for example, Tesco Extra) or focus on a specific type of goods (for example, Ikea).

Department store

A large shop that is divided into separate departments, each selling a different type of goods. An example is Debenhams. Department stores will often contain small units called concessions, each of which is a small version of a shop. These are often operated by well-known brands such as Ted Baker or Miss Selfridge.

Discussion point

Are our high streets all becoming the same? Some people argue that multiple chains are taking over the main shopping areas in every town and that it is better to have small independent retailers to add variety to the high street. As a group, discuss whether it is good to have a shopping area full of chain stores or whether it's better to have independent stores as well.

Activity Researching cooperatives

Read about The Co-operative. You can access their website by going to www.pearsonhotlinks.co.uk and searching for this title.

1 What are the similarities and differences between a cooperative and a chain store?

2 What are the benefits of being part of a cooperative?

Aspects of retailing

Non-outlet retailing

This type of retailer might not have any physical premises that customers can visit.

Mail order/catalogues

This is when a customer responds to an advert in a newspaper or magazine, for example a Brennan MP3 player. Customers simply see an advert in a newspaper, post the company an order and then wait to receive their MP3 player in the post.

Alternatively, customers read about products in a catalogue before placing an order; for example Boden, Lands' End, The Book People and Great Little Trading Co. Once goods have been ordered, they are either sent through the post or by a courier service.

Activity Analysing forms of retailing

Many retailers combine outlet and non-outlet forms of retailing. As a group, identify the advantages of combining both forms of retail and of focusing on just one.

Discussion point

Each year, Christmas Day and Boxing Day shoppers have spent more time and money buying goods online. Why do you think this was?

E-tailing

Selling products online through a website has grown in popularity over the last 10 years. Companies such as Amazon can sell through their website and through apps on smartphones or tablet PCs. E-tailers sell a mixture of digital content which customers download to their PC and physical goods which are sent through the post.

Telephone selling

Some goods can be purchased over the telephone. This involves phoning a retailer and placing an order for goods or services which are then delivered to the customer's home, for example fast-food takeaways. Customers phone a restaurant, place an order and they can pay the driver when the food is delivered to their home.

Did you know?

Sainsbury's has run trials of vending machines which sell medicine.

Vending machines

These are often used in schools and offices for snacks and drinks. Customers put money into a machine and enter a code before receiving their goods. Costa Coffee has recently developed a range of vending machines selling their branded coffee.

Shopping channels

Channels such as QVC operate on satellite and Freeview TV channels. Potential customers can watch demonstrations of products which include everything from homeware to jewellery. Customers place orders online or over the telephone before they are delivered.

Location

The location of retail business varies according to the sub-sector and retail outlet chosen.

- **City/town** – traditional shopping areas in the centre of a town or city. This is where you will find the 'high street'. These areas have declined in recent years in many towns. Parking is often hard to find or expensive.

Activity   Investigating retail locations

Print a map of your local area from a source such as Google Maps.

1 Highlight the different retail locations in your area using a different colour for each.

2 Explain why some types of retail location are more common and others are less common in your area.

- **Out of town** – areas on the outskirts of a town or city where land is cheaper. Retailers will often build superstores or hypermarkets in these locations.

- **District** – normally somewhere in the centre of a residential area. This might be a suburb of a town or city.

- **Retail parks** – large areas of land where retailers can open large outlets. They normally have a large number of free parking spaces and regular transport links provided by bus or tram.

- **Primary locations** – main shopping streets such as the high street in a town or city. Alternatively, they might be in the main concourse of large shopping centres such as the Arndale Centre in Manchester or at an airport or railway station. These locations often have higher footfall, which means that there are more potential customers, but they also have higher rents and reduced access to parking.

- **Secondary locations** – areas away from main streets. These areas normally have lower footfall, but they also have cheaper rents. This type of location is more suited to specialist retailers such as art supply stores because their customers are willing to search for these outlets.

Activity   Improving retail business

In 2011, Mary Portas published a report on how to improve retail business in town and city centres. She suggested that local councils should make it easier to open market stalls, the government should make it more difficult to open betting shops and landlords should make empty shops look attractive.

1 Do you agree with Mary's recommendations? Why?

2 How would you encourage more retailers to open stores in your local town or city centre?

Take it further

1 Find out more about Mary Portas's review of the British high street. You can access this by going to www.pearsonhotlinks.co.uk and searching for this title.

2 Do you agree with her findings?

What makes retail businesses function?

Jobs in retail business

To run effectively, a retail business needs employees to work in particular roles. Some of the common job roles in retail businesses include the following.

- **Cashiers** process transactions for customers, recording what has been purchased. They handle cash, cheques and credit cards.
- **Customer service staff** work in the front line of retail businesses, answering phone calls or working on the shop floor. Their role is to ensure that customer needs are met.
- **Retail assistants** can be divided into shop floor assistants and stockroom assistants.
- **Sales floor assistants** make sure that stock is replenished and advise customers about products. They ensure that the retail environment is safe and hygienic by cleaning as they work.
- **Sales floor supervisors** complete a rota to ensure that the sales floor is fully staffed at all times. They organise the breaks and lunchtimes of staff so that enough people are working at all times.
- **Stockroom assistants** work behind the scenes, handling stock and ensuring that it is stored correctly. They lock away valuable items, and check that items requiring special treatment such as frozen food are held in the right environment.
- **Stockroom supervisors** organise the stockroom, planning space to make sure that there is enough room for the different types of goods. They check that legal requirements such as safe handling of goods are met.
- **Receptionists** welcome customers to a shop. They might make appointments for customers to visit specialists such as opticians or sales advisers.

Why it is important that cashier's receive sufficient training before they begin to process cheques and credit cards?

Discussion point

Many retailers expect staff to do different jobs from day to day. For example, staff might be expected to move from the stockroom at busy times in order to operate tills. Do you think that it is a good idea to expect staff to know how to do different jobs? What are the advantages and disadvantages of this approach?

Did you know?

- Training is important to retailers to make sure that people do their jobs well. Asda offers over 20,000 apprenticeships to its staff every year.
- Many retailers like to promote their staff. Tesco runs a scheme called *Options* to prepare their staff for management jobs.

Just checking

1 Name three retail jobs that focus on helping customers.
2 Describe one retail job that deals with deliveries of stock.
3 Explain two ways that supervisors help to keep retailers organised.

Supporting retail business

Retail businesses can be very large and complex. For example, Sainsbury's has many shops across the UK, each of which needs regular deliveries of stock. As the business opens new stores, it must employ companies that can fit them out. It also requires legal and financial services to support its operations.

Retailers often need to make use of people with specialist skills. Although it is important to use these people to complete specific tasks, it might not be necessary to employ them permanently. Table 6.4 lists some of the functions of supporting retail businesses.

Table 6.4 Supporting retail businesses

Transport and delivery companies	These ensure that new stock arrives on time.
Suppliers and manufacturers	It is important to have suppliers who can produce the right quantity of goods to a high standard.
Computing and financial services	Many retailers use an electronic point of sale (**EPOS**). Specialist teams design these systems, providing upgrades so they continue to work properly.
Tradespeople	Workers such as carpenters or plumbers will carry out repairs in retail outlets. Workers might be hired to support specialists such as shopfitters.
Shopfitters	Shopfitters are specialist builders and decorators who are experts in preparing the retail environment, setting up the appropriate shelving and counters.
Marketing and advertising agencies	These firms carry out research into customers' needs and plan promotional campaigns to attract more customers. They might arrange advertising or produce point-of-sale material to highlight special offers.
Legal and accountancy firms	Firms of solicitors and accountants perform essential services. Accountants carry out an **audit** of a business's accounts and prepare financial statements such as profit and loss accounts annually so that managers can monitor the financial performance of their business. **Stock takes** ensure that records are accurate. Legal firms might carry out checks on legal 'due diligence' records, e.g. temperature checks on fridges.

Activity — Thinking about stock takes

Most retailers carry out a stock take at least once a year. This is normally carried out by someone independent of the store staff and managers.

1 Suggest three reasons why it might be important to check whether or not stock records are accurate.

2 Suggest one reason why stock takes might be carried out by an independent person.

Key terms

EPOS – stands for 'electronic point of sale'. These are computer systems that record transactions and process payments.

Audit – an official check on actions taken and financial claims made by a business.

Stock take – the stock in a retail outlet is counted to ensure that records are up to date.

Retail targets and performance

Introduction

Like any other business, retail businesses set themselves targets to achieve and monitor their performance against these targets.

Link

This topic links to *Unit 1: Enterprise in the Business World*.

Aims and objectives

Aims are the long-terms plans that are set by a business. **Objectives** are the steps that a retailer takes to achieve their aims.

Having aims and objectives gives the retailer a clear plan to follow. Setting targets helps to monitor the performance of individual store managers.

A retailer's aims might include:

- **survival** – a smaller business might struggle against larger competitors
- **profit maximisation** – reducing business costs and increasing revenue to make as much money as possible
- **innovation** – retailers might want to find original ways to use retail outlets or unique products that are not available to their competitors
- **securing locations** – getting the best space in a retail park or high street can be a big advantage over competitors.

Retail managers set aims and objectives which they share with their staff. Department managers review their objectives with their managers weekly, monthly or quarterly. Table 6.5 shows how retailers might use SMART objectives.

Table 6.5 SMART objectives

Specific	The objective focuses on a particular **key performance indicator** (KPI).
Measurable	Focusing on a specific KPI means you can see if you have met your target, for example 5% growth.
Achievable	You cannot increase your sales KPI to 100% if you don't have room for extra stock in your store.
Realistic	The retailer must have all of the resources that it needs to meet the objective; for example, if you want 100% more sales, you must have enough stock to achieve this.
Time-related	Clear deadlines will make it easier to see if you are on target or not.

Key term

Key performance indicator – a way of measuring how well a retail business or a retail employee is performing.

Measuring performance

Key performance indicators (KPIs) provide a way of checking how well you are progressing towards your aims and objectives. They can be set for an entire business, individual stores or groups of stores, for example all of the branches in a region.

Common KPIs include the following:

- **Sales** – this is how much revenue a retailer has earned over a period of time. This might be a day, week, month or a year.
- **Profit** – this is calculated by subtracting costs from revenue. It helps retailers to understand how well they are managing their costs.
- **Sales/profit per square metre** – this is the amount of revenue that is generated for each square metre of floor space in a store. This shows how efficiently a store is managed.
- **Sales per employee** – this is how much revenue each member of staff generates. This can help to show how hard staff are working.
- **Average revenue per customer** – this is how much money the average customer spends. This is also known as 'basket size'.
- **Service level** – this can be measured in various ways, for example by counting the number of people at checkouts, or calculating the percentage of stock on sale.
- **Customer satisfaction** – this can be measured in a number of ways, for example by looking at the rate of customer complaints or the score on a customer report.
- **Stock holding** – this is how much stock is kept in stockrooms and sales floors. If this is too high, it leads to waste when goods go out of date. If it is too low, it leads to products being out of stock.
- **Returns** – this is the number of products that are brought back to the store and the reasons why.
- **Complaints** – a business might keep records of how many customers complain, the time and date of the complaint as well as what the complaint is about.
- **Environmental performance targets** – this might be how many plastic bags are given out to customers or how much packaging is recycled.

Discussion point

Is it always fair to use sales per employee or sales per customer as a KPI? Some stores are located in busy locations or in affluent areas. Do you think that achieving good figures on your KPIs is about luck, or will a good manager achieve the targets no matter where the business is located?

Did you know?

Zara and Topshop get new deliveries of stock every few days. This keeps customers interested and helps keep the level of sales in their stores high.

Assessment activity 6.1

2A.P1 | 2A.P2 | 2A.P3 | 2A.P4 | 2A.P5 | 2A.M1 | 2A.M2 | 2A.D1

The local Chamber of Commerce would like to improve the high street in your town by encouraging more retail businesses to open stores there. They would like you to produce a website that could be used to promote the opportunities for retail in your town. You should research two contrasting retailers that already operate successfully in your area. Find out about the careers opportunities in each business and investigate local businesses that provide them with support.

1 Describe the sub-sector, channels, format, size, ownership and location of two retail businesses operating in different sub-sectors.

2 Make an assessment of how appropriate the ownership of each business is.

3 Describe how each retailer uses different forms of non-outlet retailing.

4 Outline and describe two job roles in one of your selected retailers and how you can progress in those roles.

5 Explain the role of two businesses that support a local retailer. Give examples of tasks that they carry out.

6 Describe the aims and objectives of each retailer.

7 Explain how and why each retailer uses aims and objectives.

8 Prepare a conclusion evaluating how much KPIs help each business to achieve their aims and objectives.

Tips

- When you pick your retailers for this task, make sure that they use different forms of non-outlet retail.
- You must include some evidence about why each form might be appropriate or not in an assessment. You should then conclude with a clear judgement on each business.
- Make sure that you choose two different job roles, for example a supervisor and a manager.

Retail business in the UK

Retail business and the external environment

Environmental issues

Opening a new store can lead to more people driving to visit it. This will increase traffic in local communities, causing more traffic jams and a number of road accidents.

Getting started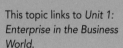

Did you know that over 7 million tons of food are thrown away in the UK every year? Groups of people called freegans visit the bins of stores in towns and cities at night, taking away food items that would otherwise be buried at a tip. Do you think it is right for retailers to simply throw goods away if they do not sell? What might be the consequences if a shop started giving away food that does not sell?

Activity	Carrying out a traffic survey

Visit a local town centre and carry out a traffic survey at different times of the day. Compare the number of cars parked and travelling through the area every two hours. What do you notice about the number of vehicles at different times of the day? What impact will this have on other travellers such as children going to school?

The amount of heating and lighting required for a large retail development might have a substantial **carbon footprint**. There is also pollution from waste packaging.

Food miles are the distance that food travels from where it is produced to where it is sold. In order to have products such as green beans all year round, many retailers import them from warm countries such as Kenya. This increases their carbon footprint.

The amount of green space in the UK is decreasing. Building out-of-town stores on **greenbelt land** is controversial. Environmentalists feel that there are already too many supermarkets and green sites should be protected. Campaigners believe that the first choice for new retail developments should be on existing **brownfield land**.

Link

This topic links to *Unit 1: Enterprise in the Business World.*

Check the packaging on the fruit and vegetables you have at home to see where they have been produced.

Key terms

Carbon footprint – the amount of greenhouse gas that a business releases into the atmosphere as a result of its activities.

Greenbelt land – an area which is protected from building and development to allow people in cities access to open space and natural environments.

Brownfield land – abandoned industrial or commercial land that can be used for new developments.

Activity	Calculating food miles

Visit Pearson hotlinks to find a link about food miles. You can access this by going to www.pearsonhotlinks.co.uk and searching for this title.

Download the spreadsheet that is available. In groups, think of a meal that you might eat this week. Calculate the number of food miles required for your meal. Suggest three ways that you could reduce the food miles in your meal.

Ethical issues

Many retailers now stock fair trade products. It is quite normal for goods such as tea and coffee to meet this standard. Fair trade is when the producer (often a farmer in a poor country) is paid a fair wage for their goods. This is good for the farmer, but it costs more for the retailer, reducing their profits.

In some poorer countries, child labour is used to produce goods. If a British retailer is found to stock goods produced by children, this causes negative publicity in the press.

Corporate responsibility has become more important to retailers in the UK in recent years. Many companies set aims and objectives relating to protecting the community and the environment.

Genetically modified foods are very controversial and no British retailers admit to selling them. The public is very worried about the impact on health of eating 'Frankenstein food'.

Organic foods have become very fashionable in the last decade. It costs more to grow food without chemicals, but customers are willing to pay more for them.

Activity   Encouraging healthy lifestyles?

Are retailers causing people to put on weight or are they helping them to live healthy lifestyles? Visit Pearson hotlinks to research stories about obesity. You can access this by going to www.pearsonhotlinks.co.uk and searching for this title.

Divide the stories up according to whether they are about retailers encouraging or discouraging healthy lifestyles.

Shoppers are increasingly interested in healthy living. People who are worried about obesity don't want to buy fatty snacks such as crisps or processed food such as ready meals. This has also helped enterprising shop managers increase sales of items such as exercise bikes and step counters.

Animal research is controversial. Britain is a nation of animal lovers and few people like the idea of using cosmetics that have been tested on dogs or rabbits. Pressure groups such as PETA often protest at companies that use animal-tested products.

Activity   Investigating animal research

Visit Pearson hotlinks to read about the uses of animal research in the UK. You can access this by going to www.pearsonhotlinks.co.uk and searching for this title.

Answer the following questions:

1 What are the arguments for and against animal testing?

2 What is animal testing used for in the UK?

3 Is it right for retailers to sell products that have been tested on animals? Explain your answer.

4 In your group, hold a debate on whether it is right or wrong to test products on animals. Divide into two teams with one team arguing for animal testing and one against.

Discussion point

Is child labour a bad thing? In poor countries where there is no formal education for young people, is it better for children to earn some money in a factory or to work on family farms? Is it better to control child labour so that it is safe or to ban it completely and make children go to school? What are the benefits and drawbacks of each situation?

Did you know?

• Asda aims to reduce the amount of waste that they send to landfill by 100 per cent by 2015.

• Greenbelt land covers 13 per cent of England. The largest greenbelt is around London and it has a total area of 486,000 hectares.

• To qualify as organic, products must follow strict British and European laws. Retailers claiming to sell organic food have to be able to trace each item back to the farm where it was grown.

CONTINUED ▶▶

Community concerns

New out-of-town developments are often blamed for the decline of city centres. Major retailers usually choose to open larger stores at these sites. This leads to town centres filling up with charity shops and betting shops.

This type of development is often blamed for a reduction in the number of small shops and independent retailers. When large firms leave town centres, this reduces footfall which means small shops struggle to attract enough customers to survive.

New retail parks can lead to new road developments. This can often improve the transport links for communities in out-of-town locations.

New retail developments create pressure on local infrastructures as there is more demand for electricity, water and local roads.

Transport systems have to be changed to accommodate new retail developments. This often provokes criticism. Who should pay the cost of this?

Discussion point

Are retail parks a good idea? In your group, discuss the benefits and drawbacks of allowing these developments in a community.

Would it be good if a supermarket was to set up next to your school/college?

Activity	Contributing to charity

How many retail businesses in your local area contribute to local charities? Carry out a survey of retailers in your local area and find out how many donate money or staff time to local causes. Who makes the biggest contribution, the major chains or the small independents?

Political issues

The amount of power held by large supermarkets is controversial. This is investigated by the Competition Commission, a government body which aims to protect the public. Limits are placed on how many stores some companies can open in certain areas to make sure no one company becomes too powerful.

Pressure groups often develop to argue against the opening of new out-of-town retail parks. Groups such as IRATE in Ilkley protest against these developments, writing letters to MPs and councillors.

Advertising campaigns by retailers are carefully watched. Most of the major supermarkets claim to have the lowest prices, but who actually does?

Activity	Researching pressure groups

Search online for 'Tescopoly' and find out about pressure groups' arguments against supermarkets. Summarise their main points. Explain whether or not you agree with their objections.

The benefits of retail developments to communities and customers

Economic benefits

New retail developments provide employment within stores and also indirectly in local companies such as wholesalers.

Donations and sponsorship are often provided, for example to local football clubs. Charities are often supported by retailers who encourage staff to arrange fundraising events in store.

A retail development will often attract new businesses to an area when it opens. If a large hypermarket opens, outlets such as cafes and taxi firms may open nearby to offer services to customers.

New people might come to live in an area near a new retail development, helping communities to grow and providing more customers for local businesses.

Social benefits

A retailer can provide meeting places for the community. People will chat while they shop. Some retailers run events such as launch nights for books where people can socialise.

Cafes and restaurants in store are often relatively cheap as a service to customers and provide a place to meet and relax.

When opening a new store, many retailers provide community facilities such as sport centres when they develop land for their store. Large superstores often have recycling facilities in their car parks.

Customer benefits

Large developments such as the Bullring in Birmingham provide facilities such as lifts and ramps for the disabled. Most large and medium-sized retailers provide wheelchairs and Shopmobility buggies for their customers.

Large out-of-town developments, such as Brent Cross in London, offer free parking to customers. This is often more convenient than paying high prices in town centre car parks.

Hypermarkets often provide cheap petrol to encourage customers to visit their stores.

Doing business with the rest of the world

The relationship between UK retailers and international markets

If a British retailer wishes to open a store abroad they must make sure that they understand their market, including the following aspects.

- **Customs:** How do people like to behave? For example, the Spanish have a siesta in the afternoon, meaning shops close for three to four hours in the day.
- **Tastes and styles:** Fashion varies greatly in different countries and it is important to sell products that meet the needs of customers.
- **Lifestyles:** People might be used to shopping in a certain way or using a particular type of goods. Tesco's Fresh and Easy stores in America struggle because American consumers are not used to the same type of ready meals as the British.
- **Location issues:** For example, will customers shop out of town or in city centres?
- **Economic and legislative environments:** For example, in India it is a legal requirement to have a local business partner.
- **Cultural considerations:** People live their lives differently in different countries. For example, the British are a nation of tea drinkers, whereas the Americans and French prefer coffee.

It is also important to choose the most appropriate method of entering the market. There are several different ways to enter foreign markets as shown in Table 6.6.

Table 6.6 Methods of entering a foreign market

Self-entry

All the work and investment comes from within your business, with the support of local advisers.

Acquisition

Buying a local company. This can be expensive.

Joint ventures

Working with a local partner. This means sharing your profits, but you can benefit from their knowledge and experience.

Franchising

Local firms can be offered the rights to operate stores under your brand name, allowing you access to expert local knowledge of customer needs.

Assessment activity 6.2 — 2B.P6 | 2B.P7 | 2B.M3 | 2B.D2

Your local Chamber of Commerce has asked you to write an article for their magazine about the issues faced by British retailers when they grow at home and abroad.

They want you to investigate two retail developments in the UK such as Bluewater in Kent and Liverpool One. You must present a balanced view of the benefits and concerns of each development. You should also investigate the issues faced by British retailers when they choose to expand abroad.

1 Explain two concerns and two benefits that have been raised about the retail developments you have investigated.

2 How have the developments benefited the community? Assess the extent to which the developments have been positive.

3 Choose one retail development and evaluate the impact that it has had on its local community.

4 Research examples of British retailers expanding abroad. Explain three different issues that British retailers should consider when they enter foreign markets.

Tip

You should include evidence that you have considered whether or not a retail development will benefit its local community. You must show that you understand potential negative impacts, such as the closure of small shops, as well as benefits, such as employment, in order to give a balanced assessment.

WorkSpace

▶ Lowri Roberts

Owner of Siop Cwlwm

Lowri Roberts has always wanted to set up a shop dedicated to selling Welsh products. She is passionate about the Welsh language and she wants to run a business that makes a contribution to the community as well as allowing her to earn a living. She runs the shop in partnership with her mum. They each have different skills to contribute to the business. Her mum is very good at organising stock takes. Lowri makes presentations to gain funding for the business.

Lowri and her mum chose a market stall because it was a low-risk way to test their idea. The rent isn't very high and they only have to give a week's notice if they want to leave. They also sell their stock online, which means they have customers all over the country, not just in Oswestry.

Lowri runs a lot of community events to encourage people to speak Welsh. They have regular 'talking shop' days where people can come in, practise speaking the language and meet other members of the community. They enjoy making a contribution to their community. Lowri and her mum also encourage children to learn Welsh. They offer lessons in Welsh and have paid a designer to make toys such as jigsaws which sell very well.

You can find out more about Lowri's shop on her website. Access this through www.pearsonhotlinks.co.uk.

Think about it

1 Which retail channel has Lowri chosen for her business?

2 How does she benefit from operating the business as a partnership?

3 How does Siop Cwlwm make a positive contribution to its community?

Introduction

Effective business support is essential for many organisations. Whether you are visiting a hotel, a hospital, a leisure club or a school or college, you will see several people carrying out a whole range of administrative activities.

These activities are absolutely vital for the organisation to function properly. Teachers, doctors and other professionals could not do their own jobs properly without administrative assistance. Neither could senior managers in business who rely on their office staff to make travel and meeting arrangements, greet visitors, answer the telephone and carry out many other necessary tasks.

Providing business support can offer fascinating opportunities. Top Personal Assistants (PAs) and Executive Assistants have interesting and well-paid jobs in major cities throughout the world.

This unit will give you the opportunity to undertake support tasks yourself and develop your skills in a practical way, as well as learning more about the importance of this role.

Assessment: This unit will be assessed through a series of assignments set by your teacher/tutor.

Learning aims

In this unit you will:

A understand the purpose of providing business support

B use office equipment safely for different purposes

C organise and provide support for meetings.

My sister works in a support role in the HR department of a company. She helps to organise interviews and prepare information for training courses and also does confidential tasks for the HR manager. It sounds really interesting and I'd like to understand more about this type of job.

Jia-li, *15-year-old Business student*

Providing Business Support

BTEC
Assessment Zone

This table shows you what you must do in order to achieve a **Pass**, **Merit** or **Distinction** grade, and where you can find activities in this book to help you.

Assessment criteria			
Level 1	**Level 2 Pass**	**Level 2 Merit**	**Level 2 Distinction**
Learning aim A: Understand the purpose of providing business support			
1A.1 Identify types of business support in two contrasting businesses	**2A.P1** Explain the purpose of different types of business support in two contrasting businesses **See Assessment activity 7.1, page 171**		
Learning aim B: Use office equipment safely for different purposes			
1B.2 Identify office equipment to meet different business requirements	**2B.P2** Describe the use of office equipment to meet different business requirements **See Assessment activity 7.2, page 179**	**2B.M1** Explain the appropriate uses of office equipment types, features and functions to suit different business purposes **See Assessment activity 7.2, page 179**	**2B.D1** Analyse the contribution that office equipment makes to the provision of business support **See Assessment activities 7.2, page 179**
1B.3 Demonstrate using different types of office equipment safely, with guidance and in accordance with health and safety legislation	**2B.P3** Demonstrate using office equipment safely, in accordance with health and safety legislation **See Assessment activity 7.2, page 179**	**2B.M2** Demonstrate understanding of the application of safe lifting techniques when using office equipment **See Assessment activity 7.2, page 179**	
Learning aim C: Organise and provide support for meetings			
1C.4 Draw up a checklist for organising and supporting either an internal or an external meeting	**2C.P4** Organise a meeting according to specified requirements using a checklist **See Assessment activity 7.3, page 191**	**2C.M3** Explain the organisation and support required for different types of meeting **See Assessment activity 7.3, page 191**	**2C.D2** Evaluate own contribution to providing support before, during and after the meeting and suggest improvements **See Assessment activity 7.3, page 191**
1C.5 English Produce a meeting brief and agenda for either an internal or an external meeting	**2C.P5** English Produce accurate documents required prior to a meeting and take notes during the meeting **See Assessment activity 7.3, page 191**	**2C.M4** English Produce accurate and detailed post-meeting documentation (including minutes) prepared from notes taken during meeting discussions **See Assessment activity 7.3, page 191**	
1C.6 Provide some support at either an internal or an external meeting and assist in clearing the venue after the meeting has finished	**2C.P6** Provide all required support for a meeting, including follow-up activities **See Assessment activity 7.3, page 191**		

English Opportunity to practise English skills

How you will be assessed

The unit will be assessed by a series of internally assessed tasks and practical activities. These are designed to enable you to demonstrate that you understand the types and purpose of business support, can use office equipment safely and can organise and provide support for a meeting.

You may need to carry out research tasks and must keep any notes you make carefully, as these will provide evidence to support your work. If you give a demonstration, make a presentation, support your teacher/tutor or other business people at an event or discuss what you have done to organise a meeting, then you will also obtain witness testimony and/or observation reports to confirm what you have done. It is important that you keep these safely, together with any documents you produce yourself.

Your assessment could be in the form of:

- a leaflet or display which illustrates how business support is different in two contrasting businesses

- a fact sheet or presentation which summarises the appropriate use of different types of office equipment and how this contributes to providing business support

- a demonstration of how to use office equipment safely

- a poster to illustrate safe lifting techniques

- a personal record of all the activities you have undertaken to organise and support a meeting and the documents you produced

- a reflective report in which you evaluate your contribution to the meeting, what you have learned from the experience and any improvements you would make in future.

Providing business support

Getting started

What type of support is provided by your school or college office? How does this help your tutors? What would happen if it didn't exist? Discuss this with your teacher/tutor to find out!

Types of support

Business support is vital in all organisations, both large and small, because it keeps the business running smoothly. There are various types of support and these are shown in Table 7.1.

Table 7.1 Types of business support

Support task	Assistance for the business
Dealing with visitors	Gives callers an immediate positive impression and enables visitor needs to be met promptly
Organising travel and accommodation	Enables staff to travel cost-effectively to meet customers and other external contacts
Managing diaries	Enables activities to be coordinated and staff to be found quickly when necessary
Using telephone systems to make, receive and transfer calls	Enables enquiries to be dealt with promptly and accurately, improves customer relations and responsiveness
Organising and supporting meetings	Helps meetings to run smoothly and a reliable and accurate record to be kept
Producing documents	Provides a written record of important information for those who need it
Processing and storing information, both manually and electronically	Enables rapid access to records so decisions are based on the latest available information

Activity   Comparing support roles

Maria works in a large doctors' practice. Justin works in the local office of his MP. Both provide business support. In pairs, suggest two differences and two similarities between the tasks they do. Compare your ideas with other groups.

What administrative support is essential at a meeting?

The purpose of providing business support

The aim of business support is to keep everything running smoothly. This is very important in both small and large organisations for several reasons.

- **To ensure consistency:** This means that support tasks are carried out in the same way, and to the same high standards, no matter who does them.

- **To make effective use of time:** In any thriving business, there are many tasks to do in a limited amount of time. Some will be urgent, some important, a few will be both. When tasks are prioritised and done by support staff, other staff can concentrate on meeting the priorities in their own jobs.

- **To support managers, teams, colleagues and departmental processes:** Managers must focus on their own responsibilities. They cannot achieve targets or run their own areas efficiently if they are distracted by administrative tasks. Other staff, too, will do a better job if they can rely on support staff for assistance.

- **To provide effective services to internal and external customers:** External customers may contact a business for information or advice, to complain or to buy products and/or services. Internal customers are people in the same workplace who need something, such as information or a copy of a document. Both types of customers want their request to be handled promptly and professionally. If this is done consistently the image and reputation of the business is enhanced.

Just checking

1 List four common business support activities and state how each one helps the work of the business.

2 What are the main purposes of providing business support?

Assessment activity 7.1

2A.P1

1 Research the job roles of three or four different business support staff in two contrasting businesses. Do this by talking to job holders, investigating job adverts online or in your local paper. Identify the types of support each job holder provides and the main purposes(s) of each person's job.

2 Use this information to prepare a leaflet that identifies and explains the types and purposes of business support provided in both businesses. Then present your findings to the rest of your group.

Tips

- Check with your teacher/tutor that the businesses you choose are 'contrasting', i.e. very different in some way(s).
- Make sure the jobs you investigate involve contrasting activities as this will give you more scope in your answer.

Did you know?

- You can find out more about business support activities by looking at *Executive PA* magazine online.

- In large organisations, support staff usually work within departments, such as HR, sales or finance and specialise in the type of work done there, for example organising interviews in HR, updating customer records in sales and checking expense claims in finance.

Remember

Support staff help a business to run more efficiently because they enable other staff to focus on their own job, knowing that important support tasks have been carried out properly.

Using office equipment for different purposes

Introduction

Many support tasks involve the use of office equipment. Using this correctly means that you get the best results in the shortest time. Using it safely is also important, as you will see later in this unit.

Types of office equipment

Computers

Most offices use both desktop computers and laptops. Laptops are preferred by staff who frequently travel or often work at home. Staff computers are usually connected on a network so that information can be shared by email or over an intranet. Users access communal software, such as word processing and database packages and an internet browser, such as Internet Explorer. Support staff must know how to use their computer system and the software packages needed for the tasks they undertake.

Printers

There are two main types of computer printers used in offices. The features and functions will depend upon the type and the price paid.

- **Inkjet printers** are small, cheaper and usually slower. They use ink cartridges which are expensive to replace if usage is high.
- **Laser printers** are larger and more expensive. They are quicker, quieter and the print quality is crisper. These printers use toner cartridges.

Table 7.2 Office printer features and functions

Feature	Function
Duplex printing	This means documents can be printed back to back.
Media capacity	This is the amount of paper the paper tray holds.
Media size	This is the maximum size of paper the printer will use (usually A4).
Media type	This is the type of paper you can use, e.g. plain paper, envelopes, labels, etc.
Memory	This is the number of pages that can be held in the printer memory.
Mono or colour	Most inkjets offer colour; laser printers may be mono or colour.
Networkable	This means the printer can be linked to several computers.
Print resolution	The higher the dots per inch (dpi) figure, the better the print quality.
Print speed	This is rated in pages per minute (ppm) and is slower for top-quality prints.

Photocopiers

Photocopiers make copies of documents, such as items received in the mail and papers in the file. They vary tremendously in terms of their size, speed and features. Some are small desktop models, others are much larger. Some are digital, use touch screen technology, provide internet access and can be linked to the computer network. Computer users can give instructions from their desk to print a document and specify how it should be produced, for example, whether it should be printed back to back.

Table 7.3 Features and functions of office photocopiers

Feature	Function
Automatic document feeder	ADFs allow multi-page documents to be stacked for copying and each page enters separately. Some also accept double-sided originals.
Copying speed	This can range from 15 pages a minute to over 100.
Duplexing	This enables two-sided copying which saves paper.
Finishing unit	This may collate multi-page documents, hole punch or staple them.
Image density adjustments	This adjusts exposure for poor text or dirty backgrounds to improve clarity.
Interrupt facility	This allows a long job to be paused while an urgent job is done.
Memory (digital copiers only)	Pages are scanned into memory before printing; routine jobs can be programmed into the machine and recalled as required.
Mono, colour or hybrid	Copies may be only black and white or colour. A hybrid saves money as the best option can be selected per task.
Paper trays and capacity	Can range from one small A4 paper tray to several different trays for different sizes of paper, e.g. a bypass tray for labels or transparencies.
Reduce/enlarge	Copies can be reduced or enlarged to fixed pre-set ratios. Some machines automatically use the best ratio.
Sample copy	This enables a test copy to be made.
User ID/counter	This calculates usage per user. Users enter a PIN to use the machine.
Zoom	This allows more precise reduction/enlargement.

Activity   Investigating photocopiers

Find out about the features available on the main photocopier you use in your centre. Then watch a demonstration that ideally includes printing on different paper sizes, collating and stapling a multi-page document, and making basic adjustments to improve print quality.

Discussion point

Are automated systems and music on hold a good thing or bad? Do they lose customers or gain them? Discuss your views as a class.

Telephone systems

There are different types of business telephone systems. In a large organisation, a designated person may operate a screen-based console that receives incoming calls. In a small business, calls are usually routed direct to extensions and answered from any phone. Many firms now have VoIP (Voice over Internet Protocol). Calls are routed over a computer network instead of traditional phone lines because this is cheaper and the quality is better.

Table 7.4 Features and functions of business telephone systems

Feature	Function
Automated attendant/ interactive voice response (IVR)	Callers are greeted with a pre-recorded message and given options to select the department they want. With an IVR system, callers can obtain information and carry out some transactions. They may be asked for ID (such as an account number) before being connected.
Automatic call distribution	This distributes incoming calls evenly among a group of operators. Used by many call centres to reduce waiting times for callers.
Caller display/ identification	This shows the caller's number plus the name and company if linked to an address book feature.
Conference calls	This allows you to speak to several people at once, either extension holders and/or outside callers.
Divert or call forwarding	This allows calls to be rerouted from one extension to another or to another phone or mobile if a person is out of the office, travelling on business.
Do not disturb	This blocks calls to an extension while it is set.
Hands free/listen on hold	This enables you to replace the handset and listen and/or talk through a speaker.
Interrupt	This indicates a waiting call, usually by a bleep on the line.
Last number redial	This automatically redials the last number you called.
Message waiting	A light or bleep shows that a voicemail message is waiting. On a computerised system, the message appears on screen.
Music on hold	This plays music and/or provides information to callers waiting to be connected.
On hold/reminder call holding	This allows incoming calls to be held while the correct person is found to deal with the call/gives a prompt that the caller is still waiting to be connected.

Table 7.4 Features and functions of business telephone systems

Feature	Function
Redirect	This enables a transferred call to be rerouted if the call has to be redirected again.
Secrecy button	Depressing this button means the caller cannot hear anything you say to a colleague (and is far better than covering the mouthpiece with your hand!).
Speed dialling	This allows abbreviated dialling for long numbers and for numbers called frequently.
Voicemail/ advanced messaging services	Callers leave voice messages in individual mailboxes when people are away or engaged on another call. Messages can be retrieved from an extension or external phone. On some systems, voicemail can be sent as text messages or as emails.

Activity — Investigating telephone systems

1 Find out the standard greeting given to telephone callers by staff at your centre. How do you think this might differ in a bank or a small retail shop?

2 Investigate the telephone system in your centre. Find out which features it has and which are most commonly used.

3 In small groups, decide on three telephone system features that would benefit **a)** a health centre, **b)** a cinema, **c)** a large retail store, **d)** a small estate agency, **e)** an international business. Compare your ideas as a class.

Office chairs

Office chairs allow staff to carry out a range of tasks comfortably and safely. They are designed to support the user's back and neck, encourage good posture and prevent discomfort. The best chairs are often described as being **ergonomic**.

You can alter the height of an office chair so that your feet are flat on the floor. You should also be able to adjust the back of the chair so that your spine is supported. The best ones also have adjustable seat depth, chair arms and tension so that the chair will tilt easily according to your weight.

You will learn more about sitting properly and safely on later in this unit.

What features can you identify that will help with good posture?

Did you know?

Most businesses instruct their staff to answer external calls with a specific greeting. This may be formal or informal, depending on the type of firm and the business it carries out. On a central switchboard, the greeting will include the name of the organisation. Individual extension users should also identify themselves by name.

Key terms

Ergonomic – designed to enable people to work safely and productively.

CONTINUED ▸▸

Instruction manuals

All office equipment is sold with an instruction booklet or manual. This explains all the features and functions and includes any other information the manufacturer thinks you should know. One important section is troubleshooting, which is normally near the end. This tells you what to do if there is a problem with the equipment. The manual also includes safety advice, which is important if you are using electrical equipment.

While you may be tempted to ignore the manual and just press a few buttons to see what happens, there are dangers with this approach. As well as making a mess of a job, you could also do something that is hazardous or break the equipment.

Training in usage

The best way to learn how to use equipment is to watch an expert who also explains what they are doing. They may make it look very easy, and you might forget what you are told, so it is sensible to take notes that you can refer to when you are doing the job yourself.

Activity   Watching a demonstration

Watch someone experienced demonstrating a range of photocopying operations and using the telephone system at your centre. Make notes so that you remember what they did.

Problem solving

All users should know the correct procedure to follow if they have a problem with a piece of equipment. If a computer printer fails to work in your centre, then you may be expected to report it to a named tutor or contact a helpline. Before you do this, however, it is sensible to make a few basic checks, such as ensuring it is plugged in and switched on.

Remember

It is normally quicker and safer to check what you should do before you start, not when you get stuck later on!

Did you know?

• Most manuals are also available on the manufacturer's website, together with help and guidance for users.

• Photocopier suppliers often provide training and show nominated members of staff how to solve problems such as paper jams and replenishing toner. Other users will not be allowed to do these tasks.

Why do staff need special training before they can solve photocopier problems?

Activity — Solving problems

In groups, look at the manuals for the printer and photocopier you use regularly. Find out what to do if the paper jams, printing stops unexpectedly, the equipment stops working or the copies are unreadable. Produce a help sheet for users.

Did you know?

It is usually more economical for a small business to have a basic copier or multifunction device (that will also print, fax and scan documents) and to pay a copy shop or local printer to prepare coloured leaflets or posters.

Meeting different business requirements

All office equipment is chosen to meet specific business requirements. The needs of a health centre are different from a bank or a cinema, and a hairdresser will have different requirements from an estate agent, a solicitor or a retail store. Factors to consider include:

- whether the business needs to produce professional documents or leaflets for clients as this will affect the type of printer or photocopier they buy
- whether there will be a large volume of telephone calls to deal with, and whether many calls will be received 'out of hours'
- whether staff are regularly travelling on business and need to keep in touch with the office.

Activity — Research office equipment

Research the type of office equipment which is routinely used in business organisations to meet different requirements, such as preparing, printing or reproducing documents, communicating with other people and providing meeting support.

You can do this by talking to the job holders you spoke to for Assessment activity 7.1 and finding out the type of office equipment that each job holder needs to use to do their work. You should also research online and you can visit large office suppliers, such as Staples, to see some items yourself.

Identify and note the main features and functions and why they are important to different users. Keep your notes safely as you will need them when you do the next Assessment activity.

Working safely

Using office equipment safely

Most people use computers every day without realising that they can cause painful ailments if they are not used correctly. This is because a computer user may be in a fixed position for hours, with their face looking at the screen, hands on the keyboard and the rest of the body immobile, resulting in musculoskeletal disorders such as repetitive strain injury (RSI) and upper-limb disorders (ULDs) to hands, wrists, arms, neck, shoulders or back. These are caused by repetitive movements, such as keying in text or using a mouse, and continual poor posture.

Laptop computers can cause more serious injuries as users sometimes rest them on their knees. The keyboard is not ergonomically designed and the screen may be small or difficult to see in bright light. This is why many businesses provide docking units for safe laptop use within the office.

The Health and Safety at Work (Display Screen Equipment) Regulations introduced minimum standards for the use of visual display screens (VDUs) and workstation design. Users are also expected to make simple changes for their own wellbeing. These include adjusting their office chairs so that their backs are well supported and their feet are flat on the floor or on a footstool, and positioning the monitor, keyboard and mouse correctly.

Getting started

A government study found that in 2010/11 1.2 million working people were suffering from a work-related illness. Can you think of the main reasons why?

Remember

Make sure you are a safe worker, not a walking hazard! Don't leave your bag on the floor where someone can fall over it, or wear a rucksack without considering people behind you.

Figure 7.1 How will sitting correctly help to avoid workplace injury?

Activity — Thinking about posture

1 Check your own posture against the illustration shown. Score yourself against each item to see if you get 10 out of 10 or rather less!

   Visit Pearson hotlinks to download the booklet *Working with VDUs* from the HSE. You can access this by going to www.pearsonhotlinks.co.uk and searching for this title.

2 Use this to design a poster which shows good positioning of a keyboard, monitor and mouse.

3 In groups, research ergonomic office chairs online, and produce a leaflet which shows how to make the necessary adjustments so the user is sitting in the correct position. Remember to test your ideas to make sure they work!

Health and safety legislation for working safely

The Health and Safety at Work Act 1974 (HASAWA) is the main legislation relating to health and safety. This states that employers have a responsibility to provide a safe working environment, and employees must take reasonable care of their own health and safety. They must also act responsibly because other people may be affected by their actions.

Other legislation regulates the space, temperature and facilities in the workplace and how equipment is maintained and used.

Safe lifting techniques

The Manual Handling Operations Regulations state that staff must never try to lift a load which is too heavy. All organisations must provide trolleys or wheeled 'sack' trucks to move heavy items. If the load is within your capabilities, then you must lift it properly by bending your knees first, so that your legs take the strain. Your legs can cope with this, whereas your back cannot.

Following instructions

Under HASAWA all employees must cooperate with their employer and follow all instructions relating to health and safety. Businesses try to prevent accidents by providing equipment manuals and training staff in how to use equipment and certain substances safely. These precautions are useless if employees ignore them.

Figure 7.2 An injury to your back could mean recurrent pain for the rest of your life.

Remember

Working safely means following workplace policies and manufacturers' instructions. It also means using your common sense and concentrating when you are doing something.

Assessment activity 7.2

 2B.P2 | 2B.P3 | 2B.M1 | 2B.M2 | 2B.D1

Your centre is hosting an event for young entrepreneurs. You have been asked to provide information about office equipment and demonstrate this to attendees.

1 Prepare facts sheets for three items of equipment, using your research findings. Each sheet should give information on how that item of office equipment is used to meet different business requirements and the type of features and functions that are valued by support staff. You should also summarise how that particular item of equipment contributes to effective business support.

2 During the event you must demonstrate that you can use a computer, printer, office chair, telephone and, ideally, a photocopier properly and safely. You must also carry out other support tasks, including greeting visitors and asking them to sign a visitor book, issuing and collecting visitor badges, finding and storing your facts sheets in a filing cabinet and producing documents.

  You must also demonstrate how to lift safely, how to sit properly at a computer and how to adjust your chair appropriately. Your teacher/tutor will observe you and will complete an observation report on your performance.

3 After the event, use your research and experience to prepare a summary in which you analyse how different items of office equipment contribute towards providing effective business support.

Tip

You should analyse your information. This means identifying the relevant features and functions that apply and explaining why each one is important.

Did you know?

• Your eyes regularly need a break from a computer screen. Look into the middle distance at intervals and blink more rapidly for a few seconds. Stretch your arms and wrists and straighten your fingers at the same time.

• RSI Action, the UK charity, warns that children as young as seven may now suffer from RSI. Read the guidelines on its website by visiting Pearson hotlinks to ensure you don't join them. You can access this by going to www.pearsonhotlinks.co.uk and searching for this title.

• If you use a telephone while you are on a computer, you should have a hands-free headset. This prevents you cradling the phone between your ear and neck while you type, which can cause serious injuries.

Organising and providing support for meetings

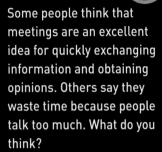

Types of meeting

There are different types of meeting and they vary in several ways.

- **Size** – some meetings involve only two or three people, whereas others involve a large number of people.
- **Internal/external** – some meetings only have internal staff present; others involve external contacts such as customers, suppliers or shareholders.
- **Formal/informal** – formal meetings have specific rules and procedures; others are informal and may just involve a small group of people chatting together.
- **Confidentiality** – meetings are confidential when sensitive information is being discussed, such as strategy meetings when directors are discussing future plans and meetings about HR issues such as a staff disciplinary interview.
- **Team meetings** – these are internal meetings held by the team leader to keep a team up to date with developments. Team members may be asked for ideas and contributions to solve a problem.

The type of meeting affects the organisational arrangements, including where and when it is held, the number of people present, how they are invited, the budget and the written record that is made.

Discussion point

As a group, suggest what problems could arise if word leaked out that the directors in a company had held a meeting to discuss possible redundancies because of a lack of orders.

Activity Investigating meetings

Find out all the different types of meetings held at your centre, both formal and informal. Discuss with your tutor the steps that are taken at confidential meetings to ensure that sensitive information is kept private.

Why is it important to check equipment is working in advance of a meeting?

Organising meetings

All meetings have several aspects in common. People are invited to attend, often by the **chairperson.** They are informed about the items to be discussed and these are often listed in an **agenda.** A record is kept to summarise the decisions taken and sent to people afterwards. These are called **minutes** and are a legal requirement for some formal meetings.

Meeting brief and agenda

The purpose of the meeting affects who is invited, what is discussed, how long the meeting lasts and where it is held. It also partly determines the budget as you will see later.

A **meeting brief** may be prepared which summarises all the key facts. This is done by the chairperson and the organiser, often by using a checklist like the one below.

Checklist for a meeting brief	
Why is the meeting being held?	
What is the agenda?	
What is the budget?	
How long will the meeting last?	
When should it be held and what time will it start/end?	
Who are the key people who must attend?	
Where will the meeting be held?	
Are refreshments required?	
Are any special equipment, resources or facilities required?	
How will people be invited?	
What information/documents will they need?	
Will anyone require accommodation?	
Will someone be required to take minutes?	
What follow-up activities are required?	

Figure 7.3 A checklist will help to ensure nothing is forgotten.

The chairperson also decides the agenda. Certain standard items are usually included and, for regular meetings, some topics may have been suggested at the last meeting. Anyone who is invited to attend may also be asked for contributions.

The agenda lists the topics in the order they will be discussed. This is helpful because if someone can only attend for a short time, they know when an item will be raised or where they will be expected to contribute.

The agenda is often linked to the notice asking people to attend as this saves sending out two sets of paperwork.

Key terms

Chairperson – the leader of a meeting.

Agenda – a list of items to be discussed at a meeting.

Minutes – the official record of the discussions and decisions taken at the meeting.

Meeting brief – a summary of the main requirements for a meeting.

Did you know?

• An Annual General Meeting (AGM) is a legal requirement for all public limited companies. This is a formal meeting to which all the shareholders are invited (see Unit 1).

• Sometimes a task group is set up to organise a specific event such as an Open Day, and will hold meetings to discuss their plans. Once the event has been held, the task group is disbanded.

• Checklists are useful because you can tick off each item as you complete it, to make sure you don't forget anything.

CONTINUED ▶▶

Checking dates

Participants in regular meetings usually know when they are expected to attend each time. Sometimes, however, the date of the next meeting is agreed at a meeting, or it may be arranged from scratch. This is more difficult because the meeting should ideally be held when everyone can attend. If this is not possible, you need to identify the key people who must be there for the meeting to achieve its purpose.

For major events where an external venue is to be used, some alternative dates should be suggested at the start because it will not be known whether a suitable venue is available on one particular date.

Confirming the budget

The budget sets the amount of money that can be spent on holding the meeting. Most organisations set a limit, which will vary according to the type of meeting and its size. For a small internal meeting the limit may be coffee/tea and biscuits. A breakfast meeting or working lunch would cost more, although this can be kept down if the catering is done internally or sandwiches are bought locally.

Meetings at an external venue, with several meals and even travel or accommodation reservations are entirely different. The budget must be agreed before any arrangements are made and quotations obtained to ensure the budget is not exceeded.

Activity   Controlling meeting costs

Most organisations have procedures staff must follow to control the costs of a meeting. Find out what happens in your centre when someone wants to hold a meeting and wants to include refreshments.

Choosing and booking venues

A meeting can be a disaster if the room is unsuitable or the facilities are poor, so space, heating, lighting, ventilation and sound-proofing are very important. The room must also be clean and tidy and not cluttered with dirty cups and papers from the previous meeting.

Internal meetings are often held in special rooms set aside for that purpose. Large organisations have a board room or committee room. Customised meeting rooms usually contain a large table and several chairs. There may be side tables for refreshments and special facilities for presentations, including blackout blinds if audio/visual equipment is regularly used.

External venues include hotels and conference centres with specialist facilities, such as seminar rooms for group discussions. Some also provide accommodation for overnight guests.

Sending meeting invitations

For a formal meeting a notice may be posted or emailed to everyone who has the right to attend giving details of the date, time and venue. This usually also includes the agenda. Other documents that may be sent include:

- **a copy of the minutes** taken at the last meeting
- **papers or reports** to be discussed at the meeting, so that attendees can read them in advance.

People are often invited to informal meetings by email. In many organisations, administrators use an electronic diary package to book the meeting in people's diaries.

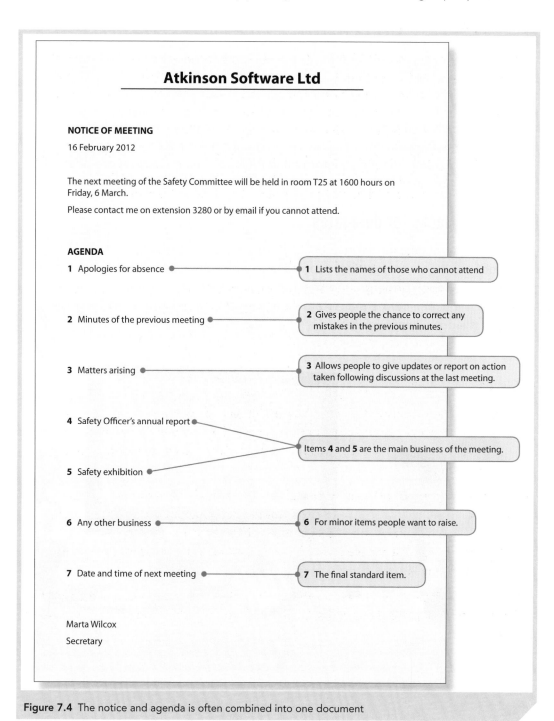

Atkinson Software Ltd

NOTICE OF MEETING

16 February 2012

The next meeting of the Safety Committee will be held in room T25 at 1600 hours on Friday, 6 March.

Please contact me on extension 3280 or by email if you cannot attend.

AGENDA

1 Apologies for absence — **1** Lists the names of those who cannot attend

2 Minutes of the previous meeting — **2** Gives people the chance to correct any mistakes in the previous minutes.

3 Matters arising — **3** Allows people to give updates or report on action taken following discussions at the last meeting.

4 Safety Officer's annual report

5 Safety exhibition — Items **4** and **5** are the main business of the meeting.

6 Any other business — **6** For minor items people want to raise.

7 Date and time of next meeting — **7** The final standard item.

Marta Wilcox
Secretary

Figure 7.4 The notice and agenda is often combined into one document

CONTINUED ▶▶

Arranging catering, equipment and resources

- **Catering requirements** depend on the length and type of meeting, the time of day and the budget. Usually, a hot drink is offered at the start and jugs of water are available on the table. A working lunch may include sandwiches.
- **Basic equipment** includes a whiteboard or flipchart on which to record ideas or decisions. There may be an overhead projector or a laptop/PC and projector so that a PowerPoint presentation can be given. A radio microphone and remote mouse allow the speaker to move around freely. There may be an interactive whiteboard, and/or a video link to an external location.

Activity	Researching equipment

Find out the functions and features of the equipment used during meetings at your centre and why each item is used.

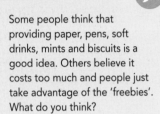
Discussion point

Some people think that providing paper, pens, soft drinks, mints and biscuits is a good idea. Others believe it costs too much and people just take advantage of the 'freebies'. What do you think?

- **Resources** include the notice and agenda, notes or minutes from the last meeting and supplementary documents. Discussion groups need notepads, pens and pencils. For external meetings, information packs and name badges are often given to delegates on arrival.

Information packs for delegates

If the meeting is at an external venue, an information pack is usually sent out. This will include a map, showing people how to reach the venue, details of any transport links (such as London Underground lines) and car parking plus information on local accommodation. The pack should state if people attending the meeting are expected to pay for their own accommodation.

What equipment can you identify in this photo?

Confirming attendance and keeping a record

An accurate record must be kept of the people who will be attending a meeting for several reasons.

- Anyone who cannot attend a formal meeting should send apologies in advance. A list is kept of these people and their reason for not attending. This enables the chairperson to check that everyone expected to arrive has done so, and the meeting can start.
- Attendees at a large meeting are normally issued with name badges on arrival. These are prepared after their responses have been received.
- The number of attendees will affect the requirements for refreshments and other resources, from pens to car parking spaces.

Identifying any special requirements

Some attendees may have physical disabilities or an impairment which means they have special requirements, for example:

- wheelchair access to the meeting room and within the room itself
- a signer on the platform for anyone who is deaf
- a hearing loop system for hearing aid users
- paperwork in large print for anyone with limited vision.

You must also ask attendees if they have any special dietary requirements. This is often included on the booking form. You will need to tell the caterer if anyone is vegetarian/ vegan or restricted by dietary requirements or cultural/religious beliefs. If you cannot check requirements beforehand, the safest option is a buffet with a good range of salads.

Did you know?

- Some people attending a meeting may need car parking. Often visitor spaces can be pre-booked for attendees.
- At most formal meetings, a minimum number of people must attend for the meeting to go ahead. This number is called the **quorum**.

Key terms

Quorum – the minimum number of people who must be present at a formal meeting to allow official decisions to be made.

Remember

Water and soft drinks are usually served at meetings, not alcoholic drinks.

Activity   Researching meeting venues

You have been asked to investigate meeting venues in your area for a one-day seminar for 50 staff. The event will start at 9 a.m. and finish at 10 p.m. Three people require accommodation overnight.

In groups, research online to find venues in your area. Check the rooms, equipment and resources plus other facilities including those for disabled attendees. Find out about catering options and calculate the likely cost.

Present your findings to the rest of the class. Then decide which venue provides the best value for money.

Just checking

1 What is a meeting brief and why is it used?

2 Identify four essential items you would need in a meeting room.

3 Explain why a formal meeting should start with apologies for absence.

4 What is meant by the term 'any other business'?

Supporting meetings and following up meetings

Getting started

The tasks that need to be done during a meeting vary according to the size of the event and where it is being held. What differences do you think there would be between supporting an informal team meeting in the workplace and supporting a formal meeting in a conference centre?

Supporting tasks

Documentation for attendees

It is sensible to have extra copies of everything that was sent to attendees in advance of the meeting, in case people forget to bring them. This includes spare copies of the agenda and also the minutes of the last meeting held by the same group. There will also be sets of documents to be given out at the meeting.

Attendance list

This is a list of everyone expected to attend and is prepared in advance. You also need to keep a list of anyone who contacts you to say that they will not be attending, and the reason.

Checking the room

The room must be set out correctly when people arrive. It is sensible to arrive early to check that the furniture is arranged properly and there are no dirty cups or papers lying around. You need to check that the resources and drinks you ordered have arrived, and that there is somewhere for people to leave coats and umbrellas.

If you have booked an external venue then you should be able to take issues such as cleanliness and equipment for granted, but it is still worth arriving early to check.

What type of problems can occur if you don't check a room in advance?

Checking the equipment

This is essential. You do not want your boss to start an important meeting and find the flipchart has only two pages left, or the radio microphone for the guest speaker is not working and no one can find a replacement. Check every item methodically by switching it on and making sure that it works properly. If someone is giving a PowerPoint® presentation, check the projector is focused and the screen is clearly visible from all parts of the room, even when the sun is shining.

Serving refreshments

Ideally, serve a hot drink before the meeting starts and have jugs of water available so people can help themselves during the meeting. Arrange for the chairperson to pause the meeting if you need to break off when the sandwiches or more hot drinks arrive. Alternatively, ask someone else to help you.

Recording who is present and who is absent

You need to know who is present and who is not. At a large meeting, pass round a piece of paper and ask people to record their names. At a small meeting, the chairperson will check who is present and you must record this. You should already have a list of people who have sent apologies in advance. Add the name of anyone else who is missing and the reason, if known.

Why is it important that the chairperson and meetings organiser work together?

Agreeing minutes of last meeting

If a meeting is held regularly, everyone must confirm at the start of the meeting that the minutes that were taken at the previous meeting are a correct record. If they contain a minor error, they are changed and approved 'as amended'. They are then signed by the chairperson. If they contain major errors, they must be rewritten and approved on another occasion.

| **Activity** | Role of a chairperson |

Research the role of a chairperson at a meeting. Then decide the main attributes of an effective chairperson and share your ideas with the rest of your class.

?   **Did you know?**

• Documents at a meeting are those that are sent out in advance, such as the agenda, and those that are given out (or tabled) at the meeting itself. The term 'tabled' simply means 'put on the table'.

• The reason why minutes of the last meeting are sent with the agenda is so that attendees can check them in advance. Therefore, they don't need to read through them at the meeting, which saves time.

CONTINUED ▶▶

Taking accurate minutes of the meeting, if appropriate

A record of what is decided is often taken at meetings for the following reasons:

- to ensure that the important points are recorded and circulated promptly
- to remind people what they have agreed to do.

Tips on taking accurate meeting notes

- You must note all essential information, that is:
  - date of the meeting
  - names of those present/those who sent apologies
  - what has been discussed/decided
  - action points (tasks people have agreed to do)
  - date and time of next meeting.
- Rule left- and right-hand margins on an A4 lined pad and write the above information at the top.
- Write the agenda heading, the initials of the speaker in the left margin and a summary of what they say next to it.
- In the right-hand column, put the initials of people who agree to do something.
- Listen carefully to what people are saying.
- Summarise – just write down the main points of what was agreed.
- Don't panic if you miss something. Put an asterisk where the gap is and ask the chairperson for help later.
- Use 'text speak', if it helps.
- Write up your notes promptly, while the discussions are fresh in your memory.
- Use complete sentences and the past tense, i.e. 'Luke said that . . . ', not 'Luke says that'.
- Check you have spelled everyone's name correctly.
- Be prepared to redraft your notes several times.

◤ Follow-up activities

You may think that your job is done once the meeting is finished, but there are several other tasks still to do.

Writing up minutes after the meeting

Write up your minutes promptly, especially if you have any queries, or the chairperson may forget what happened. An example of the minutes of a meeting is given opposite. You should note that:

- the chairperson is listed first and other members are then listed in alphabetical order
- the headings match those in the agenda
- the minutes are written in the past tense and specific dates are given (not 'tomorrow' or 'next year' as this could be confusing)
- the minutes are a summary (details of discussions are not included)
- the action column shows the initials of everyone who agreed to do a task.

Atkinson Software Ltd

MINUTES OF MEETING

A meeting of the Safety Committee was held in room T25 at 1600 hours on Tuesday 6th March 2012.

PRESENT
Annika Hall (Chair)
Uzma Ahmed
David Blunt
Neelam Rani
Marc Salazar (Safety Officer)
Marta Wilcox

		Action
1	**Apologies for absence** Sean Fox sent his apologies.	
2	**Minutes of previous meeting** These were agreed as a true and correct record and signed by the Chairperson.	
3	**Matters arising** David Blunt said he had received a quotation from Brands Electrical for new emergency lighting at a cost of £12,500. He would chase up the two quotes still outstanding.	DB
4	**Safety Officer's annual report** Marc Salazar circulated copies and outlined key items – in particular accident figures which were down 8 per cent from the previous year.	
5	**Safety exhibition** Annika Hall said this would be held at the NEC on 12 and 13 November and suggested two members should attend. Uzma Ahmed and Neelam Rani agreed to do so and to report back at the next meeting.	UA/NR
6	**Any other business** David Blunt said several safety signs had been vandalised at the Northfield Road depot. Marc Salazar agreed to investigate.	MS
7	**Date and time of next meeting** The next meeting will be held at 1600 hours on Friday 6th April 2012.	

Signed ………………………… (Chairperson) Date ………………………..

Figure 7.5 An example of minutes.

CONTINUED ▶▶

◤ Other tasks

Clearing the venue

Always leave the room as you would wish to find it. Check all waste paper is in the bin, the table is clear, equipment is unplugged and tidied away, all spare papers and resources have been collected and the furniture is where it should be. Check, too, that no one has left anything behind.

Why is it particularly important to make sure equipment is put away safely when using an external venue for meetings?

Remember

All documents should be circulated in time for people to carry out the actions they agreed to take before the next meeting.

Did you know?

People who receive the minutes of a meeting usually look first to see where their name appears – and then check what they promised to do.

Circulating documents to attendees

Once the chairperson agrees that your minutes are accurate, you must send them out together with any other documents that were agreed. These are sent to everyone, whether they attended the meeting or not, so that they know what happened and have the information they need for the next meeting.

Monitoring completion of agreed actions

People agree to do things at a meeting for many reasons. They may want to impress their boss or feel they cannot refuse. They may genuinely want to be involved, but then find themselves very busy immediately afterwards. The danger is that action tasks may get forgotten.

For this reason, many administrators keep a separate list of the actions people promised to take. They can then check that progress has been made, and give a gentle reminder if necessary.

Activity   Investigating meeting documents

Look at two or three past agendas, related minutes and meeting papers issued at meetings at your centre (preferably in sequence). In groups, discuss the contents and check how those who attended responded to the different agenda items and action points listed.

Just checking

1 Suggest three reasons why meetings are held.

2 Why is it important to know who cannot attend a meeting?

3 Why is an action column useful in the notes of a meeting?

4 Suggest three tasks you may have to carry out if external visitors were invited to a meeting venue some distance away.

Assessment activity 7.3   *English*   2C.P4 | 2C.P5 | 2C.P6 | 2C.M3 | 2C.M4 | 2C.D2

For this assessment activity, you will form your own meetings group (or groups) and hold a series of meetings. Your first task is to make sure that you do not forget anything when you are organising and supporting these.

1. a) Prepare to organise the first meeting by drawing up a checklist with suitable headings. This should include all the aspects involved in organising and supporting a meeting that you have read about in this unit.

   b) Attach to your checklist an explanation of the organisation and support that is required for different types of meetings.

2. When you are personally responsible for organising a group meeting, you will undertake the following tasks:

   a) Update your checklist to ensure it includes all specified requirements. You will organise the meeting according to these requirements.

   b) Produce accurate documents needed for a meeting, for example the meeting brief and agenda.

   c) Take notes during the meeting.

   d) Produce accurate and detailed post-meeting documentation, including minutes, for at least one meeting.

   e) Provide the support required including follow-up activities when the meeting has ended.

   f) Afterwards, reflect on your own contribution. Identify what went well and what did not, and think about what you could have done better at all stages, that is before, during and after the meeting. Prepare a short report, suggesting changes that would enable you to improve your contribution in the future.

Tips

- Prepare your checklist using similar headings to the ones in this book, for example: meeting brief/agenda, dates, budget, venue, equipment and resources, refreshments, documents. You might also find it easier to write about organisation and support under the headings of before, during and after the meeting.

- Identify the difference between formal and informal meetings and those held internally and in an external venue.

- A good way to start thinking about your contribution is to look back at your checklist. Compare what actually happened with what you planned to happen. What differences were there, and why? Then think about everything you have learned since you started. What advice would you give someone who was organising next week's meeting, and why?

In this unit is an activity to help you to prepare for the meetings you will hold. You will find it helpful to read this, and the Workspace case study that follows, before you undertake Assessment Activity 7.3.

Activity   Preparing for meetings

You now need to make some preparations before you hold the first meeting. As a group, decide the focus for your meetings. This could be to hold an event (see suggestions below), to raise money for charity, to form a student council, or your group or teacher/tutor may have some better ideas.

You should now plan the first meeting. Decide when and where it will be held and make any required bookings. Decide what equipment you might need (e.g. a flipchart, projector and computer) and book this. Ask for a volunteer to be meetings organiser the first time. This duty must then be done by everyone in turn.

The meetings organiser should prepare a meeting brief, notice and agenda. The notice will be straightforward. The agenda should be as follows:

1 Apologies
2 Election of chairperson
3 Rota for meetings organiser
4 Main business of meeting (e.g. selection of event, charity to support, role of student council)
5 Any other business
6 Time and date of next meeting

The first item must be done properly. Anyone unable to attend must send apologies to the meetings organiser beforehand, together with a reason.

Your group must decide a fair way to elect a chairperson. You might want to start by thinking of the qualities a good chairperson would need. Note the chairperson has the casting vote if there are any later disagreements.

The main item of business should be the key focus. Don't be too ambitious or plan to spend any money unless you know how to raise some. The meetings should be held over the next two to three months, which should give you some idea of the time you have available.

If you can't reach a decision at the first meeting, everyone should be asked to go away to think about other options, check ideas with family members and report back at the next meeting. This is what happens at many business meetings!

Finally, ask if anyone has anything to raise under AOB. The meetings organiser must then prepare the notes and circulate them, and all participants must carry out any agreed action before the next meeting.

Event suggestions include:

- A one- or two-hour workshop with visiting speakers
- An away day for the group as a whole
- A quiz event with prizes
- A visit to an interesting local business
- A mini conference lasting half a day with various activities.

It is even better if you can choose an event that will help you with other aspects of your course.

WorkSpace

▶ Caroline Gooder

Engineering Administrator, Cummins Turbo Technologies

Cummins is a large, global organisation which employs over 1000 people in Huddersfield, West Yorkshire. It produces Holset turbochargers which improve the efficiency of an engine, and sells these mainly to large truck makers. More than 350 engineers are employed in the Engineering Department where Caroline works.

Caroline's boss is Joanne Worthington, the Engineering Global Capacity Project Leader, but she also provides administrative support to the seven engineering directors and other departmental staff.

Caroline's role includes dealing with visitors, organising travel and accommodation, organising and supporting meetings and producing documents. She organises two different types of meetings: the monthly staff meeting of the directors, and the site facilities meeting with the engineering staff. She books the meeting rooms, prepares and issues the agenda and takes the minutes. Refreshments are only arranged if external clients are present. Caroline types the minutes on a laptop in the meeting room. The image is projected on screen so that the directors can comment on items as she types them. At the end of each section Caroline notes any action required in bold type.

The meeting rooms also have conference call phones with a speaker, so that other Cummins staff can be involved in any discussions. In addition to the projector, there is also an electronic whiteboard.

Caroline's most essential item of equipment is her computer. She uses this to communicate by email, rather than telephone. Cummins has its own instant messaging (IM) service which enables her to talk to Cummins staff all over the world when they are travelling on business. The company has a policy of being paper-free so all information is held on the computer system and only printed out when absolutely necessary.

Think about it

1 What equipment does Caroline find the most useful, and why?

2 Cummins' engineers travel to many places, including China. What will Caroline have to consider before she tries to talk to someone visiting Shanghai?

3 Suggest two reasons why an interactive whiteboard is useful in a meeting room.

4 Why do you think Cummins only provides refreshments at meetings when there are external visitors?

5 Suggest three benefits for Cummins of having a paper-free policy.

Introduction

In this unit, you will learn how businesses are structured, or organised, so that people can do their jobs effectively. All businesses need to carry out certain functions and these are usually represented by specific departments, such as sales, finance and production. You will find out about different job roles and how the structure of the organisation can affect these.

All functions within an organisation are important but one key area is human resources (HR) which is responsible for ensuring the best person is recruited for each job vacancy. You will learn about the documents that inform candidates about a specific vacancy and the correct way to apply for a job. You will prepare for, and attend, a job interview and carry out a personal audit to produce your own career development plan.

Assessment: This unit will be assessed through a series of assignments set by your teacher/tutor.

Learning aims

In this unit you will:

A know about job roles and functional areas in business

B produce documentation for specific job roles

C demonstrate interview skills and plan career development.

> I am really interested in this unit because one day I will be applying for jobs. I want to find out about different job roles and how businesses decide what sort of candidate they want when they have a vacancy. Knowing what they look for when people apply for a job will help me to make a good impression and do well in an interview.
>
> Harry, *16-year-old Business student*

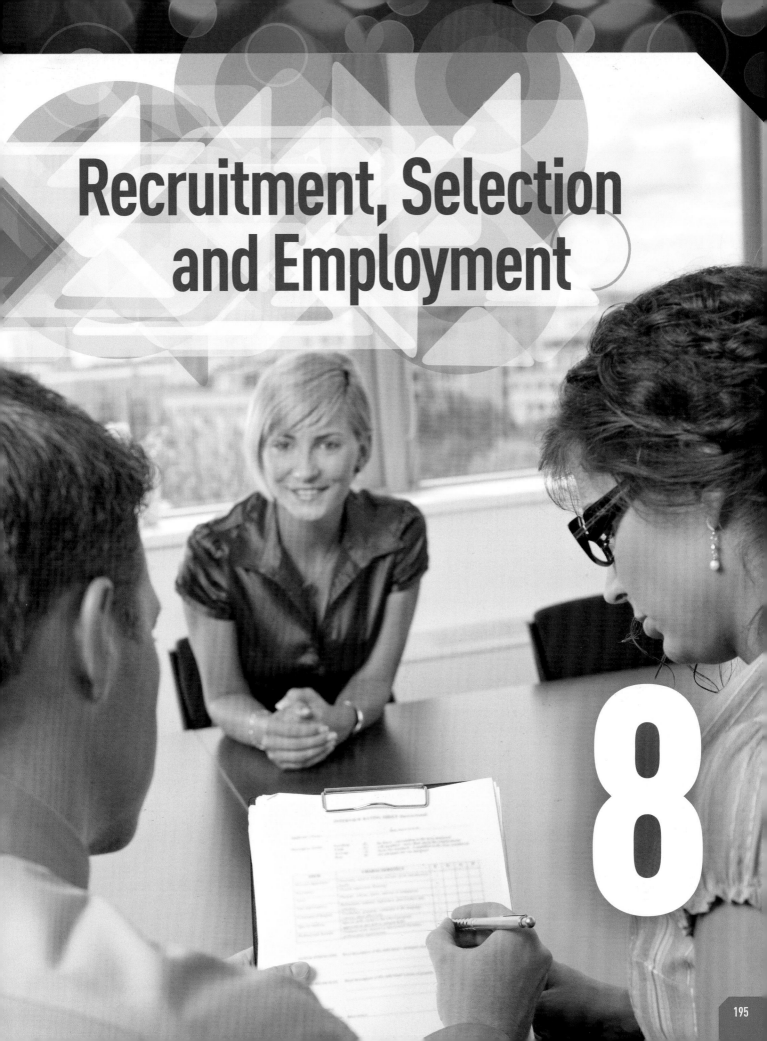

Recruitment, Selection and Employment

Assessment Zone

This table shows you what you must do in order to achieve a **Pass**, **Merit** or **Distinction** grade, and where you can find activities in this book to help you.

Assessment criteria			
Level 1	**Level 2 Pass**	**Level 2 Merit**	**Level 2 Distinction**
Learning aim A: Know about job roles and functional areas in business			
1A.1 Describe the purpose of two functional areas in two contrasting businesses	**2A.P1** Explain the purpose of different functional areas in two contrasting businesses **See Assessment activity 8.1, page 207**	**2A.M1** Compare two job roles and responsibilities from different functional areas in two contrasting businesses **See Assessment activity 8.1, page 207**	**2A.D1** Analyse the impact of organisational structure on job roles and functional areas in a selected business, using appropriate examples **See Assessment activity 8.1, page 207**
1A.2 Identify the responsibilities of two different job roles in a selected business	**2A.P2** Describe the responsibilities of two different job roles in two contrasting businesses **See Assessment activity 8.1, page 207**		
Learning aim B: Produce documentation for specific job roles			
1B.3 English Produce a job description for a specific job	**2B.P3** English Produce an appropriate and detailed job description and person specification for a specific job **See Assessment activity 8.2, page 218**	**2B.M2** English Produce an appropriate and detailed job description and person specification for a specific job, justifying why the documents will encourage effective recruitment **See Assessment activity 8.2, page 218**	**2B.D2** Analyse gaps in knowledge and skills that might require further training or development to match the requirements of a given person specification and job description **See Assessment activity 8.2, page 218**
1B.4 English Produce, with guidance, a curriculum vitae and letter of application to apply for a suitable job role	**2B.P4** English Produce a curriculum vitae, letter of application and completed application form to apply for a suitable job role **See Assessment activity 8.2, page 218**	**2B.M3** Justify how current knowledge and skills meet those required in a given person specification and job description **See Assessment activity 8.2, page 218**	

Assessment criteria			
Level 1	Level 2 **Pass**	Level 2 **Merit**	Level 2 **Distinction**
Learning aim C: Demonstrate interview skills and plan career development			
1C.5 English Provide some appropriate responses to interview questions for a specific job role	**2C.P5** English Provide appropriate responses to interview questions for a specific job role. **See Assessment activity 8.3, page 223**	**2C.M4** English Demonstrate prior research and preparation when providing appropriate responses to interview questions for a specific job role **See Assessment activity 8.3, page 223**	**2C.D3** Evaluate the suitability of a realistic career development plan using interview performance feedback and own reflection **See Assessment activity 8.3, page 223**
1C.6 English Produce, with guidance, a personal career development plan	**2C.P6** English Produce a realistic personal career development plan **See Assessment activity 8.3, page 223**	**2C.M5** English Produce a realistic personal career development plan showing independent research and planning **See Assessment activity 8.3, page 223**	

English / Opportunity to practise English skills

How you will be assessed

This unit will be assessed by a series of internally assessed tasks. These will enable you to demonstrate that you understand how functional areas and job roles can differ between organisations. You will prepare a job description and job specification and apply for a suitable job role. You will attend an interview and produce your own career development plan.

Your assessment could be in the form of:

- a leaflet or presentation in which you explain the differences between two contrasting organisations

- a recruitment pack that you prepare for candidates

- your own application for a suitable job role and attendance at an interview

- your career development plan with reasons for the items you have included.

Organisational structures and functional areas

Introduction

In all businesses, whether large or small, it is important to **coordinate** staff job roles so that everyone contributes to the overall purpose of the business and work is not duplicated unnecessarily.

Key term

Coordinate – work together in an organised and complementary way so that everyone can do their job more easily and efficiently.

Understanding organisational structures

All organisations need some form of structure. Having specific job roles means each person knows what they are responsible for doing. At a medical practice, for example, there may be doctors, nurses, a practice manager, office staff, receptionists and cleaners. Their responsibilities are different, but together they ensure the practice is run efficiently.

In most businesses, staff are divided into different groups. At your school or college, there are teaching and support staff. The way an organisation is structured depends on its size and type.

Hierarchical structures

Large organisations may have several levels of managers and supervisors. Staff have specific job roles and only carry out tasks related to their own role. There may be fixed rules and procedures and little scope for staff to use creativity and imagination. Examples include the army, local government and large supermarket chains such as Sainsbury's.

Flat structures

Flat structures have only two or three levels, for example a recruitment agency with one manager, several interviewers and a few support staff. Flat structures are used when staff need little supervision. Many creative businesses prefer this structure as staff can exchange ideas more easily.

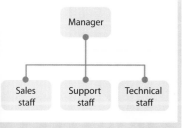

Figure 8.2 Flat organisation structure

Figure 8.1 Hierarchical organisation structure

Matrix structures

This structure is used when a business is involved with major projects such as building hospitals or installing large IT systems. Each project is undertaken by a team controlled by a project leader. All teams are supported by the departments who provide specialised services such as finance and human resources (HR). When a project is completed, the team is disbanded and assigned to a new one.

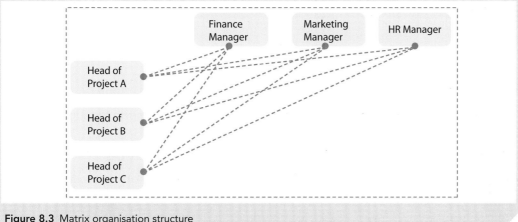

Figure 8.3 Matrix organisation structure

Functional structures

Many organisations are divided into functional areas, each based on one aspect of the organisation's overall purpose, such as finance, marketing or HR, as you will see later in this unit.

In other organisations, some of the main functions may be different and this affects what the areas are called. For example, airport functions include air traffic control, security, retail, catering and baggage handling.

Activity   Identifying different functions

Divide into groups and research the type of functions carried out by hospitals, hotels and newspapers (or magazines). Then compare your results.

Divisional structures

Some businesses structure their operations into different divisions, based on location, type of customers, what they do, or a combination of these.

Many international organisations, for example Kraft Foods, are structured by geographical area, such as the Americas, the Middle East, Asia/the Pacific and Europe. Other businesses focus on their products, for example, Alliance Boots has two divisions: Health and Beauty and Pharmaceutical Wholesale operations.

Just checking

1 What does the term 'organisation structure' mean?

2 Identify four types of organisation structure you may find in business.

3 Describe the main differences between a hierarchical organisation and a flat structure.

Functional areas

Introduction

Many business organisations are divided into functional areas, each specialising in a group of related tasks. Some of these activities are undertaken by all businesses, such as finance, sales and HR, whereas others vary. Only a manufacturer has a production department.

Sales

Businesses earn money by selling goods and services and this is the function of the sales staff. Their responsibilities include:

- meeting or telephoning customers to promote goods and services
- responding to customer enquiries and providing technical information and advice
- preparing quotations or estimates; negotiating discounts or financial terms
- organising sales promotions and other events and keeping customer records up to date.

In what situations is it possible to negotiate a discount?

Production

Production is the key activity of all manufacturing businesses. Some focus on manufacturing the components that are used in the finished product, others assemble the components. Their responsibilities include:

- planning production schedules to maximise the use of available equipment
- producing or assembling the product and checking quality throughout the process to avoid producing any rejects
- resolving any delays or problems
- routinely inspecting and maintaining production machinery.

In groups, research the difference between **job, batch and flow** production processes. Then find an example of each on YouTube. Products could include. crisps, bread, cars, fizzy drinks, submarines, cosmetics, paper, chocolate, glass and cruise liners. You decide which is which!

Purchasing

The purchasing department is responsible for buying materials and components for production, consumables such as stationery and small capital items such as office furniture and computers. Their responsibilities include:

- obtaining raw materials, stock and consumable items from approved suppliers
- evaluating suppliers and negotiating to obtain the best value for the business
- resolving any supply or quality problems and chasing late deliveries
- taking account of customer needs and current fashions and trends in the case of retail buyers (see Zara case study).

Administration

Administrators carry out a variety of support activities in order to help business operations run smoothly. Senior administrators may also monitor budgets and interview new staff for their departments. Their responsibilities include:

- dealing with incoming and outgoing mail and telephone messages; receiving visitors
- organising, storing and retrieving paper and electronic records
- making travel arrangements and organising events such as conferences and interviews
- organising meetings and preparing meetings documents
- preparing and distributing documents by post and electronically.

Customer service

Customer service staff assist customers who have an enquiry, concern or complaint. Customer service staff must be helpful, personable and aware of customers' legal rights. Their responsibilities include:

- providing specialist information and advice about products and services
- responding to complaints and solving customers' problems
- supplying spare parts, arranging for repairs and replacing damaged goods
- giving feedback to departments to improve service and satisfaction
- ensuring the business complies with consumer laws.

Did you know?

- A quotation is a price which the supplier is bound to keep to, but an estimate is an indication of cost which could change.
- The term 'supply chain' is sometimes used to describe each stage of the process from goods leaving a factory to arriving in a store.

Discussion point

Many customer service staff help customers who use the company's website to buy goods. Discuss the additional skills that these staff will need to help customers who are having problems ordering goods online.

Distribution

Distribution ensures that finished goods are delivered to the right place, on time and in the right condition. Their responsibilities include:

- storing and labelling goods correctly before despatch
- completing delivery documents, loading vehicles safely and despatching on an agreed date
- scheduling vehicle routes to minimise overall journey time
- dealing with problems, such as delays due to vehicle breakdown
- completing any required paperwork for shipping goods abroad.

Activity	Delivering just in time

Some manufacturers such as car makers ask for deliveries to be made in a narrow time slot called 'just in time'. This system is designed to keep the stock of components to a minimum. Suggest two benefits of doing this.

Finance

There are two main tasks undertaken by finance: providing information to help managers run the business (management accounting), and keeping accurate records of financial transactions undertaken by the business (financial accounting). Their responsibilities include:

- preparing and sending invoices and checking that correct payments are received
- checking and paying invoices received
- preparing the payroll and ensuring staff are paid correctly and on time
- producing departmental budgets and budget reports
- producing cash flow forecasts and other financial reports
- producing the annual statutory accounts (including the profit and loss account and balance sheet).

Human resources (HR)

Discussion point

Why is it important for businesses to retain good staff as long as possible? How can they do this? Discuss your ideas as a group.

The human resources (HR) of a business are its employees. HR staff are responsible for all aspects of recruitment and training. Their responsibilities include:

- advertising job vacancies and promotion opportunities, dealing with job applications and arranging interviews
- issuing a contract of employment to new staff and arranging induction
- maintaining staff records including leave entitlement and absenteeism due to sickness
- arranging staff training and development activities
- checking health and safety and keeping accident records
- liaising with staff associations or trade unions
- ensuring compliance with current employment legislation.

ICT (Information and Communications Technology)

Even small businesses today have a computer system or network and most also have a website. The ICT department's responsibilities include:

- maintaining current computer systems and software
- advising on and installing updates, upgrades and new equipment and software (including maintaining security against viruses and hackers)
- training and assisting users
- maintaining the company website in conjunction with the marketing department
- operating a backup system so that critical data can be restored quickly.

What other ways can you think of to advertise a product?

Marketing

Marketing is all about identifying and meeting customer needs and promoting products to potential customers. The responsibilities of the marketing department include:

- conducting market research to obtain customer views on products and services
- summarising market research findings to managers and designers
- promoting products and services by advertising and promotional methods (press, TV, online, direct mail, sponsorship and trade shows), and coordinating publicity campaigns
- producing and distributing leaflets and catalogues
- designing, updating and promoting the company website.

Research and development (R & D)

Research, development and design are three stages in bringing a new or adapted product to the market. The responsibilities of people working in this area include:

- identifying future customer needs, and keeping up to date with technological and scientific developments through research
- developing outline drawings together with a model and/or a prototype for any new products
- designing detailed drawings and specifications so that the item can be produced.

Did you know?

- Induction programmes aim to familiarise new employees quickly with the company, what it does and its rules and procedures.

- Beyoncé and Jay-Z applied to patent their baby's name, Blue Ivy, to stop anyone else from using it. Normally patents are used to prevent people copying new product ideas.

- The pharmaceutical (drugs) industry spends billions of pounds on R & D, yet only 1 in 10,000 potential drugs actually reach the market.

Activity — Researching functions

With the agreement of your teacher/tutor, arrange to research functional areas in a local business. Divide into groups and prepare to interview someone who is involved with marketing, HR, finance, ICT and administration. Prepare questions in advance and then present your findings to the rest of the class.

Just checking

1 Why would you find a production department only in some businesses?
2 What is the difference between the sales department and the marketing department?
3 Why is the finance department so important?
4 What is the main function of the HR department?

Purposes of functional areas and links between them

Supporting business aims and objectives

The purpose of functional areas is to ensure that vital business activities are carried out promptly and efficiently so that the business achieves its aims and objectives. Specific areas support certain types of aims and objectives.

- Sales and marketing are involved achieving targets linked to developing new markets or increasing sales.
- R & D and production are involved developing new products and may use feedback from sales, marketing or customer service.
- ICT maintains communication links between different functional areas.
- Finance supports financial targets such as keeping costs low and monitoring budgets.

Links between functional areas

No functional area in a business organisation can work in isolation. In a small firm, people responsible for different functions usually interact informally and on a continuous basis. Sales staff know which customers pay their bills promptly and which ones still owe money. Managers know, without being told, which members of staff are hard-working. A customer query can be answered quickly by asking others in the office for advice. In a larger organisation, people may work in separate areas and rarely meet each other, but they still need information and support to work effectively. The main departmental links in an organisation are shown in Table 8.1.

Table 8.1 Information flows between functional areas

Functional areas	Examples of links with...
Sales	production about delivery dates for customers
	finance about customer credit ratings, discounts or late payments
	marketing about sales promotions
Production	purchasing about raw materials required
	sales if there are delays or production problems
Purchasing	finance to confirm that deliveries are received
Distribution	sales/customer service if there are delivery problems
	finance to confirm deliveries are despatched so invoices can be sent
HR	all departments about staff vacancies and training
	finance about salary increases and bonuses
R & D	production, marketing and customer service about new or adapted products
Finance	all departments about budgets and financial targets
ICT	all departments about maintenance or security
Administration	all departments whenever information is required or to organise meetings between departments.

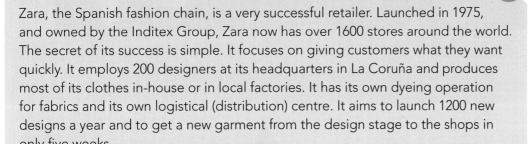

Case study

Zara, the Spanish fashion chain, is a very successful retailer. Launched in 1975, and owned by the Inditex Group, Zara now has over 1600 stores around the world. The secret of its success is simple. It focuses on giving customers what they want quickly. It employs 200 designers at its headquarters in La Coruña and produces most of its clothes in-house or in local factories. It has its own dyeing operation for fabrics and its own logistical (distribution) centre. It aims to launch 1200 new designs a year and to get a new garment from the design stage to the shops in only five weeks.

Zara does not have a hierarchical structure because it wants decisions to be made quickly. This is not possible if there are many levels of managers. Store managers and staff compile new orders quickly, based on demand in their own store. Twice a week, customers can expect new deliveries in the stores, all located in prime locations.

Find out more about the company and see what it would be like to work in one of its stores by visiting Pearson hotlinks. You can access this by going to www.pearsonhotlinks.co.uk and searching for this title.

1 Identify two main aims Zara has.

2 Identify how design, production, distribution and the retail stores all contribute towards achieving Zara's aims and objectives.

3 Unlike many fashion retailers, Zara has not **outsourced** its production to Asia to save money. Instead, it keeps control over its supply chain from design to distribution. What does it gain by doing this?

4 How does Zara's organisation structure benefit **a)** its operations, **b)** its customers?

5 Zara stores are in expensive prime locations, yet it spends less on advertising than most of its competitors. Suggest two reasons for this strategy.

Key term

Outsource – hire an outside firm to do a task, such as distributing goods or installing an ICT system.

Job roles and responsibilities

Introduction

In most large organisations, staff are employed at several different levels.

Figure 8.4 Job roles at different organisational levels

What do people at these levels do?

Table 8.2 Job roles and responsibilities you may find at each level

Job role	Responsibilities	This involves...
Director	Looking after shareholders' interests Deciding **policy** or **strategy**	Deciding where the business is going Agreeing how it should get there Being successful so shareholders get a good return on their investment
Manager	Motivating staff, setting targets Recruiting and dismissing staff Allocating work, communicating Planning and decision making Problem solving	Focusing on the objectives their department must achieve Organising the work to produce the required results Quickly solving any problems that may prevent this
Supervisor and team leader	Managing operatives Motivating staff Allocating tasks	Allocating work and checking it is being done Solving day-to-day problems
Operational and support staff/assistant	Day-to-day general work or clerical duties	Completing tasks on time and to the right quality standards

Impact on roles of different organisational structures

Zara does not want a hierarchical structure because it wants staff to be able to make rapid decisions about stock (see case study). Many retail chains make these types of decision at head office, and this is an example of how organisational structures can impact on different job roles. Other examples are given in Table 8.3.

Table 8.3 The impact of organisational structure on job roles

Structure	Impact
Small firm/ flat structure	Usually informal, all staff may undertake different tasks, be expected to work flexibly and make suggestions. No specific functional areas – staff roles cover main functions required. Owner/ manager undertakes a wide range of tasks and is known to all staff.
Matrix structure	Team members report to team leader who is responsible for the success of a project. Some members may belong to more than one team.
Hierarchical structure	More formal, specific job roles, salary grades and rules. Training programmes provided for staff. Instructions from above are passed on by managers and supervisors. There is less flexibility and permission is required to make major changes.

Did you know?

- The number of staff a manager is responsible for is called their '**span of control**'. Normally this is between eight and twelve. It is easier to supervise staff doing routine operations, such as packing, than complex or varied jobs.
- You can find out about the organisational structure and the responsibilities of different job holders in many large businesses by looking at the careers section of their website.

Assessment activity 8.1

2A.P1 | 2A.P2 | 2A.M1 | 2A.D1

You have been asked to contribute to a local careers exhibition by preparing an information leaflet on functional areas and job roles in business. Your leaflet will also show how the organisational structure can affect job roles and functional areas. You may work in small groups to research specific businesses, but the information leaflet you produce must be all your own work.

Prepare for this task by choosing two contrasting businesses. Find out the titles of their functional areas, the work they do and how they link with each other. Then investigate the organisational structure of each business. You might find it helpful to draw charts to illustrate these. Then investigate two different job roles in each organisation. Make sure they are from different functional areas so they are easier to compare. Find out the responsibilities of each job holder.

- Start your leaflet by explaining the purpose of the different functional areas in each business. If one of your businesses is too small to have functional areas, explain the main functions carried out by different employees.
- Identify and describe the responsibilities of two different job roles in each business.
- In a separate section, compare two job roles and responsibilities. They should be in different functional areas and different businesses.
- For one of the businesses you have investigated, analyse the impact of the organisational structure on both the job roles and functional areas. Use appropriate examples from your research to provide evidence for your conclusions.

Tip

You will find this activity easier if your two businesses are totally different, for example a small charity and a large retailer, or a large manufacturing organisation and a small service provider such as a solicitor or estate agent.

Recruitment

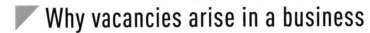

Why vacancies arise in a business

There are several reasons why vacancies arise:

- **An employee leaves:** People may retire, move away from the area or find a job which suits them better, pays more or involves less travel.
- **High staff turnover:** This can happen if working conditions are poor, the hours are long or the wages are lower than at similar companies.
- **Extra work:** As businesses expand, they often need extra staff. This can include managers and supervisors as well as support staff.
- **Sickness:** If staff members are ill and need to stay off work for some time, temporary cover may be needed to ensure their work is done.
- **Different job roles required:** If a business starts to carry out new types of work, then job roles will change.
- **Maternity and paternity cover:** Maternity leave enables expectant mothers to take up to 12 months' leave; new fathers can have up to two weeks' leave. Parents of young children can apply for parental leave. Employers can fill these vacancies on a temporary basis.

Ways of recruiting staff

Businesses can fill a vacancy in several ways:

Jobcentre Plus: This is a government-funded service that accepts job advertisements by phone or email. They focus on helping people who are unemployed to find work.

Consultants: They specialise in filling senior positions that need someone with specialist skills and experience. Some are called 'headhunters' because they try to poach top executives from one company to work for another.

Recruitment agencies: They advertise permanent and temporary vacancies on behalf of their business clients, who only pay a fee if a permanent vacancy is filled. Temporary staff ('temps') are usually paid by the agency which charges the client a higher rate.

From within the business itself: This happens if there are suitable internal applicants who can apply for promotion. The business must still follow a proper recruitment procedure to ensure equal opportunities for all applicants.

Advertising: Many businesses advertise vacancies, which may involve posting them online at sites such as Fish4jobs, or advertising them in a local or national newspaper or relevant trade journal.

Why is it important to ask all candidates the same questions?

Activity Investigating Jobcentre Plus and recruitment agencies

Find out more about Jobcentre Plus by visiting Pearson hotlinks. You can access this by going to www.pearsonhotlinks.co.uk and searching for this title.

Research some recruitment agencies (either locally or online) to find out what kind of vacancies they advertise.

Types of recruitment

The first decision the business must make is whether to recruit from within the organisation (internal), or to look outside (external) for applicants. There are advantages and disadvantages to both methods, as shown in Table 8.4.

Table 8.4 Advantages and disadvantages of internal and external recruitment

Recruitment option	Advantages	Disadvantages
Internal	• Candidates' strengths and weaknesses are known. • Cheaper to advertise. • Vacancy can be filled more quickly. • Staff see that there are opportunities for advancement.	• Only suitable when there is a potential promotion involved. • The person appointed is unlikely to bring fresh ideas to the job. • It still leaves a job to fill within the company as the internal candidate must be replaced.
External	• External person has outside experience and new ideas. • Suitable for basic level jobs where there is no promotion opportunity.	• Not easy to judge applicants – some people are good at selling themselves at interview. • May not fit into the existing team. • May take time to fill vacancy. • New employees may need training.

Cost and legal considerations

• **Cost:** The costs involved depend on the method of recruitment. An agency advertises and carries out preliminary interviews, but charges a fee if they provide a candidate who is appointed. If the business itself carries out the recruitment tasks, costs involve staff time preparing the documentation and interviewing, and paying for press advertising. For some vacancies, travelling expenses may be paid to candidates.

• **Legal considerations:** By law, all applicants must be treated fairly and equally at all stages of recruitment. A business can ensure this happens, by only allowing candidates who meet an essential list of requirements to be interviewed. All applicants must be asked the same questions at the interview.

Activity　　Researching equal opportunities policies

Find out about the equal opportunities policies at your centre to ensure all staff and learners are treated fairly.

Just checking

1 Identify four reasons why a vacancy may occur in a business.

2 Why must all candidates be treated in the same way?

3 Identify two advantages and two disadvantage of filling a job vacancy with an internal candidate.

?　**Did you know?**

• Some businesses are busier at certain times of the year. For example, many retail stores recruit extra staff on temporary contracts over Christmas, and some holiday companies recruit temporary staff over the summer months.

• Online recruitment saves money. Advertisements in the press are expensive, but promoting vacancies on the company website is free.

• In the UK it is unlawful to treat someone differently or unfairly because of gender, race, disability, age, religion and beliefs, sexual orientation or transsexuality.

Job descriptions and person specifications

Introduction

Job descriptions and person specifications help applicants to understand more about a potential job, and therefore help to prevent unsuitable applications that would waste people's time.

Job descriptions and person specifications can be developed in several ways.

- **By department:** Staff in the department where the vacancy arises may prepare a description of what the job entails. This allows departmental staff to contribute ideas and suggestions.

- **By job holder:** The current job holder may list the tasks and duties that are involved. The benefit is that this person will know the job better than anyone, but may exaggerate some of the tasks or duties!

- **By interview:** The job holder may be interviewed to find out what is involved. This enables their views to be considered, but also allows for extra input by a specialist. This is useful if the business wants to change or update the job role.

Contents of a job description

A **job description** summarises the main facts about a job. It helps an applicant to understand exactly what type of work they will be asked to do. An example is shown in Figure 8.5.

SAFETY FIRST LTD – JOB DESCRIPTION	
Job title	Customer Services Team Member
Contract type	Permanent
Location	Main Street, Danesbury DN3 9JL
Description of business	Safety First provides safety equipment and protective clothing.
Purpose of job	To ensure all customers are satisfied with the products and service they receive.
Main tasks	Answering customer queries by phone and email; processing customer orders; informing customers about any issues with their orders; resolving customer problems; processing refunds; updating customer records; liaising with other team members.
Hours of work	37.5 hours per week
Pay and benefits	£12,000 – £13,500 per annum
Promotion prospects	After appropriate training and experience, the successful candidate may be eligible for promotion to Team Leader.
Lines of reporting Responsible to: Responsible for:	Customer Services Team Leader N/A

Figure 8.5 A job description for a customer service team member

Contents of a person specification

A **person specification** lists the essential and desirable qualifications, skills and attributes of the person required. Applicants chosen for interview are normally those who have all the essential requirements and several of the desirable ones, too.

Depending upon the vacancy, the person specification may include information on:

- attainments, e.g. qualifications, membership of professional bodies
- competency profiles, e.g. what the candidate should be able to do
- special aptitudes or skills, e.g. numeracy, problem solving
- essential and desirable attributes, e.g. previous relevant experience and product knowledge, relevant interests
- disposition, e.g. leadership qualities
- circumstances, e.g. whether mobile or not.

SAFETY FIRST LTD – PERSON SPECIFICATION		
Department	Customer Service	
Job title	Customer Services Team Member	
Vacancy no.	474	
	Essential	**Desirable**
Attainments	Educated to GCSE level	Level 2 Business or
	IT literate	Customer Service qualification
Competency profile	Can deal effectively with customers	Able to use database software
	Can contribute to the work of the team	
Special aptitudes	Good communication skills	Good numeracy skills
Disposition	Good organisational skills	Calm and patient
	Friendly personality	

Figure 8.6 A person specification for a Customer Services Team Member

Activity   Identifying attributes

1 In groups, identify two jobs where each of the following attributes would be important: **a)** high level of qualifications; **b)** good at maths; **c)** interest in animals; **d)** ability to travel; **e)** patience; **f)** good IT skills. Compare your ideas.

2 Research job descriptions and person specifications online for vacancies in large companies such as Boots and Marks & Spencer. Expect them to vary in layout and content.

Assessment activity 8.2   Preparation

Research job vacancies that would appeal to, and be relevant to you. You can use printed and online sources, or your own experience if you have a part-time job. Find out as much information as possible about the organisations and how the jobs contribute to the overall purpose of the businesses.

You are working in a business and need to draft an appropriate and detailed job description and person

specification for your chosen job. To encourage effective recruitment, check that the essential and desirable requirements are appropriate for the candidates you want to attract.

Keep your documents safely. You will use them again when you complete Assessment activity 8.2.

Applying for jobs

Introduction

Businesses vary in the way they advertise jobs and in their application process. You may have to request a job description and person specification, or they may be available online. You may be required to complete an application form, or send your CV and a covering letter of application.

Application forms

Although these are important documents, many applicants make careless mistakes, from incorrect spellings to missing out important information. This may mean they are immediately eliminated from the application process.

Table 8.5 Dos and don'ts when completing an application form

Do...	Don't...
… print out (or photocopy) the form to practise on	… complete the original until your practice form is perfect
… read the form through first	… try to do it in a rush
… collect all important information, e.g. examination results, before you start	… guess anything important, such as grades or dates
… check whether you must use a black pen, or can submit the form online	… use an old pen that might put blobs of ink on the form
… check where you should use block capitals	… write your town or postcode in the wrong place
… write neatly and think about what you are doing	… put the current year for your date of birth
… check whether you need to include names of referees	… include someone's name without permission
… use the space for answers wisely	… make any spelling errors
… check where you need to sign and date the form	… complete any section marked 'for official use'
… ask someone to help you check the form	… sulk if they criticise anything
… proofread the form carefully	… cross out errors – use a tiny amount of correction fluid
… make a copy before you post it.	… attend an interview without rereading the form.

Activity   Completing an application form

Many sample application forms are available online. Print one out, complete it and ask your tutor to check you have done it correctly.

Curriculum vitae

A curriculum vitae (CV) is a summary about you and your achievements. It must look professional and be printed on good-quality white A4 paper. It should be quite short – one or two pages at the most – and divided into sections under clear headings to include the following information.

- **Your personal details:** Your name, address, phone number and email address are vital. Your date of birth is optional.
- **Your education:** Put this in date order with your most recent qualification or course first. Include your school or college, dates attended, qualifications obtained, or examinations where you are still awaiting the result.

Activity   Preparing a profile

Some people start their CV with their name and then write a brief personal profile. This short, opening statement summarises their strengths to attract the reader's attention. Read some examples online and try doing it yourself. Then compare statements to see whose are best.

- **Your work history:** This should be in date order, with the most recent job first. Include part-time or temporary jobs you have undertaken, giving examples of your responsibilities.
- **Other useful information:** This makes your CV stand out from the rest. Include any positions of responsibility you have held, hobbies, sports, voluntary work or organisations you belong to, and any other relevant information (such as fluency in a language).
- **Referees:** Many CVs say 'references available on request'. This means if you are offered an interview you will have to provide names. One should be a current teacher/tutor and the other someone who knows how you work, such as a work experience supervisor. Always obtain permission before you give someone's name.

Why is it important to include your hobbies on your CV?

Activity   Creating your own CV

Find out more about CVs on the National Careers Service website by visiting Pearson hotlinks. You can access this by going to www.pearsonhotlinks.co.uk and searching for this title.

Use the CV builder to prepare your own and obtain expert advice if you need it.

Letters of application

Most employers expect you to write a letter of application, to which you will attach your CV. This letter must tempt the reader to read your CV. Your letter should 'sell yourself' to the prospective employer so there must be no spelling, punctuation or grammatical errors.

CONTINUED ▶▶

Activity   Checking Jack's letter

Jack writes a covering letter of application to send to Safety First Ltd. Read the letter on the next page, and then identify where he relates his application to the essential and desirable requirements in the person specification. Could he have done any better? Discuss your ideas as a group.

Other requirements

Most job applicants are expected to produce documents to support their application, for example copies of qualification certificates. They may also need to provide evidence of a CRB (Criminal Records Bureau) check. This lists all convictions held on a person's police record and is essential for anyone working with young people or vulnerable adults.

Pre-application tests

Prospective employers use application forms, CVs and letters of application to assess candidates applying for a job. They may also use other forms of assessment, such as:

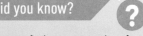

Did you know?

You can find many examples of psychometric tests online if you want to practice.

- **Online psychometric tests:** These use questionnaires to assess a person's knowledge, abilities, attitude and personality traits.
- **Physical fitness test:** This applies to jobs where fitness, strength and stamina are needed, such as the police, fire service and armed forces.
- **Sight test:** Some jobs require first-class vision such as air traffic controllers and driving instructors. Sight tests also check for colour blindness, which is necessary for jobs where colour awareness is important, such as interior designers and personal shoppers.
- **Health checks:** These are often essential for candidates for senior positions where long absences could cause serious problems.

Next steps after applying for a job

When applications are received, they are logged, and once the closing date has passed, they are assessed by HR or a senior manager.

- **Shortlisting** means identifying which candidates meet all the essential requirements and should be interviewed.
- **Invitation to interview or assessment centre:** Shortlisted candidates are invited to attend an interview or an assessment centre where they are tested against criteria for the job.
- **Feedback:** After the interview or assessment, the best candidate(s) for the job(s) are identified and offered the position. Unsuccessful applicants should be given the opportunity to receive constructive feedback on their performance.

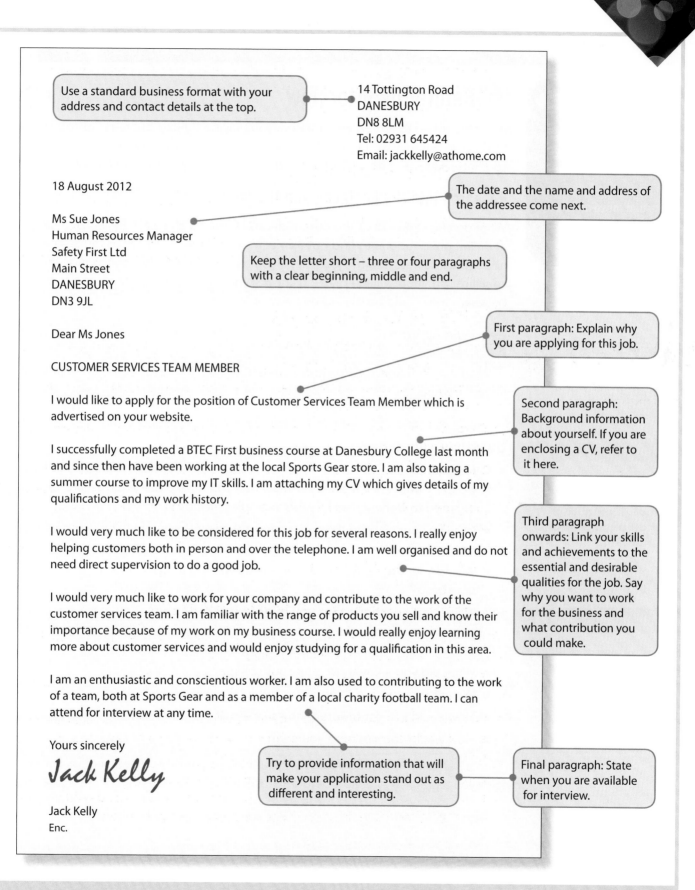

Use a standard business format with your address and contact details at the top.

14 Tottington Road
DANESBURY
DN8 8LM
Tel: 02931 645424
Email: jackkelly@athome.com

18 August 2012

Ms Sue Jones
Human Resources Manager
Safety First Ltd
Main Street
DANESBURY
DN3 9JL

The date and the name and address of the addressee come next.

Keep the letter short – three or four paragraphs with a clear beginning, middle and end.

Dear Ms Jones

CUSTOMER SERVICES TEAM MEMBER

First paragraph: Explain why you are applying for this job.

I would like to apply for the position of Customer Services Team Member which is advertised on your website.

Second paragraph: Background information about yourself. If you are enclosing a CV, refer to it here.

I successfully completed a BTEC First business course at Danesbury College last month and since then have been working at the local Sports Gear store. I am also taking a summer course to improve my IT skills. I am attaching my CV which gives details of my qualifications and my work history.

Third paragraph onwards: Link your skills and achievements to the essential and desirable qualities for the job. Say why you want to work for the business and what contribution you could make.

I would very much like to be considered for this job for several reasons. I really enjoy helping customers both in person and over the telephone. I am well organised and do not need direct supervision to do a good job.

I would very much like to work for your company and contribute to the work of the customer services team. I am familiar with the range of products you sell and know their importance because of my work on my business course. I would really enjoy learning more about customer services and would enjoy studying for a qualification in this area.

I am an enthusiastic and conscientious worker. I am also used to contributing to the work of a team, both at Sports Gear and as a member of a local charity football team. I can attend for interview at any time.

Yours sincerely

Jack Kelly

Try to provide information that will make your application stand out as different and interesting.

Final paragraph: State when you are available for interview.

Jack Kelly
Enc.

Figure 8.7 Jack's letter

Job interviews

⯈ Before the interview

If you are asked to attend an interview, you may be thrilled but nervous too. You want to do well, but may worry because you do not know what to expect or how to impress your interviewer(s). The answer is good preparation so that you can do your best.

Research into the business and the job role

What do you know about the organisation? Have you checked the website and looked at online press reports to find out as much as possible? Find out as much as you can about the business and the job role. If you have received a job description and person specification, these will help. If you know someone who works there, talk to them, but be aware they could be biased one way or another!

Activity	Preparing for interview

Read the WorkSpace case study to see how one HR manager recommends that you prepare.

Questions, questions

- **Questions to ask** should *not* focus on holidays or pay rises. Instead try to fill in any gaps in your knowledge and show that you have done your research and are committed to working hard. Good examples include:
  - ■ I saw on your website that you support the local community by doing various projects. Can all staff get involved with these?
  - ■ Would your organisation support me if I wanted to carry on studying on a part-time basis?
- **Anticipating questions that you might be asked** helps you to have some good answers ready. Usually the first questions are the easiest as these are meant to relax you. Later they will get slightly harder. Typical questions include:
  - ■ What did you enjoy most at school/college?
  - ■ Why did you decide to apply for this job?
  - ■ How could you contribute to the success of this business?
  - ■ How would you describe yourself?

Prepare an answer for each question you think you may be asked and ask someone to give you a practice interview beforehand.

Activity | Deciding on questions for Jack

In groups, decide what questions you would ask Jack if you were interviewing him for the job of Customer Services Team Member at Safety First Ltd. Look back at the job description and person specification for clues. Then compare your ideas with other groups.

Preparing for an interview

Think about your appearance. Remember that the interviewer is probably of your parents' generation, so dress with this in mind. Choose an outfit you like which is comfortable, ideally one that boosts your confidence.

Making sure your clothes are freshly washed and pressed, and check your hair and nails are clean too. Good personal hygiene is essential, and this means having fresh breath too.

Check the day, date and time of the interview, and allow plenty of time to get there. Check where the business is located and the bus or train times. If it is somewhere unfamiliar, do a practice run to find the premises a day or so before.

Behaviour during the interview

Displaying confidence

Experts say that confidence is a state of mind, but this is not much use if you are feeling just the opposite. Instead, focus on the practical.

- Wear clothes that boost your confidence.
- Rehearse so that you are well prepared.
- Remind yourself that an interview is a two-way process. Perhaps you will find out you do not want to work for the company.
- Remember you can only do your best. You cannot control who else has applied.
- Tell yourself an interview is an opportunity to sell yourself to an employer. If they decide not to buy, it is their loss.

Body language

Confident people stand tall and look people in the eye. They have a firm (but not terrifying!) handshake. They sit upright, do not fidget and smile at appropriate times. They send positive signals to people watching them. For an example of confidence in action watch Barack Obama on YouTube.

Tone and clarity of voice

There is no point rehearsing appropriate answers if the interviewer cannot tell what you are saying because you are not speaking clearly. Avoid slang, but speak naturally and don't mutter or shout. Your tone must be respectful, but this does not mean you have to grovel. Just be polite!

Remember that you will feel more confident if you are well prepared.

CONTINUED ▶▶

Active listening

You should pay attention to the questions to make sure that you understand what you are being asked. If you are not sure what the question means, it is better to say, 'I'm sorry, but could you repeat that, please?' than to answer the wrong question.

Showing interest

At the interview, you should use appropriate body language, tone of voice and questions to show that you are very interested in working for the business. The questions you ask can show an in-depth interest in the work involved.

Activity	Using body language

In groups, suggest four ways in which you can show boredom or interest through your body language. Then compare your ideas as a class.

Assessment activity 8.2	*English*	2B.P3	2B.P4	2B.M2	2B.M3	2B.D2

On your own, finalise the draft job description and person specification for the specific job role that you researched earlier. Present these to your class and your tutor, explaining why your documents will encourage effective recruitment. Divide into small groups, decide which of the jobs appeals most to your group, and prepare an attractive job advertisement. Advise applicants to apply by completing an application form and submitting their CV and a letter of application. Then prepare an application form that candidates can complete, and circulate the advertisement to the rest of your class.

1 On your own, apply for one of the advertisements circulated by producing your CV, application letter and completed application form. Prepare a personal statement that justifies how your current knowledge and skills meet those required in the job description and person specification.

2 Prepare a checklist or personal statement that justifies your choice of job by showing how your current knowledge and skills meet those required in the job description and person specification.

3 Research the job role and prepare your responses to possible interview questions. Prepare interview notes in which you analyse any gaps in your knowledge and skills that might require further training or development. Keep these safely.

WorkSpace

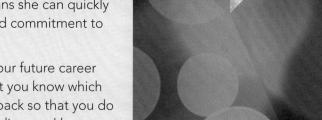

▶ Sonya Clarkson

Head of Employment Services, East Lancashire Hospitals NHS Trust

When Sonya Clarkson's personal circumstances prevented her from going to university, she promptly focused on finding a career she would enjoy. She knew she liked dealing with people, so HR was a natural choice. She obtained a job as an HR Assistant and worked hard, studying part-time for three years to obtain the Chartered Institute of Personnel and Development (CIPD) Diploma and then an MA degree. She steadily climbed the ranks and is now Head of Employment Services for a large NHS Trust. Her experience means she can quickly spot when young candidates have the potential and commitment to build a successful career.

To impress Sonya, you must think carefully about your future career path. Assess your strengths and weaknesses so that you know which skills to develop. Sonya recommends getting feedback so that you do this honestly. Setting career goals for the short, medium and long term means you can seize the right opportunities to help you progress.

Read the job description and person specification for a job carefully and be realistic about whether you have the skills or not. If you apply, then you must be able to justify your claims.

Sonya is always impressed by applicants who ask to speak to her informally to find out more about the job, organisation and team they will be working with.

Finally, Sonya expects interviewees to make an effort to stand out – by preparing well, dressing smartly, being friendly and open, and interested in the job and the organisation.

Think about it

1 How has Sonya demonstrated that she sees setbacks as potential learning experiences and can set realistic goals?

2 Identify two skills that you possess. Then prepare a statement for each that demonstrates that you have applied that skill.

3 Research an organisation that interests you, and prepare two questions you can ask an interviewer to demonstrate your knowledge and to find out more.

Personal audit

Key term

Personal audit – a summary of your knowledge, skills, attributes and interests.

Remember

Sonya Clarkson recommends getting feedback from someone after you have prepared a personal audit to check you have done it honestly.

Personal audit

A **personal audit** is a useful first stage in preparing for employment. It involves assessing your current knowledge and skills, then identifying areas where you are strong and those you need to develop.

Knowledge and skills

You can gain knowledge in many ways. Studying for qualifications is just one. Going to work (either part-time or work experience), or helping out in a family business will increase your knowledge. Similarly, you may travel or learn a language.

Skills may be technical or practical, such as being able to swim, ride a bike, drive a car, draw or use a computer. In business, your communication and numeracy skills are vital. Potential employers will expect you to have proof of knowledge or skills you claim to possess, such as exam certificates and school or college reports.

Interests

Sometimes your interests and leisure activities can be relevant to a job application. Demonstrating team-working skills through sport may be useful for a job, but playing computer games would not normally be relevant, unless you are applying to work in a games shop.

Activity — Carrying out a personal audit

Carry out a personal audit, using the format shown opposite, or using a pre-prepared form provided by your centre. Then discuss your conclusions with your teacher/tutor.

Matching knowledge and skills

Many people apply for jobs with no hope of an interview because they do not have the necessary experience and/or qualifications. All good job advertisements clearly state the essential knowledge and experience required. As an applicant, you need to check you possess these. You may be successful without all the desirable attributes, providing you can persuade the interviewer that you are keen to develop these areas.

You need to match your knowledge and skills to jobs you would like to do in the future. Look at the requirements in advertisements, and then identify the knowledge and skills you need to develop so that you can apply with confidence for the position.

Just checking

1 Identify two benefits of carrying out a personal audit.
2 Why is it useful to identify and list your personal interests?

PERSONAL AUDIT

Name ....   Date ....

KNOWLEDGE
Knowledge gained   **Evidence**

....

....

....

....

SKILLS
Communication skills
Speaking to people face to face   Speaking clearly on the telephone
Listening carefully   Expressing my ideas and opinions
Joining in a group discussion   Persuading other people
Using correct punctuation and spelling Writing clearly and concisely

Technical skills
Using ICT equipment   Using office equipment
Using a range of software   Using the internet
Keyboarding   Producing professional documents

Practical and work skills
Working with details   Punctuality
Finding and correcting own mistakes   Tidiness
Organisational ability   Meeting deadlines
Planning how to do a job   Using initiative to solve problems
Making decisions   Accepting responsibility

Numeracy
Simple calculations   Percentages
Accuracy

INTERESTS

> Identify knowledge you have gained from other sources, such as work experience, e.g. first aid or how to do stock-taking for a retail firm.

> For each skill listed, score yourself from 1–5 where 1 = I am very good at this skill; 2 = I am good, but it could be improved; 3 = I definitely need to improve this skill; 4 = I would have to work hard to develop this skill; 5 = I have not had the chance yet to develop this skill.

> List your interests and identify how each of these has contributed to your personal development.

Figure 8.8 Example of a personal audit form

Career development

Getting started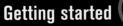

Sonya Clarkson in the WorkSpace case study decided she wanted a career not a job. What is the difference? And does it matter? What is your view?

◢ Information and advice

Many learners have only a vague idea about possible careers. It is all too easy to drift into a job if one comes your way, or to be influenced by family or friends. While their input can be invaluable, there are many other useful sources that can reveal types of work and jobs that you might not have thought about. Your main options are listed in Table 8.6.

Table 8.6 Sources of careers information and advice

Source of advice	Type of advice available
Careers advice services	Most schools and colleges have careers advisers who provide information about career paths. You can also contact a specialist adviser online at the National Careers Service.
Advertisements	You can find job advertisements in newspapers and online. Those in your local paper will identify opportunities in your own area.
Word of mouth	Ask people you know about the work they do, particularly family and friends.
Careers fairs	Here you can visit stands set up by employers and educational establishments to talk about types of jobs and courses.
Teachers/tutors	Your teachers/tutors know about the careers previous learners have followed. They can advise you, knowing your strengths and weaknesses, which is an advantage.
Previous and current employers	You will have your own views about the type of work you are doing. What do you like and dislike about it?
Network connections	Networks are people you know and (sometimes) people they know. They can be useful if there is someone you know who is doing the type of work you are interested in.

Employment and government agencies

Employment agencies such as Adecco, Reed and Kelly Services specialise in finding employees for clients and provide useful advice online. Visit Pearson hotlinks to find a link to the National Careers service website.

You can access this by going to www.pearsonhotlinks.co.uk and searching for this title.

Activity   Researching careers

Check out the Career Tools and the Careers Advice provided by the National Careers Service and find out more about those that interest you.

Developing a career plan

Your career plan is your rough map to the place where you one day want to be. It is 'rough' because you may change your mind several times as you progress. It identifies your aims and ambitions, and helps you to decide which courses to take and to identify opportunities which would give you useful experience. Your options include:

- **Choosing between an academic or vocational pathway:** Academic courses focus on specific subjects such as maths or physics; vocational courses are aimed at particular careers, such as business or engineering. Some are full-time courses; others are designed so that people can learn as they are working, such as apprenticeships which include taking NVQ qualifications.

- **Full- or part-time employment:** Full-time employment means working around 40 hours per week. A part-time job means you could study for additional qualifications in your spare time. Many students in higher education have part-time jobs so that they can earn money.

- **Training needs, development plans, personal targets:**
  - Your training needs relate to the skills you need to develop to work in a certain job or for a particular employer.
  - Development plans identify the activities that would help you to improve your abilities, such as learning a language.

  Personal targets are the aims you set yourself to achieve your needs and plan.

- **Professional and career-specific qualifications:** Most major careers have professional qualifications linked to them (see WorkSpace case study). There are specific qualifications in many professions including accountancy, law, teaching and food hygiene.

Did you know?

- LinkedIn is a social media site where professionals can find and contact each other online.
- If you leave school at 18 and study for a degree, you will be in higher education. If you study after leaving school, but not at degree level, this is called further education.

Discussion point

Some young people offer to work for nothing to get experience in an industry. Is this a good idea or not?

Activity — Designing a career development form

In small groups, design a form for a career development plan. Allow space for your name, date of plan, career aims (short, medium and long term), current strengths, skills and weaknesses, and training/qualification needs (short, medium and long term). Include an action plan (with dates for review). Compare the forms as a class and choose the best one.

Assessment activity 8.3 *English*   2C.P5 | 2C.P6 | 2C.M4 | 2C.M5 | 2C.D3

- Produce a realistic personal career development plan for yourself. This should show evidence of independent research and planning and identify how you would realistically achieve the skills you are currently lacking.

- You have been asked to attend an interview for the job role for which you applied. Attend as requested by your teacher/tutor, and provide appropriate responses to the questions you

are asked. These should show that you have researched the role and have prepared well.

- After the interview, write a report in which you evaluate the suitability of your career plan. Do this by referring back to your interview performance feedback, your own reflection on this, and the gaps in your knowledge and skills that you identified in Assessment activity 8.2. Identify any changes you would make.

Tip

Your career development plan must show evidence that you have researched career paths you are interested in, and identified the qualifications and skills you will need to attain.

Introduction

Marketing is an important activity for all businesses, both large and small. There is usually a direct link between how well a business or brand is marketed and its success. There is no point in producing a product or offering a service that customers do not want, do not understand or do not know exists.

In this unit you will learn about marketing, its importance and the different types of markets that exist. You will consider the importance of branding and how businesses research the market and use the information they find to improve their business prospects. You will explore the components of the marketing mix and the factors that affect this.

You will apply what you have learnt by reading and discussing examples of actual business marketing techniques and strategies. This will help to prepare you for your case study assessment and for working in business yourself in the future.

Assessment: You will be assessed using a paper-based test lasting 1 hour 30 minutes.

Learning aims

In this unit you will:

A explore the role of marketing within businesses

B consider how businesses use market research to make marketing decisions

C explore the use of the marketing mix.

I want to run my own business in the future and am very aware of the importance of marketing. Today consumers can easily compare products and services online so it is hard to compete unless you know what you are doing.

Zak, 16-year-old Business student

Principles of Marketing

9

Principles of marketing

Defining marketing

Getting started

There are many definitions of marketing. These may vary, but most focus on one person. Can you think who this is?

Some people think that marketing is the same as promoting, selling and advertising. It is how potential **customers** know about what you offer.

However, this is only a small part of marketing. You can only sell things that customers want and this means understanding their needs, where they buy and how they find out what is on offer. Therefore any definition of marketing must include several factors.

An American marketing guru, Peter Drucker, thought that, to be successful at marketing, businesses had to think about how their business looked from the customer's point of view. Another, Philip Kotler, thought that marketing meant that a business met its customer's needs whilst making a profit.

Did you know?

Marketing should be at the heart of the business and reflected in everything that the staff do and say to customers.

Activity   Understanding marketing

Most definitions of marketing focus on the customers. Individually, research the below and find the different definitions of marketing they provide.

- The Chartered Institute of Marketing (CIM)
- Philip Kotler.

Visit Pearson hotlinks at www.pearsonhotlinks.co.uk and search for this title to visit the websites for the CIM and for Philip Kotler. You already have an idea of how Philip Kotler defined marketing, but research to find out more.

In groups, think about the above definitions. Look carefully at Kotler's definition. Then suggest four activities marketing involves. Exchange your ideas.

Key terms

Customer – an individual who makes a purchase from a business to use themselves or to give to others.

Market share – the percentage of the total sales of a product accounted for by one company.

The importance of marketing

Businesses undertake marketing activities because they gain several benefits.

Table 9.1 The benefits of marketing

- Helps the business to understand customer needs and develop products to meet these needs.
- Gains/increases **market share**.
- Boosts sales, usually resulting in increased revenue and higher profits.
- Increases brand awareness, recognition and recall.
- Helps to launch new products successfully.
- Enables them to sell in new markets.
- Encourages customer retention and loyalty.
- Builds/enhances the reputation of the organisation.

How businesses use marketing

Businesses use marketing in several ways. These include:

To understand customer needs

Customers can be grouped in several ways and their needs analysed, so that businesses can focus on the needs of their target customers.

To keep ahead of competitors

In a competitive market several suppliers offer similar items. Knowing the actions of competitors means a business can identify how to make its own product or service different or more appealing. This is known as gaining **competitive advantage**.

To communicate effectively with the public

Marketing identifies the most appropriate channels, both offline and online, to reach the target market and keep their attention.

To increase sales and profitability

Reducing prices may increase sales but lower profits. Marketing aims to increase value so that buyers obtain a distinct benefit when they interact with the business or make a purchase. This increases both sales and profits.

Marketing and corporate objectives

The **corporate objectives** state the aims the business wants to achieve. They may include targets such as increasing market share, selling overseas and/or improving customer relations. These corporate objectives affect the content of the **marketing plan.**

SMART objectives

The marketing plan identifies the activities required to achieve the corporate objectives. For example, if an objective is to increase profits by 5 per cent, a marketing objective may be to increase online sales by 20 per cent in the next 12 months.

This is a SMART objective because it is:

- **Specific**: it states an exact, numerical goal related to online sales
- **Measureable**: it can be checked by monitoring online sales figures
- **Achievable**: the target must be possible with the resources available
- **Realistic**: it must be sensible, based on the number of existing online sales
- **Time-based**: it has a deadline date for achievement.

Key terms

Competitive advantage – the advantage gained by offering more superior goods or services than competitors.

Corporate objectives – the actions necessary to achieve the aims set by the business.

Marketing plan – the document which sets out the marketing activities necessary to achieve the business aims.

Did you know?

In most businesses, repeat customers contribute more to profits than new ones – and adding value increases customer loyalty.

Remember

It is important that the marketing plan reflects the corporate objectives.

Link

SMART objectives are covered in *Unit 1: Enterprise in the Business World.*

Remember

It is easier to increase sales by a large percentage if you are starting from a low base point.

Just checking

1 Why do most marketing definitions include the word 'customer'?
2 What does marketing involve in addition to promoting, selling and advertising?
3 Explain why the marketing plan should reflect the corporate objectives.
4 Give three reasons why marketing is important to businesses.

What is a market?

Introduction

A market comprises all the possible customers who might buy a product or service. There are many different types of market and a business must first identify the market in which it is operating.

Types of market

Markets may be identified by product, location, size or type of customer. One important difference is whether you are selling to businesses or **consumers**.

- **Business to Business (B2B)** is selling to industrial buyers or retailers and not direct to the public. Businesses purchase goods for resale, raw materials to make other products and **consumables** and services needed for their day-to-day operations.
- **Business to Consumer (B2C)** is selling to private individuals and households who buy goods and services for their own use, such as clothes retailers and hairdressers.

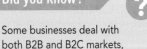

Why is it more likely that this business operates in the B2B market?

Related market activities

The type of market targeted will have a direct effect on the marketing activities that are undertaken.

- **Marketing to business buyers** involves promoting the product at trade fairs, networking with contacts in the industry and talking to potential purchasers face-to-face.

  Business buyers are focused on price and benefits and expect to receive detailed information about a product, see demonstrations or presentations, negotiate discounts and payment terms, discuss delivery, installation and receive after-sales support. The decision to buy may be made by several people and is unlikely to be made quickly.

  Large retail buyers only purchase products that link with their reputation and image, or that can provide additional or different benefits to their customers.

- **Marketing to consumers** involves persuading people to purchase (this decision may be made on impulse), carrying out market research to find out about customer wants and buying habits, promoting a brand, identifying the benefits and communicating this to potential customers through targeted advertising and promotions that are appropriate to the product.

  A business needs to provide excellent customer service to enhance its reputation and operate a returns policy that reflects this.

What incentives do stationery providers like Staples offer to business buyers?

Activity   Give it a name!

Jarrad has invented a new type of play dough which he calls 'dough ball'. It doesn't stick to fabric or dry out, and unless it's rolled together, colours can be separated.

Work in groups to come up with a better name for Jarrad's invention. Then identify the factors he must consider before deciding whether to sell direct to other businesses, such as supermarkets and toy shops, or direct to consumers, and the advantages and disadvantages of each method.

You can look at the British Toy and Hobby Association website for ideas. To do this, visit Pearson hotlinks at www.pearsonhotlinks.co.uk and search for this title. Then compare your suggestions.

CONTINUED ▶▶

Different types of markets

Consumers and customers

If you market to consumers, it is useful to know who these are, and how they differ from customers.

- **Consumers** are the individuals or groups who use (consume) different items. They are the end user, such as the child who plays with Jarrad's dough ball.
- **Customers** are those people who actually make a purchase. They may be a private individual, such as the parent or grandparent who buys a dough ball, or a business, such as the toy shop or supermarket that bought it direct from Jarrad to sell to the end user.

Activity	Identifying features

Jarrad must think about the features that will help him sell his product. Make a list of those which will be most important to a store and those which will be most important to consumers and customers. Compare your ideas.

Goods and services markets

Some businesses produce or supply goods, while others offer a service to their customers. Some do both. A hairdresser provides a service but may also sell hair and beauty products in the salon.

Did you know?

Convenience goods are inexpensive items we buy often such as chocolate, milk and magazines. Durable goods are those that last such as televisions and furniture.

What features do nail bars stress when they market their services to consumers?

- **Goods markets** relate to buyers and sellers of different products, from crisps to computers. These can be sub-divided into different types, such as convenience goods, durable goods and luxury goods.

- **Services markets** relate to the sales of different types of services, from hotels to nail bars. These can be sub-divided, for example into financial services, personal services and business services.

Capital and consumer goods markets

Only businesses buy capital goods. An example of a capital good is the machine that makes the tubs into which Jarrad puts his dough balls, or the machine that makes the dough. The dough itself is a consumer good.

- **Capital goods** are used to make another product.
- **Consumer goods** are items bought from a shop or online store for, or by, an end user.

Mass and niche markets

You already know that a 'market' represents all the possible consumers for a product or service. Some large producers aim to produce items that will appeal to everyone, whereas some small firms do exactly the opposite.

- The **mass market** is the largest market possible for an item, without any allowances for income, personal interests or preferences. Mass market clothing retailers include Next and Marks & Spencer.
- A **niche market** is a much smaller market for a specialist product which takes into account specific needs. For example, Long Tall Sally is a niche retailer because it specifically stocks clothes for tall women.

What benefits do niche markets offer to suppliers?

Market and product orientated businesses

Businesses vary in their reason for making a new product.

- **Market orientated** businesses identify the needs and wants of their prospective customers and then make their product to meet these. An example is the Glo-Clock seen in Unit 1 which was developed to meet the needs of parents.
- **Product orientated** businesses focus on their areas of expertise to produce innovative items. Examples include the Dyson bladeless fan and Apple's iPad.

Discussion point

Gillette regularly launches new razors. Is this because it is fulfilling customer needs, further developing successful products, or both? Look at its latest advertising online before you answer this.

CONTINUED ▸▸

Business models

The business model is how the business makes money and/or adds value, as you saw in Unit 1. There are three basic types: the sales, advertising and marketing model. The main features of each are summarised below.

Table 9.2 Features of the different types of business model

Type of model	Focus	Feature	Examples
Sales model	The focus is on selling goods that have already been produced or a 'no frills' service. Sales may be door-to-door, by catalogue, online, party plan or by phone.	Revenue comes from sales or commissions. The aim is to maximise sales by making items freely available or low priced and offering incentives to encourage the customer to buy.	Skype, Amazon, Avon, Kleeneeze, Ryanair, Primark, H&M, eBay, EAT
Advertising model	The focus is on earning revenue from advertisers because they will benefit from the link.	Revenue comes from other businesses advertising and promoting their goods and services. Many bloggers make money this way.	Commercial radio stations, Google, ITV, Sky, Facebook, London Evening Standard, Mumsnet, YouTube
Marketing model	The focus is on relating to customers and responding to their needs.	Revenue is enhanced by the relationship between the brand and the consumer. The business aims to be responsive to customer needs and engage with the customer in other ways, such as sponsoring community and social events.	Nike, John Lewis, Kelloggs, Cadbury, Virgin, Honda UK, M&S, Boots, Red Bull

What types of goods are suitable for selling door-to-door?

Business orientation and choice of model

A product orientated business is more likely to operate a sales model. The goods are produced and the income of sales staff is often related to the number of sales. A business which is customer focused will be more likely to operate a marketing model.

Most businesses do not choose just one model. Many operate a hybrid. For example, ASDA and Tesco focus on cheap prices and want high sales, but also use focus groups, analyse sales to decide which items to stock and sponsor different projects. Most newspapers and magazines receive money from advertisers *and* also charge people who make a purchase.

A business can also change its model. Facebook has only recently started to make money through advertising.

Within these broad categories there are also other options, such as the 'bait and hook' model where the product is cheap to tempt the purchaser, but subsequent add-ons are expensive. This was started by Gillette, which sold cheap razors with expensive blades. Many printer firms copied this idea, charging high prices for cartridges. Today many apps are sold in this way, especially those featuring virtual worlds.

Activity   Investigating brand activities

As a brand, Red Bull is incredibly effective at marketing. They partnered with Felix Baumgartner to envision, develop and execute the Red Bull Stratos project that saw the Austrian freefall from 24 miles above earth, breaking the sound barrier.

Without Red Bull's lead role as a driver of the mission, including sourcing an expert team and using their own communications and moving image team to promote the event, this scientific project would not have taken place – or been shared with a global audience.

In groups, research two or three famous brands of your choice and find out about their sponsorship and community activities. Then summarise how you think this helps the brand to develop customer relationships.

Principles of branding

◢ The distinctive nature of branding

Branding separates the business, product or service and makes it stand out from its competitors. This makes it easier to sell in a new market and easier for customers to recognise in an established market.

◢ The different dimensions of a distinctive brand

A brand is not just a name. It is everything associated with it – from the price and quality to the image and the feeling customers get when they think about the brand.

Consistency is vital. Whether the brand is focused on luxury, quality, fun, reliability or value for money, all the elements associated with it must reinforce that image to the customer.

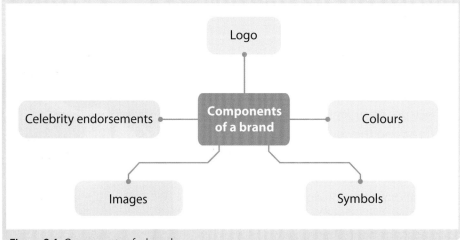

Figure 9.1 Components of a brand

- A **logo** makes the brand instantly recognisable. The distinctive lettering used is called logotype, e.g. IKEA, Argos and Google.
- **Symbols** can be used instead, e.g. Hello Kitty, Apple, BMW and Twitter. Other brands combine a symbol with logotype, e.g. British Airways and BP.
- **Colours** make the brand instantly recognisable on a retail display, and the colours themselves can reflect the image. Broadly, black, gold or silver denote luxury; green reflects nature; yellow links to sunshine; white to cleanliness and red/orange to speed or danger.

Activity   Identifying logos and symbols

The black horse of Lloyds Banking Group would give a different impression in jazzy stripes! In groups, identify six logos or symbols and suggest the colour significance. Then find out why McDonald's changed its colour scheme from red and yellow to green in Europe but not in America.

- **Images** are visual representations used by the brand. Flawless skin is an essential image for skincare products. Banks show friendly staff to imply they are customer focused. Often the same images are used on packaging, leaflets, point-of-sale displays and in advertisements.
- **Celebrity endorsements** add value, for example most people associate Walkers Crisps with Gary Lineker and when Cheryl Cole endorsed L'Oréal's Elnett hairspray, sales increased by 14 per cent. Smaller businesses can gain too. Myfirstyears.com gained valuable free publicity by sending free gifts to celebrities with new babies, including Mo Farah, Danni Minogue and Sir Elton John.

The benefits of building brands

Building a brand provides several benefits for a business:

- **Value** is added through increased recognition and customer loyalty. Brand lovers will pay more to get their preferred brand which gives the brand a value. Premier Foods received £41 million for Sarson's Vinegar when it sold the brand. Marketing costs can be reduced because loyal customers make repeat purchases and often promote the brand to others on Facebook and Twitter.
- **Brand personality** endows it with human attributes and is reflected in how people 'feel' about the brand. This can be reinforced by the brand itself. Churchill Insurance uses a bulldog to characterise solidity and strength. Pixar is seen as clever, young, creative, lively and inquisitive, and their use of an animated lamp, Luxo, in their logo adds to this.
- Strong brands can spread their image to other products more easily and cheaply.
  - **Brand extensions** are new or adapted products, for example Mars and Galaxy went from chocolate bars to ice cream and Ariel from washing powder to stain remover.
  - **Brand stretch** is when unrelated products are added. Caterpillar started making bulldozers and now makes boots, toys and clothing!

Activity   Assessing brands

1   A good test of the distinctive nature of branding is to write down what you associate with each of the following brands and to compare your ideas:

Adidas; Apple; Halifax; Mini Cooper; Blackberry; GHD; Nokia; Ted Baker; Spotify; Topshop; Starbucks.

2   In groups, identify the different dimensions related to each brand and suggest how these link to its personality.

3   List **two** brands you admire and **two** you do not. Be prepared to give reasons to support your opinion.

? Did you know?

When sales at Mothercare fell, the company recruited Jools Oliver to promote her own range of children's clothes at the stores.

💬 Discussion point

When Brad Pitt promoted Chanel No 5, the script was criticised and spoof versions were posted on YouTube. Was this bad for Chanel or is there no such thing as bad publicity?

? Did you know?

You can find out why Caterpillar footwear 'fits' the caterpillar image on its website. You can also find examples of failed brand extensions on The Market Hipster website. To do this, visit Pearson hotlinks at www.pearsonhotlinks.co.uk and search for this title.

Researching the market

Introduction

Researching the market means investigating the needs of today's customers, what similar items competitors offer and what gaps exist for new products and services. It also means evaluating new ideas to see if they are feasible, and assessing whether the business has the skills or abilities to meet the challenge. The first step is to obtain relevant data.

Types and sources of data

There are different types and sources of data.

Primary and secondary data

- **Primary data** is obtained from customers themselves. Methods include interviews, questionnaires, analysing sales records and focus/feedback groups.

- **Secondary data** is published information that already exists or another organisation has obtained. This includes electoral rolls, newspaper reports, articles in trade journals and online sources. Obtaining secondary data is known as **desk research.**

Quantitative and qualitative data

- **Quantitative data** involves numbers, such as sales figures, the numerical analysis of a survey and statistics taken from published reports issued by government departments and the Office for National Statistics and by firms such as Mintel and Keynote.

- **Qualitative data** explains why people hold certain views. Their opinions may be found through interviews, focus groups and surveys designed to find out more precisely what people think.

The uses of different types of data

Quantitative and qualitative data

Most businesses obtain both types of data when they are carrying out research. This data should enable them to

- **Understand trends and make predictions**: Some markets grow over time, others are static and some shrink in size. For example, tablet sales are growing, laptops are fairly static and desktop sales are falling. Trends can also relate to lifestyle and population changes. Today there is greater demand for beauty treatments and casual/sports clothing as well as health supplements and holidays for the over 50s.

- **Identify areas of interest or gaps in the market**: These will depend upon the product or service offered and what customers usually buy. Market reports help to identify emerging customer needs that are not currently satisfied.

 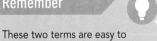

Internal and external data

Internal data is collected by the business itself such as stock figures, customer data and customer feedback. Past sales data, for example, can be used to analyse which stock sells the best and should be reordered, and which should not. External data includes market trends, competitor information and customer spending habits generally. Both types are used for:

- **benchmarking against competitors**, which is a way of comparing one business with others on certain issues. For example, by checking a competitor's website, you could see whether their product range, prices, delivery charges and customer return policies were better, or worse, than yours

- **producing a SWOT and PESTLE (situational analysis)**, which are two different ways in which a business can examine its own position in the market. They let businesses assess how they could be affected by future trends and developments and then work out their possible response.

◤ The use and benefits of situational analysis

- A PESTLE analysis focuses on outside forces (see Topic B.3).
- A SWOT analysis identifies the Strengths and Weaknesses in the business itself, as well as the Opportunities and Threats in the market. It is usually completed after doing a PESTLE analysis, as you will see in Topic B.3.

> **🔑 Key term**
>
> **Situational analysis** – when a business looks at its own position in the market and assesses how it could be affected by trends and developments.

> **❓ Did you know?**
>
> To match their competitors and increase sales, many online retailers have added 'click and collect' and 'next day delivery' to their services.

Activity Researching data for Petra

Research relevant information on cheese and frozen yoghurt.

- Group 1 should investigate the information available from Mintel, Key Note and IBISWorld.

- Group 2 should study the *Food Statistics Pocketbook*, published annually by Defra and available online.

- Group 3 should study *Dairy Statistics: An insider's guide* (also available online).

- Group 4 should search on Google for trends and analysis in cheese/frozen yoghurt industry.

Compare your findings and decide how this could help Petra.

NOTE: Although Mintel, Key Note and others charge for specialist reports, you can find out a lot about market trends by reading their blogs and press releases.

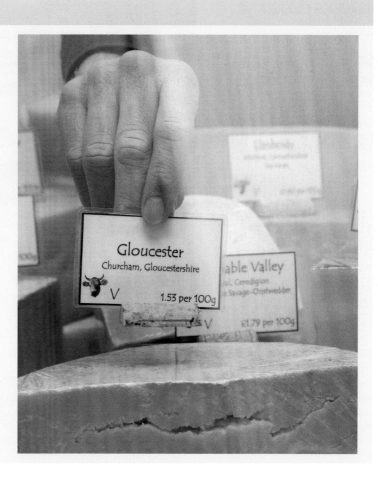

Using market research in businesses

Understand the purpose of research and analysis

The purpose of market research is to help a business answer the following questions:

- Who are we selling to?
- What do they want to buy and who else provides it?
- When and where do they want it, and how much are they prepared to pay for it?
- Is this market growing or declining and how easy will it be to enter it?

These issues are the focus of this section.

Identifying target markets

A business should start by identifying its **target market**, that is, the specific group of customers the business aims to supply. As customers have different wants and needs, most markets include different **market segments**. These are sub-groups of people or organisations that share certain characteristics which lead them to have similar needs. For example, the soap market includes baby soap, liquid soap, budget soap, antiseptic soap, luxury soaps, and so on – all targeted at different groups of customers.

Why do famous brands like Elvive make so many varieties of shampoo?

A useful step is to build up a profile of the **target customer**. This information may include:

- Personal factors, such as age, gender, culture, occupation, income, family size, lifestyle and leisure activities.
- Location.
- Attitude to price.
- The products currently available and used by these customers.
- The products currently offered often have strengths and weaknesses. By analysing these, it may be possible to identify a **gap in the market** which can be filled either by changing the product or service, offering it in a different way or using different distribution channels.

Identifying competitor activity

Businesses usually want to stay ahead of their competitors. To do this they need to identify their key competitors and observe their behaviour. This can be done by studying their website, visiting the premises, talking to their customers, analysing their advertisements, looking at their displays and promotional materials and reading press reports on their activities.

There are usually three steps to analysing competitors and their activities:

- Identify and list the main competitors.
- Summarise the key points about them, for example their location, types of products, quality, customer service features, advertising and promotional methods used.
- Identify their strengths and weaknesses from a customer's point of view.

A business should then look for new initiatives or good ideas that can be adapted or improved. This may include offering to a broader range of customers or to those whose needs are not currently met by the competition.

Always ensure that your new gap in the market actually meets a customer need.

Understanding consumer behaviour and motivations

Customers are motivated to make a purchase to fulfil a need. Understanding the factors that influence a customer's behaviour and trigger a decision to buy helps a business to find the best ways to appeal to its customers.

Many of our needs are basic; if you are hungry, you need food, and if you are cold, you need warmth. Higher level needs relate to aspects such as our social needs, our egos and our ambitions. If you are short of money, you will focus on meeting your basic needs. If you have money left over, you can spend this on meeting your other needs, but these vary greatly according to personal preferences.

Businesses need to know why, how and where their customers buy, how much they spend, what else they buy and what they ignore. They need to find out how their business plans and practices fit with the needs and wants of customers, what customers think of the business and what it offers, or plans to offer.

? **Did you know?**

All customers are influenced by various factors in their life, including their income, personality, friends and family, lifestyle, interests, culture and previous experiences.

CONTINUED ▸▸

Table 9.3 Descriptions of some of the methods companies use to find out information

Focus groups	Used to generate new ideas or find out opinions about new proposals or the business itself. Members may meet or be asked their views online.
Customer panels	Formed to represent a typical cross-section of customers, they meet regularly to give feedback on products, services and other relevant business aspects.
Mystery shoppers	Hired to visit the business anonymously and then give feedback on their experience and the information they were given by staff.
Observation	Store managers/supervisors observe customer behaviour, in particular which displays/products attract attention and which do not, how long customers stay in the store or in a particular area, which products they purchase.
Foot counting	Checking the number of people who come or visit is used to test the popularity of an event, peak times of activity and the most popular areas visited.
Analysing customer data	Customer data and sales records can be analysed to identify patterns of spending and used to build up customer profiles. This is a major advantage of operating loyalty programmes such as Tesco's reward card as all spending can be tracked and monitored.
Surveys	Market research companies such as YouGov ask people's opinions and publish their findings.

Did you know?

Some businesses specialise in profiling customers by collecting data on their behaviour and then classifying them into different groups to predict future behaviour and buying habits. An example is Dunnhumby, which works with Tesco and other brands.

Remember

Businesses should analyse how their current business practice fits with the identified needs and wants of their potential customers and assess customer reactions to future proposed offerings.

Activity   Investigating customer profiling

Divide into two groups to find out more about the ACORN system of classification and Experian's Mosaic UK classification. To access the websites for this, visit Pearson hotlinks. You can access this by going to www.pearsonhotlinks.co.uk and searching for this title. Then summarise the main benefits of using profiling techniques to analyse customer behaviour.

Identifying market trends

Market research can be used to identify the key components of a market and to assess whether there are opportunities, or whether it is a **saturated market** or declining and not worth entering.

- **Value:** this shows the size of the market and how much people spend. It is usually given in government and commercial research reports and available from many trade associations. For example, according to Mintel, in the UK people spent £1.4 billion going to the cinema in 2011. This information is useful to film makers, cinema chains, advertisers and competitors such as television companies.

  However, data on markets is often sub-divided or segmented by area or product and this will be more relevant to some businesses. A Hollywood film company would want to know about global attendance figures, whereas a small business thinking of advertising at the cinema would only want local attendance figures.

- **Market growth rate:** some markets are growing rapidly, others slowly and some are static or declining. This can be assessed by obtaining data over several years as well as looking at the success – or otherwise – of businesses that operate in the market. Mintel forecasts that UK cinema attendance could grow to £1.6 billion by 2017. This information is used by cinema chains when they are assessing whether to invest in new cinemas or extra facilities.

- **The level of competition:** this means finding out the number of direct competitors and checking what they offer. In the UK, the main cinema chains are Vue, Odeon and Cineworld. They can find out about each other from their websites, from visiting each other's premises and from company reports. Each will want to differentiate their own business in some way.

- **The number of products in the market:** this information can be found by checking the products or services offered. It is usually easier for small businesses to enter a niche market where there are only a few specialised products or suppliers. It is even better to be first to market with a new or different product which will boost sales. For example, cinema attendances increased when 3D films were first launched.

Key term

Saturated market – a market which is full of similar products which now have little value to consumers.

Discussion point

A recent newspaper report claimed that cinemas are dying out and in ten years' time all films will be watched at home as downloads. As a group, decide what research on the market you would carry out to confirm or contradict this claim.

Just checking

1 What is meant by the term 'target market'?

2 What type of secondary data would be useful for assessing market trends?

3 List four ways in which businesses can use research to find out about customer behaviour.

The value of market research to businesses

▶ Interpreting key research findings

Market size

Most markets are quite complex and can be calculated in different ways.

- **By value** – Liam could find out total sales of the UK coffee market.
- **By product/brand** – Liam could find out which are the most popular brands and if the market is segmented at all, so that he can find information more relevant to his own situation.
- **By customer** – Liam could investigate customer behaviour and spending habits.

Market growth

Market growth is important but rates vary. Liam could check the percentage change over time to identify whether growth is fast or slow. There are implications related to both fast and slow growing markets.

- **A fast-growing market** offers opportunities for higher sales, greater sales revenue and more profit. This can attract powerful producers which can drive prices down. They can afford greater investment, making it harder for small firms to compete.
- **A slow-growing market** offers less immediate reward but involves fewer competitor challenges. Products can evolve based on customer feedback and new technological developments. The focus can be on quality and prices are probably more stable.

Market share

This is usually the percentage of the total sales of a product accounted for by one company but is sometimes calculated by the number of outlets. Liam may want to find which companies have the largest market share and why they are so popular.

Why is it important to research market growth before launching a new product?

Table 9.4 Benefits of different levels of market share

Benefits of a high market share	Benefits of a lower market share
More sales will result in increased profits especially if marketing and production costs per unit are less.	The focus can be on specialist products which may be sold at a premium price.
Brand recognition increases, which contributes to higher sales.	The business is not seen as a threat by larger suppliers who may otherwise try to undercut its prices.
Powerful companies can obtain supplies at lower cost because they buy in bulk.	The business can selectively advertise and promote its products to its target market.
If the market is static, increasing market share enables a business to increase sales revenue.	Additional expenses related to expansion (e.g. more buildings or equipment) can be avoided.

The desirability of different levels of market share

Most large firms aim for a high market share but there are advantages in operating at a different level. For example, many small independent coffee shops are thriving.

PESTLE analysis

Businesses also need to research data relating to the wider environment to find out about issues that might affect them. This is normally obtained for six key areas, known as PESTLE. Each letter stands for a key area to investigate.

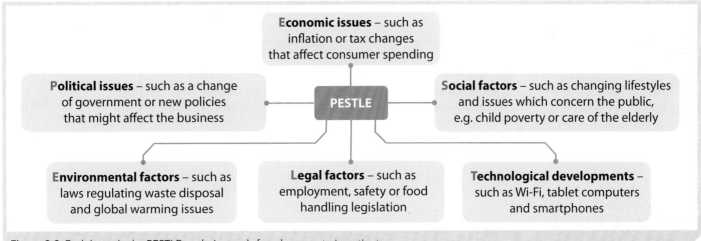

Economic issues – such as inflation or tax changes that affect consumer spending

Political issues – such as a change of government or new policies that might affect the business

PESTLE

Social factors – such as changing lifestyles and issues which concern the public, e.g. child poverty or care of the elderly

Environmental factors – such as laws regulating waste disposal and global warming issues

Legal factors – such as employment, safety or food handling legislation

Technological developments – such as Wi-Fi, tablet computers and smartphones

Figure 9.2 Each letter in the PESTLE analysis stands for a key area to investigate

Case study

You have agreed to research and analyse the data Liam needs. In groups, carry out the following activities and then present your findings to the rest of the class.

1 Read the extract from the Project Cafe 12 report below, then summarise the key facts that Liam needs. Justify your choice and state how Liam could use the information.

2 Liam wants his coffee shop to be special. Research the market further to identify factors that customers value about coffee shops (particularly independents) before you advise him.

3 Research the potential for different locations in your own area. Then justify your choice.

4 Research the data for a PESTLE analysis and summarise the key factors you find.

Extracts from Allegra UK Project Café 12

The value of the total coffee market in the UK was £5.8 billion. This covers branded chains, non-specialists and independents. By 2017 these sales could reach £8 billion from over 20,000 outlets.

In 2012, total sales for branded chains were £2.34 billion – up from £2.1 billion in 2011 and more than twice the size of the market in 2005. By 2017, branded sales could reach £3.8 billion. This group includes well-known coffee shops with the highest market shares – Costa Coffee with 28%, Starbucks 18% and Café Nero 9% – and food-focused outlets such as Pret A Manger, EAT and Greggs. Non-specialist operators include department store cafés, supermarket cafés and pub chains. Their sales amounted to £1.77 billion in 2012 and sales by independents were £1.69 billion.

More than 600 new coffee outlets opened in the UK during 2011. Allegra predicts this growth will continue and for branded chains to exceed 7,000 outlets by 2017. High quality independent coffee shops are thriving, too, though weaker outlets are not. One in 10 adults now visits a coffee shop daily. In 2009, they spent £3.50. This fell to £3.18 in 2011 but increased to £3.77 in 2012.

The most critical consideration for any successful operator is location. Second is quality of coffee and food. Other factors include ambiance and atmosphere of the environment, food choice, beverage choice, service and barista skills.

Information provided courtesy of Allegra Strategies Ltd

The 4 Ps of the marketing mix

Introduction

The marketing mix consists of all the elements a business must consider to sell its products or services successfully. It is called a 'mix' because these elements (like ingredients) can be changed to achieve different results. This is often essential because demand may fall as new products come on the market or customer tastes change.

Key terms

Core product – the basic product designed to meet user needs.

Augmented product – the core product plus additional benefits or services.

Unique Selling Point (USP) – a special feature of a product (or service) that makes it easy to promote and sell.

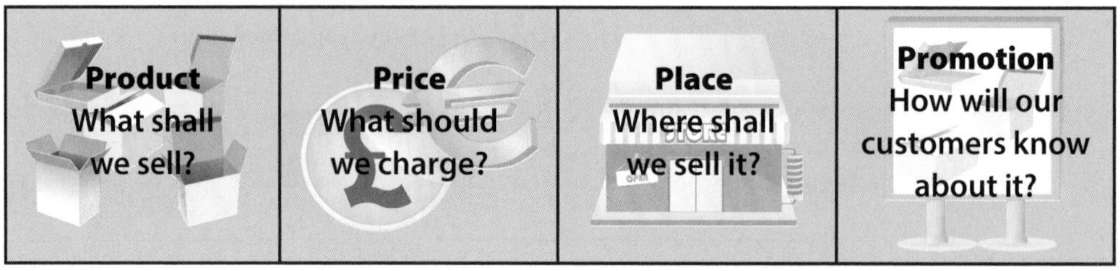

Figure 9.3 The 4 Ps of the marketing mix

Did you know?

To be successful, businesses must continually change or reinvent themselves. This is why Apple has released an iPad mini, and Argos now focuses on online sales and click and collect, rather than its traditional catalogues.

Product

The product refers to the goods or service that is offered. It should be something customers want to buy because it meets their needs. Ideally a new product will fill a gap in the market, preferably in an area where sales are growing.

Core and augmented product

- The **core product** is the basic product, such as a smartphone or computer.
- An **augmented product** is one with 'extras' that make it even more desirable, for example guarantees, warranties or superb quality.

Did you know?

A product that has something 'extra' and stands out from its rivals is even more desirable. This is known as product differentiation.

Unique Selling Point (USP)

The **Unique Selling Point (USP)** is the major aspect of a product, service or brand that makes it easy to promote and sell. For example, the Dyson Airblade hand-dryer is the fastest, most hygienic dryer on the market so it is very attractive to buyers. Service providers can also have a USP by offering extras, such as a hairdresser who offers evening appointments or operates a loyalty scheme with discounts for regular customers.

Activity — Finding USPs

Both small and large businesses need a USP. Check out the most watched entrepreneurs on *Dragon's Den*. To do this, visit Pearson hotlinks at www.pearsonhotlinks.co.uk and search for this title. In each case, identify the USP that made them special.

Product life cycle

All markets and products have a life cycle which means there is a starting point and, at some stage, an end point. In some markets, such as bread, the life cycle may be hundreds of years, but often it is much shorter than this.

A business should locate the life cycle position of each of its products or services. At the saturation or decline stage, businesses may decide on an **extension strategy** to renew interest in the product. This was why Nintendo launched the WiiU in 2012, six years after the Wii when sales and interest had fallen. Another option is to go for 'retro' appeal, as BMW did with the Mini relaunch, or to sell in new markets (e.g. overseas) where the product may still be a novelty.

Key terms

Extension strategy – a plan to revive sales by adapting a product or launching in new markets.

Product portfolio – the range of products produced by a business.

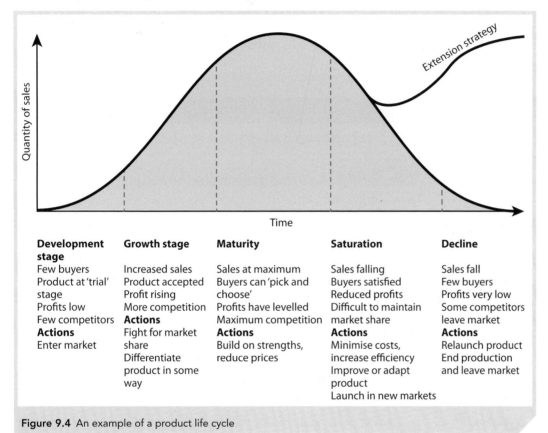

Figure 9.4 An example of a product life cycle

Remember

The products in the portfolio should complement each other or fit the image and/or specialities of the business. So Heinz shouldn't make vacuum cleaners and Dyson shouldn't make soup.

The life cycle diagram shows Quantity of sales (y-axis) against Time (x-axis), with an Extension strategy curve extending from the decline. The stages below the graph are:

Development stage
Few buyers
Product at 'trial' stage
Profits low
Few competitors
Actions
Enter market

Growth stage
Increased sales
Product accepted
Profit rising
More competition
Actions
Fight for market share
Differentiate product in some way

Maturity
Sales at maximum
Buyers can 'pick and choose'
Profits have levelled
Maximum competition
Actions
Build on strengths, reduce prices

Saturation
Sales falling
Buyers satisfied
Reduced profits
Difficult to maintain market share
Actions
Minimise costs, increase efficiency
Improve or adapt product
Launch in new markets

Decline
Sales fall
Few buyers
Profits very low
Some competitors leave market
Actions
Relaunch product
End production and leave market

Product portfolio

A **product portfolio** is the range of products offered by a business, such as all the Heinz varieties of food products. Many businesses offer more than one because:

- products have different life cycles. The business must replace or revamp products in decline to keep overall sales high
- some products are more successful than others, so it is risky to depend upon the sales of one item alone. Having several products reduces this risk
- offering related products or services can increase revenue, such as a hairdresser selling beauty products or opening a nail bar in the salon
- they want to broaden their target market. Currys sells both household appliances and electronics to broaden its appeal to more customers
- they want to extend the brand. Tesco has increased its product portfolio to include banking, insurance, mobile phone services and petrol.

Activity

Identifying disadvantages

A large product portfolio is not always a good thing. Work in groups to identify the dangers of this approach. Discuss your ideas as a class.

CONTINUED ▶▶

Discussion point

Deciding the right price is vital. If you set it too low, you may fail to make potential profits, but if it is too high, people may think you are too expensive and go somewhere else. So how do you decide what to charge?

Key term

Pricing strategies – alternative methods of deciding the best price to charge.

Did you know?

A loss leader is a product sold below cost for a short time to boost sales or market share.

What is the advantage to a business of offering products on sale for a set period of time?

▸ Price

Pricing strategies

Producers have several options when deciding what price to charge. These are called **pricing strategies.** The best one will depend upon the type of product and the competition. There are two main options:

1 **Focus on costs**: this is possible when the customer considers aspects such as skill and expertise, not just price. It is often used by tradesman, such as decorators, who calculate the cost of their materials and time before working out how much to charge the customer.

2 **Focus on the market**: this is important in a competitive market, when the business wants to attract customers away from its rivals.

Table 9.5 Pricing strategies

Focus on costs	
Cost plus pricing	Calculate how much the product costs to make. Add on a percentage profit.
Mark-up pricing	Calculate how much the product costs to make. Add on a percentage mark-up.
Focus on the market	
Competitive pricing	Check the price that competitors charge, ask about the same. This is used by supermarkets and mass market clothes shops.
Price taking	Check the 'going' price and ask exactly the same. This is used for identical products that customers can compare, such as eggs or tomatoes on market stalls.
Skimming	Ask a high price at the start to take advantage of the 'novelty' value. This is often used for high tech products, such as blu ray and 3D televisions.
Penetration pricing	Ask a low price at the start, to interest people. This is often used for new food brands, sweets or chocolate.
Premium pricing	Ask a high price for a luxury item that consumers will get prestige from owning. This is used by brands such as Gucci and Porsche.

Activity | Evaluating pricing strategies

A new device has been launched in Sacramento called a Hicural. This is a small stick that quickly cures hiccups. If this was your invention, how would you price it? Divide into groups and identify the strengths and weaknesses of each of the strategies above. Then compare your ideas and suggest the best one for the Hicural.

Elasticity of demand

The law of demand says that sales increase as prices fall (and vice versa). This is why discount prices tempt you to buy more and why you buy less (or something else) when prices increase. This affects some products more than others and is known as the **elasticity of demand.**

- **Essential items** such as food and fuel are needed no matter what they cost – although we might buy less or switch brands to save money. Motorists may switch to train or bus and reduce leisure trips. Food and fuel are relatively inelastic because demand does not change much when prices change.

- **Non-essential items** are more elastic because demand falls more quickly if prices increase. Examples include cars, chocolate and televisions. This is because you can do without or buy an alternative.

Calculating elasticity shows the responsiveness of an item to changes in price and is done by using the following formula.

$$\text{Price elasticity of demand (PED)} = \frac{\%\text{ change in quantity demanded}}{\%\text{ change in price}}$$

A worked example

When beauty shop owner, Sara, increased her prices by 5 per cent, sales of bath products fell by 10 per cent, whereas sales of skin care items fell by only 2.5 per cent. What can PED tell her about these goods?

Sara calculates her PED for bath products as 10/5 = 2. Here the percentage quantity sold fell by *more* than the price increase, so demand is **elastic**. A PED >1 shows that demand for an item is elastic.

However, her PED for skin care items is 2.5/5 = 0.5. Here the percentage quantity sold fell by *less* than the price increase, so demand is inelastic. A PED of <1 means that demand for an item is inelastic.

Sara now knows that she has more scope to increase skin care prices without affecting her sales revenue. Therefore, she should consider lowering the price of bath products to regain sales and perhaps increase skin care prices further.

Just checking

1. What pricing strategy would most likely be used by a) a builder, b) a DIY store, c) an exclusive art gallery?

2. The University of Sheffield reported that if the price per unit of alcohol was 45p then 2,040 lives could be saved a year and if the price was 50p, 3,060 lives a year could be saved. What does this suggest about the price elasticity of alcohol?

3. The USP of pound shops is the fact that all their goods sell at the same low price. Suggest one advantage and one disadvantage of this pricing strategy.

Key term

Elasticity of demand – the degree to which demand (and sales) increases as prices fall, and vice versa.

Did you know?

An exception to the law of demand is luxury goods, where sales may increase when prices rise because ownership is so prized.

Did you know?

If the change is identical for both quantity and price, this is unitary demand.

Remember

If you are given different selling prices or quantities, then you must be able to calculate the percentage difference. If there is an increase, e.g. £10 to £12, divide the difference by the lower (original) figure then × 100 = 2/10 × 100 = 20%. If there is a fall, e.g. 200 sales fall to 150, divide the difference by the higher (original) figure then × 100 = 50/200 × 100 = 25%.

CONTINUED ▶▶

◤ Place

In the marketing mix, this relates to the way in which the product will be distributed (or the service offered) to the customer. The aim is always to get the product to the key customer in the right condition and at the right time.

Within the market

The positioning of the product, or where goods are found within the market, depends upon the type of product or service being sold.

- Fast moving consumer goods (FMCGs), are low-cost items, such as chocolate and crisps. They are widely available in many shops and stores.
- Certain goods are available in specialist outlets, from pharmaceuticals and wedding dresses to plumbers' supplies.
- Luxury goods are sold in different retail outlets from discount items.

The key point is that the target customer must be able to locate them quickly and easily.

Distribution channels

Producers can decide whether to sell goods direct to the consumer or indirectly via a wholesaler or other intermediary.

Did you know? ❓

Genuine Gemstone, the jewellery retailer, sells direct to customers on its own Gems TV channel.

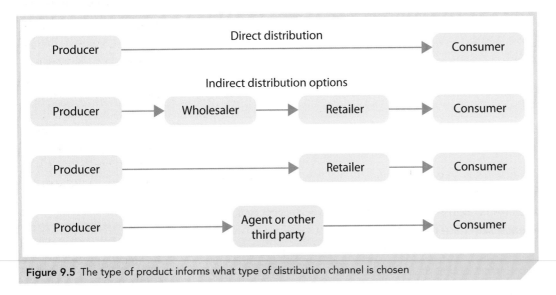

Figure 9.5 The type of product informs what type of distribution channel is chosen

- **Direct channels:** today many goods are sold direct to consumers either from the business website, by catalogue, door-to-door, over the telephone, in factory and farm shops and by party plan.

- **Indirect channels:** this means involving other people in the process. There are three main options.

Did you know? ❓

According to the *Retail Times*, over 4,000 specialist furniture stores will close in the future. High cost items will be bought more in general stores, such as John Lewis, and cheaper products online.

1 Mass produced items, such as ball point pens, go to a wholesaler who breaks down bulk quantities for retailers. They then sell to the consumer in small quantities.

2 The producer sells direct to the retailer. Sainsbury's buys direct from Heinz and B&Q direct from Crown Paints.

3 This option involves a specialist agent or third party. Ticketmaster is an agency which sells theatre tickets online, the Trainline.com offers a similar service for train tickets. Travel agents sell holidays and brokers sell insurance. Many department stores rent space to other businesses called concessions, e.g. MAC cosmetics in Selfridges.

Location within a distribution channel

The location within a distribution channel will affect the way a business operates. Some producers and wholesalers do not deal directly with consumers. B2B businesses like these are concerned with pricing and promoting their goods for their own buyers.

Specialist intermediaries are interested in obtaining and promoting items that will interest customers, and widening their choice of suppliers.

All B2C companies, such as high street retailers, focus on customer needs and wants and aim to satisfy these at a price they are willing to pay.

Locational factors for a physical business

The location of a physical business is affected by many factors (see Unit 1).

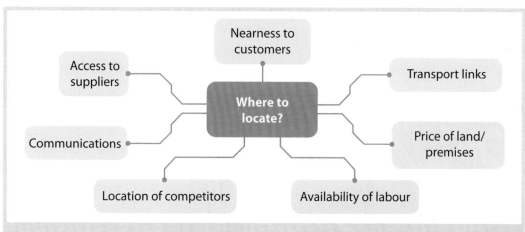

Figure 9.6 The main factors that businesses have to consider when deciding where to locate

Ecommerce

According to industry experts IMRG, the value of the UK's online retail market in 2012 was £77 billion. Popular goods bought online are groceries, fashion, entertainment, alcohol, beauty, telecoms and toiletries/health products. The growth of ecommerce has affected all retailers and offers many benefits. Many businesses no longer need a high street presence, which reduces costs. Selling direct also means there are no intermediaries to pay.

Relevance of channels to the size and type of the business

Many businesses use multiple channels, for example you can buy Boden clothes online and by catalogue. When a business decides which channels to use, there are three key points to note.

- The channel(s) must be appropriate to the product and the target customer(s).
- The channels should be appropriate to the size of business. A small business is unlikely to be able to produce items quickly to meet large orders from major retailers without incurring considerable additional costs.
- There should be no conflict between channels. For example, party plan participants or door-to-door sales people are unlikely to be successful if the goods are also widely on sale in retail outlets.

CONTINUED ▶▶

Did you know?

Websites such as notonthehighstreet.com and etsy.com act as agents by showcasing products and charging a fee or commission on sales.

Discussion point

Where is a cinema located in a distribution channel? How would that affect the marketing mix of a business like Vue or Odeon?

Activity

Identifying location factors

In groups, decide on the main factors that would influence the location of each of the following businesses: an estate agent; a newsagent; a radio station; a timber merchant; a tourist hotel; a car factory. Then compare your ideas.

Activity

Investigating Jamie's channels

Jamie Oliver promotes and sells his books, meals, cookery equipment – all through a variety of different distribution channels. Investigate these in groups and see how many you can identify. For each one, suggest the reason that channel was chosen.

Promotion

We are bombarded with images and messages about businesses and their products every day and in many places. What is the aim of these and what type of promotions are best to use?

The promotional mix

The **promotional mix** is the combination of methods chosen by a business to advertise and promote their brand or products. The best promotional mix will depend upon the type of product, the target customer, the actions of competitors and the available budget.

The promotional budget

This is the amount of money that can be spent on advertising and promotion to ensure that the brand or product retains a high profile. Having a budget means the business is less likely to overspend. Some methods are very expensive, others are cheaper and some are free. Choosing the most cost-effective is an important skill.

Businesses that produce and sell goods globally can spend vast amounts on promotions. It is estimated that Coca Cola spends around $3 billion a year and McDonald's $2 billion a year. They can afford it because the cost per item produced is very low.

A small business has a far smaller budget and must choose carefully how to spend its money to get the best results. It should assess the success of different methods to see if they were worth the amount spent.

It is important that your promotional budget is used wisely.

Promotional channels

Table 9.6 The main promotional channels

Promotional channel	Examples
Advertising	Television and commercial radio; cinemas; newspapers and magazines; billboards and posters; buses and taxis; tube stations and bus stops.
Sales promotions	Vouchers; coupons; competitions; point-of-sale materials, e.g. posters; display stands; LED displays; free samples; free gifts (e.g. balloons, pens); carrier bags.
Public relations and publicity	News stories; feature articles; sponsorship of special events.
Direct marketing	Mail shots; email newsletters; telesales; flyers.
Personal selling	Trade fairs; craft shows; exhibitions; visits by reps to large organisations.
Emarketing	SMS or text messages; internet adverts; promotions by social media; viral marketing and blogs; search engine optimisation (to ensure site is ranked highly in searches).

Viral marketing and social media

Viral marketing means encouraging people to spread a message about your product to their contacts. An example is the 'Sent from my iPhone' tag that appears on the bottom of those emails. Viral marketing started when people forwarded emails with website links, now it is more often done by social media, such as Twitter or Facebook.

By encouraging customers to subscribe to their news feed on a social media site, businesses can build a following and provide updates that people share with others. Facebook and Twitter can also be used to find out customer opinions. Another method is to produce a short video and post this on YouTube with links sent out via social media. The more the content appeals to the audience, the greater the chance of success.

'Above the line' and 'below the line' promotions

Traditionally all promotions were divided into two types:

- **'Above the line'** are paid for promotions. They include all forms of advertising, for example on TV, in the press, or to Google on a pay per click basis for a high search ranking.
- **'Below the line'** are all other types of promotions. They include sales promotions, direct mail, press features, celebrity endorsements, personal selling and telesales.

Guerrilla advertising

These are unusual and unconventional tactics used to promote a brand, product or idea. They include the use of flash mobs and graffiti and often happen in unusual places. The aim is to do something unusual and creative on a low budget to attract masses of attention. Successful campaigns often go viral, which gains maximum publicity for a small outlay.

 Did you know?

The Gangnam Style video holds the record for viral spread with over 1.5 billion viewings on YouTube. This has made a global star of Korean singer, PSY, increased the value of his recording company and his father's business and contributed to increased advertising revenue for Google, which owns YouTube.

Activity

Investigating guerrilla advertising

For a brilliant example of a flash mob, visit Pearson hotlinks at www.pearsonhotlinks. co.uk and search for this title. Now search online yourself to find an example of guerrilla advertising that attracts you. Present it to the group with reasons why it appeals. Then vote for the best five.

CONTINUED ▶▶

Did you know? ❓

Shops selling budget items, such as Farmfoods, Lidl and Aldi usually look for locations that are cheap. This keeps costs down and doesn't conflict with their brand image. Conversely, a shop selling luxury items will want a premium location, usually in a city centre or a well-known shopping mall.

Consistency and the marketing mix

All businesses have to identify the most appropriate elements of the marketing mix for their own product or service, for example what product(s) to make or stock, what price(s) to charge, how to distribute the product and what promotional methods to use. An important factor here is consistency. This means that the customer always receives the same 'message' and this will depend upon the desired brand image and the target customer.

- Budget products aimed at the mass market are priced cheaply and competitively. They are available in appropriate outlets, such as markets and discount stores. Promotions may include leaflets delivered door-to-door or point-of-sale materials in store.

- Producers of luxury items adopt a premium pricing strategy. The goods are available in concessions in department stores or in the brand's own stores in city locations or shopping malls. Promotions include press advertisements in appropriate magazines.

A smaller business should take the same approach. If it wants to be known for high quality and excellent service, then its website, promotional materials and the outlets it chooses must reflect that. Similarly, if it wants to promote a young, fun image, then all its marketing materials should give that message.

Discussion point 💬

Originally Thornton's chocolates were seen as luxury items and only available in their own shops. When sales fell, the business cut costs by closing many stores and selling in supermarkets. Was this a good idea or has this changed the image of the brand? What has this meant for its main competitor, Hotel Chocolat? Discuss your ideas as a group.

Do you think your opinion is influenced by where something has been purchased?

The difference between ebusiness and ecommerce

Although these words are often used interchangeably, there is an important difference.

- **Ecommerce** means buying or selling goods over the internet. It also includes offering customer service online.

- **Ebusiness** includes other business operations such as production and product development, stock control systems, financial systems, human resources and customer relationship management (CRM). All the major business functions are linked by technology.

> **Activity** / Investigating Sage
>
> Sage produces a wide range of software for all types of businesses that can integrate selling online with other office systems. Check the range available on their website. To do this, visit Pearson hotlinks at www.pearsonhotlinks.co.uk and search for this title.

Benefits of ebusiness and ecommerce

Many small businesses that sell online operate manual 'back office' systems – they record orders manually and keep customer records on paper. However, as businesses grow they benefit from electronic systems. For example, **customer relationship management (CRM)** is used to target customers more precisely, reward loyal customers and develop customer relationships. Customer information is held in a central database, accessible to all staff to help them work more efficiently.

> **Key terms**
>
> **Customer relationship management (CRM)** – obtaining data on customers and using this to improve customer relationships and encourage customer loyalty.
>
> **Productivity** – the amount of output produced by a person or industry.
>
> **Efficiency** – being competent and making the best use of resources, such as time or money.

Table 9.7 The benefits of ebusiness and ecommerce

Benefits of ecommerce	Benefits of ebusiness
Enables sales to be made 24/7.	Saves money as there is less duplication of activities in the business.
Cheaper than being on the high street as no premises are required.	The business can respond promptly and effectively to enquiries.
Enables more orders to be received and processed.	Increases staff **productivity** and **efficiency**.
Can promote the product to overseas markets.	Detailed customer records can be analysed to check responses.
Can sell to people on the move through mobile sites and apps.	Can send email newsletters and target customers effectively.
Can promote the product through social media sites.	Can analyse effectiveness of marketing and sales campaigns more easily.

> **Just checking**
>
> 1 Identify three direct and three indirect channels of distribution.
> 2 State four factors a retailer would take into account when choosing a physical location.
> 3 What is the link between viral marketing and social media?
> 4 Give two examples of 'above the line' and two examples of 'below the line' promotions.
> 5 Explain the difference between ecommerce and ebusiness.

Factors affecting the marketing mix

Activity

Researching areas of influence

In groups, research **two** other examples for each area of influence. Then decide how all the examples might impact on each of the four Ps of a business – product, price, place and promotion.

Kirsty's SMART objectives

Specific – Kirsty's first target was orders for 100 a month.

Measurable – She could check this number against the orders received.

Achievable – Kirsty knew that she could make these dresses in that time without compromising quality.

Realistic – She knew she had the stock and resources to achieve this goal.

Time-based – Kirsty's goal was to achieve this number of orders each month.

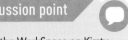
Discussion point

Read the WorkSpace on Kirsty Hartley's business. When you have completed the questions, discuss the type of external influences that could affect her marketing mix in the future, and decide the best response in each case.

Influences on the marketing mix

Businesses should regularly review their marketing mix to ensure they keep pace with new developments and external challenges. This is better than reacting only when there is a crisis.

Table 9.8 Key areas of influence on the marketing mix

Area of influence	Example
Technology	Fast 4G mobile networks make it easier to watch TV and downloads on smartphones and tablets.
Economic issues	During a recession, customers have less money to spend.
Cultural issues	Sensitivity to religious and age differences and respect for other beliefs.
Social issues	The population in the UK is ageing because people are living longer. There is greater focus on preventative health, such as exercising and eating fruit and vegetables.
Ethical issues	Paying very low wages while making high profits is considered unacceptable.
Political issues	If business rates are increased, costs will increase for businesses.

If the business also carries out a PESTLE analysis, it will consider environmental issues, such as pollution and packaging, and legal issues, such as changes to consumer legislation.

Evaluating the effectiveness of a marketing mix

The aim of marketing is to operate a business successfully in a competitive market and to increase sales and profits. All aspects of marketing should be regularly reviewed to check this is happening.

The best way to do this is to quantify responses. Kirsty Hartley of Wild Things Dresses (see opposite) analyses her response rates on different websites to check their effectiveness. She checks if orders have increased following articles in the press or promotions by bloggers. She links activity on Facebook and Twitter with her order book, and sets herself regular sales targets to achieve and checks the outcome. Kirsty's SMART objectives are shown in the feature box. (You learnt about SMART objectives at the start of this unit.) You can see how Kirsty markets her dresses when you research the WorkSpace questions.

WorkSpace

▶ Kirsty Hartley

Owner of Wild Things Dresses

Kirsty Hartley is the perfect example of how to grow a small business successfully through a combination of skill, creativity and excellent marketing. From a £50 roll of fabric two years ago, Kirsty now sells her quirky, fun dresses all over the world to buyers, including Charlotte Church and Lily Allen. In her first 18 months, her sales turnover rose by 300 per cent and orders continue to increase.

So what formula has Kirsty used to make her business a success? Key to her success is that she knows her market well. Before she had children, Kirsty taught design and worked as a freelance designer for many high street stores, including Mothercare. She identified a gap in the market for good quality, handmade clothes in original designs, and two years ago decided to trial her ideas at craft fairs. She identified her target market as young mothers, like herself, who wanted to buy bright, contemporary, good quality dresses in designs that their children would adore. With two young daughters, Kirsty could not only gain instant feedback on her designs, but also had no problem finding models to wear the clothes.

Projected costs for her own website were high, so Kirsty researched other alternatives. Her first choice was Etsy, the global brand leader in shop window websites. She set up her shop on Etsy in June 2011. The shop featured her trademark character dresses and is today featured on 10 similar sites including Folksy.com, Bouf.com, notonthehighstreet.com and Peanut and Pip. Her dresses are priced to take account of the commission she pays to the sites to ensure that each sale is still profitable. Kirsty's next step was social media. She created a Facebook page and joined Pinterest and Twitter. She sent samples to bloggers of relevant sites such as Babyccino Kids and Bambino Goodies. As word spread, journalists contacted Kirsty for features. One such feature in the *Telegraph*'s Saturday magazine, *Stella*, resulted in several orders – all from men!

Kirsty wants to continue to grow the business and design her own prints. She is also developing a range of boys' clothes and looking at accessories like tights to go with her dresses. She plans to set up her own website so that she can send mailshots and email newsletters to her regular customers. She might even obtain a few celebrity endorsements, too!

Think about it

1 What type of market research did Kirsty carry out and how did her own background help her?

2 What advantages does Kirsty gain by showcasing her products on Etsy and similar sites?

3 How can using social media help Kirsty to grow her business?

4 What benefits does Kirsty gain by focusing on 'below the line' promotions?

5 Is Kirsty's marketing mix consistent and how does it relate to her USP and her brand? Before you answer, research some of the sites listed and read the Etsy and Folksy blogs about Wild Things Dresses to find out more about her business.

BTEC
Assessment Zone

This section has been written to help you to do your best when you take the assessment test. Read it through carefully and ask your teacher/tutor if there is anything you are not certain about.

Hints and tips

Before the test

Remember

You will have 1 hour 30 minutes to do the test and should answer all the questions.

You will improve your chances if you make sure that you have revised all the key areas that are likely to be covered.

You will need a black pen to complete the assessment. Arrive in good time so that you are not in a panic. Remember to put your name, centre number and candidate number at the top of the page.

Key revision topics (your teacher/tutor may add to these)

1   When revising ensure you consider all the key marketing terms that have been covered in this unit. Think about appropriate examples that you can use in the test, such as:

- Target customer and target market
- Marketing plan
- Competitive advantage
- SMART objectives and corporate objectives
- Situational analysis, e.g. SWOT and PESTLE
- Gap in the market
- Benchmarking
- Market share and market trends
- The marketing mix

- USP
- Brand image
- Market segment
- Product life cycle and extension strategy
- Product portfolio
- Elasticity of demand
- Distribution channels
- The promotional mix
- Viral marketing and guerrilla advertising.

2   Think about how to define and explain the difference between certain terms and think about examples for them, such as:

- B2B and B2C
- Customer and consumer
- Goods and services markets
- Capital and consumer goods markets
- Niche and mass markets
- Market and product orientated businesses

- Primary and secondary data
- Quantitative and qualitative data
- SWOT and PESTLE analyses
- Core and augmented product
- Ebusiness and ecommerce
- 'Above the line' and 'below the line' promotions.

3 Ensure you think about the following:

- The importance and benefits of marketing to business and how it is used by businesses
- The benefits of distinctive branding and the dimensions of a brand
- The use and purpose of market research in business and how to interpret research findings
- The marketing mix, including product portfolio of a business, pricing strategies, promotional budget/mix and distribution strategies
- Competitors, customer behaviour and other factors that affect the market for a product
- Factors that influence the marketing mix
- How to evaluate the marketing mix.

During the test

The test is in TWO sections. Section A has mainly individual questions. Section B starts with a case study on which all the questions in that section are based. All the questions are compulsory and you should attempt an answer for each one. Remember that you will never lose marks for a wrong answer, but you cannot gain a mark for a blank space!

Allocate your time wisely. You will need to spend longer on Section B because you need to fully understand the case study before you answer any questions. You should also allow more time for questions that ask you to 'evaluate' as these need more thought. Also, allow ten minutes at the end to check through your work before you hand it in.

Use the number of marks alongside a question to give you guidance on how detailed your answer should be or how many points you should list. If you are asked for two examples, you cannot gain full marks if you only provide one.

Interpret command words correctly, such as 'state', 'describe' or 'evaluate'. Further guidance is given on this later in this section.

Section A

Read through all the questions in Section A first, before you write any answers. This gives you time to settle your nerves. Some short questions will be very straightforward and, if you are clear about what is being asked, you may be able to answer these quickly.

Expect at least one question in Section A to be longer and to require more thought. You may wish to make notes on some rough paper before you start to answer this.

Section B

Start by reading the case study – but don't expect to get your head around it in the first reading. Simply note the main points about the business and the product.

Now read the questions. This will give you a clearer focus as you will now know which items of information are important. Note key terms that are asked so that you can underline or highlight these as you reread the case study.

Read the case study again and look for the information you need. This may relate to:

- the product, its USP and/or the product portfolio
- the target market and/or target customer

- the entrepreneur, business model and business orientation
- the marketing mix of the business, e.g. distribution channels, pricing policy, promotional methods
- the competition and market conditions
- market research that has been, or could be, carried out.

Relate to the business by imagining that you are running it and facing the challenges and opportunities that are described. This will help you identify with the owner and the situation.

Keep referring back to the case study to make sure that your answers are relevant and focus on the situation you have been given.

If you are completely stuck on a question, then leave it for now and come back to it later. Or write a brief answer and leave room to expand it.

Always read through your work at the end to check it makes sense and you haven't made any silly errors or omissions.

Sample questions

Below you will find some sample questions with answers. Read these carefully and note the hints and tips that are given. Then answer the remaining questions yourself and check your answers with your teacher/tutor.

If you are asked to define a marketing term, simply state what it means.

Section A

1 State the missing 'P' in the marketing mix (1)

i Product

ii Price

iii Promotion

iv .... Place

Write clearly in black ink on the line or space provided for your answer.

2 **What** is the meaning of the term 'product portfolio'? (1)

This is the range of products or services produced and supplied by a business.

'**Outline**' means giving the main points without going into too much detail.

3 Outline **two** purposes of having a promotional budget. (2)

1 A promotional budget means the business has money available to promote its goods or services.

2 Having a budget helps to ensure that the business will not overspend on promotions.

Always give the correct number of points asked for. Often there may be several acceptable answers.

4 Explain **two** ways in which economic issues can influence the marketing mix of a business. (4)

    1 A business may have to change its pricing strategy if there is a recession and people have less money to spend. In this case, it might have to offer discounts or lower prices.

    2 If prices rise because of inflation, a business may not be able to afford to spend as much on advertising and promotion and may have to review the methods it uses.

You **explain** by providing details and reasons to support the points you are making. As this is harder than 'outlining' or giving a definition, these questions are worth more marks.

This answer would gain full marks because the learner has shown a clear link between economic issues and two aspects of the marketing mix, price and promotion.

5 After Daniel won a TV contest to find young, talented chefs, he was offered the opportunity to set up his own business.

(a) Identify **two** factors he should take into account when choosing a location for his restaurant. (2)

    1 A restaurant must be convenient for customers so it needs to be in a city centre or easy to reach by car.

    2 The location should be appropriate for his brand image. For example, if he wants to open a top class restaurant, then this needs to be in a good area, even if the premises will cost more.

(b) Daniel is convinced that bookings will be very high because he is well known and his food is unusual, so he decides on a premium pricing strategy. Explain why Daniel thinks this pricing strategy is appropriate. (2)

Premium pricing is used for luxury items that people are proud to own. Daniel thinks that customers will be willing to pay a high price because he is famous and cooks unusual food and they can tell people about their visit.

(c) Customers complain that prices are too high. Daniel is considering issuing discount vouchers of 20% for a month to see if this results in an increase in the number of bookings.

    i) State how he could use this information to calculate the price elasticity of demand (PED) for his food. (1)

Daniel can calculate PED for his food by dividing the percentage change in bookings by the percentage change in price.

    ii) Explain how calculating the PED can help Daniel to decide whether or not to lower prices. (4)

If demand is elastic (>1), it means that bookings will increase by more than the percentage fall in price, so it would be a good idea to lower prices.

If demand is inelastic (<1), then it means bookings will increase by less than the fall in price, so his total revenue is likely to fall if he lowers his prices.

If you are given a specific business situation, make sure all your answers are appropriate and take it into account.

One question in Section A may be longer and involve a business situation with several questions. It is useful to read through it all before you start to answer.

This answer tells the examiner that the learner understands what is meant by 'brand image'.

'Identify' means give the basic facts about the topic.

You may be given the percentage change in demand, too, and asked to calculate the PED.

You should **describe** by giving a clear description that includes all the main points.

In this case you must explain what to do if PED is elastic and what to do if it is inelastic.

Evaluate by looking at all the information and making a judgement. Give reasons to justify your decision.

(d) Daniel has refused to accept reservations, insisting tables are allocated on a first come, first served basis. But the number of people dining in the restaurant is falling and some evenings are very quiet. A friend suggests Daniel should change the business orientation, as he is still very focused on his unusual food, and then review his marketing mix.

Evaluate whether this would be a good idea. (8)

Demonstrate to the examiner that you understand the key terms in the question. Here these are 'business orientation' and 'marketing mix'.

Daniel has been product orientated so far because he has focused on his skills as a chef to produce different food. If he changes his business orientation to be market focused, then he will find out more about what his customers want and take their needs into consideration.

He could find out by carrying out a survey or chatting to people as they dine. He could also find out what other restaurants do – especially his main competitors.

Using the correct marketing term, where appropriate, shows the examiner you understand the topic.

Daniel's marketing mix comprises his price, product, place and promotion. He can check his prices against competitors who serve similar food in the area and adjust these if necessary. He can find out which of his dishes are most and least popular with his customers and review his menu. He can make sure that the atmosphere and service at the restaurant is excellent. He should also review his decision not to accept reservations. Customers may dislike not being able to make a reservation in case they cannot get a table when they arrive. They will then go elsewhere and may never return. Daniel should also find out the best ways to advertise and promote his restaurant to his target customers once the initial publicity has faded.

In your final paragraph, make your recommendations and reasons crystal clear.

It is therefore a good idea for Daniel to be market orientated. If he understands the needs of his customers and is responsive to these, then he should be able to increase business and keep ahead of his main competitors. This is better than just focusing on the food he prepares as this is only likely to be successful if he was very famous or had far more experience. Even then, it is never sensible to think you can ignore the needs and opinions of your customers.

Over to you!

Section B

This section starts with a case study of 300–400 words on which all the questions are based. This case study is shorter, but will give you practice in reading carefully and then applying your knowledge of marketing to a situation. Check all your answers with your teacher/tutor.

Anya's 1bag

Three years ago, Anya produced and launched the '1bag' – a multi-coloured fabric bag, available in various sizes, and priced between £50 and £95. Its main selling point was that it was the only bag women ever needed as it toned with any outfit. She sold the bag at craft fairs where it was very popular, and cleverly got it featured in several women's magazines and newspapers. This publicity boosted sales and enabled her to pitch her product to several large department stores and gain substantial orders.

Last year Anya started her own website to boost interest in her brand. She encouraged customers who bought a 1bag to register their purchase on her site. If they then have any problems with the bag – such as a zip failing or the strap breaking – they can send it back to have it repaired. Promoting this service in the department stores boosted sales, as did Anya's use of Facebook and Twitter to promote the 1bag.

Now, though, orders have started to fall. Anya paid for a few press advertisements to try to increase sales but is unsure whether these are having any effect. She is reluctant to lower prices as she thinks this could affect the image of the brand.

Anya thinks there is scope for a leather unisex 1bag, but to keep costs down, these would have to be made quite cheaply abroad. She also thinks there could be opportunities to extend her brand by producing related fashion accessories, but knows she will have to research this market further before she decides what to do.

1 Anya's 1bag has a distinct USP. Give **two** benefits of this to her business. (2)

2 Anya uses various methods to promote the 1bag. Identify **two** 'below the line' methods she uses. (2)

3 Give **two** reasons why these are more suitable than 'above the line' methods. (2)

4 Give **one** advantage and **one** disadvantage of selling the 1bag in the B2B market only. (2)

5 a) Identify **two** examples of quantitative data that will give Anya information on the fashion accessories market. (2)

b) For each of your examples, explain how she could use this information to help her to make a decision. (4)

6 Anya finds that the market for fashion accessories is growing rapidly. Describe **one** advantage and **one** disadvantage of operating in this type of market. (4)

7 Describe **one** ethical factor that could affect Anya's decision to make leather 1bags overseas. (2)

8 Anya is concerned that the 1bag could be reaching the end of its product life cycle. Evaluate this possibility and the options open to her. (8)

Introduction

Businesses produce millions of different documents every day. They write letters and reports, send emails, prepare agendas for meetings and purchase orders for supplies they need. They respond to enquiries and complaints and provide information to people both inside and outside the company.

Wherever you work, your own written communication skills will be on display. If you cannot write a proper sentence, spell words correctly or use the right punctuation, this will quickly become obvious.

This unit will enable you to develop your written communication skills. You will learn about the types of communication that are confidential and the care you must take when you are preparing and copying documents for other people. You will learn about the different types of documents used to communicate with people in business, both internally and externally. This information will enable you to develop your knowledge of the documents you will see, read and write when you start work.

Assessment: This unit will be assessed through a series of assignments set by your teacher/tutor.

Learning aims

In this unit you will:

A know the purpose of written communication in business contexts

B plan and select appropriate business documents to communicate in different business contexts

C produce business documents for communication in a business.

> I am looking forward to learning more about business documents and improving what I write. I know this will help me when I am preparing my assignments as well as when I go to work.
>
> Farzana, *16-year-old Business student*

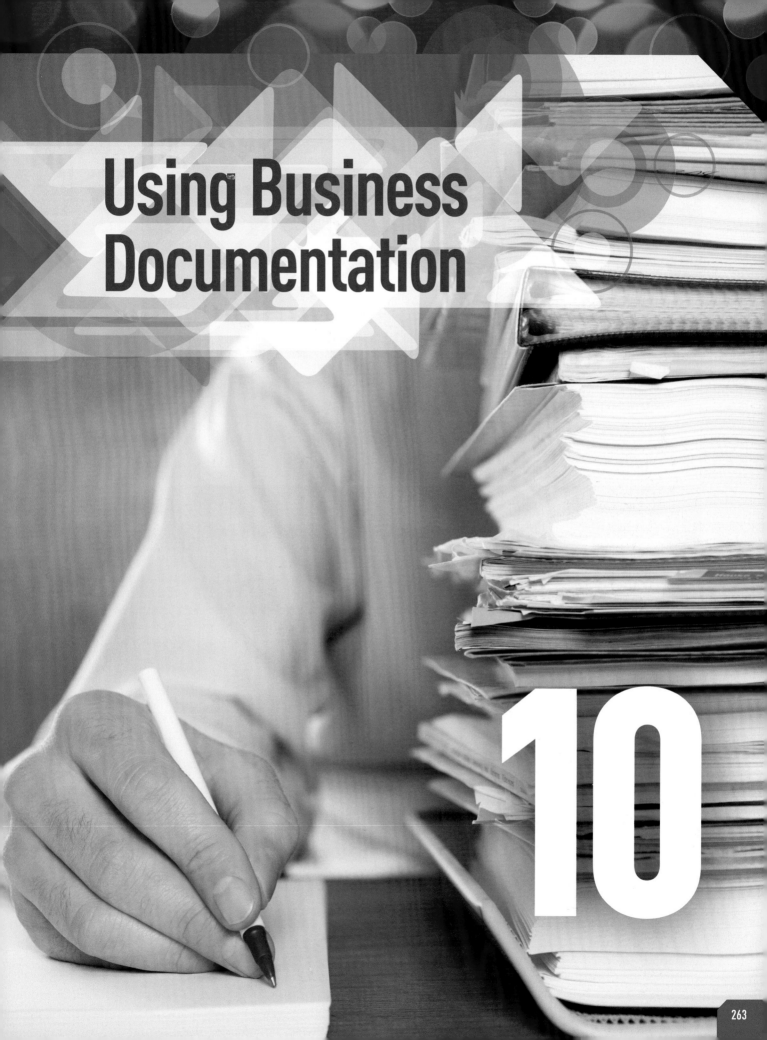

Using Business Documentation

10

BTEC
Assessment Zone

This table shows you what you must do in order to achieve a **Pass**, **Merit** or **Distinction** grade, and where you can find activities in this book to help you.

Assessment criteria			
Level 1	**Level 2 Pass**	**Level 2 Merit**	**Level 2 Distinction**
Learning aim A: Know the purpose of written communication in business contexts			
1A.1 Identify four different business documents used in a selected business	**2A.P1** English Describe the purpose of four different business documents used in a selected business **See Assessment activity 10.1, page 277**	**2A.M1** English Compare the purpose of both formal and informal documents from different business contexts in a selected business **See Assessment activity 10.1, page 277**	**2A.D1** English Evaluate the impact of written communications in different business contexts in a selected business **See Assessment activity 10.1, page 277**
1A.2 English Outline the business contexts that influence the format of four business documents in a selected business	**2A.P2** English Explain how the business context influences the format of four business documents in a selected business **See Assessment activity 10.1, page 277**		
Level 1	**Level 2 Pass**	**Level 2 Merit**	**Level 2 Distinction**
Learning aim B: Plan and select appropriate business documents to communicate in different business contexts			
1B.3 List the factors to be considered when planning and selecting appropriate business documents in four different business contexts	**2B.P3** Describe the factors to be considered when planning and selecting appropriate business documents in four different business contexts **See Assessment activity 10.1, page 277**	**2B.M2** English Compare the effectiveness of business documents to meet the needs of different audiences in four different business contexts **See Assessment activity 10.1, page 277**	**2B.D2** English Evaluate the effectiveness of business documents to meet the needs of confidentiality and audit requirements **See Assessment activity 10.1, page 277**
1B.4 English Outline the suitability of business documents in meeting the needs of the audience in four different business contexts	**2B.P4** English Explain the suitability of business documents in meeting the needs of the audience in four different business contexts, including the need for confidentiality **See Assessment activity 10.1, page 277**		

Level 1	Level 2 Pass	Level 2 Merit	Level 2 Distinction
Learning aim C: Produce business documents for communication in a business			
1C.5 English Produce two business documents of different types to support business tasks for internal communication in a selected business	**2C.P5** English Produce three accurate business documents of different types to support business tasks for internal communication in a selected business **See Assessment activity 10.2, page 287**	**2C.M3** English Assess the factors that influenced the production of internal and external documents, including reaching the intended audience by the agreed deadlines **See Assessment activity 10.2, page 287**	**2C.D3** English Justify the suitability of the internal and external documents produced in meeting the needs of the intended audience **See Assessment activity 10.2, page 287**
1C.6 English Produce two business documents of different types to support business tasks for external communication in a selected business	**2C.P6** English Produce three accurate business documents of different types to support business tasks for external communication in a selected business **See Assessment activity 10.2, page 287**		

English / Opportunity to practise English skills

How you will be assessed

This unit will be assessed by a series of internally assessed tasks and activities. These will enable you to demonstrate your understanding of the different types of documents used within a business and the factors that are considered when these are being selected for use. You will also demonstrate that you can produce business documents yourself that are suitable for both internal and external communications.

Your assessment could be in the form of:

- a leaflet or brochure about the different types of documents used in business and the reasons these are used

- a display illustrating different types of business documents used for internal and external communications in a selected business

- a range of documents prepared in response to certain business situations

- a report of the main factors that affect the choice of different documents to communicate in business.

The purpose of written communication in business contexts

 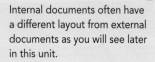
Purposes and formats of different types of business documents

The purposes of business documents

People in business communicate for a reason. This may be to inform other people about a situation or event; confirm an arrangement or agreement; promote an idea, product or service; provide instructions; make a request.

Types of business documents

There are many different types of business documents. Some are only used to communicate internally (within the business). Others are used to communicate externally (with contacts outside the business). The main purposes of the documents you must know about are summarised in Table 10.2.

Table 10.1 Types of business documents

	Recipient	Document
Internal	Supervisor, manager or colleague within an organisation	Handwritten message or note; text; memo; email; notice; agenda; minutes; organisation chart; flow chart; report
External	Customer, supplier and others outside the business	Email; text; business letter; report; purchase order; invoice; meetings document (if external contacts involved in meeting); flyer; press release; mail shot

Did you know?

Internal documents often have a different layout from external documents as you will see later in this unit.

Table 10.2 Types of written documents and their main purpose and features

Type of document	Main purpose	Main features
Letter	Provides information to internal and external contacts	Slower than email; formal and impersonal; provides a permanent written record
Memo	Provides important information to staff	More formal than email; provides a permanent record if filed
Email	Provides or requests information internally and externally	Informal; rapid; other documents can be attached; can be sent worldwide very easily
Report	Gives an account of an event or investigation	States method of investigation, conclusions and recommendations for action
Notice	Provides information to many people. Meeting notices specify when and where a meeting will be held	Provides essential instructions or key information in an attractive, easy-to-read format

Table 10.2 Types of written documents and their main purpose and features (continued)

Type of document	Main purpose	Main features
Agenda	Gives information to meeting participants	Provides a list of items to be discussed in order
Minutes of a meeting		Summarises discussions, action to be taken and by whom
Purchase order	Authorises a supplier to provide goods at a stated price	Includes details of goods, number required, price and delivery method
Invoice	Demands payment for goods supplied on credit	Includes details of the items purchased, the unit price, VAT payable and the total price
Organisation chart	Shows the structure of the organisation as a diagram	Identifies different levels of staff, their job roles and the links between them
Flow chart	Shows a sequence of events or a process	Includes symbols and arrows and identifies when decisions or actions must be taken
Flyer	Advertises forthcoming events, services or goods for sale	Includes bold headlines and graphics to attract attention
Press release	Aims to obtain free publicity in a newspaper or magazine	Summarises key information about a forthcoming event or promotion
Mail shot	Promotes products or services in a letter or leaflet	May be targeted at certain customers or distributed to householders in an area

Formats

The format of the document relates to the way it has been prepared.

- **Handwritten** documents are written with pen or pencil. Always write neatly and use a dictionary if your spelling is poor.
- **Electronic** documents are sent from one computer to another, such as email or attachments.
- **Word processed** documents are prepared on computer using a package such as Microsoft Word®.
- **Text** messages are sent to staff and customers to provide information or reminders quickly.
- **Virtual** documents are viewed on an electronic device such as an iPad or a courier's handheld PDA which you can sign using a stylus.

Did you know?

Some virtual office services produce professional business documents for small or start-up businesses. You can find an example by going to www.pearsonhotlinks.co.uk and searching for this title.

Activity Comparing business documents

In small groups, use books and the internet to find examples of each of the business documents listed in Table 10.2. Compare the type of information provided on each one and the layout used.

Business contexts and business documents

Introduction

The **business context** is the situation that exists when people are communicating. For example, a context may be responding to a customer enquiry or complaint, asking for payment or making a presentation.

Activity   Identifying business contexts

In groups, identify three more business contexts. Then share your ideas.

Formal and informal documents used in a business context

The type of work a business carries out affects the formality of its communications. Accountants and solicitors often write formal letters, even to clients they know well, because these include information on serious financial and legal matters.

Table 10.3 Formal and informal methods of communication

	Used when...	Examples
Formal	... the matter is important or serious ... you do not know the recipient very well ... you want a written record	Business letters, memos and reports Job interviews Important meetings
Informal	... people know each other well ... people are in frequent contact	Email Internal notices to staff

- **Meetings** can be formal or informal. Formal meetings include the Annual General Meeting (AGM) of a company, Directors' meetings and Governors' meetings in schools and colleges. The minutes record the discussions and actions agreed. Other meetings are more informal, such as team briefings held to update a team with matters of common interest. You can learn about meetings in Unit 7.

- **Notices** are internal documents that provide information or give instructions to staff. A notice announcing a leaving party will be more informal than one about health and safety. Notices must be clearly worded and contain all the details that people need.

- **Reports** may be prepared for internal or external use. They are often written following research or an investigation, or to give an account of an event. For example, a report may investigate a proposal to change opening hours or to update the computer system and summarise the advantages and costs of taking these actions.

- **Technical enquiries** include requests for estimates, queries about a product and detailed quotations. Some are informal, but many are not, such as an enquiry about the supply and installation of expensive equipment. The information is always put in writing to avoid any confusion. Any technical information given verbally should also be confirmed in writing to prevent misunderstandings.

- **Communicating with supervisor, colleagues, suppliers or customers** involves responding to a communication or initiating a communication yourself. The purpose and the type of recipient should influence your method of communication (e.g. letter or email), as well as the words you use, the layout and your 'tone'.

Create a poster for a cake sale. Make sure you think of all the details you need to include.

- **Complaints** may be received verbally or in writing and staff may have to follow a set procedure in response. This includes replying in writing so there is a written record. This is important because a complaint could result in legal action if it cannot be resolved amicably.

- **Presentations** are used to give information to a group and are more formal than a chat or discussion. Handouts can provide further information. The style and tone will vary according to whether the presentation is internal or external, and whether or not senior managers and/or important customers are attending.

- **Confidentiality** relates to information that the business – or your manager – does not want to share with other people. This may relate to personal information about staff or customers, or future business plans which a competitor would benefit from knowing.

? **Did you know?**

You should avoid using contracted words such as 'isn't' or 'can't', and expressions such as 'OK' in business documents.

Activity Checking your tone

Your tone is how you phrase your sentences. This can indicate formality or courtesy. Reorder the following sentences with the most formal first and the most informal last. Then suggest who would be an appropriate recipient of each one, and compare your ideas.

1 Is there any chance you can let me know today?

2 We would be grateful if you could let us have this information promptly.

3 Please could you let me know as soon as possible?

4 I really need to know ASAP.

CONTINUED ▸▸

◤ The influence of internal audiences, external stakeholders and the public

Your audience consists of all those people who will see a document and whose opinions, needs and possible responses must be considered.

- **Your internal audience** are people who work in the same organisation as you. They may include senior managers or colleagues you do not know. There may be some restrictions on the communications you can send and to whom. For example, junior employees do not usually email the managing director. In a large organisation more formal communications such as memos or reports may be circulated quite widely. In a small business, communications may be more informal, and include internal emails between staff and the owner or manager.

- **External stakeholders** are those people outside the organisation who have an interest in the business, for example customers, suppliers, the government (and tax authorities), the bank and the local community. This will affect the type of document used, the information it contains and how it is worded. Direct communications may often involve a business letter, particularly about formal or important matters.

- **The public** may be interested in any future business plans as these may affect them as potential customers or job seekers. The image of the business is important so information available to the public must be totally accurate and professional. Information may be provided by means of leaflets, flyers, mail shots or press releases.

Did you know? ❓

The existence of social media means that silly errors in an external business document can become common knowledge very quickly.

Businesses have to communicate effectively with their audience. How would the audience and the situation affect the wording of this communication?

Selecting appropriate documents to meet the business context

The business context affects the purpose of the communication and therefore the formality of the communication, the type of document that is best and its content. For example:

- You can promote a product or service to customers by writing a letter, sending an email or having flyers printed. You could promote an event to staff by email or by creating a notice. It will depend upon the complexity of the information and how best to communicate it.

- Certain types of document are used in specific business contexts. Purchase orders and invoices are used when you are buying or selling goods. Agendas and minutes are used in relation to meetings. Organisation charts and flow charts are two ways of presenting information graphically.

What information would need to be included on a flyer or an email to make you want to attend an event?

Impact of effective and ineffective written communication in businesses

Effective written communications have a major impact on the reader. They can persuade them to take action, buy a product or attend an event. They can give customers a positive view of the organisation. As written documents provide a permanent record, any major errors may come back to haunt you for years to come!

Remember

People communicate in writing, rather than verbally, when the information is long, complex, may be used several times or must be recorded to prevent later disputes.

Table 10.4 A summary of the impact of effective and ineffective communications

Impact of effective written communications	Impact of ineffective written communications
Gives a positive image of the business	Gives a negative impression of the business
Improves and enhances customer relationships	Loses and alienates customers
Improves organisational efficiency	Wastes time and money
Motivates employees	Demotivates employees
Gets the right results quickly	Causes errors and misunderstandings
Makes new ideas and suggestions more acceptable	Creates stress and conflict
Gives customers confidence	Creates problems and arguments

Just checking

1 List four purposes of creating business documents.
2 Give two examples of internal business documents and two examples of external documents.
3 Why are many documents more formal in a large organisation?
4 What is meant by the term 'business context'?

Planning and selecting appropriate business documents

When you are planning and selecting the most appropriate document to use, there are several factors to consider.

The needs of the audience

Your audience may be internal, external or both. You need to consider the purpose of the communication, what your audience already knows about the topic, how formal you need to be and whether they have regular access to email or text messages. Your audience may include:

- **your line manager** who is directly responsible for you. You should obviously not communicate with your line manager in the same way you would with your best friend
- **a colleague** who may work in the same department as you or in another part of the organisation
- **a customer** who may be a business customer or a private individual. In either case, your organisation will normally have specific methods of communicating with contacts external to the business.

Did you know?

Choosing the best document to meet the needs of your audience increases its effectiveness and impact.

Costs and availability of resources

Businesses try to keep costs down. Postage rates are high, so electronic methods such as email are cheaper. However, email is not an option if your audience does not have regular internet access.

Special software and skills are needed to produce high-quality leaflets and flyers. Unless the business has the resources and expertise available in-house, it is usually better to use a specialist design and print service which can provide expert advice.

Speed and urgency required

Electronic methods of communication are quicker than 'snail mail', especially when you are sending a document overseas. An email is instant whereas an airmail letter can take over a week to arrive. Email attachments can also include other documents such as reports, meetings papers, purchase orders and invoices.

The need to plan research and gather information

Preparation time is important for some formal documents. You cannot put together a presentation or prepare a formal report very quickly. This is because you will need to decide what information you will need, research this and then analyse the results before you start to write anything.

Activity Investigating design and print services

Check out the services available at Kall Kwik and identify the benefits for a small business like Karen's (see WorkSpace) of using a specialist organisation like this. You can access the website by going to www.pearsonhotlinks.co.uk and searching for this title.

WorkSpace

Karen Neild

Director, J A McNulty Ltd

In 2010, Karen and her husband Roger took over J A McNulty Ltd from her father, who started the business in 1988. They now run a well-established double glazing and repair company in Bollington, Cheshire.

The business supplies private customers, trade customers (such as glaziers and builders) and commercial businesses, including shops, hospitals and the local council. Prompt, accurate and courteous written communications are essential for the business to operate efficiently. Enquiries are received by email, telephone and through the website. Once measurements have been taken and items are costed, a quotation is prepared. This is sent by email – or by post for customers without IT access. If they phone to accept, Karen asks them to confirm their order in writing.

Karen then issues a purchase order to suppliers, either by fax or by email. Once the job is completed, an invoice is sent asking for payment in seven days. Most customers pay promptly, but if there are delays, Karen sends a business letter as a reminder. This is more formal than an email so more appropriate in this situation.

To promote the business, Karen has designed flyers focusing on boosting repairs or increasing demand for windows or doors. She also writes a blog on a website to inform customers about new developments and products. To give instructions to staff, Karen may prepare a notice and put this on the board above the job trays, so that everyone will see it. If the matter is important or personal she writes a confidential memo with a tear-off slip, which the recipient must sign and return to prove they have read the information.

Karen knows that information about customers and employees is confidential. This information is kept securely and retained only for as long as necessary, to comply with the requirements of the Data Protection Act.

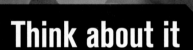

Think about it

1 Explain why Karen always asks a customer for written confirmation of an order.

2 Suggest two reasons why small businesses prefer to communicate by email than by post.

3 Identify two occasions when Karen does communicate by post and give a reason in each case.

4 Give two reasons why Karen does not use email to communicate important or personal information to staff.

5 Suggest three items of information about customers or employees that will be confidential.

Choice of content, style and format

- The content, style and format (or layout) will depend upon your choice of document and the reason for sending it. For example, a mailshot will focus on promoting an item, a response to a complaint will show concern and a report will provide factual information.
- In all documents, the meaning must be clear and the style and format appropriate for that type of document, as you will see in the next section.

Remember

Although emoticons may feature in your communications to friends, they are not appropriate for business documents.

Activity   Writing a press release

A good press release has an attention-grabbing headline, is easy to understand and vital information comes first. Subsequent paragraphs provide more detail so that if the article is cut to fit the space available, key facts are retained. Paragraphs are short, focus on what is happening and where, when, why and who is involved. Further details can be put in Editor's notes below.

Read the example in Figure 10.1 and note the format. Then imagine that a famous celebrity is visiting your school or college and write a press release about it. Invent any details you want and put your own contact details at the end.

Did you know?

An embargo on a press release until a certain date means the item must not be published until that date has passed.

NEWS RELEASE – 5 SEPTEMBER

Zenith
FITNESS AND WELLNESS CENTRE

FOR IMMEDIATE RELEASE

GOLD MEDALLIST VISITS DALESBURY
Sarah French to open latest Zenith centre

Sarah French, UK gold medallist at London 2012, will be opening the new Zenith Fitness and Wellness Centre in Dalesbury on Saturday 20 October. Sarah, winner of the women's modern pentathlon, has been a friend of Zenith's owner, Bob Prest, since their school days.

The new centre is on Castle Rise and facilities include a large, air-conditioned gym, swimming pool, sauna and steam rooms and exercise studios. Therapies include acupuncture, reflexology and Indian head massage, and a wide range of beauty treatments are available. The healthy food café, fully-equipped crèche and free parking guarantee a relaxing visit for all the family.

Zenith Fitness and Wellness was formed in 1999 and the first centre was opened in Covent Garden, London. There are now 12 centres throughout the UK.

-ends-

For further information contact Celeste Bishop
Mobile: 07700900356
Email: Celeste@acme.co.uk

Figure 10.1 Think about the features that make this a good press release

Channel of communication

Business communications can flow in different directions, as shown in Figure 10.2.

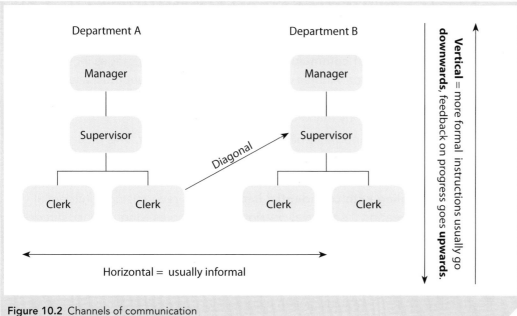

Figure 10.2 Channels of communication

Within the business, vertical communications go upwards or downwards between people at different levels. The most obvious example is an instruction from the boss to all the staff. Horizontal communications are sent between colleagues at the same level, whether they are managers, supervisors or more junior staff. Diagonal communications are a feature of larger organisations, when people at different levels in different departments communicate directly.

Clarity of language

The amount of detail in a communication must be appropriate for your audience. For example, you should not design a notice for young children in the way you would for adults.

- **The fog index** calculates how easy it is to read something you have written. It uses a mathematical formula based on the number of words in a sentence and the number of complex (multi-syllable) words. The final number equals the number of years of education someone needs to understand it, using the US year grade system.
- **The crystal mark** is a symbol awarded by the Plain English Campaign for documents that are easy for everyone to read and understand. The society also issues guides on writing different types of documents and has downloadable software to help check for lack of clarity. It also welcomes nominations for awards, both good and bad.

Activity   Finding Plain English winners

Visit the Plain English Campaign website to find out about recent winners of Plain English awards and Golden Bulls (not good to win), and read the useful guidance to improve your written communications. You can access the website by going to www.pearsonhotlinks.co.uk and searching for this title.

?   **Did you know?**

Critics of the fog index say that just because a word has multiple syllables does not mean it is hard to understand. Every child knows the word 'banana' (ba-na-na) which has three syllables, whereas 'shrewd' has only one syllable, but fewer people know what it means.

Activity

Fog index

Find out the fog index for a paragraph you have written by inputting it online. You can access the website by going to www.pearsonhotlinks.co.uk and searching for this title.

The crystal mark logo.

CONTINUED ▶▶

Confidentiality

Confidential or sensitive information can cause worry, offence, embarrassment or even loss of business if it is made public. If you are handling confidential information, this will affect the type of document you should write and how it is prepared, stored and distributed.

- **Appropriate methods of communication** for confidential messages include business letters, reports or minutes of meetings. The document must always be clearly marked as PERSONAL or PRIVATE AND CONFIDENTIAL and distributed in a sealed envelope also clearly marked CONFIDENTIAL.
- Confidential documents normally have a restricted circulation. This means that only a limited number of copies are made for specified recipients. Office copies are kept in a locked file. Draft or spoiled documents are shredded.
- **Sensitivity in dealing with confidential issues** means recognising confidential information and treating it sensitively by not leaving copies lying around, shredding spoiled copies and not discussing the contents.
- **Material that might be confidential** includes:
  - personal details about staff or customers
  - payroll details, staff work and health records
  - product information, company plans for the future and financial information useful to competitors
  - notes taken at a disciplinary hearing or minutes of a meeting at which possible internal changes were discussed.

Did you know?

Email should never be used to communicate sensitive or confidential information.

Remember

The Data Protection Act aims to prevent information held by an organisation from being misused. This includes confidential employee data as well as data on customers, potential customers and suppliers.

Activity   Investigating confidential information

In groups, suggest the type of information held by your centre that might be confidential. Then talk to your teacher/tutor about the measures taken to ensure it is kept secure.

Keeping records for audit requirements

Key term

Audit – an official check on actions taken and financial claims made by a business.

Written business documents provide evidence of discussions and actions. An **audit** is an official check. There are a variety of types of audit such as financial audits generally carried out by a firm of accountants, quality audits and audits of internal communications. The auditors check that claims made by the company are genuine by referring to the supporting documents.

Documents that may be required during an audit must be kept safely. Some are kept for a minimum length of time for legal reasons, including accounts documents, accident reports, attendance records, payroll records and tax documents. Businesses are recommended to keep various staff records and agreements for six years or more, including disciplinary records, health and safety records and trade union agreements.

Talk to your teacher/tutor about the types of written communication that are required and stored at your centre because they may be needed by an auditor, or to prove something during an Ofsted inspection.

Assessment activity 10.1 *English* 2A.P1 | 2A.P2 | 2B.P3 | 2B.P4 | 2A.M1 | 2B.M2 | 2A.D1 | 2B.D2

You are asked to give a short presentation on the use, purpose, impact and effectiveness of **four** business documents in a selected business of your own choice. Choose a variety of different types of documents, ensure that some are for internal use and some for external use. You should compare how effective these documents are in meeting the needs of their different audiences and evaluate whether they meet the audit and confidentiality requirements of the business. To accompany this presentation, prepare a leaflet or poster to circulate that illustrates the purpose of these different documents in your selected business.

Your presentation and leaflet or poster should focus on the following aspects of business documentation.

- Two of these should be informal and two should be formal. You should include information on the type of document, the business context in which it would be used and how this has influenced the format chosen (i.e. handwritten, text, word processed, electronic or virtual, the types of audience).

- A comparison of the different purposes of the formal and informal documents used by your chosen business and an evaluation of their impact in different business contexts.

- The factors to consider when planning and selecting business documents in different business contexts, to ensure the documents are appropriate and meet the needs of each particular audience, including the need for confidentiality.

Tip

You will find this assessment activity easier if the documents you choose are as different as possible. Select some documents which are for internal audiences and some which are for external audiences. Make sure that the documents are from different business contexts, some formal and some informal, some open and some confidential.

Discussion point

All organisations are advised to keep copies of application forms and interview notes on unsuccessful candidates for one year after the interview was held. As a group, suggest reasons for this.

Produce business documents for communication in a business

Steps involved in producing business documents

Entering, editing and formatting text

When you have decided on the most appropriate words to write, you need to key these into the document you create on a computer and then check your work, making amendments as necessary. You must also decide how your text will be formatted, i.e. the size of your headings, whether or when to use bold or italics, what spaces to leave between headings and paragraphs, and so on.

For business documents, the golden rule is 'less is more'. No one wants to read a cluttered document with different features, so keep it simple.

Use of different formats and styles

The format of a document relates to how it will look when it is produced.

- **The font** determines the way the typeface will look. This must be clear and easy to read. Arial, Verdana and Trebuchet MS are popular choices for business documents, but you can be more creative if you are designing a notice. Each document should have one font only throughout, although the size may change for different headings.

- **Headings** range from main 'A' headings, to 'B' sub-headings and 'C' smaller headings. There are examples of all of these on this page. It is important to use these consistently throughout the document.

- **Images** may be included in some types of documents to provide additional information, but are not usually appropriate in a business letter.

- **Pagination** is important in a long document. You can put a page number at the top or bottom, to the left, in the centre or to the right. **Headers and footers** enable you to have a separate text area at the top and bottom of the page for certain types of information. For example, the name of the business could be in a **header** at the top of each page in a multipage report and the date and page numbers included in the **footer**.

Did you know?

'White space' is the term used for blank areas between features. This helps to make the page easy to read and is essential in a notice or flyer.

Key terms

Header – the top section of a document.

Footer – the bottom section of a document.

Why are images acceptable in leaflets and brochures but not in a business letter?

Drafting and redrafting

It is not easy to write a clear, concise and consistent document at your first attempt. You need to check your spelling, punctuation and grammar, make sure that your information is in a logical order and nothing has been missed out, and that the tone is right and your reader will understand it. It is likely to take a few attempts before you get it right.

Proofreading

Good proofreading skills are vital. Running a spell check is not enough because these miss errors where the result is another 'real' word, for example, form/from; too/two; stationery/stationary; draft/draught. Checking involves reading through your work carefully and asking for advice if you are unsure about anything.

Use of standard/appropriate layouts

The layout of a document relates to how it is set out. This should focus on ensuring that the key information is clearly seen.

Some organisations have a house style that specifies how documents should be set out, including the font to be used and the style of headings, pagination and headers and footers. This helps to ensure that all documents are consistent.

> **Remember**
>
> It is not appropriate to use textspeak in any texts or emails you send on behalf of a business organisation.

Not proofreading properly can cause a lot of embarrassment

Fitness for purpose

The document selected must be fit for purpose and appropriate to the task and the audience, whether internal or external. Purchase orders and invoices are sent to external contacts; the former aims to obtain goods and the latter demands payment. Letters and memos both provide information, but letters are sent to external contacts and memos are only sent internally. Email is the best option if you want information to arrive quickly.

Activity   Checking out meetings documents

In Unit 7 you can see meetings documents. The purpose of these is to provide information to participants before and after a meeting. You can also read tips on taking accurate notes. Go to this section now to see how to do this.

CONTINUED ▶▶

Using relevant technical language, graphical information and conventions

- **Technical language** is only appropriate if the recipient understands it. This normally means restricting it to specialists who work in the same industry.
- **Graphics** are usually tables, charts or diagrams although images are included in flyers and notices and a photograph may be sent with a press release. The type and frequency of images will depend upon the purpose of the document and the audience.
- **Conventions** are standard ways of doing things. These are illustrated in the next section.

Recording and reporting

Notes may be taken during conversations or discussions and then typed up so there is evidence of what was said or agreed. They may be prepared as minutes of a meeting or as a report following a visit to a customer.

Any written record must be accurate and complete. This does not mean writing down every word, but does mean ensuring that nothing important is left out.

Copying documents

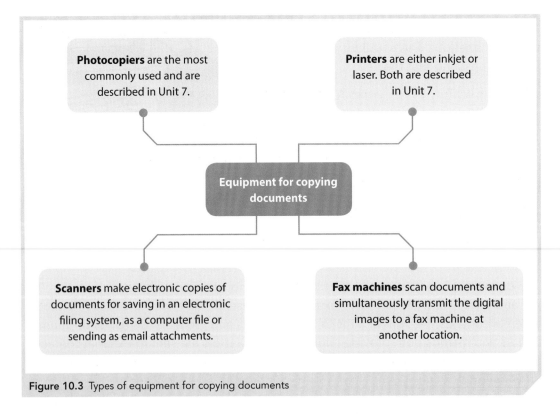

Figure 10.3 Types of equipment for copying documents

Whichever type of equipment you use, you must ensure you produce quality **hard copies** and do not waste paper. The key points are shown in the checklist below.

Table 10.5 Checklist for copying documents and minimising wastage

✔	Read the handbook (or ask for a demonstration) before you use any new equipment.
✔	Follow health and safety requirements, e.g. keep liquids away from electrical equipment, ensure the equipment is on a stable surface and there are no trailing wires.
✔	Check the number of copies you are expected to produce.
✔	Check the quality of your original document is good and it has no errors.
✔	Take one test copy. Then make any adjustments that are needed. (On a scanner you can preview the image to check it.)
✔	Ensure the correct paper is in the tray. This should usually be 'fanned' so that pages do not stick together. Refill the tray if necessary.
✔	Check no warning lights are indicating that your ink or toner is low, or some copies will be unreadable. If you do not know how to replace the ink or toner, ask someone to show you.
✔	Be vigilant, particularly if you are making many copies, in case there is a problem part way through.
✔	On some photocopiers you can collate multiple pages and have these stapled or bound automatically. If you are stapling pages yourself, check the pages are in the right order and that the staple(s) do not obscure any text.

Working within given time frames to meet deadlines

An urgent document should be top priority. It must be prepared promptly and sent using the most appropriate method to ensure the recipient(s) gets the information in time. If you have a complex document to produce, agree a deadline and then plan your work, bearing in mind your other jobs.

Ensuring documents reach intended audience

There are specific methods you can use to ensure that important and urgent documents are received safely.

- You can send a document by courier, but this is expensive. Another option is to use the Royal Mail Recorded Delivery service so you can track when it is delivered. The recipient must sign for it, too, which provides proof that it was received.

- You can check the 'read receipt' option when you send an email. This asks the recipient to click to confirm they have received it, though the request can be ignored. A safer option is to telephone to check it has arrived safely.

Key term

Hard copy – the term used for a paper copy of a document.

Did you know?

If you are producing a multi-page document that will be stapled or bound, it is sensible to have wide margins so that no text will be obscured.

Just checking

1 What is the difference between a header and a footer?
2 Identify three ways you can reduce paper wastage when copying a document.
3 Why can you never rely on a spell check to find all your mistakes?

Document conventions

Memos and emails

Memos

- Memos are internal documents which may be used for complex or important matters. They are normally quite short and focus on just one topic. The most usual layout is shown in Figure 10.4.
- The formality of a memo will depend on the recipient and the subject matter. A memo about a social event will be worded very differently from one about a serious customer complaint.
- Slang expressions should be avoided but abbreviated words are sometimes used, for example, 'thanks', 'I'll' or 'haven't'.

Did you know?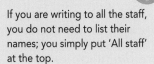

If you are writing to all the staff, you do not need to list their names; you simply put 'All staff' at the top.

Activity

Writing a memo

Write a memo to your teacher/tutor asking if you can be excused from classes next Monday. Explain that your father has his own business and has an urgent order to fulfil. He would like you to help out and thinks it would be good experience, but only with your teacher/tutor's agreement. Reassure them this is an exception and that you will catch up with any work you miss.

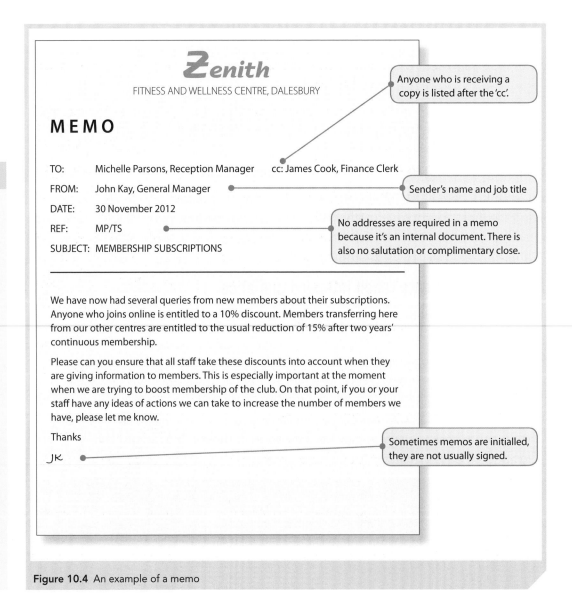

Zenith

FITNESS AND WELLNESS CENTRE, DALESBURY

MEMO

TO: Michelle Parsons, Reception Manager   cc: James Cook, Finance Clerk

FROM: John Kay, General Manager

DATE: 30 November 2012

REF: MP/TS

SUBJECT: MEMBERSHIP SUBSCRIPTIONS

We have now had several queries from new members about their subscriptions. Anyone who joins online is entitled to a 10% discount. Members transferring here from our other centres are entitled to the usual reduction of 15% after two years' continuous membership.

Please can you ensure that all staff take these discounts into account when they are giving information to members. This is especially important at the moment when we are trying to boost membership of the club. On that point, if you or your staff have any ideas of actions we can take to increase the number of members we have, please let me know.

Thanks

JK

Anyone who is receiving a copy is listed after the 'cc'.

Sender's name and job title

No addresses are required in a memo because it's an internal document. There is also no salutation or complimentary close.

Sometimes memos are initialled, they are not usually signed.

Figure 10.4 An example of a memo

Emails

Emails can be sent internally or externally. If John had emailed Michelle, the wording would be the same but not the format. This is because the header on an email is set up by the software and includes:

- **the sender's name** – which is inserted automatically
- **the recipient's name** – this is inserted automatically when you reply
- **the date and time** – again, this is inserted automatically
- **the subject** – enter a brief title to summarise the content.

When you send an email, you have several options.

- You can copy an email to other people and have two choices: 'cc' copies include the name(s) of the recipient(s) at the top which everyone can see; 'bcc' copies are blind copies that have the recipients' names hidden.
- You can forward an email you have received to other people.
- You can attach electronic files containing text, graphics, sound clips or images. Compress (zip) any large files so they transmit more quickly.
- You can include a high priority level for important emails on some email programmes. Only use this when it is appropriate or people will ignore it.

Writing business emails is different from sending them to your friends. The rules shown in Table 10.6 should be followed at all times.

Remember

In an external email you may need to be more formal, start with 'Dear' (at least on the first occasion) and sign off with 'Best wishes'.

Table 10.6 Business email rules

DO...	DON'T...
… reply promptly to emails you receive.	… use the same phrases you would use to a friend.
… copy the style of salutations and complimentary closes used on emails where you work.	… include confidential information.
… use proper sentences and paragraphs and correct English (i.e. normal spelling, grammar and punctuation).	… SHOUT by using all capitals or use emoticons such as :) or : (, or abbreviations such as LOL.
… get to the point quickly and keep your sentences relatively short.	… use 'Reply to All' unless it is essential.
… use bullets or numbered points for a list of items.	… forward and copy emails unnecessarily, particularly if they include other people's email addresses.
… send separate emails if you are communicating on different topics.	… use technical words or jargon your recipient will not understand.
… carry out a spell check and then proof-read.	… delete the message thread – it can be useful to refresh people's memory.
… check it makes sense and is error-free before you press 'send'.	… print out messages unless it is really necessary.
… add 'thanks' at the end if you are asking a favour.	… reply to spam, forward chainmail or virus hoax emails.
… check you are sending it to the correct recipient and that you have included the attachments you mentioned.	… assume all emails arrive. If you do not receive a response, telephone instead.

CONTINUED ▸▸

Notices and reports

Notices

Notices aim to provide essential information in order of importance. The style and layout will depend upon the formality of the message, the amount of text and the target audience. They often include a striking graphic or image to attract attention.

Points to note:

- Use a large, clear, short heading that says what it is about.
- Keep the text short and break up longer sections by using sub-headings or bullet points.
- Use terms and language that everyone will understand.
- Include all the key details: what, when, where and who to contact.
- Add the date and your name, if people may need to contact you.

Activity | Designing a notice

Design a notice to advertise a 5K Fancy Dress Fun Run in aid of the local hospice which will start at Zenith four weeks on Sunday at 10 am. Invent any further details to make it realistic.

Reports

Reports may be prepared for internal or external use. They are often written after carrying out research, undertaking an investigation or to report on an event. Before you start there is some preparation to be done.

- **Consider the aim**: Why are you writing it? Who is it for? What do they want to know?
- **Draft the introduction**: Say who asked you for the report and why.
- **Organise your information**: Put your facts into a logical order and then decide how to separate them to keep them clear.
- **Decide appropriate recommendations**: If you are asked for these, they must be sensible and relevant to the rest of your report.

Points to note:

- The headings and spacing must be consistent and no slang or abbreviated words should be used.
- Add an appropriate title at the top and your name and the date at the end.
- There are usually three sections: an introduction, which states the reason for writing the report; the body of the report, which gives the information you have obtained; a conclusion, which sums up the information and says whether or not any action is needed.
- Only add your recommendations if you have been asked to provide them.

Activity   Writing a report

The Healthy Food Café at Zenith, which is open to members and non-members, is not doing well. John Kay recently had complaints about poor service which the staff have strongly denied. He has asked Julie Marshall, a market researcher, to visit and report on her experience. Read the report in Figure 10.5 and then decide what recommendations she might add. Draft these using the same format.

For one experience you have in the next week (such as eating out, going to the cinema, buying something in a shop), write a report to summarise it. Decide on appropriate headings and then add recommendations you think the business could make to improve customers' experiences (if any). Present your report to the rest of your group.

? Did you know?

It is clearer to divide up lengthy information into separate paragraphs or numbered or bulleted points. Bullets are better when there is no specific order.

REPORT ON VISIT TO ZENITH FITNESS AND WELLNESS CENTRE, DALESBURY, 18 FEBRUARY 2013

Introduction

As requested, I visited the Healthy Food Café at Zenith Fitness and Wellness Centre in Dalesbury last week. This report summarises my experience.

First impressions

I arrived at 12.30 p.m. with a friend.

1. I had previously telephoned and asked if I could reserve a table but was told that this service is not available. Fortunately there were several vacant tables.
2. The eating area was clean, light and airy, but some empty tables still needed to be cleared of dirty dishes.

Food and drink

The short menu on the table was supplemented by a blackboard listing daily specials.

1. Several hot meat, fish and vegetarian dishes were available as well as cakes and puddings. No sandwich options were listed and only one salad dish.
2. A range of hot and cold soft drinks was available. The café does not have a licence to sell alcoholic drinks.
3. The food that I ate was well-cooked and attractively presented. The price was reasonable.

Service

Although the café is self-service, there were no notices explaining this.

1. At the counter, it took a few moments before the staff broke off from their conversation to serve me.
2. Both assistants were smartly dressed in clean, white overalls with their hair tied back.
3. When I queried the ingredients in a dish, the young woman went to the kitchen to ask. I was then told it would take 20 minutes to prepare.
4. There were no trays available and the staff did not offer to help carry any items to the table.

Conclusions

My conclusions are as follows:

1. The café area is modern and attractive and the food quality is good.
2. The level of service is poor and with no reservation system or drinks licence, I would not choose to visit the café for social reasons.

Julie Marshall
18 February 2013

Figure 10.5 Julie's report

CONTINUED ▶▶

Business letters

Business letters are used for external communications and written on headed paper. This gives key information about the organisation, such as its name, address, telephone number, website address and often the address of the registered office. A standard layout is shown below.

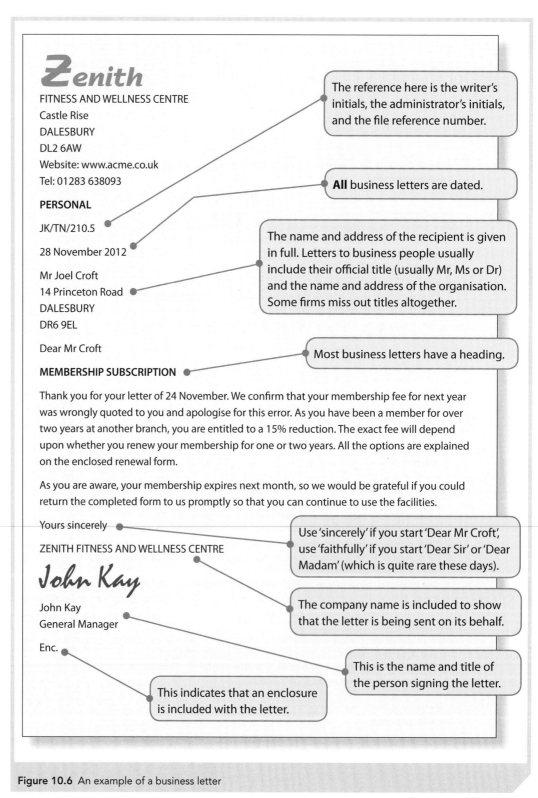

Figure 10.6 An example of a business letter

Points to note:

- Slang and contracted words, such as 'don't' are never used in a business letter.

- The style and tone should suit the purpose: a sales letter is upbeat, a written complaint should be factual and the response should be apologetic.

- Letters must be polite – use the word 'please' if you want something, but avoid its overuse with other phrases such as 'we would be grateful if…' or 'it would help us if…'

- Letters should never end just with 'thank you'. Instead use a more business-like phrase such as 'We appreciate your help in this matter.'

- There are usually three of four paragraphs: the first gives the reason for writing and introduces the main topic; the second (and possibly the third) provide more detail; the closing paragraph says what will happen next or the action expected.

> **? Did you know?**
>
> Many businesses use open punctuation where commas are inserted only in the body of the letter to help understanding, but are not used in abbreviations or at the end of address or date lines.

Assessment activity 10.2 *English* | 2C.P5 | 2C.P6 | 2C.M3 | 2C.D3

1 You work for Zenith Fitness and Wellness Centre. Your manager, John Kay wants you to undertake several tasks which will involve you preparing suitable business documents for the below situations. Note that although some employees have email access, there is also a staff notice board.

a) John wants to offer 'women only' spa days starting four weeks on Thursday. These will include pool and spa access, lunch and two beauty treatments for £80 per person. Publicise this information to the staff. Then notify the local paper.

b) Lisa Wright has emailed, enquiring about the cost of having a hen day at the centre before her June wedding. John says to offer her a variation on the spa day. For 10 people it would cost £70 each and include sparkling wine at lunch – but she must book it in the next two weeks and pay a deposit of 25 per cent.

c) Since Julie's visit, the café has a new supervisor, tables can now be reserved, there is a Lite Bites menu, a licence to serve alcohol and full waitress service. Brian Short of 23 Watery Lane, Westbridge, WE2 9PL complained about the café last month. John wants you to apologise, explain the improvements and include a £20 voucher to tempt him to return.

d) Although staff can normally eat in the café, on Friday it has been reserved by a local business group from 12 noon to 2.30 pm. John wants all staff to know so they can make alternative arrangements.

e) John wants you to work in a group to devise an alternative programme to the spa day for men. Hold this discussion, then write a report containing your ideas, conclusions and recommendations.

2 You have produced six documents. Look at the format and style of each document and think about how the documents you have produced are suitable for your intended audience and why they are fit for purpose, bearing in mind the context and the alternatives available. Write a summary, assessing the factors that influenced the way in which you produced each document, including how you could reach your intended audience in time.

Tip

You should explain why the format and style of each document made it fit for purpose and how your choice of document relates to the context of the situation.

Introduction

If you look at job advertisements, you will often see that they require a team player. Is this you? Surveys of employers reveal that team skills are very important. Why is teamwork essential in business? Is it because of the special energy that is created when individuals come together and share their skills and talents in the pursuit of a common goal? Or is it because a good team can achieve far more than the same number of individuals?

Teamwork will stretch your talents and harness your creativity. Some of your best moments at work are likely to be when working in a team with people who share your dreams and aspirations. At some point in your career, you may take on the role of team leader. This role comes with more responsibilities and to do it well, you will need special qualities. This unit explores the importance of teams and teamworking, the role of a team leader and the skills needed for effective teamworking.

Assessment: This unit will be assessed through a series of assignments set by your teacher/tutor.

Learning aims

In this unit you will:

A investigate the importance of teams and teamworking

B understand the role of the team leader

C use skills to demonstrate effective teamworking.

> This unit made me realise how important it is to be able to work well in a team. It was good to be able to practise my teamworking skills and I enjoyed finding out about what makes a good team leader.
>
> Amelie, *16-year-old Business student*

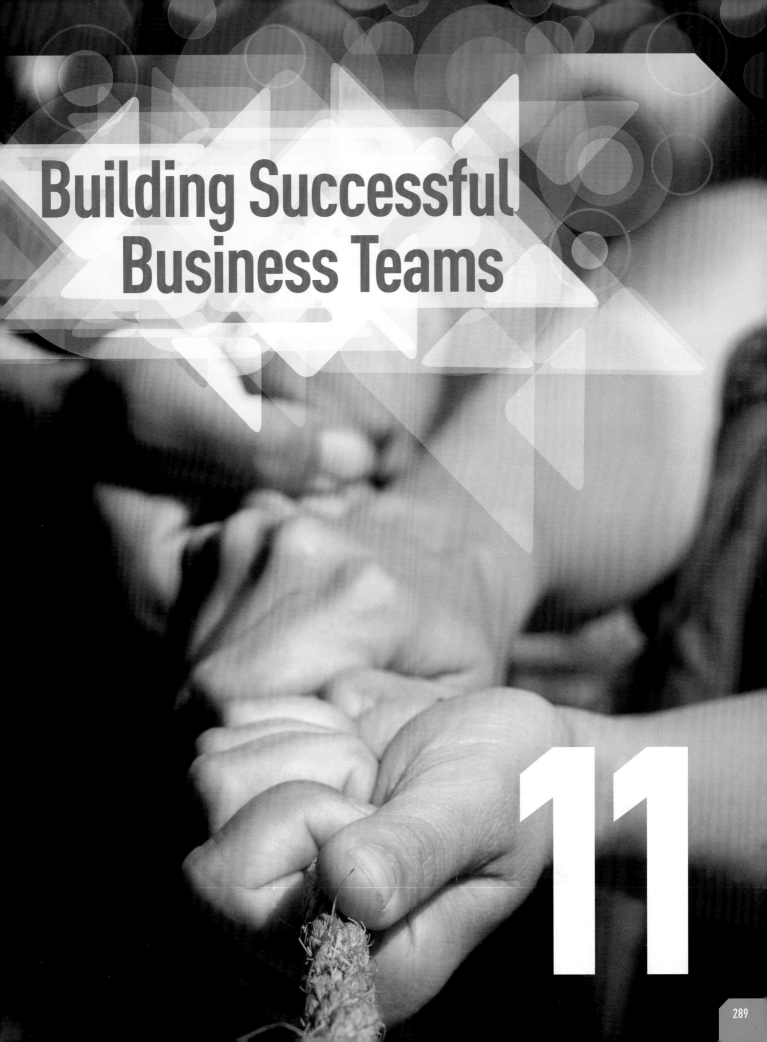

Building Successful Business Teams

11

Assessment Zone

This table shows you what you must do in order to achieve a **Pass**, **Merit** or **Distinction** grade, and where you can find activities in this book to help you.

Assessment criteria			
Level 1	Level 2 Pass	Level 2 Merit	Level 2 Distinction
Learning aim A: Investigate the importance of teams and teamworking			
1A.1 Identify the characteristics of two effective business teams	**2A.P1** Describe the characteristics of two effective business teams **See Assessment activity 11.1, page 304**	**2A.M1** Assess, using examples, the importance of the stages of team development and team role theory in developing an effective business team **See Assessment activity 11.1, page 304**	**2A.D1** Evaluate the effectiveness of a selected business team **See Assessment activity 11.1, page 304**
1A.2 Outline the importance of the stages of team development in a selected business team	**2A.P2** Explain the importance of the stages of team development in a selected business team **See Assessment activity 11.1, page 304**		
1A.3 Outline the importance of team role theory in a selected business team	**2A.P3** Explain the importance of team role theory in a selected business team **See Assessment activity 11.1, page 304**	**2A.M2** Assess the benefits of teamworking for the business and individual team member of a selected business **See Assessment activity 11.1, page 304**	
1A.4 Identify the behaviours needed for effective teamwork	**2A.P4** Describe, using examples, the behaviours needed for effective teamwork **See Assessment activity 11.1, page 304**		
Learning aim B: Understand the role of the team leader			
1B.5 Outline the role and responsibilities of a team leader in two business teams	**2B.P5** Explain the importance of the role and responsibilities of the team leader in two contrasting business teams **See Assessment activity 11.1, page 304**	**2B.M3** Assess how the team leader contributes to the effectiveness of a selected business team **See Assessment activity 11.1, page 304**	**2B.D2** Evaluate the effectiveness of a team leader in ensuring a selected business team meets its objectives **See Assessment activity 11.1, page 304**
1B.6 Identify the attributes and qualities of the team leader in two business teams	**2B.P6** Describe the attributes and qualities of the team leader in two contrasting business teams **See Assessment activity 11.1, page 304**		

Level 1	Level 2 Pass	Level 2 Merit	Level 2 Distinction
Learning Aim C: Use skills to demonstrate effective teamworking			
1C.7 English Demonstrate appropriate teamworking skills that contribute to meeting the objectives of a business team	**2C.P7** English Demonstrate effective teamworking skills that contribute to meeting the objectives of a business team, including taking responsibility for own work **See Assessment activity 11.2, page 309**	**2C.M4** English Demonstrate effective teamworking skills that contribute to meeting the objectives of a business team, including taking responsibility for own work and overcoming barriers **See Assessment activity 11.2, page 309**	**2C.D3** Evaluate own contribution to the effectiveness of a business team in meeting its objectives **See Assessment activity 11.2, page 309**
1C.8 Describe how well the team performed, including own role in the team	**2C.P8** Assess how well the team performed in meeting its objectives **See Assessment activity 11.2, page 309**	**2C.M5** Assess how well the team performed in meeting its objectives, including how conflict was managed and resolved and how barriers were overcome **See Assessment activity 11.2, page 309**	**2C.D4** Recommend improvements to the performance of the team to ensure it continues to meet its objectives in the future **See Assessment activity 11.2, page 309**

English / Opportunity to practise English skills

How you will be assessed

You will be set assignments in which you will investigate the importance of teams, teamworking and the role of team leaders in business teams. You will also complete tasks that require you to demonstrate and provide evidence of your own teamworking skills.

Your evidence of assessment could be in the form of:

- a written account or presentation detailing your investigations of business teams
- written observational evidence of effective teamworking skills
- a personal statement reflecting on own teamworking skills.

Effective teams

Introduction

Can you think of a job that does not involve teamwork? Even people who appear to work alone, are usually part of a team. For example, when you visit the dentist, you normally see a team of people including the dentist, dental nurse, hygienist and receptionist.

Some teams, such as top sports teams, work together on a daily basis, whereas other teams may appear to operate as individuals, but work together towards shared goals by meeting regularly and supporting one another.

What is a team?

A team can be defined as 'a collection of people who have a commitment to work together to achieve a common goal'. This is different from a **group** which is a collection of individuals who have something in common, such as being in the same place at the same time or sharing the same interests.

Teams can be powerful. People in teams are more likely to have the same values, to rely on each other, to listen to each other and to trust each other than people in groups.

Activity

Identifying teams and groups

Which of the following are teams and which are groups? Give a reason for your choices.

- football fans;
- the cast of a play;
- a crowd at a music festival;
- the staff at a McDonald's outlet;
- your business teachers/tutors;
- friends who go out together on a Saturday night.

What is the common goal for the team in this picture?

Types of business teams

Not all teams are the same. Some teams are permanent; others are temporary and work on a specific project before disbanding.

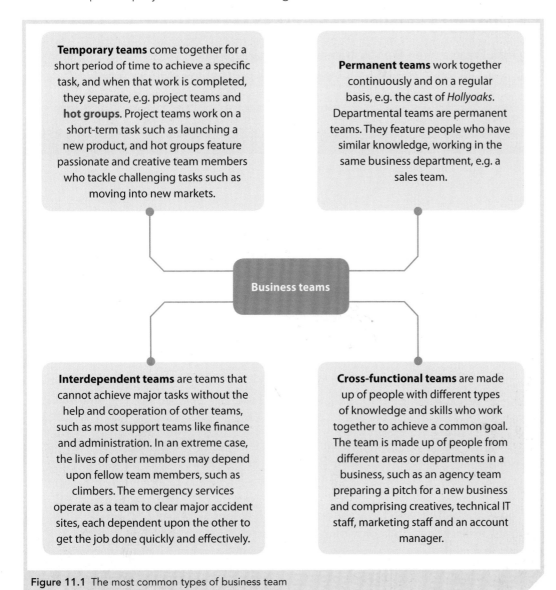

Temporary teams come together for a short period of time to achieve a specific task, and when that work is completed, they separate, e.g. project teams and **hot groups**. Project teams work on a short-term task such as launching a new product, and hot groups feature passionate and creative team members who tackle challenging tasks such as moving into new markets.

Permanent teams work together continuously and on a regular basis, e.g. the cast of *Hollyoaks*. Departmental teams are permanent teams. They feature people who have similar knowledge, working in the same business department, e.g. a sales team.

Business teams

Interdependent teams are teams that cannot achieve major tasks without the help and cooperation of other teams, such as most support teams like finance and administration. In an extreme case, the lives of other members may depend upon fellow team members, such as climbers. The emergency services operate as a team to clear major accident sites, each dependent upon the other to get the job done quickly and effectively.

Cross-functional teams are made up of people with different types of knowledge and skills who work together to achieve a common goal. The team is made up of people from different areas or departments in a business, such as an agency team preparing a pitch for a new business and comprising creatives, technical IT staff, marketing staff and an account manager.

Figure 11.1 The most common types of business team

Key term

Hot group – a group of highly motivated employees who work together on a project that is above and beyond their normal duties.

Did you know?

Many businesses arrange for their employees to go on team-building days where they participate in activities such as white water rafting, rock climbing and team-building challenges. This is done to improve the way in which they work together by building trust among the team and improving communication.

Just checking

1 What is the difference between a team and a group?
2 What is an interdependent team?
3 What is a hot group?
4 What is a cross-functional team?

What makes a team effective?

◤ Characteristics

Successful teams often demonstrate specific characteristics. These reinforce the purpose of the team and help individual members act in the team's interest.

Table 11.1 Characteristics of an effective team

Characteristic	What this means for the team
Importance of each team member's contribution whatever their role	Everybody must feel valued in the team.
United in a common purpose	It is essential that everybody is working towards the same goal and puts this ahead of their personal goals.
Complementary skills	Some team members are strong in the areas in which others are weak, so they are more successful together than on their own, e.g. in a sales team one person may be a technical expert while another colleague might be very good at dealing with difficult customers.
Loyalty to the team	At all times, team members act in the best interest of the team, and not themselves.
Development of Identity	Individuals feel proud to belong to that team and this will increase their commitment to the team.
Trust	You can rely on your team members without constantly checking on them, so you get more done.
Cooperation	This is vital if everybody is to work together.
Good communication	Listening to each other and being understood are essential to avoid misunderstandings, and so is providing timely and accurate information to other members in a tactful way.
Reaching consensus	All teams are likely to have disagreements, but it is important that the team can talk things over and come to an agreement. This may mean that individual members have to compromise to reach agreement.
Supporting each other	People are happier and more productive when team members help one another and know they can rely on their colleagues for help in a crisis.
Managing conflict	Disagreements are common in all teams, but being able to manage that conflict well prevents people becoming resentful and opting out.

Activity Handling conflict

Discuss ways in which a team leader could handle a conflict situation that has arisen with a team.

Stages in team development

It can take time for a team to become effective. Bruce Tuckman studied teams and found that they go through various stages before they are at their most effective.

Forming
This is when the team first comes together. Individuals begin to get to know each other, but at this stage there is little shared purpose.

Storming
Individuals in the group put forward their own ideas. They may challenge each other and the team still lacks direction and structure.

Norming
The team starts to come together. They establish their goals and put together a plan to achieve them. The plan outlines who is to do what.

Performing
The team achieves its goals. It is well organised and its members are working well together. At this stage, you will see many of the characteristics of an effective team outlined in Table 11.1.

Transforming
As times goes by, teams change. People leave and people join, or existing team members take on new roles. These changes mean that the team is unlikely to remain in the performing stage. People may feel uncertain about what is expected of them and their colleagues, and this feels like the forming stage. People may want to put forward new ideas, which is the storming stage, or new people or people with different roles may need to be allocated jobs, which is the norming stage.

Figure 11.2 The stages in team development

Take it further

A stage that has more recently been suggested is 'mourning'. This occurs when the team breaks up and members of the team miss their colleagues and go through a grieving process. Television programmes such as *X Factor* and *Strictly Come Dancing* feature people who work very closely together and then they are suddenly knocked out of the competition. Do you think that they go through a mourning stage? Have you ever felt empty or sad at the end of a project?

Just checking

1 Identify four characteristics of a successful team.
2 What happens in the forming stage?
3 What happens in the norming stage?

Activity   Acting out the stages in team development

You are going on a week's holiday with four friends and will be sharing self-catering accommodation. In groups, devise a role-play to illustrate an example of the first four stages. A year later, three of you go away again, but this time with two new members. Suggest how this might 'transform' the team.

Team roles

Introduction

Each person in an effective team has a clear role. This ensures that all team members know what they should be doing and helps to avoid several people doing the same task.

◢ Belbin's Team Roles

Dr Meredith Belbin devised a popular theory of **Team Roles** from years of studying teams in different workplaces. Belbin claims that when people get together in a team, they take on specific roles. He identified nine major team roles and found that some people take on more than one.

He argued that for a team to work well, all Roles must be covered and there needs to be a balance in the Roles. For instance, if a team has no Coordinator or Shaper, there is no one to lead the team or to help it focus on its goals.

Table 11.2 shows Belbin's Team Roles. You can see that each Role has its strengths and its allowable weaknesses. Team members understand that the flipside of being good at one thing may be that you are not so good at something else. For instance, if you are a Shaper, working in a team designing a new logo, you should appreciate that your artistic colleague (a Plant) will suggest many ideas even if some of them are too wacky to be useful.

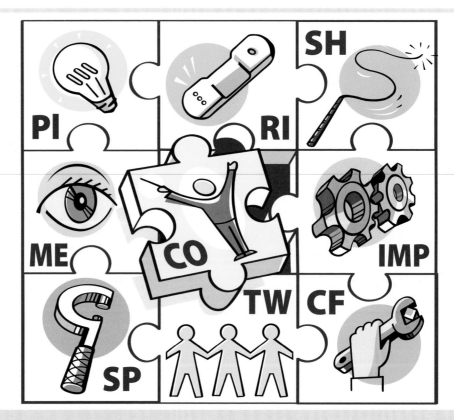

Figure 11.3 Belbin's Team Roles

Table 11.2 Belbin's Team Roles

Role	Contribution to the team	Allowable weaknesses of role
Plant	Creative, imaginative, free thinking. Generates ideas and solves difficult problems.	Ignores incidentals. Too preoccupied to communicate effectively.
Resource Investigator	Outgoing, enthusiastic, communicative. Explores opportunities and develops contacts.	Over-optimistic. Loses interest once initial enthusiasm has passed.
Co-ordinator	Mature, confident, identifies talent. Clarifies goals. **Delegates** effectively.	Can be seen as manipulative. Offloads own share of the work.
Shaper	Challenging, dynamic, thrives on pressure. Has the drive and courage to overcome obstacles.	Prone to provocation. Offends people's feelings.
Monitor Evaluator	Sober, strategic and discerning. Sees all options and judges accurately.	Lacks drive and ability to inspire others. Can be overly critical.
Teamworker	Co-operative, perceptive and diplomatic. Listens and averts friction.	Indecisive in crunch situations. Avoids confrontation.
Implementer	Practical, reliable, efficient. Turns ideas into actions and organises work that needs to be done.	Somewhat inflexible. Slow to respond to new possibilities.
Completer Finisher	Painstaking, conscientious, anxious. Searches out errors. Polishes and perfects.	Inclined to worry unduly. Reluctant to delegate.
Specialist	Single-minded, self-starting, dedicated. Provides knowledge and skills in rare supply.	Contributes only on a narrow front. Dwells on technicalities.

Activity   Understanding Belbin's Team Roles

In pairs, identify one Team Role from the table above to research further online. Check with your teacher/tutor if there are any terms that you do not understand. Then prepare a short description that summarises the strengths and weaknesses of that type of person for the rest of your class.

Key term

Delegate – to assign work to someone within the team.

Activity

Which roles do you play?

Think about your experience of working in teams and try to identify the role(s) you play. Discover the role you play in the team by asking your fellow learners and teacher/tutor if they agree with you.

Just checking

1. Which Belbin Team Role comes up with the initial idea?
2. Which Belbin Team Role might overly delegate the team's jobs?
3. Which Belbin Team Role is good at finding out information?
4. Which Belbin Team Role makes sure that the work is completed?
5. Who is likely to have a special skill?

Effective teamworking

 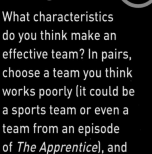
Team behaviours

If team members can demonstrate certain behaviours, the team should work well together. These behaviours will boost team morale, bond a team, build trust, make people feel valued, ease tensions, aid communication and move the team forward.

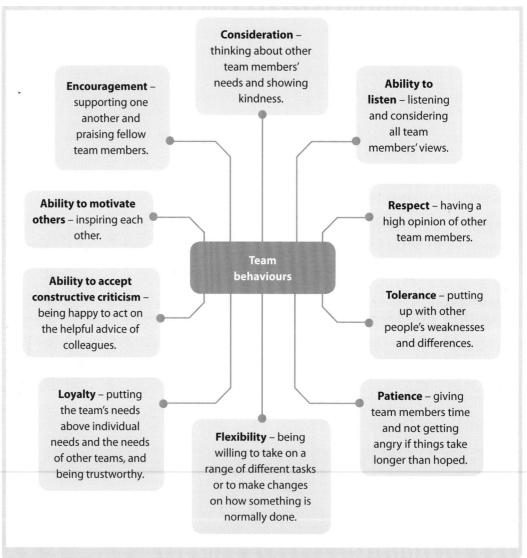

Figure 11.4 The above behaviours all contribute to ensuring a team work well together

Activity   Practising good teamworking behaviours

Select three behaviours of effective teamworking and demonstrate them at some point during the day, whether at school, college or work placement. Record your experiences and be prepared to discuss them with the rest of your class.

The benefits of effective team working

There are many benefits of effective teamworking, both for the business and the individuals within the team.

Table 11.3 Benefits of effective teamworking

Benefits for the business	Benefits for the individual
Contributing to business objectives: teams focus on specific tasks that help the business to achieve its main goals.	**Opportunities to stretch talents and take on new responsibilities:** you get the chance to learn from one another and when the team divides up the work, you might take charge of new things outside of your normal job role.
Making best use of people's strengths: putting people in the role for which they are best fitted.	**Increased motivation:** it can be lonely and boring working on your own. Most of us enjoy working with others and working together towards a goal can be exciting. There is also a greater sense of belonging and commitment when working in a team.
Better internal communication: being part of a team means that you are in constant close contact with your colleagues and you communicate with them frequently which should mean that people find it easy to talk to each other.	**Opportunities for creativity and showing initiative:** you can bounce ideas off one another and show people what you are capable of achieving.
Increased efficiency and productivity: good teams outperform individuals because teams have a special energy from bringing different talents together.	
Less duplication of tasks: working in a team means that you can sort out who is doing what, which avoids several people doing the same thing without realising it.	
Less risk by sharing work: businesses do not like to rely on one person to do a key job because if they leave, the business may be left with no one knowing how to do that particular job.	
More flexible workforce: teams offer more skills, knowledge and together can achieve far more than any individual.	

Activity   Why join 'Team'?

The Prince's Trust is an organisation that helps to change the lives of young people who are not in education, employment or training. One way in which they do this is through a very successful 12-week programme called 'Team'. Go on the Prince's Trust website and find out more about this programme and identify the benefits to be gained. You can access the website by going to www.pearsonhotlinks.co.uk and searching for this title.

Roles and responsibilities of the team leader

Key term

Team leader – the individual who has overall responsibility for the team and its goals.

Introduction

One definition of a **team leader**'s role is to 'meet the needs of the task, team and individual'. When a team leader can balance these three things well, team morale and productivity should improve. Therefore a team leader such as David Moyes should aim to get their team to successfully achieve the task (for example, winning the FA cup) while managing the needs of the team (for example, agreeing and communicating a training regime) and the needs of the individual (for example, helping players cope with injury).

Think of three team needs that the manager of FC Barcelona would have managed to ensure that the team won Champions League.

Team leader responsibilities

Team leaders have a number of responsibilities to ensure that the team is effective. Some of these responsibilities are listed below:

- **Planning the work of the team:** this means considering all the different tasks for which the team is responsible and deciding which areas individual members should focus on, bearing in mind their strengths, experience and interests.
- **Setting objectives and deadlines:** objectives are short-term and focus on the achievement of individual tasks by the agreed deadline. Objectives should be SMART (specific, measurable, achievable, realistic and time-based).
- **Giving instructions:** team leaders give the team clear and specific instructions so that everyone knows what they are doing and by when.
- **Monitoring the work of the team:** the team leader checks how the task is being carried out compared with the plan.
- **Motivating the team:** team leaders embolden the team to achieve its objectives by offering incentives and exciting tasks, inspiring people with their personality and being supportive.

- **Communicating with the team:** team leaders ensure the team knows what is expected of them and keep them informed. Communication occurs through meetings and through technology, e.g. phone, email and video-conferencing.

- **Making decisions:** team leaders are responsible for making decisions, such as deciding on the best way of doing something or allocating team members to different activities. Some decisions, such as how to solve a problem, often involve all team members.

- **Providing feedback:** team leaders provide feedback to the team and to individual team members on performance of a task. This may be done in the form of a written report, **appraisal** or verbal feedback.

- **Leading meetings:** team leaders run team meetings and briefings. Meetings need a clear purpose and should involve the whole team.

- **Managing conflict:** team leaders should monitor and manage conflict in the team, e.g. by stepping in when there is a disagreement and negotiating a solution that keeps everyone happy.

- **Providing support:** team leaders support the team by getting to know people individually so that their needs are understood, by providing assistance or extra training and praising people for their achievements.

Key terms

Appraisal – the process by which a manager examines and evaluates an employee's work.

Activity Researching team leader responsibilities

1 Identify which of these tasks your teacher/tutor carries out as your team leader.

2 Prepare questions and interview a team leader from your school or college to find out about their job and how they plan the work of their team.

Remember

Team leaders should regularly review their team's performance. This may mean making changes to achieve an objective. When Prime Ministers review their government's performance, they carry out cabinet reshuffles where MPs are given different jobs. When television directors review a soap's success, they bring in new characters and write out old ones.

How the team leader contributes to overall effectiveness

The team leader's role is important to the effectiveness of the team, including:

- **ensuring business needs are met:** this is achieved through delegation of tasks, or dividing the work among the team members, and through checking and ensuring that work is being completed to the right quality

- **integrating a leadership role into day-to-day activities:** this means the leader is working closely with the employees on day-to-day activities (e.g. in team meetings, one-to-one meetings and informal contact), which should raise the standards of work and provide opportunities to bring out people's talents.

Just checking

1 Why is it important that objectives are SMART?

2 What is an appraisal?

3 Can you think of any examples of what is likely to cause conflict in a team?

Attributes and qualities of an effective leader

Introduction

If you are a team leader, you should expect a lot from your team, but you will only get the best out of people if you treat them well.

If you want to be an effective leader, you should do the following:

What qualities do you think make Sir Alan Sugar successful?

- **Treat others fairly** – divide the work up fairly among the team and give people enough time to do it. Do not show favouritism by giving your friends the best jobs.
- **Involve team members** – do not leave anybody out and make sure that everyone is heard.
- **Value team members' contributions** – show that you value team members, e.g. point out their achievements.
- **Respect others' opinions** – ask for your team's opinions and use their ideas to make decisions. People then feel involved in the decision making.
- **Support team members** – encourage people and help them where needed.
- **Lead by example** – if you want people to work hard, you will have to work hard and be disciplined. Get your hands dirty and show people that you are not too special to do the jobs that you expect them to do.
- **Accept responsibility** – if somebody in your team makes a mistake or if the team does not achieve its objectives, do not blame the people in your team. Accept that you were in charge so their failings are your fault. Perhaps you could have done more to support the team? Maybe your plan was not right? Maybe an individual needed more training?
- **Communicate effectively with the team** – try to be persuasive and clear in the way you communicate the team's goals and duties. Engage in **active listening** and questioning.
- **Show integrity, fairness and consistency** – show **integrity** through being honest and truthful. You could demonstrate this quality by owning up to something if you have made a mistake, or through working in an honest way by always following company rules and procedures. To show consistency, you need to be predictable. Avoid going back on your decisions, do not blow hot and cold with your moods. If you are consistent, people will know where they stand with you.

Activity   Communicating effectively

Good communicators are active listeners and use questioning effectively.

Active listening is making an effort to hear what people are really saying. To do this, pay close attention to what the person is saying, do not get distracted by other things around you and do not allow yourself to get bored or lose focus on what the person is saying. When you are really struggling, try repeating what they are saying back to yourself in your head.

Questioning can be used to help the team.

- It can be used to find out information: 'Does anybody know …?'
- Questions can be used to clarify things: 'Did you mean…?'
- They can also be used to find out what the team thinks: 'How many of you think…?'

Next time you work in a team, try to use active listening and questioning techniques to see how they affect the way you work. Write a short reflective log, recording your thoughts about whether these techniques have helped you to communicate better.

Link

You can learn more about listening and verbal communications in different business situations in *Unit 5: Sales and Personal Selling*.

Did you know?

Research reveals that we only remember between 25 and 50 per cent of what somebody tells us. This means that when the team is communicating, they may forget up to half of what they have discussed, which can lead to misunderstandings and conflicts. This is the reason why many team leaders issue minutes of team meetings afterwards.

Just checking

1 List three ways effective leaders get the best out of their teams.

2 Explain how you could demonstrate that you had integrity.

3 What action should you take if someone in your team makes a mistake?

4 Why is consistency important for effective leadership?

CONTINUED ▸▸

Assessment activity 11.1

2A.P1 | 2A.P2 | 2A.P3 | 2A.P4 | 2B.P5 | 2B.P6 | 2A.M1 | 2A.M2 | 2B.M3 | 2A.D1 | 2B.D2

Use the information you gather from your interviews to evaluate the effectiveness of the team. Consider all the factors that contribute to this, in particular you should think about how effective the team leader is in ensuring that the business team meets their objectives. Ensure that you ask questions that will help you find out the correct information, prepare all your questions beforehand but be ready to ask further questions where necessary. You can choose how to present your findings. Suitable ways include a PowerPoint® presentation, an information booklet, posters and/ or a written report. To collect the information, you can work in a group or with a partner, but you must write up your findings individually.

You work for an outdoor education centre where people learn how to do water sports such as canoeing, sailing and raft building. Your manager wants to start selling team-building days for businesses. You have been asked to find out about teams and team leaders and present your findings to your colleagues.

You will research two contrasting business teams. Your teacher/tutor might arrange for team leaders to visit your group or you might have to find people yourself. One team could be from your own school or college, for example the canteen staff, the administrative staff or the Business tutors. The other could be someone you know who is in a team at work, for example a leader of a small business. Your teacher/tutor should check your choice of teams to ensure they are suitable before you start your research. To gather the information, you will interview someone from each team and ask questions about their team and their team leader.

- Consider the characteristics that make teams effective and describe three effective characteristics for each of your chosen teams. Comment on the behaviours that individual members display, using examples, that also contribute to effective teamworking and assess the benefit of these behaviours for the team members and the business.

- For one team, explain the importance of stages of team development and of Belbin's Team Role theory and assess, using examples, how they make the team effective.

- Explain the importance of the team leader's role and responsibilities for both of your teams, describing the attributes and qualities that make them effective. To evaluate the effectiveness of the team leader you could select one team leader and assess them in detail.

Tips

- Discuss how each of Tuckman's stages (forming, norming, etc.) is important to the team's development.
- Ask a team member if they can identify any of Belbin's Team Roles within their team and find out how people playing these different roles contribute to the business team's objectives.
- You must include why the team leader's role and responsibilities are important to the team.
- Comment on how effective the team leader is at helping the team to achieve its goals.

WorkSpace

Philip Johnson

Architect

Philip Johnson led the team of architects and design consultants that designed the London 2012 stadium. This enormous achievement was recognised in 2010 when he won 'Team Player of the Year'.

The project's tight deadline was a big challenge. Teamwork and effective communication were essential as it enabled people to work on different aspects of the design at the same time. Regular team meetings were held to review the team's progress and discuss plans, and after each meeting people were emailed an updated actions list. Sharing an office enabled the team to discuss issues as they arose, which Philip stresses is always better than communicating by email.

So what can Philip tell us about effective team working? He emphasises that you have to trust that people know what they are doing and accept that you will not always agree with your colleagues, but that you have to find a way of working together for the good of the project.

When leading a team, Philip says it is important to build a team with the range of skills that are needed to complete the work. He says that you must identify and make use of people's strengths and make sure you don't overlook quiet team members who may not put themselves forward as forcefully as others. Philip says that team leaders must be patient and give people the chance to prove themselves.

Despite the challenges this team faced on such an important project, Philip recalls that a good team spirit developed where people helped one another and celebrated individual successes. Philip appreciates that people are happiest when they are working on projects they believe in, and working on the stadium for the city in which the team lived and worked was definitely a once-in-a-lifetime experience.

Think about it

1   What were the benefits of working in a team to design the London 2012 stadium?

2   Identify two skills that you possess. Then prepare a statement for each that demonstrates how you have applied that skill.

3   Research an organisation that interests you, and prepare two questions you can ask an interviewer to demonstrate your knowledge and to find out more.

Effective teamworking skills

Introduction

Job application forms often ask you to provide evidence of a time when you have worked well in a team. If you are asked in an interview whether you work well in a team, it is not enough to simply say that you are a good team worker; you need to explain what good team skills are and give examples to show you have them.

Teamworking skills

Table 11.4 should help you to demonstrate effective teamworking skills.

Table 11.4 How to demonstrate effective teamworking skills

Teamworking skill	How to demonstrate this skill
Showing a positive attitude and respecting others	• Participate enthusiastically without dominating other team members. • Treat all team members with equal respect, courtesy and consideration at all times.
Taking responsibility for own work	• Clarify objectives, agree task allocation and complete tasks to agreed deadlines and to the best of your ability.
Supporting other team members	• Share information, knowledge and experience. • Be aware of what other people in your team are doing and offer help and support if you can.
Responding positively to constructive feedback	• Thank the person giving the feedback, even if they are pointing out weaknesses in your work. • Listen and be open to their comments. • Respond by making changes to your work/ behaviour where appropriate.
Recognising and dealing with conflict situations	• Identify problems in the team and be willing to discuss the issues. • Criticise ideas, not people, and offer feedback on tasks rather than individuals' performance.
Communicating effectively	• Listen to other people's views/ideas. • Speak to colleagues frequently and try to explain things clearly. • Use body language to enhance communication, e.g. smile and nod when someone has a good idea and be aware of other people's facial expressions to understand their feelings. • Demonstrate assertiveness through standing up for yourself, without disrespecting someone else. • Speak calmly, at a normal pace and volume, and keep to the point.
Cooperating with other team members	• Work well with all types of people, even if they are much older than you or are unfamiliar to you. • Accept team members' help or advice and try out their ideas.

Link

You can learn more about communicating effectively in *Unit 5: Sales and Personal Selling*.

Activity   Preparing for a job interview

You are invited to an interview for a part-time job that involves teamwork. Prepare for the interview by thinking of some examples where you have demonstrated effective teamworking skills. You can use your experiences of working on projects at college or school, playing in teams or at work.

Potential barriers to effective team performance

Unfortunately, things do not always run smoothly when working in a team, but being aware of potential barriers that prevent the team working well together can help in overcoming the issues and getting the team back on track.

- **Lack of commitment from team leader, team members or self:** How would it make you feel if some members of your team were not committed? Can you think of any footballers who have been criticised for drinking alcohol the night before an important match?

- **Poor communication:** How can you share the goals of the company if they are not communicated to the team? How can conflicts ever be resolved if people are not communicating well? What would happen if nobody listened to one another and everyone talked over one another?

- **Lack of appropriate skills:** Teams should be made up of individuals who have skills that complement one another. How successful would a netball or ice hockey team be with lots of defenders, but no attackers?

- **Resource issues:** Even the best teams cannot achieve great things without adequate resources, e.g. financial, physical and staff.

- **Personal factors:** Personal issues such as not respecting authority or a lack of cooperation can prevent the team from working well together.

- **Conflict between team members:** How would team members making personal attacks or aggressive gestures towards one another affect the team?

? Did you know?

The band Oasis split up because of the ongoing conflict between brothers Liam and Noel Gallagher.

? Did you know?

Bands like One Direction, JLS and Little Mix all need financial backing, music studios, world-class concert venues and a talented support team to be successful.

Activity   Identifying and removing barriers

In small groups, identify which barrier(s) may be the source of the problem in the following comments that have been made by unhappy team members. Then decide how an effective team leader should respond. Compare your ideas with other groups.

- 'I'm not sure what I'm meant to be doing.'
- 'I really can't be bothered.'
- 'How can I do my job properly when there's no money to buy the equipment I need?'
- 'I'm not working with him! He's horrid.'
- 'None of us can speak French, so how are we meant to talk to the customer?'

The role of the team leader is to promote harmony!

Developing effective teamworking skills

Introduction

Have you ever worked on a project where some members of the team appear to opt out? Perhaps they sat back and let others do all the work and avoided being part of the discussions. This behaviour is likely to cause tension in the team.

Teams that work well together are made up of individuals who all contribute to the work of the whole team. Each member plays a valuable role in achieving the team's goals and developing teamworking skills. For example, an individual who helps a colleague who is struggling with their tasks, will help the team meet its overall goal. Demonstrating this positive behaviour will enhance the way in which the team works together.

Activity   Thinking about Team Roles

Look again at Belbin's Team Roles to see how each Role contributes to the work of the whole team and its teamworking skills.

We know that our individual contributions are important to the team's overall success.

We do our best to support and respect each other by offering help and praise when it's needed.

We take **collective responsibility** and are all responsible for getting the work done, for our successes and our failures.

We try to overcome barriers to communication and ensure that we all put forward ideas as to how we might complete a task.

We change our behaviour or the way we do things in response to feedback from the team.

We offer help to other team members if they need it as we are all committed to the team's success.

How we contribute to the work of the whole team.

Activity | Making improvements to a team

Your friend has been promoted to team leader at a local retail store. The team leader she is replacing was absent a lot which affected the team. They squabble and do not work well together. She is concerned that some older members may ignore what she says. In groups, discuss how she can overcome these barriers and how she can show by example the skills needed for a team to be effective.

Just checking

1 Identify three teamworking skills.

2 Describe how you could demonstrate those teamworking skills.

3 What is 'collective responsibility'?

4 Describe how an individual's contributions in a team situation can help the whole team to achieve its goals.

5 Describe how one team member's behaviour can help the whole team develop good teamworking skills.

Assessment activity 11.2 | *English*

2C.P7 | 2C.P8 | 2C.M4 | 2C.M5 | 2C.D3 | 2C.D4

This assignment requires you to work in a business team and participate in a business task, such as running a fund raising event. Alternatively, this assignment could be completed in conjunction with assessment activity 11.1 and your business task could be gathering the information needed for assessment activity 11.1.

To successfully complete this activity, you should have at least two team meetings in which your teacher/tutor will observe and assess your performance. Your teacher/tutor will provide a written observation record for your portfolio. You must also provide written evidence in a reflective journal reviewing your experiences of working in a team, especially consider how effective you think your contribution was and ensure that you consider at least two ways that the team could improve its performance to meet future objectives.

- Hold at least two team meetings where, through effective teamworking skills, the objectives of your team must be determined. Tasks should then be discussed and decided upon, considering any barriers that may arise. Tasks can then be delegated to team members as appropriate. Show your teamworking skills by discussing team roles in relation to assigned tasks and ensuring you take on responsibility for appropriate work. Teachers/tutors will review meetings and look for demonstration of at least three effective teamworking skills.

- After your meetings, use your journal to review your list of business team objectives and consider whether you have achieved them all. You should evaluate how effective your contribution was to meeting team objectives and how your team overall has met your determined objectives. Think about how you all overcome any conflict and barriers.

Tips

- Identify two or more things that may be preventing the team from making progress and do something positive to help overcome each barrier.
- Ensure you include positive things that happened as well as things that did not go so well.

Introduction

You probably take it for granted that you have legal rights as a customer. Although you might not know precisely what these rights are, you would undoubtedly complain if your new mobile stopped working after a day or a T-shirt you bought shrank dramatically when you washed it.

In the UK, many laws have been passed to give consumers specific legal rights and these are regularly amended (updated) to keep them relevant for modern consumer activities such as buying online.

In this unit, you will learn about the most important laws that protect consumers. You will also find out about the law of contract and what is meant by negligence, as well as the legal remedies that are available to buyers and sellers. You will learn about the difference between civil and criminal law as well as the different courts that administer the law and the roles of the people who work in the legal profession.

Assessment: This unit will be assessed through a series of assignments set by your teacher/tutor.

Learning aims

In this unit you will:

A investigate civil and criminal law and their courts and personnel

B understand the law relating to consumers and their protection

C apply appropriate legal remedies available to buyers and sellers.

> I am really interested in the idea of working in the legal profession but I sometimes think about starting my own business. This unit will help me whatever I decide to do, as well as whenever I buy something myself, which is great.
>
> Adam, *16-year old Business student*

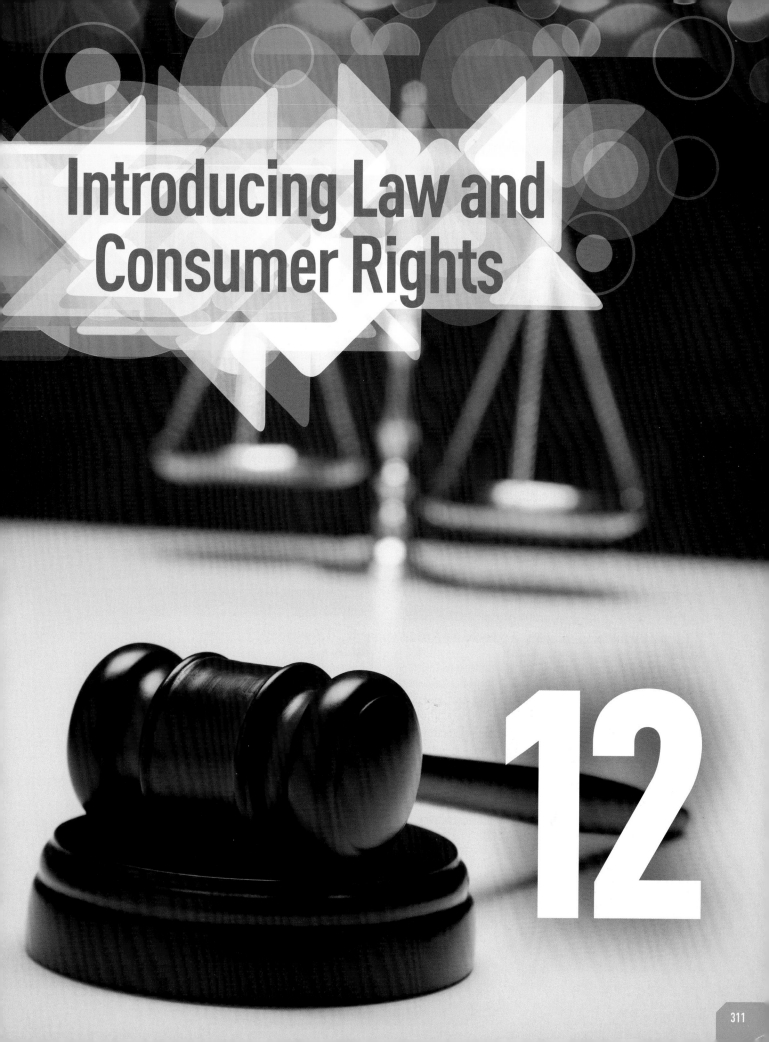

Introducing Law and Consumer Rights

12

BTEC Assessment Zone

This table shows you what you must do in order to achieve a **Pass**, **Merit** or **Distinction** grade, and where you can find activities in this book to help you.

Assessment criteria			
Level 1	Level 2 Pass	Level 2 Merit	Level 2 Distinction
Learning Aim A: Investigate civil and criminal law and their courts and personnel			
1A.1 Outline the role of the civil law and courts in a given situation.	**2A.P1** Explain the role of the civil law and courts in two different situations. **See Assessment activity 12.1, page 325**	**2A.M1** Compare, using examples, the process of the law and the use of the courts in civil and criminal law cases. **See Assessment activity 12.1, page 325**	**2A.D1** Evaluate how civil or criminal law, courts and personnel have been used in a selected case. **See Assessment activity 12.1, page 325**
1A.2 Outline the role of the criminal law and courts in a given situation.	**2A.P2** Explain the role of the criminal law and courts in two different situations. **See Assessment activity 12.1, page 325**	**2A.M2** Assess the importance of using magistrates and juries in criminal courts. **See Assessment activity 12.1, page 325**	
1A.3 Identify the roles and responsibilities of people involved in the law in given situations.	**2A.P3** Explain the roles and responsibilities of people involved in the law in both a criminal and a civil situation. **See Assessment activity 12.1, page 325**		
Level 1	Level 2 Pass	Level 2 Merit	Level 2 Distinction
Learning Aim B: Understand the law relating to consumers and their protection			
1B.4 Outline how the requirements of contract law are relevant to consumers in a given situation.	**2B.P4** Explain how the requirements of contract law protect consumers, with reference to different contract formats. **See Assessment activity 12.2, page 340**	**2B.M3** Compare the effectiveness of the law of contract and negligence in protecting consumers in given situations. **See Assessment activity 12.2, page 340**	**2B.D2** Evaluate, using recent cases, the effectiveness of consumer protection law. **See Assessment activity 12.2, page 340**
1B.5 Outline the relevance of negligence in a given situation.	**2B.P5** Explain how negligence protects consumers in given situations. **See Assessment activity 12.2, page 340**		

312   BTEC First Business

Assessment criteria

Level 1	Level 2 Pass	Level 2 Merit	Level 2 Distinction
Learning Aim B: Understand the law relating to consumers and their protection			
1B.6 Identify the legislation that protects consumers in given situations relating to: • a contract for the sale of goods • a contract for the provision of services • defective goods or negligence • a breach of criminal law.	**2B.P6** Describe how legislation protects customers in given situations relating to: • a contract for the sale of goods • a contract for the provision of services • defective goods or negligence • a breach of criminal law. **See Assessment activity 12.2, page 340**	**2B.M4** Compare the consumer protection provided by different legislation in a given situation. **See Assessment activity 12.2, page 340**	
Level 1	**Level 2 Pass**	**Level 2 Merit**	**Level 2 Distinction**
Learning Aim C: Apply appropriate legal remedies available to buyers and sellers			
1C.7 Outline why consumers may have a claim in three situations.	**2C.P7** Explain why consumers may have a legal claim in three different situations. **See Assessment activity 12.3, page 345**	**2C.M5** Compare the benefits of the remedies available to buyers and sellers in three different situations. **See Assessment activity 12.3, page 345**	**2C.D3** Evaluate the appropriateness of legal remedies decided in recent consumer protection cases. **See Assessment activity 12.3, page 345**
1C.8 Identify remedies available to buyers and/or sellers in three situations.	**2C.P8** Describe the remedies available to buyers and sellers in three different situations. **See Assessment activity 12.3, page 345**		

How you will be assessed

This unit will be assessed by a series of internally assessed tasks and activities. These will enable you to demonstrate your own understanding of consumer law, including negligence and the law of contract, and apply your knowledge in several different situations, including recent case examples. You will also show that you understand the difference between civil and criminal courts as well as the importance of the roles of those who work there. Your assessment could be in the form of:

- a leaflet, report or presentation about civil and criminal law, their courts and those who work there
- a report or presentation analysing legal disputes, identifying how the law protects consumers and the legal claim/remedy available
- a report or email advising a client on a particular dispute and quoting the outcome of a recent relevant case.

Role of civil law and its courts

Civil law

The meaning and purpose of civil law is to govern disputes between private individuals and/or organisations.

Almost every day, we interact with other people and businesses, for example buying a magazine from a newsagent or going on a bus. Sometimes, our interactions lead to disputes when something goes wrong. Perhaps the magazine has pages missing, or a car collides with the bus and you are injured.

If something goes wrong, you, as an individual, must take steps to resolve the dispute. In the example, your **remedy** may be as simple as returning to the newsagent and getting your money back or exchanging the magazine.

If the dispute cannot be sorted out between the parties, the conflict may need to be taken to a civil court where the court will decide. Most civil claims are resolved by the payment of a sum of money called **compensation**. Occasionally, a court may order a party to do something (this is called **specific performance**), or prevent them from doing something.

Civil courts

The different courts involved in civil cases and their jurisdiction are outlined below. These cases may involve consumer protection claims, which are usually disagreements over the meaning of an agreement (see contracts), damages for personal injury or property damage caused by negligence. Other areas of civil law dealt with by the civil courts are family law (divorce and child custody), employment law, land law and company law.

County Court

- Local courts are situated in most large towns. Claims can usually be started in any county court.
- It deals with straightforward cases up to £50,000, except defamation.

High Court

- The main court is in London, with branches around England and Wales. It consists of the Queen's Bench Division (hears contract and negligence claims), the Family Division and the Chancery Division.
- It deals with higher value civil claims over £50,000. Claims worth over £25,000, except personal injury claims, may also begin here but it is usually more complex claims. It also hears appeals from the County Court.

Court of Appeal (Civil Division)

- It is located in London and hears appeals from several tribunals, the County Court and High Court.
- Cases are usually heard by a panel of three judges and occasionally five in important cases.

Supreme Court (formerly the House of Lords)

- Located in London, this is the highest Court in England and it hears appeals only on points of law.
- Cases are heard by a panel of Justices of the Supreme Court. They must always sit as an uneven number, and this is normally five.

European Court of Justice (ECJ)

- It is based in Luxembourg. Any court can refer a case to the ECJ if the case involves a point of European law. The case will still be decided in the English court guided by the ECJ's ruling.

Which courts are based at the Royal Courts of Justice in the Strand, London?

Activity — Finding your nearest civil court

Find out the location of your nearest civil court. You can access Her Majesty's Courts & Tribunals Service website by going to www.pearsonhotlinks.co.uk and searching for this title.

CONTINUED ▶▶

Link

You will learn more about the people involved in *Topic A.3.*

Civil procedure

Figure 12.1 shows the sequence of events that takes place. Those involved are the claimant, the defendant and the judge. A solicitor or barrister may be involved, but usually only in complex cases. However, in any case a witness or expert witness may be called.

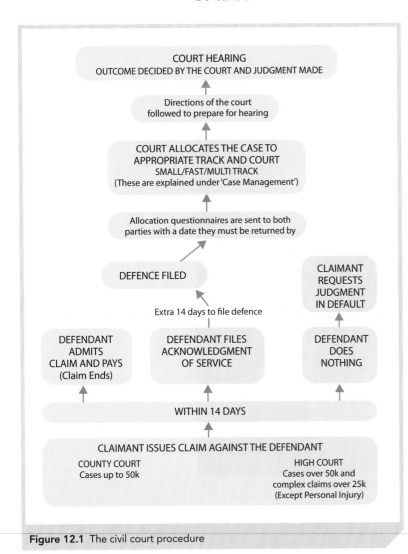

Figure 12.1 The civil court procedure

Case management

Once a defence is filed, the judge will allocate the claim to one of the following three tracks.

Small claims track

- This deals with simple claims under £5000, any personal injury or tenant's repair element under £1000, otherwise it will be a fast track case.
- Hearings are usually informal and round the table in the Judge's Chambers (office) in the County Court.
- Parties are encouraged to represent themselves. A lawyer (a solicitor or barrister) can be used but their legal costs cannot be recovered.

Fast track

- This usually deals with claims valued at between £5000 and £25,000 that are suitable for a one-day trial.
- The hearing will be in a courtroom with the parties represented by lawyers. The loser usually pays the other party's reasonable legal costs.
- A strict timetable is given, aiming to get the case to a final hearing within 30 weeks from allocation.

Multi-track

- This deals with claims over £25,000 or complex claims.
- Claims at this level can be started in either the High or County Court and the case usually stays in that court, although the judge can transfer it.
- Parties are usually represented by lawyers, and the loser pays the other party's reasonable legal costs.

Did you know?

Civil claims hearings are generally open to the public to attend. However, the judge can hear the case in private if both parties agree. In some instances, such as cases involving children, where confidential information is involved or it is in the interests of justice, the case will be heard in private.

Alternative methods of resolving disputes and their uses

Parties in dispute should always attempt resolution without resorting to the courts. This is known as **Alternative Dispute Resolution (ADR)**. The following methods are examples.

- **Negotiation** is direct discussion between two disputing parties to find a solution. This is often the parties themselves, but once solicitors are involved they will continue trying to negotiate a settlement even when the case is with the court.

- **Mediation** is where an independent third party helps the disputing parties find neutral ground to settle the dispute. The mediator does not usually give an opinion, but simply goes between the parties to attempt a settlement. A face-to-face meeting with the mediator can be used, as can a mini trial.

- **Conciliation** is like mediation because an independent person is used to assist making a settlement. However, they will play a more active role and make suggestions to the parties.

- **Arbitration** is where the parties agree to let a third party decide. The dispute can be decided by just one arbitrator or a panel of up to three. If the parties cannot decide how many to use, the Arbitration Act 1996 states that just one should be used. The decision of the arbitrator is legally binding on the parties and can be enforced through the courts. There is usually a formal hearing, where witness and expert evidence can be given. However, the parties may agree to a different method, such as making written submissions.

- **Tribunals** exist alongside the court system to deal with cases involving social rights and state welfare. Thousands of cases are decided by tribunals each year. Tribunals are divided into two tiers; the first tier hears cases initially and the other tier hears any appeals.

> **? Did you know?**
>
> In commercial contracts the parties often elect in advance to have disputes settled by arbitration if they arise (this is known as a Scott v Avery clause).

Activity Investigating the process

In groups, access the courts' website by going to www.pearsonhotlinks.co.uk and searching for this title. Download leaflets EX301, EX304, EX305 and EX306. Prepare a summary on one particular leaflet (your teacher/tutor will tell you which one) and present this to the class. Then look at leaflet EX50. Assume you are claiming £1000 to settle a dispute. What track would this be allocated to and in what court would the case commence?

Just checking ✔

1 What is the name of the person making a claim in a civil court?

2 Two large businesses are in a dispute. One claims that the other has copied its designs for a product and is claiming over £1 million of lost revenue. In which court would this claim be heard?

3 Explain three ways that a dispute may be settled before it reaches the courts.

Role of criminal law and its courts

Criminal law

The purpose of criminal law is to punish people who break the law, to maintain law and order and to protect the public. Someone who commits a serious crime, such as armed robbery, will go to prison. For lesser offences, the punishment may be a fine or community sentence. Motorists who break the law may be given penalty points or banned from driving.

Criminal courts

- **The Magistrates' Court** is the local court which initially deals with all criminal cases although, after a preliminary hearing, it may refer serious cases to the Crown Court. Relatively minor cases are tried and dealt with by the magistrates, and some cases may be heard in either court. Magistrates can issue warrants for arrest and decide on bail applications. They also try defendants aged between 10 and 17 in the Youth Court. These hearings are held in private.

- **The Crown Court** tries all serious cases such as murder, and lesser cases such as theft, where the defendant has opted for trial by jury. It passes sentences on cases passed to it by the Magistrates' Court and hears appeals from defendants tried in the Magistrates' Court against their sentence. A defendant who pleads not guilty may also appeal against their conviction.

- **The Court of Appeal (Criminal Division)** also hears appeals, but only on points of law.

Did you know?

Committing a crime is known as 'an offence against the state' and legal action is taken in the Queen's name.

Did you know?

Magistrates were originally charged with helping to keep the peace, which is why they are also known as JPs (Justices of the Peace).

Did you know?

On the continent a different system (known as inquisitorial) is sometimes used where the judge is involved in obtaining and researching the facts of the case.

The adversarial system

In the UK, the adversarial system of law is used. This means that two 'adversaries' or opponents – the prosecution and the defence – research and present their case to the judge and the jury, who stay neutral throughout and listen to the evidence.

- **The prosecution** aims to prove the defendant guilty and studies the evidence, brings witnesses and cross-examines defence witnesses.

- **The defence** aims to prove the defendant is innocent and also brings witnesses and cross-examines prosecution witnesses.

Why are the prosecution and defence called adversaries?

The judge is the referee, making sure everything is undertaken properly and in accordance with the law, and giving instruction to the jury at the end of the trial in the 'summing-up' to guide them on points of law.

Types of offence

There are three types of criminal offence ranging from minor to very serious. This affects where they are tried.

Table 12.1 Types of offence

Type of offence	Court in which tried
Summary, e.g. driving without due care and attention; drunk and disorderly; common assault	Magistrates' Court only
Either way, e.g. theft ; drugs; assault causing actual bodily harm	Magistrates' Court or Crown Court
Indictable, e.g. murder; manslaughter; arson; robbery	Crown Court only

Bail or remand

When someone is charged with a criminal offence, a decision has to be made as to whether to allow **bail** (they retain their freedom until the trial), or to **remand** (keep) them in custody.

If the police do not want to allow bail, then the Magistrates' or Crown Court make this decision. They weigh up the issue of depriving the accused (who may be innocent) of their freedom against other factors, such as the risk to the public if they are released. The 1976 Bail Act presumes that everyone has the right to bail, so the court starts from this point and then considers the factors below.

Key terms

Bail – allowing an accused person to retain their freedom until the trial, often under certain conditions.

Remand – keeping someone in custody.

Table 12.2 Factors to consider for bail

If bail is granted, might the defendant:	Defendant's history:	Should a condition be imposed such as:
• Fail to surrender (disappear)? • Commit another offence? • Influence a witness? • Be in danger because of the nature of the case?	• How serious is this offence? • What is the evidence? • Have they got a criminal record? • Are they already on bail? • Are they known in the community? • Have they failed to surrender on bail before?	• Wear an electronic tag? • Abide by a curfew? • Report regularly to the police? • Reside at a stated address? • Arrange for someone to agree to pay a surety (money) if the defendant fails to attend court?

Mode of trial

This refers to where the trial will be held, which depends upon the seriousness of the offence and the plea entered.

• A trial for a summary offence starts when a person receives a summons to appear in court. It is held in front of a District Judge or a panel of three lay magistrates in the Magistrates' Court.

• A trial for an indictable offence is always held in the Crown Court. A defendant who pleads guilty is sentenced by the judge. A defendant who pleads innocent will have the case heard by a judge and jury.

Remember

The prosecution or defence may appeal against the bail decision. The defence may appeal if bail is denied. The prosecution can appeal if bail is allowed and the maximum sentence would be less than five years' imprisonment.

CONTINUED ▸▸

- A person charged with an 'either way' offence is asked whether they plead guilty or not guilty.
- If they plead guilty, the Magistrates may pass sentence or refer this to the Crown Court if the punishment is likely to exceed their maximum powers.
- If the defendant pleads not guilty, a 'mode of trial' meeting is held to decide where the case will be held. The magistrates may agree to hear it or decide the case should be referred to the Crown Court, or the defendant may choose to be tried by a jury.
- At the Crown Court a plea and case management hearing (PCMH) is held. The judge will pass sentence if the defendant pleads guilty. Otherwise, the prosecution and defence complete a questionnaire to summarise key aspects of the case for the court. The defendant may ask for advice from the judge to see if it may be better to change the plea. The judge will issue any further directions required to ensure the trial can be dealt with efficiently and set a date.

At the trial

The phrase 'innocent until proved guilty' means that it is up to the prosecution to prove that the defendant is guilty – not the other way round. This is called the **burden of proof**. The jury must be sure, beyond reasonable doubt (they must be 99 per cent sure) that the defendant intentionally committed the guilty act. The Crown Court procedure is shown in Table 12.3.

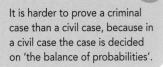

Remember

It is harder to prove a criminal case than a civil case, because in a civil case the case is decided on 'the balance of probabilities'.

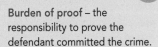

Key term

Burden of proof – the responsibility to prove the defendant committed the crime.

Table 12.3 The Crown Court procedure
The charge is read to the court.
The jury is sworn in. The judge explains what will happen.
The prosecution gives its opening speech, presents evidence and witnesses.
The defence gives its opening speech, presents evidence and witnesses.
The prosecution sums up. The defence sums up.
The judge sums up and directs the jury who retire to consider their verdict.
If the verdict is 'guilty', any previous convictions are read to the court and the judge usually pronounces sentence. If the verdict is 'not guilty', the judge dismisses the case.

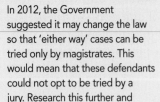

Discussion point

In 2012, the Government suggested it may change the law so that 'either way' cases can be tried only by magistrates. This would mean that these defendants could not opt to be tried by a jury. Research this further and then discuss the benefits and drawbacks of this change.

Just checking

1 What is the difference between bail and remand?

2 What is meant by the 'adversarial system'?

3 Which type of cases cannot be heard in a Magistrates' Court, and why?

WorkSpace

▶ Dan Michaels

Office Administrator

When Dan was summoned for jury service he was 20 years old and his first thought was whether he would be allowed time off. However, his boss, Miranda, knew that she had to agree to Dan's attendance. She also generously offered to top-up the allowance he would receive from the court to his normal pay so that he wouldn't be any worse off.

Dan was told to attend his local Crown Court and was surprised to find so many jurors there. He had not realised that trials go on simultaneously in different courts – and jurors are needed for all of them. They were shown a film about their role and then told to wait. Miranda had advised Dan to take a book in case he had to wait around, and he was grateful for her advice.

Dan wondered if he would be called at all. His aunt was excused from being on a jury for a trial that was expected to last 12 weeks, because she was about to take an exam. She was called a second time, but was again excused when she discovered that the defendant was a neighbour!

Fortunately that never happened to Dan. He was called twice. The first was a simple case of theft and was over quickly, but Dan was surprised how nervous he felt. He wondered what would happen if he couldn't make his mind up, or disagreed with everyone else. After listening to persuasive arguments from the prosecution and defence, he was relieved when the judge summed up the legal arguments at the end and made things much clearer.

The second trial involved an armed robbery. Dan looked at the two men in the dock – tall, good-looking and self-assured. They answered questions with ease and Dan struggled to envisage them committing a crime. After the jury found them guilty, a list of their previous convictions was read to the court. They had both been in prison several times for other serious offences. Dan felt a bit silly for thinking they could have been innocent and wondered if he would have been less gullible if he was older.

Think about it

1 Why are some jurors who are asked to attend court never called to be on a jury?*

2 State two reasons why a juror who is called may be excused from witnessing a trial.

3 Explain why Dan found the judge so helpful.

4 Explain why juries are not told about any previous convictions until after the trial.

5 Do you think Dan would have done better if he had been older?

* You will find it helpful to read about jurors in Topic A3 of this unit before answering these questions.

Working in the law

Barristers

These are self-employed legal experts who mainly act as advocates for clients by representing them in court and presenting their case to the judge and/or jury. They have the rights of audience in all courts in England and Wales. They are usually instructed through a solicitor, although in civil cases clients can go direct to them.

Barristers draft legal documents and provide independent expert opinions to clients. Some work for the Crown Prosecution Service and may appear in criminal courts from the Magistrates' Court up to the Appeal Courts.

Solicitors

Solicitors often work in 'high street' private practices and provide legal advice and assistance to clients on many aspects of the law including personal injury claims, writing wills and family issues such as divorce. They may appear in court and often represent a client in the Magistrates' Court and County Court. Some solicitors are qualified to conduct hearings in the higher courts. Some specialist firms concentrate on commercial aspects of the law and advise business clients.

Legal executives

Legal executives are members of CILEx (the Chartered Institute of Legal Executives) and have obtained a professional qualification in Law. This enables experienced staff in solicitors' firms to obtain recognition as qualified lawyers, specialise in certain areas of law and advise clients. They have restricted rights to appear in court on behalf of clients.

Paralegals

These are involved in legal work but are not qualified as solicitors or legal executives. They may work for solicitors, in local government or for a charitable organisation. They may carry out a range of activities from dealing with clients to preparing legal documents.

Did you know?

Becoming qualified as a barrister is often referred to as 'being called to the bar'. The top 10 per cent of barristers are known as QCs (Queen's Counsel). A term for this is 'taking silk' because of the type of gown that is worn in court.

Activity

Finding out about being a barrister

Find out more about being a barrister at the Bar Council and how to become one by going to www.pearsonhotlinks.co.uk and searching for this title.

Activity   Investigating legal executives and paralegals

Find out more about being a legal executive and a paralegal by going to www.pearsonhotlinks.co.uk and searching for this title.

Did you know?

The duty solicitor scheme means that anyone arrested and charged at a police station, or anyone in custody and appearing at the Magistrates' Court, can be represented by a solicitor.

Judges

Judges are at the top of the legal profession. Superior judges sit in the High Court, the Court of Appeal and the Supreme Court. Inferior judges include Circuit judges who sit in the County Court or Crown Court (referred to as 'Recorder' if they are part-time) and District judges who sit in the County Court and Magistrates' Court.

The judge's role will depend upon the court they are working in.

Find out more about judges and what they do on the Judiciary website. You can access the website by going to www.pearsonhotlinks.co.uk and searching for this title.

Table 12.4 The role of judges in different courts

Type of court	Role of judge
High Court, Court of Appeal, Supreme Court	• Hears appeals against a sentence or conviction in the criminal courts or the decision/compensation awarded in a civil case.
Crown Court	• Tries cases and directs the jury, notes the evidence and ensures the trial is fair. • Prepares for the case and may decide whether bail should be allowed. • Decides and passes sentence if the defendant is found guilty.
County Court	• Responsible for case management and allocates the track to be followed. • During a case, listens to the evidence, cross-examines those present and decides on matters of procedure. • Decides the liability, the appropriate remedy, damages that must be paid and who will pay the costs of the trial.
Magistrates' Court	Decides how the law applies to the case, the verdict and passes sentence on defendants who plead guilty.

Lay magistrates

These are unpaid members of the public who have volunteered to work as a magistrate for at least 26 half days every year. They hear less serious criminal cases and commit others to a higher court. Magistrates must be aged between 18 and 70 and need no special qualifications, but must possess six specific personal qualities shown in Figure 12.2.

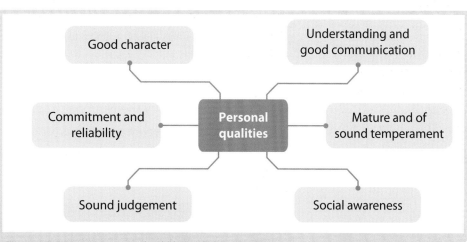

Figure 12.2 Lay magistrates should have all these qualities.

Anyone can apply but certain professions are ineligible, such as the police, because of possible conflicts of interest. Magistrates must have no serious convictions themselves. Ideally the magistrates in an area will represent their local community with a mix of men and women and different races.

There is a rigorous application process and all new magistrates receive extensive training before they can sit in court.

CONTINUED ▸▸

Discussion point

Some people think that the jury system is not appropriate in very long or complex trials (such as for money laundering or computer hacking) and argue a team of experts would be better.

Divide into two groups and research the matter further. Then hold a debate: 'Juries are past their sell-by date'. One team should argue for the motion and one against. Then vote.

Jurors

You are eligible to be a juror if you are between 18 and 70 years of age, registered on the electoral role and have been resident in the UK for at least five consecutive years since you were 13. You are not eligible if you have previously been sentenced or are on bail or probation.

Jurors are randomly chosen both to attend, and when they are selected for a trial, to ensure that the process is as fair, independent and democratic as possible. The counsel for the prosecution or defence may object to a selected juror but must have a good reason and the final decision will be that of the judge. If a juror knows anyone else involved in the trial at all, they must say so and will then be asked to stand down.

Juries are seen to underpin the right of an individual to have a fair trial. The jury is impartial and assesses the merits of the case only on the evidence they hear.

Sources of information

- **The National Trading Standards Board** is responsible for coordinating investigations into major business issues such as internet scams and illegal money lending. Trading standards officers, funded by local authorities, also visit local premises to enforce the law, particularly in the areas of animal health and food safety.
- **Citizens Advice Bureaux (CAB)** is the first stop for customers to make a complaint and receive advice about rogue traders. CAB also provides information and advice for consumers online.

Activity   Investigating sources of information

Divide into three groups. Each group should find out more about one of the following and summarise their findings for the rest of the class.

1 Work undertaken by the National Trading Standards Board.
2 Information and services available for consumers at CAB.
3 Help provided by *Which*? (Consumers' Association).

Just checking

1 What is the difference between a barrister and a solicitor?
2 How are lay magistrates selected?
3 What is the role of a judge in a criminal trial?

Assessment activity 12.1

Your task is to consider legal cases and situations heard in the civil and criminal courts and use your information to prepare a report which evaluates how civil or criminal law, courts or personnel have been used in a selected case. Your report should explain the role of the civil and criminal courts and the roles and responsibilities of the people involved in two situations in each court.

Do this by carrying out the following activities.

1 After you have read the two scenarios below, prepare notes to explain the role of the civil law and its courts in *each* situation and the roles and responsibilities of the people usually involved in a civil case.

Jake buys a second-hand Scott mountain bike from his local bike shop for £500. Within a month the gears start slipping. Jake takes the bike back to the shop three times for repair but the problem is not fixed and the shop refuses to give him a refund or replacement. Jake wants to go to the civil court to get his money back.

Ashley, a talented young tennis player with a glittering future, is involved in a serious accident. She is driving home from practice when her car is hit from behind by a large truck. Ashley suffers serious spinal injuries and is still in hospital. She is bringing a personal injury claim against the driver of the truck.

2 When 19-year-old Tina is arrested for shoplifting and charged with theft, she is allowed police bail, on condition she lives at the family home. She is very upset and is denying the charge. Her mother, Maria, tells their solicitor that she wants Tina tried by a legal professional, such as a judge, and not a lay person like a magistrate or a juror.

Prepare notes that will explain to Maria how the law is applied in this type of situation and the courts and people involved. Because being tried by a judge is not an option under English law, include an assessment of the importance of using magistrates and juries in criminal courts.

Your teacher/tutor will either provide you with a recent criminal case to study or arrange for you to see a case being heard in the Magistrates' Court or Crown Court.

- Write a review in which you explain the case, the personnel involved and how the law was applied.

- Add to your review by comparing the process of the law and the use of the courts in civil and criminal law cases. Include examples of different cases to illustrate the points you make.

- Complete your review by reconsidering all your material to evaluate the effectiveness of the law in this particular case.

Tips

- Highlight the differences between the type of cases that are dealt with in civil and criminal courts as well as the different processes that are followed.

- Evaluate the process that took place and the roles of those involved, as well as the effectiveness of the law in that particular case.

How contract and negligence relate to consumers

 ## Contract

A contract is a legal agreement entered into voluntarily by two or more people. In a contract of sale, there are specific terms and conditions that bind both the buyer and the seller.

Contracts for goods and/or services

Contracts of sale for providing goods and those relating to services are treated differently in law.

- **A contract of sale for goods**: this is an agreement that a supplier will 'transfer or agree to transfer property in goods to a buyer for a monetary consideration, called the price.' This is the definition given in Section 2 of the Sale of Goods Act 1979 (SOGA). This Act is very important as it sets down the main terms relating to the sale of goods.

- **A contract for the sale of services**: this is an agreement for someone to do something for you, such as clean your jacket or mend your car. Under the Supply of Goods and Services Act 1982, these services must be carried out for a reasonable charge, within a reasonable time and with reasonable care and skill.

Contract requirements

For a contract to be valid, certain basic requirements must be met.

Offer

In most contracts, the buyer must offer to buy an item from the seller. This must be a specific offer, either verbally or in writing, to buy a particular item at a stated price. It must be communicated directly to the seller. If you post an order form to a company, the offer is not actually made until your document is received.

The retailer does not have to accept your offer, even if the goods are on a shelf and you offer the asking price. As long as the retailer is not discriminating against you (for example, on grounds of race or gender), there is nothing you can do if you are refused the item.

An offer does not last indefinitely. If either party dies or if there is no acceptance within a reasonable time, then the offer will lapse. The offer will also lapse if it is made subject to a particular condition which is not met. If you agree to buy a watch, but want it gift-wrapped and are told this service is not available, then the offer will lapse. You can also revoke (withdraw) your offer at any time *before* it has been accepted.

Acceptance

If the offer is accepted, this must be communicated to the person making the offer. It may be:

- **by verbal or written statement** (e.g. the company emails confirmation of your order)
- **by conduct** (e.g. an assistant gives you the item and takes your money).

The acceptance must be unqualified which means that it must exactly match the offer. If you offer to buy a DVD for £15 and you are told it is really £20, then this is a counter offer. It is then up to you whether you offer to buy one at the new price or refuse to make a further offer.

Does the retailer have to sell you a product at the price shown?

Price (or consideration)

In England and Wales (but not Scotland), a contract must involve some kind of payment or other consideration. The law is not usually interested in how much you paid. If you manage to buy a bargain, that is your good luck. Only if the price seems very odd (for example, an iPhone for £10) might there be some concern, in case undue pressure has been placed by one party to the contract upon the other.

Capacity of under 18s

Each person making the contract must be capable of understanding what they are doing. If someone has a mental disorder or is drunk when they make the agreement, the contract is probably invalid. If you are under 18 (a minor), then you can only enter a binding contract for necessaries – essential goods and services such as food and clothing. This is why under 18s can only have a pay-as-you-go mobile contract and not a monthly one, and cannot own a credit card.

 Did you know?

An invitation to treat is not an offer. It is a statement intended to encourage offers, such as a price label in a shop. If this price is wrong and you must pay more, there is nothing you can do. Invitations to treat include articles displayed in a shop window or on a shelf in a self-service store and adverts in the press, in catalogues and online.

Did you know?

Another basic requirement is that you want to enter into the transaction. The legal term is 'intention to create legal relations'. When you buy something from a shop, the courts will always presume this unless it can be proved otherwise.

Activity

Investigating a case

Investigate the case of Harrow London Borough Council v Shah (1999) and find out why the shop assistant should not have accepted the customer's offer to buy.

CONTINUED ▶▶

Format of contracts

Contracts can be formed in many ways:

- Verbally – by an explicit agreement between two or more people.
- Written – such as a contract of sale for a house.
- Standard form – such as a holiday booking form in a brochure.
- Online – by completing an online order form.
- Mail order – by completing the order form you received with a catalogue and posting it.

Did you know?

Although a contract does not have to be in written form, it is obviously advisable to have written proof of a contract that involves a considerable sum of money.

Why should contracts for expensive items always be in writing?

Terms and exclusion clauses

Key term

Breach of contract – fail to comply with one or more terms of a contract.

Some terms in a contract are express and others are implied. If one party fails to abide by these, and breaks the contract, they have **breached** the terms of the contract.

Table 12.5 Express and implied terms

Express terms	Implied terms
• These are specifically stated, verbally or in writing. • These are included as a condition in a contract and the seller must comply, e.g. a specific date for delivery. In this case the correct phrase to use is 'time is of the essence'.	• The courts accept that these are the clear, but unexpressed intentions of both parties, for example, it is implied that you will pay a reasonable price for an item – you cannot expect to receive it for nothing. • Terms can also be implied by Acts of Parliament.

Note: A court will always look first at the express terms and not usually imply a term which contradicts an express term.

A condition in a contract is a vital term.

An **exclusion clause** is a term that attempts to limit or restrict the liability of the supplier or limit the rights of the consumer. The Unfair Contract Terms Act 1977 states these are only valid when they are considered 'fair and reasonable'. If the dry cleaner ruins your best jacket, they must prove they took reasonable care of it. If the damage is through an employee's negligence, you would probably be entitled to compensation. Another Act which regulates contract terms is the Unfair Terms in Consumer Contracts Regulations (1999) which you will learn about later in this section.

Key term

Exclusion clause – a term which attempts to limit or restrict the liability of the supplier or limit the rights of the consumer.

Case study

Read the following case study and the task that follows. Then compare your ideas.

In January 2012 both M&S and Next mistakenly advertised products on their websites with the wrong price. M&S advertised Panasonic 50 inch 3D plasma televisions costing £1,099 for £199, while Next listed two sofas worth £1,198 for £98.

M&S apologised and credited customers who had placed an order with a £25 voucher as a goodwill gesture, but when those customers started an online petition arguing that the company was in breach of contract, M&S agreed to supply the TVs at the advertised price. Next contacted all the customers to explain the error and said its standard terms and conditions gave it the right to cancel an order at any time prior to dispatch.

Your task: In small groups, decide whether a valid contract of sale existed between both M&S and its customers, and Next and its customers. Your answer should refer to the difference between an offer and an invitation to treat, the requirements of a valid contract and fair terms and conditions in a contract of sale.

Just checking

1 How would you define a contract of sale?

2 What is the difference between an express term and an implied term in a contract?

3 What does it mean if someone has 'breached' a contract?

CONTINUED ▶▶

◢ Negligence

In law, negligence means either failing to do something or not acting with reasonable care so that someone else suffers because of your actions.

Differences between contract and negligence

A contract is a legal agreement. If one party breaches the contract, then the other party can take legal action to recover any monetary loss they suffered as a result. If the builder you have paid to mend your wall is incompetent and the wall falls down after two days, you can take action for breach of contract.

Negligence occurs when someone is hurt or injured or their property is damaged because of the negligent act or omission of someone else. If the wall injured passers-by when it collapsed, the builder has not taken reasonable care and has been negligent. The aim of any award for damages is to put the claimant(s) back into the position they were in before the incident occurred.

You can sue someone for breach only if you have a contract with them. The passers-by injured by the wall did not have a contract with the builder but can still claim for their injuries under negligence.

Activity

Which is which?

An internet shopping company delivers damaged goods to number 24 and then knocks down the gatepost of number 26. Which of these is a breach of contract and which is negligence?

Case study

In August 1928, May Donoghue went to a café with a friend who bought her a drink in an opaque bottle (May couldn't see inside it). When May refilled her glass, a partly decomposed snail fell out of the bottle. May was later taken ill with gastroenteritis and went to hospital.

As May had not bought the drink, she could not sue under the law of contract. Instead she sued the maker, Mr Stephenson, for negligence, arguing it was their duty not to produce contaminated drinks. May won her case in 1932.

One judge, Lord Aitkin, famously argued that people had a duty in law not to injure their 'neighbour' – 'someone so closely and directly affected by my act, that I must think about them when I am doing something (or not doing something) that would affect them'.

All food and drink manufacturers in the UK today have a duty of care to their customers to ensure that their products are not contaminated and have statutory responsibilities under the Consumer Protection Act (see section B.2).

Discussion point

What do you think the penalties should be for businesses that ignore their 'duty of care'? Would you reduce these if the problem had been caused accidentally? Discuss your ideas as a group.

Concepts of duty, breach and damage in the context of consumers

The law of negligence has now developed further. In the case of Caparo v Dickman (1990), an investor who lost money in a company blamed the auditors for producing inaccurate accounts. The court devised a three-fold test shown in Table 12.6 to show how it can be proved that a duty of care exists.

Table 12.6 The three-fold test

It should be possible to foresee that some damage or harm will result. If the damage was not foreseeable, a court may decide this is a pure accident and negligence is not an issue.
The relationship between the parties should be proximate (close) enough (e.g. in time and space) for the two to be linked.
It must be fair, just and reasonable to impose a duty of care on the defendant.

If a duty of care is established, the claimant must prove that this has been broken by the defendant. When deciding this, the court will look at the standard of care required by a 'reasonable man' who may take greater risks or more precautions depending upon the circumstances.

Did you know?

If a legal case sets a precedent, the court judgement applies to all future cases with the same features. As these may be affected by new laws and judgements, you should check if any new cases reaffirm this.

Activity   Investigating a test case

Your brother is learning to drive and you tell him that all road users have a duty of care to one another. He says this doesn't apply to learners. Is he right? Research Nettleship v Weston (1971) to find out.

Remember

A test case is one that sets a precedent for other cases involving the same legal aspects.

Is the law different for learner drivers?

How legislation protects consumers

Introduction

Specific legislation exists to protect customers when they buy goods and services and to provide protection against negligence, fraud and theft.

Contracts for the sale of goods

There are four main laws that relate to the sale of goods. These are summarised in this section.

- The Sale of Goods Act 1979
- The Unfair Terms in Consumer Contracts Regulations (1999)
- The Consumer Protection (Distance Selling) Regulations (2000)
- The Consumer Protection from Unfair Trading Regulations (2008)

Sale of Goods Act (1979) (as amended)

This states that all goods sold, whether new or second-hand, must be:

- **as described** by the seller, the package or on any display sign or in any advertisement, for example, waterproof boots must not leak
- **of satisfactory quality** in relation to the price paid, description and age of the item. The quality of the goods includes their state and condition, including appearance and finish. They should be free from minor defects, safe and durable
- **be fit for the purpose for which they are intended**, e.g. walking boots should be sturdy. The goods must also be suitable for any specific purpose you made clear when you bought or ordered the goods, e.g. you said you want the boots for climbing.

If these conditions are not met, the buyer can reject the goods and the seller must refund the buyer or, if reasonable, allow the buyer to opt instead for a repair or replacement. A free repair can be offered but does not have to be accepted. If it is, but is not satisfactory, the buyer still has the right to a refund. Sale goods are also covered, unless the fault was clearly obvious or pointed out at the time of sale and was the reason for the reduction.

Faulty goods can be returned by post if this is more convenient, or the customer can ask the shop to collect at its own expense. All goods posted by a supplier are at the seller's risk.

The retailer can ask for some proof of purchase, but this does not have to be a receipt. A bank or credit card statement would also suffice.

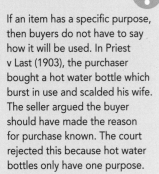

Did you know?

If an item has a specific purpose, then buyers do not have to say how it will be used. In Priest v Last (1903), the purchaser bought a hot water bottle which burst in use and scalded his wife. The seller argued the buyer should have made the reason for purchase known. The court rejected this because hot water bottles only have one purpose.

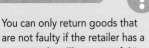

Did you know?

You can only return goods that are not faulty if the retailer has a returns policy. The terms of this are up to the retailer. Most stores have a time limit for a full refund and ask for proof of purchase.

Points to note

- The buyer's claim is always against the retailer, not the manufacturer.
- Goods cannot be rejected because of defects pointed out by the seller at the time of the sale.
- An item should be rejected within a reasonable time, normally a few weeks, but it does depend upon the product and the nature of the fault.
- Defective goods must be repaired or replaced free of charge within six months of purchase or up to six years if they could reasonably be expected to last that long.
- If the buyer claims within six months of purchase and the retailer rejects it, the retailer must prove the product was not faulty. If the claim is made after six months, the retailer can ask the buyer to prove the fault is not due to normal wear and tear, for example, by getting an expert's report.
- Second-hand and sales goods are covered by the Act, but it is reasonable for these not to be the same condition as new or full price goods.

| Activity | Researching the Sale of Goods Act |

In groups, research the Sale of Goods Act further and identify the rights of the following consumers.

1 Paula orders two matching lamps, a new dining table with six chairs and curtains from a fabric sample she was given in the store. When the goods arrive, one of the lamps is damaged, the curtains do not match the sample and the chairs are missing. The store says they will credit her for one lamp and the chairs will be delivered next month.

2 Imran buys an expensive new coat in October which starts to fray in February. The retailer says that because he has been wearing it, he is only entitled to a partial refund.

3 Jane uses an expensive kitchen knife to prise open a can and the end chips off. When she explains to the retailer what happened, they refuse to give her a refund.

4 Fatima agrees that her faulty printer can be repaired, but three months later is still waiting for it to be returned.

5 Lindsey buys a self-assembly wardrobe but cannot build it because the instructions are in Chinese.

How long should it take to repair faulty equipment?

CONTINUED ▶▶

Unfair Terms in Consumer Contracts Regulations (1999)

This legislation protects consumers from unfair terms that may be included in a contract. Consumers can report a term they consider is unfair to their local Trading Standards department or the Office of Fair Trading. If a term is considered unfair then the consumer cannot be held to it.

A term is considered unfair if:

- it causes a significant imbalance in the parties' rights and obligations, so that the consumer is at a disadvantage
- the standard terms of the contract do not take into account the interests and legal rights of the consumer.

All standard terms must be written clearly and be easy to understand. If there is any doubt about what a term might mean, the meaning most favourable to the consumer will apply.

Points to note

- Terms relating to the actual product or service or the price are 'core terms' and cannot be challenged, so a consumer cannot say a price is unfair because the item is on sale at a lower price elsewhere.
- Terms that have been individually negotiated, business-to-business contracts and purchases from private individuals are also exempt.

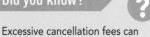

Did you know?

Excessive cancellation fees can be unfair. Only essential costs and loss of profit can be claimed.

> **Activity** Applying the regulations
>
> Explain why the following would be considered unfair under the regulations.
>
> 1 Gym membership where you have to give three months' notice to cancel, but the gym can cancel it in one week.
> 2 A trader delivers a red rug when you specifically ordered a blue one and says it is in the terms and conditions.

Consumer Protection (Distance Selling) Regulations (2000) (as amended)

The Distance Selling Regulations protect customers who buy goods and services on the internet, by mail order, by digital television, phone or fax. The seller must:

- provide clear information to consumers on all aspects of goods being sold, including the name and address of the supplier, a description of the goods or services, the price, when payment will be taken and the customer's right to cancel
- send written confirmation by post or email
- give customers a cooling off period of seven working days
- give a refund if the goods are not provided by the agreed date or within 30 days from the order.

Points to note

- If the consumer cancels, then their money must be made available within 30 days.
- Companies must not send out unsolicited goods and must offer customers an opt-out from receiving junk mail, emails and phone calls.

Did you know?

Some goods and services are exempt. Consumers cannot cancel perishable goods such as food and flowers, travel and tailor-made items. Computer games, magazines, CDs and DVDs cannot be returned once the packaging is opened.

It is only lawful for an online seller to ask for payment in advance if they provide their full geographic address. Can you think why?

The Consumer Protection from Unfair Trading Regulations (2008) (CPRs)

These regulations stop traders from misleading, behaving aggressively or acting unfairly towards consumers. They prohibit any practices that deliberately set out to cause consumers to take a different decision than the one they would have made if they were dealing with an honest and fair trader. These include:

- misleading actions, such as lying about the features of a product, passing them off as another brand or advertising goods that do not exist
- misleading omissions, such as missing out important information or giving it too late to be of use
- aggressive practices that harass or coerce a consumer in some way, such as refusing to leave until a contract is signed or making threats
- specific banned practices, e.g. bogus sales, falsely stating a product has limited availability and persistent cold-calling.

Consumers should report a suspected offence to Trading Standards, which can take action in the civil or criminal courts. Trading Standards can apply to the civil courts for an enforcement order. Breach of the order is punishable in the criminal courts with an unlimited fine and up to two years' imprisonment.

Points to note

- The CPRs apply to commercial practices that occur before, during and after a transaction. This means they also include after-sales services and the cancellation of an existing contract.
- They include business-to-business practices connected to consumers, for example, a trader supplying canned food to a supermarket must ensure its labels comply with the CPRs.
- Consumers cannot bring an action under the Act, but could use the trader's actions to end the contract and get their money back, for example by claiming that the goods were not 'as described' or 'fit for purpose'.

What type of behaviour could harass or coerce a customer to sign?

CONTINUED ▶▶

Contracts for the provision of services

Supply of Goods and Services Act (1982)

These cover buyers against services such as car repairs and building work. The Act states that all services should be carried out:

- for a reasonable charge
- within a reasonable time
- with reasonable care and skill
- using satisfactory materials.

Points to note

- Any materials supplied must comply with the same requirements as those laid down in the Sale of Goods Act, for example they should be of satisfactory quality, as described etc.
- If the work is done *without* reasonable care and skill, the buyer may be able to terminate the contract or may only be able to claim damages. It will depend upon the problem.
- The time to be taken may be specified in the contract. Otherwise, how reasonable it is will depend upon what is being done and whether the materials are easily available.
- The 'reasonable' price depends upon the work being carried out, but the courts can vary (change) a price they consider to be excessive. One aim of this is to thwart 'cowboy builders'.

What rights do you have if a business fails to carry out a service in a reasonable time?

Activity   Advising Amy

Amy is redoing her bedroom. She orders new fitted wardrobe units from Wardrobe World and John, a local decorator, tells her how many rolls of wallpaper to order from the designer interiors store. The wardrobes are a disappointment – one door is an odd shade and slightly scratched, and the units do not fit properly. John over-estimates the expensive wallpaper so Amy has a roll left over. She is fed up. Amy wants Wardrobe World to give her a refund and says she is not going to pay John. Is she right?

Negligence or defective goods

Consumer Protection Act (1987)

It can be difficult to prove negligence, even when someone has been hurt by a defective product. To make this easier for consumers, the Consumer Protection Act (CPA) was passed. This Act has two separate aspects, one relating to civil law and product liability; the other relating to criminal law and product safety. The Act has also been strengthened by the General Product Safety Regulations (2005).

- Product liability is the civil aspect. It enables someone to sue the manufacturer in the civil courts if they are hurt by a defective product.
- Product safety is the criminal aspect. This makes selling an unsafe product a criminal offence. This part of the CPA is enforced by Trading Standards officers. If the producer is prosecuted and found guilty, there is a maximum fine of £5000 and/or imprisonment of up to six months.

Points to note (civil aspect)

- This Act places a major responsibility on anyone producing consumer goods to ensure they are safe. 'Goods' means all types of consumer goods, as well as food.
- Someone who is injured by a product they bought can sue under the Sale of Goods Act. The CPA enables any injured person to sue, so an adult can claim on behalf of a child injured by a dangerous toy.
- If damage is caused by a defective product, then compensation can be claimed. If you lend your hair straighteners to your friend, and they became so hot they burn her, she can sue the manufacturer. If the straighteners also catch fire and cause serious damage to the room, she can also claim compensation, providing the damage is £275 or more.
- Court action must be taken within three years of the date of the injury and it is up to the claimant to prove that, on the balance of probability, the injury was caused by the defective product. The court would consider how the product had been sold and marketed, the instructions and any warnings that came with it, when it was supplied, and how it was used. If it was used carelessly or not according to the instructions, then any settlement could be reduced because of contributory negligence on the part of the user.

> **Remember**
>
> The limit of £275 is to stop claims for very small amounts, known as 'spurious' claims.

Activity · Product recalls

In 2012, BMW recalled 1.3 million cars worldwide because of a battery fault which could cause a fire. In 2010, Toyota recalled thousands of cars because of a problem with the accelerator pedal.

In groups, discuss the issues that car manufacturers have to face when deciding on a recall. Why might some be tempted not to take this action and what could be the result? Do you think that the growth of social media could influence their decision?

Then research current recalls in the UK on the Trading Standards website. You can access this site by going to www.pearsonhotlinks.co.uk and searching for this title.

> **Did you know?**
>
> As foreign producers may be casual about product safety, the EU operates the RAPEX scheme to get dangerous goods quickly off the shelves. You can find out what goods are on the database this week by visiting the website.

Just checking

1 State two benefits that consumers have gained because of the Consumer Protection Act.
2 What are spurious claims?

CONTINUED ▶▶

Breaches of criminal law

Manufacturers of unsafe goods can be prosecuted under the Consumer Protection Act (1999) by a law enforcement agency. Usually this is Trading Standards, which can also take action if traders do not comply with the requirements of the Consumer Protection from Unfair Trading Regulations (2008).

The aim of making certain actions a criminal offence is two-fold: firstly, to protect consumers from duress, fraud or misrepresentation by an unscrupulous trader; secondly, to act as a deterrent to anyone considering behaving in this way, not just because there is the possibility they may be fined or imprisoned, but also because of the resulting publicity.

Cases that would be difficult or expensive to prove by an individual in a civil court can be dealt with in the criminal courts, with the overall aim of protecting future buyers.

These are the breaches you need to understand.

False trade descriptions

This is contained in the Consumer Protection from Unfair Trading Regulations. It is an offence for a seller to falsely describe an item in any way – verbally, in an advertisement, on a label or in the shop window. It is also a criminal offence to supply goods that are falsely described, such as bogus 'designer' perfumes and handbags.

The Consumer Protection from Unfair Trading Regulations (2008)

As described earlier, these make misleading actions and omissions, as well as aggressive practices, an offence, and ban certain specific practices.

Did you know?

Trading Standards officers may choose to advise a small business owner, or issue a caution as a first step. They will only start a prosecution if the caution is ignored or the offence is serious.

Activity Applying the Consumer Protection from Unfair Trading Regulations

Reread the information about the Consumer Protection from Unfair Trading Regulations. Then investigate these further and identify which of the following actions is an offence.

1 The same shop has had six 'closing down' sales in the last three months.
2 Your local grocery store is offering 'buy one get one free' deals.
3 The owner of a take-away decides to use a similar logo to KFC to attract customers.
4 Your friend boasts that he is selling lots of disposable cameras because these were a 'special purchase', so they are only available at that price for a limited time.
5 A friend says you will get rich quickly if you join his pyramid selling scheme.

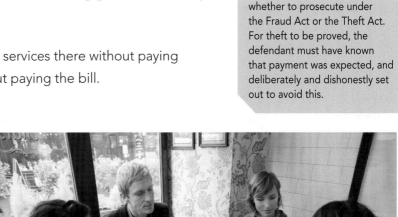

Fraud Act (2006) – Sections 2 and 11

Fraud is deception. The aim of a fraudster is to mislead someone so that they can obtain what is not rightfully theirs, whether this is money or goods.

Fraud by false representation (Section 2) is when a person behaves dishonestly or lies to obtain something, such as using a stolen credit card to buy goods.

Obtaining services dishonestly (Section 11) relates to obtaining goods without any intention of paying for them. Examples include:

- ordering goods online with a stolen credit card
- pretending to be a member of a club to use the services there without paying
- ordering food in a restaurant and leaving without paying the bill.

Theft Act 1978 (Section 3)

Making off without payment, such as shoplifting, is an offence under Section 3 of the Theft Act. This also relates to payments that are usually made on the spot for goods supplied or a service offered, such as filling a car with fuel and driving away without paying, or staying in a hotel and leaving without paying the bill.

> **Remember**
>
> A prosecutor looks at all the facts in a case before deciding whether to prosecute under the Fraud Act or the Theft Act. For theft to be proved, the defendant must have known that payment was expected, and deliberately and dishonestly set out to avoid this.

If you dislike the food, can you leave without paying?

Activity   Who is the thief?

Research fraud and theft further. Then, in groups, decide whether either party was guilty of fraud, theft or both. Give examples of cases to support your opinions.

1 Sarah and Sue go to a café for a meal every week. Usually they each take turns to pay. Today it is Sue's turn. Sarah has to leave early and chats to the owner on the way out. Sue is confused, thinking Sarah has paid, and also leaves.

2 Bilal and Afzal each get a taxi to take them home. Bilal's taxi driver gets lost, there is an argument and Bilal gets out without paying and walks home. Afzal's taxi driver asks him for £10, which Afzal refuses to pay and he runs off.

> **Did you know?**
>
> According to the Retail Fraud Study, store theft cost retailers £3.4 billion in 2012.

CONTINUED ▶▶

Assessment activity 12.2

2B.P4 | 2B.P5 | 1B.6 | 2B.P6 | 2B.M3 | 2B.M4 | 2B.D2

Before starting a business it is important to have an understanding of what is meant by 'the law' and how it affects consumers. You have been asked to write reports on the effectiveness of consumer protection in law for some recent cases. This will involve researching and commenting on several specific scenarios that your teacher/tutor will give you. You will then present your findings in a short report.

Task 1

Read the scenario below (or an alternative provided by your teacher or tutor) and write a report on whether this consumer should sue for breach of contract or negligence. Your report must:

- compare recent consumer protection law cases to assess the effectiveness of consumer legislation in law and how it is used to protect consumers in this situation
- compare the effectiveness of the law of contract and the law of negligence and include information about the different contract formats
- cite a famous case to support your conclusion.

Scenario

Holly made a hotel booking for her and her mother online and paid for the reservation in advance. They had a horrible time. Her mother, who is blind, slipped on some spilt food in the dining room. The spill had been reported to staff but they had not cleaned it up. Her mother broke her foot and now cannot walk. When Holly is told she is protected by contract law she is confused because she didn't sign a contract. Holly is considering whether to sue the hotel or not and is unsure whether she should sue them for breach of contract or negligence.

Task 2

Read the scenarios below (or alternatives provided by your teacher or tutor) and provide a report on the effectiveness of consumer protection law. For each scenario your report must:

- compare the effectiveness of consumer protection law/the relevant legislation
- describe how legislation protects the consumer
- cite past case(s) to support your conclusion.

Scenario A

Hamida buys a sponge cake for her father's birthday from the bakery. When he bites into it, he breaks his front tooth on a small screw. When she complains to the bakery they argue that she did not specify why she wanted the cake. Refer to the case of Priest v Last (1903) or Godley v Perry (1960).

Scenario B

When Holly makes the hotel booking she pays extra for a large twin bedroom and butler service, which is advertised on the hotel website and in the press as a special feature. However, when they arrive, Holly and her mother are shown to a small room and told the butler is off sick. When Holly asks for a refund she is told that the payment is non-refundable.

The next day, in the village tea shop, a local woman tells Holly that she used to work in the hotel, there are no luxury rooms and there has never been a butler. She feels the 'package' is a trick to get guests to make more expensive bookings. Identify what action Holly can take about the butler service she did not receive. Refer to the case of R v Mears and another (2011).

Scenario C

Max is selling imported fan heaters from abroad and has just signed a contract to supply 10,000 to a large store. The casing is metal and brightly painted. If you touch it after you switch it on you receive an electric shock and if you leave it turned on it gets very hot. Refer to the case of R v Zoostation Ltd (2010).

Scenario D

Anthony is thinking of having some plastic bags printed to look like charity collection bags and using them to collect donated items, but then selling the donated items at car boot sales and keeping the money rather than giving the items to the charity. Refer to recent cases where Trading Standards have taken action.

Task 3

Looking at all the cases you have researched for Tasks 1 and 2 evaluate how effective you think consumer protection in law is. You should also research other recent cases to support your evaluation.

Tips

- Take each situation in turn. Then refer to the legal principles you have learned and the appropriate statute where it applies.
- Remember that you can normally only take action under the Sale of Goods Act or the Supply of Goods and Services Act if you are the purchaser and there is a contract between you and the seller.
- Use recent examples to show the effectiveness of consumer protection.

Situations and legal remedies

Activity

Importance of 'time is of the essence'

Suggest three occasions when it would be important to state that 'time is of the essence' on a contract for the sale of goods.

Introduction

There may be different situations when a buyer is unhappy and requires a remedy to put things right. These are summarised below.

▼ Situations where consumers may have a legal claim

In each of the following situations, the consumer may have a legal claim.

The buyer wants to end the contract

You cannot cancel a contract because you feel like it. Many contracts contain specific information about cancellation, so you need to check the terms that apply in each case.

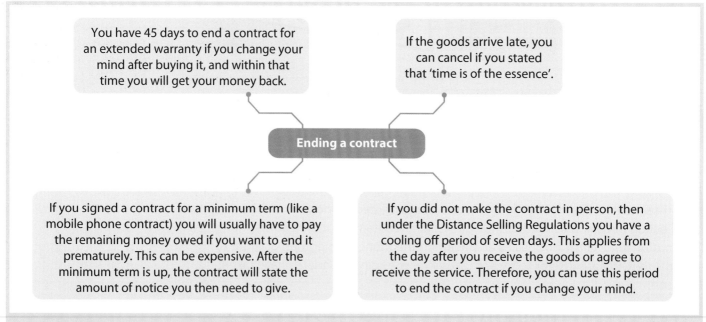

Figure 12.3 Ending a contract

The goods were defective

If the goods are unsatisfactory and do not meet the terms of the Sale of Goods Act, the seller has breached the terms of the contract. You can reject them, ask for a refund and end the contract. The same applies if you bought goods under the Distance Selling Regulations.

The goods caused injury or damage

It is a criminal offence to sell unsafe goods or food that it is unfit to eat or contaminated. If you, or someone else, are injured by a product you have bought, then the retailer must tell you who supplied it or be liable themself. If the goods are imported, you can claim against the importer.

Did you know?   ?

A manufacturer's defence for food could be that the product had no defects when it was sold to the retailer and the contamination was introduced while it was on the shelves. In this case, the retailer would be liable under the Sale of Goods Act.

Services have not been provided or provided poorly

Under the terms of the Supply of Goods and Services Act, if a service is not provided by the date agreed, or to an acceptable standard, then the buyer may be able to cancel the contract and claim damages.

> **Activity**   Advising your parents
>
> A professional photographer took photos for your parents when your brother emigrated to Australia. The photos are all out of focus. He says his camera was faulty but argues that the contract they signed says that he is not responsible for any problems caused by faulty equipment. In groups, decide whether this exclusion term is reasonable or unreasonable, what your parents should do and what damages they might be able to claim. To find out, research the case of Woodman v Photo Trade Processing Ltd (1981).

The wrong goods were provided

If an online seller sends you the wrong goods by mistake, you are protected by the terms of the Consumer Protection (Distance Selling) Regulations (2000). You should return them promptly for a refund or exchange. If you go into a shop and buy the wrong goods by mistake, the situation is different. Unless the goods are damaged or defective, you are reliant on the goodwill of the seller to give you an exchange or a refund.

Only part goods were provided

If the goods are part of a set, you do not have to accept them. Nor do you have to agree to delivery in instalments unless this was negotiated at the outset. You have the right to return goods but must pay for anything you keep.

The goods were falsely described or misrepresented

You have rights under the Sale of Goods Act and may notify Trading Standards if the seller is in breach of the Consumer Protection from Unfair Trading Regulations.

> **? Did you know?**
>
> You cannot claim damages for distress or disappointment unless the aim of the contract is to provide pleasure, for example, a holiday.

The rights and duties of buyers and sellers

It is important that both buyers and sellers know their rights and duties and the type of remedies that they must provide or can receive. These will vary depending on the situation and whether the law of contract applies, negligence is an issue, there has been a crime or there is a specific legislation to cover a transaction or provide protection.

For example, if you buy a defective product, you have the right to a refund, a repair or a replacement. If it has caused injury, you may have the right to compensation. If you signed a contract, for example for a broadband service that keeps failing, you may be able to end this prematurely because the supplier is in breach.

> **? Did you know?**
>
> Many small traders are not aware that they do not have the right to issue a credit note if a buyer returns defective goods.

Remedies and their benefits

Damages

These are the same as compensation, but the amount can vary. If a product is faulty, the amount is normally equal to the cost of a replacement or a repair.

Consequential loss covers other losses, such as injury or damage to other property by a faulty product, or other expenses, such as loss of earnings. In some cases, additional damages are allowed for distress, inconvenience or disappointment.

Termination

In this case, the contract has existed and then it is ended. An example is cancelling a mobile phone contract which has been running for several months.

A contract may be terminated because of breach of contract, such as being sold faulty goods. In this case, the contract did exist, and if the buyer suffered a wrong during this time, action can still be taken to remedy this. This may include claiming compensation or damages.

A contract may be terminated by mutual agreement when there is no breach.

Recission

This remedy is explained in the case study below.

Case Study

Amina always wanted her own business. When she sees a local coffee shop for sale she immediately goes to chat to Keith, the owner. He tells her she would make a good living from the business, just like him. What he does not tell her is that he is selling because a branch of Starbucks is to open round the corner. Amina buys the business. Two weeks later Starbucks opens and takes most of her trade. She is desperate until her solicitor tells her she can take action to rescind the contract.

In this situation, both parties are put back into the situation they were in before the contract existed. Amina no longer owns the coffee shop and gets her money back, and Keith gets the shop back again.

Assessment Activity 12.3

2C.P7 | 2C.P8 | 2C.M5 | 2C.D3

The reputation of a business you work for could be damaged if it was breaking the law or refusing to replace faulty goods. You are involved in a presentation on legal remedies for both buyers and sellers in recent cases.

Task 1

Re-use the scenarios below (or alternatives provided by your teacher or tutor). Prepare a presentation on the legal remedies available. Which legal remedy would be most appropriate in each scenario? For **each scenario** your presentation must:

- consider recent past consumer cases
- explain why the consumer may have a legal claim
- compare the legal remedies available to the buyer (if there is one)
- compare the legal remedies available to the seller.

Scenario A

Hamida buys a sponge cake for her father's birthday from the bakery. When he bites into it, he breaks his front tooth on a small screw. When she complains to the bakery they argue that she did not specify why she wanted the cake. Refer to the case of Priest v Last (1903) or Godley v Perry (1960).

Scenario B

When Holly makes the hotel booking she pays extra for a large twin bedroom and butler service, which is advertised on the hotel website and in the press as a special feature. However, when they arrive Holly and her mother are shown to a small room and told the butler is off sick. When Holly asks for a refund she is told that the payment is non-refundable.

The next day, in the village tea shop, a local woman tells Holly that she used to work in the hotel, there are no luxury rooms and there has never been a butler. She feels the 'package' is a trick to get guests to make more expensive bookings. Identify what action Holly can take about the butler service she did not receive. Refer to the case of R v Mears and another (2011).

Scenario C

Max is selling imported fan heaters from abroad and has just signed a contract to supply 10,000 to a large store. The casing is metal and brightly painted. If you touch it after you switch it on you receive an electric shock and if you leave it turned on it gets very hot. Refer to the case of R v Zoostation Ltd (2010).

Task 2

Look at the various legal remedies that you have researched for the above scenarios and then research some recent consumer protection cases. Evaluate the appropriateness of the remedies decided in these legal cases.

Tip

- A legal precedent is set when a court decision made in a case becomes the rule for similar cases in future. Identifying a relevant recent case gives you guidance on the outcome in the same or similar situations.

Introduction

The importance of good financial management in a business cannot be overestimated. Every year, many businesses fail because the owners or managers do not realise, or understand, the vital role of planning and forecasting in relation to controlling revenue and expenditure to achieve a profit.

Successful businesses thrive because money is used wisely. Unprofitable activities can be avoided through techniques such as breakeven analysis. Income and payments are monitored and cash flow is forecast so that potential problems can be identified in advance. Action can then be taken to avoid expensive loans and surplus funds reinvested or used to pay off any debts. The process of budgeting enables expenditure to be planned and controlled. This helps to prevent any unpleasant surprises that might jeopardise profits.

Understanding these techniques is vital for all business owners.

This unit builds on *Unit 2: Finance for Business* to give you a more in-depth knowledge of financial planning and forecasting in business.

Learning aims

In this unit you will:

A demonstrate the use of breakeven analysis in business

B demonstrate the use of cash flow forecasting in business

C investigate the use of budgets and budgetary control in business.

My cousin was surprised when his business failed because he knew he was working really hard. He never realised that he was losing money all the time until an accountant worked out the figures for him. I would hate to do that, which is why I want to study this unit. I want to be able to monitor my own finances to make sure my own business would be profitable.

Louise, *15-year-old Business student*

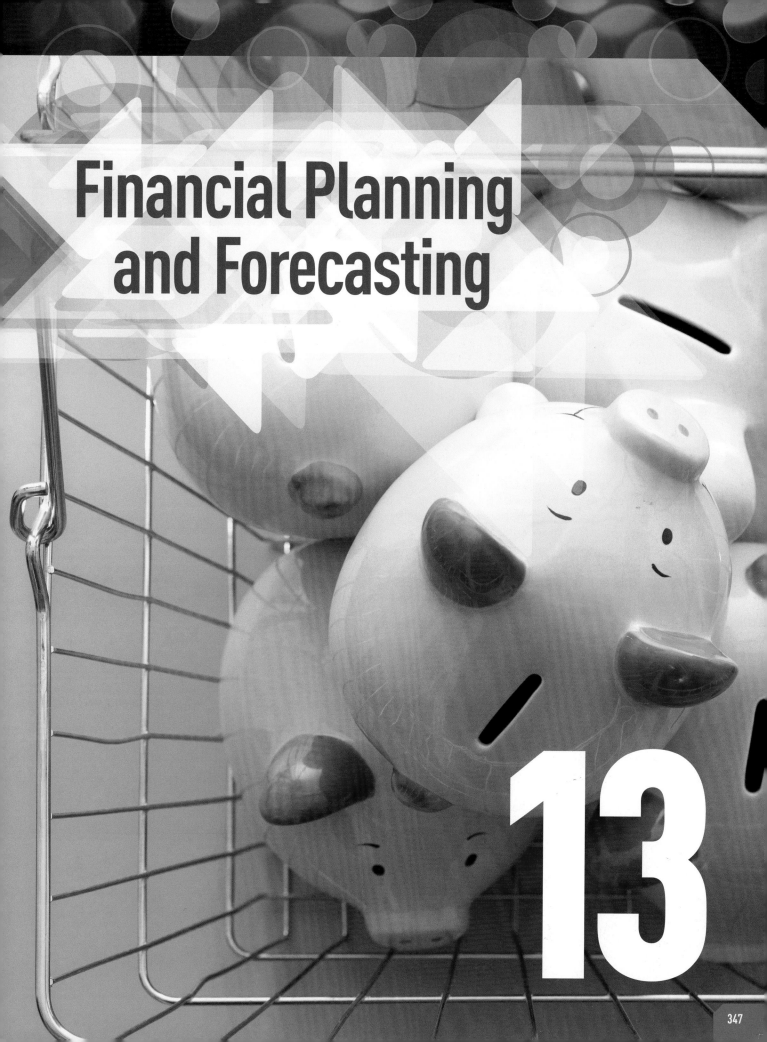

Financial Planning and Forecasting

BTEC
Assessment Zone

This table shows you what you must do in order to achieve a **Pass**, **Merit** or **Distinction** grade, and where you can find activities in this book to help you.

Assessment criteria			
Level 1	Level 2 Pass	Level 2 Merit	Level 2 Distinction
Learning aim A: Demonstrate the use of breakeven analysis in business			
1A.1 Maths Calculate, with guidance, breakeven using given sets of data.	**2A.P1** Maths Calculate breakeven using given sets of data. **See Assessment activity 13.1, page 355**	**2A.M1** Maths Assess the impact of changing cost and revenue data on the break-even point for a selected business. **See Assessment activity 13.1, page 355**	**2A.D1** Evaluate the importance of breakeven analysis to a selected business. **See Assessment activity 13.1, page 355**
1A.2 Maths Present an accurate breakeven graph.	**2A.P2** Maths Present the breakeven using an appropriately annotated, accurate graph. **See Assessment activity 13.1, page 355**		
1A.3 Outline the uses of breakeven in a given situation.	**2A.P3** Explain how a selected business can use breakeven analysis in a given situation. **See Assessment activity 13.1, page 355**		
Level 1	Level 2 Pass	Level 2 Merit	Level 2 Distinction
Learning aim B: Demonstrate the use of cash flow forecasting in business			
1B.4 Maths Prepare an annual cash flow forecast for a selected business using monthly data.	**2B.P4** Maths Prepare an accurate annual cash flow forecast for a selected business using monthly data. **See Assessment activity 13.2, page 361**	**2B.M2** Maths Analyse a cash flow forecast to identify issues and appropriate actions for a selected business. **See Assessment activity 13.2, page 361**	**2B.D2** Evaluate cash flow forecasting as a tool for managing the finances for a selected business. **See Assessment activity 13.2, page 361**
1B.5 Describe the effect of regular and irregular cash inflows and outflows on a selected business.	**2B.P5** Explain the implications of regular and irregular cash inflows and outflows for a selected business. **See Assessment activity 13.2, page 361**		

Level 1	Level 2 Pass	Level 2 Merit	Level 2 Distinction
Learning aim C: Investigate the use of budgets and budgetary control in business			
1C.6 Identify the types of budgets used by two contrasting businesses.	**2C.P6** Describe the purpose of specific budgets used in two contrasting businesses. **See Assessment activity 13.3, page 369**	**2C.M3** Compare how budgetary control is used in two contrasting businesses. **See Assessment activity 13.3, page 369**	**2C.D3** Evaluate the influence of variances on financial decisions made by a business. **See Assessment activity 13.3, page 369**
1C.7 Outline how budgetary control is used in a selected business.	**2C.P7** Explain how budgetary control is used in two contrasting businesses. **See Assessment activity 13.3, page 369**		
1C.8 Identify, with guidance, favourable and adverse variances in a given business budget.	**2C.P8** Identify favourable and adverse variances in a given business budget. **See Assessment activity 13.3, page 369**		

Maths Opportunity to practise mathematical skills

How you will be assessed

This unit will be assessed by a series of internally assessed tasks and activities. These will enable you to demonstrate your own understanding of financial planning and forecasting and apply your knowledge in several different situations. You will also show that you understand the importance of breakeven analysis and cash flow forecasting and how the outcomes of the budgeting process can impact upon the financial decisions made in business. Your assessment could be in the form of:

- a clearly annotated breakeven graph for a business, with an accompanying report analysing the information and explaining the likely outcome of changes that would affect cost and revenue data, together with your recommendations for the business owner

- a spreadsheet showing an annual cash flow forecast for a business using supplied data, together with your analysis and recommended actions. A separate document should summarise why preparing and analysing cash flow forecasts is an essential tool for managing business finances

- a presentation on budgets and budgetary control where you compare the budgets of two contrasting businesses, explain how each is used and discuss the types of decisions that may be made as a result.

Calculating breakeven

Introduction

Successful business people are very financially aware. They always know how much money they have, how much they are owed and how much they owe to other people. They know when income is expected and regularly think of ways to make more money. If you have your own business one day, hopefully you will think like this!

The concept of breakeven

You learned in *Unit 2: Finance for Business* that all businesses have income (revenue) and expenditure (costs). If income is *less than* expenditure, the business is making a loss and some form of corrective action will probably be needed. However, if income is *greater than* expenditure, the business is making a profit and this extra money can be put to good use.

The point in between profit and loss, where income and expenditure are equal, is known as the **breakeven point**.

Definition of breakeven point

A breakeven situation is achieved when the cost of producing goods or delivering a service is equal to the total income received. Breakeven is often used to monitor the progress of a new product. It is quite normal for a new product to make a loss in the early stages of sales but if it is successful the income will rise and pass the breakeven point to generate a profit.

Methods of calculating breakeven

There are two principal methods of calculating breakeven:

- Using a formula.
- Producing a chart or graph.

Using a formula

The formula used to calculate breakeven is:

$$\text{Breakeven point} = \frac{\text{fixed costs}}{\text{selling price per unit} - \text{variable cost per unit}}$$

Remember

Costs fall into two categories – fixed and variable. Both types are involved in breakeven analysis. Can you remember the difference between them? If not, look back at Unit 2, Topic A.1.

Calculating the breakeven point

1 For each of the following sets of figures, calculate the breakeven point.

Product	Selling price per item (£)	Fixed costs (£)	Variable cost per item (£)
a) Toy dress up doll	12.00	10,000	4.00
b) Printed T-shirt	10.00	500	5.00
c) Cheese sandwich	1.75	200	0.5
d) Sports car	20,000	1 million	15,000

2 The sports cars are not selling well and the manufacturer decides to reduce the price to £17,500. How many must now be sold to breakeven?

Link

A breakeven graph can also be referred to as a breakeven chart. You covered these in *Unit 2: Finance for Business*.

Key term

Margin of safety – the amount by which sales would have to fall to reach the breakeven point.

Producing a chart or graph

A graph provides far more detail than the formula. For example, for different levels of output, it shows the total costs and total revenue of the business and how much profit (or loss) will be made.

Although drawing a graph takes longer than using the formula, it allows a business to see their financial situation visually and this can make it easier to analyse the situation, to plan the best way forward.

A breakeven graph is a visual representation of a business's financial situation.

Drawing and analysing a graph

Look back at Unit 2 to refresh your memory about breakeven graphs. Work through Table 2.2 and revise all the features. Use the following information to draw a breakeven graph and label the features listed below.

Ben runs a local business selling home delivery pizzas. He wants to know how to calculate his breakeven point and how to find his **margin of safety**. He has given you the following figures for a typical week's trading.

Average selling price of a pizza = £7.00

Variable cost = £2.00 per pizza

Fixed costs = £500

Items to be labelled: costs and revenue axis and number sold axis, fixed costs, total costs, variable costs, sales revenue, breakeven point, profit area, loss area, margin of safety if sales are 140 per week.

Read off the breakeven point and double-check this figure using the formula. Check and discuss your graph and calculations with your teacher/tutor.

Breakeven analysis

 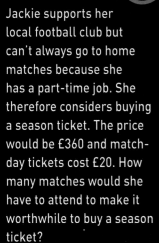
Discussion point

Breakeven analysis assumes that all items sell at the same price, and that prices will remain the same at all levels of sales. Is this true in real life, or do prices vary?

Key term

'What if approach' – a way in which managers plan for the future. They look beyond the current situation to consider what might be the result if they make certain changes.

The concept of breakeven analysis

The main use of breakeven is to analyse the consequences of possible actions. In Jackie's case, this is whether it is worth buying a season ticket.

All businesses must make many decisions, particularly about costs and prices. They need to keep costs low and sell at the best price to be successful. Breakeven analysis shows what will happen if costs or prices change. If it is impossible to make a profit at a competitive price, then the business may not be able to sell a particular item.

Breakeven analysis is therefore a tool which helps managers make the best decisions. It can be used when they are using the **'what if approach'**.

Identifying areas of profit and loss

The graph you produced for Ben should look like the one shown below.

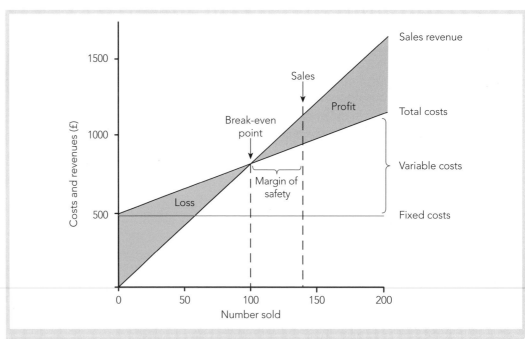

Figure 13.1 The breakeven graph for Ben's pizza delivery business

The profit and loss areas are shown in blue (profit) and green (loss). They are the areas between the total cost line and the total sales income line. You should see that:

- at all levels of sales below the breakeven point, Ben is making a loss. The further away from the breakeven point, the greater the loss he incurs
- at all levels of sales above the breakeven point, Ben is making a profit. This increases, as you move to the right of the breakeven point
- the amount of profit or loss at any level of sales is seen by calculating the distance between the cost and sales revenue lines.

Margin of safety

The margin of safety is the amount of profit forecast above the breakeven point. It is the amount by which sales would have to fall before the planned activity would start to make a loss. This is like a safety net for a business which will want the margin to be as large as possible. It is also a measure of the level of risk the business would be taking with a new project because the lower the margin of safety, the greater the risk of failure.

Remember

Total costs = fixed costs + variable costs

Costs (fixed, variable, total)

In Unit 2 you learned about these costs. They are all vital components of breakeven calculations.

Contribution

If a business produces several different items, it can be difficult to decide how to allocate fixed costs between them. One solution is to use the idea of **contribution**. For example, a bakery produces various types of bread and cakes. As it cannot decide how to allocate fixed costs to each one, it subtracts the variable cost of making each item from the selling price. The result is the contribution each item makes to the fixed cost figure.

The contribution for a certain type of bread could be calculated as follows:

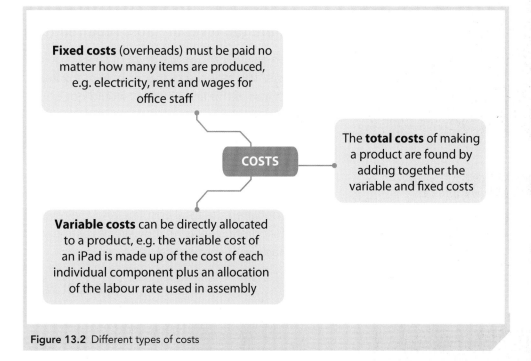

Figure 13.2 Different types of costs

Variable cost = 30p   Selling price = £1.40   Number made and sold = 2000

Contribution per loaf = £1.40 – 30p = £1.10

Total contribution for this type of bread = £1.10 × 2000 = £2,200

The total contribution figure for all the products should equal the total fixed cost figure.

Key term

Contribution – the selling price minus the variable cost of a product. This is the contribution the product makes to the fixed or overhead costs.

Total revenue

The total revenue is the number of sales of an item multiplied by the price. This line always starts at zero on the breakeven graph because if there are no sales, no income is being earned. Varying either the number of items sold or the price of the goods will change the total revenue.

Did you know?

If a business makes several items, it may need to carry out a breakeven analysis on each one and then add all the sales figures together to calculate the total revenue figure for the business.

CONTINUED ▶▶

Presenting and interpreting breakeven information graphically

A breakeven graph provides a visual presentation of key financial matters related to a project or the sale of an item, such as the breakeven point and the potential profit or loss. If a spreadsheet package is used to produce a breakeven graph, the figures relating to costs and price can be easily changed, giving an immediate display of the results.

The relevance of breakeven analysis to a business

Breakeven analysis can be used in several ways.

To estimate the level of sales required to break even

Breakeven analysis shows the level of sales required for the sales revenue to at least cover costs. This tells the manager how many items *must* be sold if the business is not to make a loss. If this level of sales would not be possible, the project may have to be abandoned.

To estimate profitability

If the breakeven analysis shows that the forecast level of sales is above the breakeven point, the product is profitable. The amount of profit is found by measuring the distance between the total cost line and the revenue line for the forecast sales level. If the forecast profit level is healthy, any investment needed to introduce a new product can be made with confidence.

As a tool when making future business decisions

If the graph shows the situation is close to the breakeven point, the managers will want to take action to improve profitability, for example by increasing income or cutting costs. However, while reducing costs always increases profitability, changing prices is more difficult. If prices are reduced, sales revenue will only increase if more items are sold. If prices are increased, then fewer items may be sold.

Managers must also consider the effect of other factors on breakeven (Figure 13.3). Events of this kind mean breakeven analysis needs to be regularly undertaken to take account of any changes.

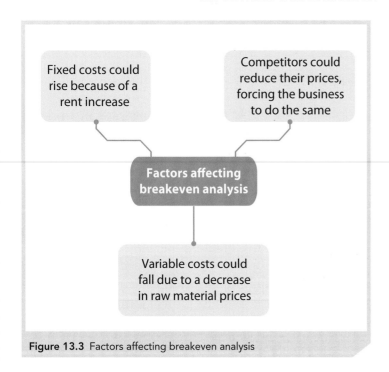

Figure 13.3 Factors affecting breakeven analysis

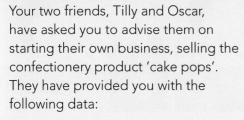

Activity   Making the right decision

A competitor opens near Ben, selling pizzas at an average price of £6. Can Ben compete at this price? His insurance premiums and business rates increase next month by £50 a week, but he could save money by changing supplier and reducing his variable costs to £1.50 per pizza. Use breakeven analysis to advise Ben and suggest what he should do. Then compare your ideas with other members of your class.

Just checking

1 How would you define the breakeven point?

2 Explain the importance of the margin of safety.

3 A firm produces three different items. How can it allocate overheads, such as electricity, accurately between them?

Assessment activity 13.1   *Maths*   2A.P1 | 2A.P2 | 2A.P3 | 2A.M1 | 2A.D1

Your two friends, Tilly and Oscar, have asked you to advise them on starting their own business, selling the confectionery product 'cake pops'. They have provided you with the following data:

Estimated variable cost of making each cake pop = 50p

Other (fixed) costs: £150 a week

Proposed selling price: 80p

They estimate they can make 800 each week, but Oscar is unsure whether they could sell all the cake pops they make. A local store has offered them a contract to buy 400 each week, but will only pay 75p per cake pop. Tilly reckons that if they allow for an extra £30 a week to be spent on local advertising, then they will sell plenty at the higher price.

Prepare a report for them which includes their break-even output and a breakeven graph to illustrate their basic business plan and evaluates the importance of breakeven analysis to their business. In your report, explain how they can use break-even to help them make business decisions before assessing how their different options will affect the breakeven point. Summarise how this will change if they supply the store and/or increase their advertising.

Preparing a cash flow forecast

Getting started

You first learned about cash flow forecasts in Unit 2. Can you remember why they are used and their benefits? What are the dangers for business owners who know nothing about cash flow?

Identifying cash inflows

All businesses receive money. On a cash flow forecast these are known as cash inflows. The main types are given below.

Capital

All new businesses need money for essential items, such as equipment or premises. The money invested in the business at the outset is called **capital** and it is mainly used to buy **assets**, such as a van or computer. These normally last a long time but can be sold if necessary.

Additional capital may be needed at a later date, for example to buy new equipment if the business is expanding.

Investors who buy shares in the business in return for **dividends**.

Banks who provide a loan in return for regular interest payments.

Friends or family who lend money to help the business owner(s).

Money for capital expenditure can come from three places.

Sales

This is income received from customers who buy the products or services offered by a business. They may pay in two ways:

- **Cash sales** are retail transactions where the customer pays when the goods are purchased, whether this is in actual cash, by cheque or debit/credit card. In all cases, the business receives the money when it makes the sale.
- **Payments from debtors** concern business-to-business transactions which are conducted on a credit basis. This means that payment is made a short time after the goods or services have been supplied. Businesses which owe money to other businesses are known as debtors and this type of business transaction is known as **credit trading**.

Loans

Businesses may need to borrow money from banks or other sources, usually for capital investment. The loan is taken out for a fixed length of time, after which the money has to be repaid. The lender also charges interest to the borrower. Sometimes repayment of the capital amount and the interest are made together, so that the borrower owes nothing at the end of the loan period.

An **overdraft** is another source of additional money but occurs when a business is allowed to spend more money than it has in its bank account. This must be agreed in advance and a limit is set. The rate of interest charged is quite high and is calculated on a daily basis.

Other inflows

Businesses may have other sources of income. Some allow posters or displays on their premises or include advertisements on their website. Others may rent out part of a building which they own to another business.

Regular and irregular inflows

Running a business would be easier if all payments were regular and predictable. Unfortunately they are not.

- Cash sales vary from week to week as customers allowed credit may take longer than agreed to pay their account.
- Seasonal factors are important. Hairdressers, toy shops and restaurants are much busier in December than January. Many seaside businesses close down in the winter.
- The weather can affect many trades. A builder, roofer or gardener may be delayed and therefore do not receive payment as expected.

How the timing of inflows influences the cash flow of a business

Inflows of money directly affect the amount of money the business has available. Unpredictable inflows may mean that there is at times a surplus of cash, at other times cash is in short supply. If a large payment is late, the business may not have enough money in the bank to pay its own bills that month.

> **Key term**
>
> **Overdraft** – this occurs if a business pays more out of its bank account that it has in credit. The bank may allow this but will make an extra charge.

> **Did you know?**
>
> Airports, retail stores, garden centres and sporting arenas all make extra money from concessions, when another firm uses a space on the premises to sell its goods, such as Ted Baker, MAC and the White Company in Selfridges.

Why do these businesses close down in winter?

Activity Choosing who to pay

Your business is short of cash this month. Will you pay an important supplier an overdue bill, or pay wages to your two staff? Why? What could be the consequences? Compare your ideas with other members of your group.

> **Did you know?**
>
> Ryanair is a seasonal business. It does not use a quarter of its aircraft in the winter months.

Identifying cash outflows

All businesses must spend money to operate. The payments they make are called cash outflows and the main types are given below.

Purchases

Businesses make two types of purchases.

- **Cash purchases** are transactions paid for immediately in cash, by cheque or by a debit or credit card, e.g. small stationery items, train and taxi fares and vehicle fuel.
- **Payments to creditors** are usually payments to suppliers who have provided stock or raw materials on a credit basis. Expensive equipment or motor vehicles may also be paid for each month.

Repayments

Any business that has borrowed money must make repayments.

- **Loans** are usually repaid on a monthly basis.
- A **mortgage** is a loan used to buy property, usually over a long period such as 15 or 20 years. Repayments are usually made monthly.
- An **overdraft** must be kept within the agreed limit by making regular repayments. The bank may insist on personal guarantees or additional security to protect itself in case the borrower defaults.

Expenses

Business expenses are all those items of expenditure which are required for the business to operate.

- **Wages** – paid to employees either weekly or monthly.
- **Rent** – paid to the property owner if the building is not owned by the business.
- **Advertising** – used to promote the business and maintain or boost sales.
- **Interest** – due to the bank on any loan, mortgage or overdraft held.

Regular and irregular outflows

Whereas some outflows will be regular payments that have been agreed in advance, such as rent, others will be irregular and some may be unpredictable.

- The wage bill may vary, particularly if some employees are paid overtime or bonuses, or if additional staff are hired at busy periods.
- Additional stock may be needed before a busy season which means higher supplier bills.
- Emergency payments may be necessary if an important item of equipment breaks down, such as a heating boiler.
- Assets, such as vehicles or computers, eventually wear out or become out of date and need replacing.

How the timing of outflows influences the cash flow of a business

Although there are similar issues with outflows, the business usually has more control over the timing of these, so it could delay payment to a supplier until the bank balance has improved. The danger is that if payment is delayed too long, that supplier may refuse to supply goods in future.

◤ Cash balances

A cash flow forecast is made up of several totals or balances. These enable you to calculate the amount that a business will have in the bank at the end of a period, usually a month. These balances are as follows:

Opening balance

This is the amount of money planned to be in the bank account on a certain day, normally the first of the month.

Income per period

This is the total receipts or inflows the business expects to receive during the period.

Expenditure per period

This is the total payments or outflows the business expects to make during the period.

Net cash flow

This is the difference between total income and expenditure for the period. If the business has spent more than it earned, this figure will be negative.

Closing balance

This is the opening balance figure plus the net cash flow figure (or minus a negative figure). It shows how much money the business has left at the end of the period.

How can late or irregular payments affect a business?

Activity   Suzie's cash flow forecast

Suzie has started to prepare her forecast. Look at this carefully and then answer the questions below. Keep your work safe as you will use Suzie's forecast again later.

1 Write a brief definition of each of the following terms: opening balance, closing balance, income per period, expenditure per period.
2 How did Suzie calculate a net cash flow figure of £12,000 for January?
3 How did Suzie reach an opening balance of £63,000 for February?

Table 13.1 Suzie's cash flow forecast (£'000)

Item	Jan	Feb	Mar	Apr	May	Jun	Jul	Aug	Sep	Oct	Nov	Dec
Income	56	58	60	55	60	30	20	25	80	70	75	70
Expenditure	44	48	47	43	140	40	42	40	40	42	45	90
Net cash flow	12	10	13	12	−80	−10	−22	−15	40	28	30	−20
Opening balance	51	63	73	86	98	18	8	−14	−29	11	39	69
Closing balance	63	73	86	98	18	8	−14	−29	11	39	69	49

Analysing a cash flow forecast

The purpose of analysing a cash flow forecast

To identify a potential surplus or deficit

Cash flow forecasts contain vital information about the financial health of the business. The closing balance is a very important figure because it tells you how much money the business has at the start of the next month.

- **A potential surplus:** if a large balance is forecast, this potential surplus should be used productively, for example to buy additional resources, such as more productive equipment or new computers.
- **A potential deficit:** if the closing balance figure is low or negative, different action must be taken, for example:
  - Borrowing money by taking out a bank loan or asking the bank to agree an overdraft.
  - Reducing spending as much as possible, such as by finding cheaper sources of stock or raw materials.
  - Increasing inflows by chasing up overdue debts and holding a discount sale to sell old stock.

To inform business planning and forecasting

A business must compare its cash flow forecast with its actual cash flow each month. A fairly accurate forecast indicates business planning is sound, either because reliable data has been used or the owner is experienced. Any substantial differences should ring warning bells. A business must question whether its forecast is too optimistic (or pessimistic) and why, so that it can be more accurate in the future.

A cash flow forecast shows predicted trends over time. If the business is seasonal, the owner can identify problems and look for additional sources of revenue. If the overall trend is upwards, the owner can plan how to improve the business. If it is downwards, then inflows need increasing and outflows need reducing through careful budgeting. Some items may need to be reduced and others cut out completely.

How cash flow forecasting can be used to manage business finances

Cash flow forecasting is an important tool which can be used to effectively measure and control business finances. However, it is not perfect as you will see in Table 13.2.

Table 13.2 Strengths and limitations of cash flow forecasting

Strengths	Limitations
It provides advance warning of potential surpluses and deficits, so that action can be taken.	A forecast is based on estimates which could be wrong, particularly for a new business with no past data.
It identifies the main sources of revenue and any slow-paying customers.	A long range forecast may be inaccurate given unforeseen factors, e.g. tax and price increases and competitor behaviour.
It enables enough money to be available so bills and wages are always paid on time.	It gives only one view, e.g. it does not include valuable assets that could be sold if there was a serious problem.
It shows the main outflows (vital when preparing budgets) and helps identify over-spending.	It cannot predict when customers may not pay their bills or fail to place another order.
It ensures that a close check is kept on finances and helps appropriate business decisions to be made.	Mistakes in the forecast can result in the wrong decisions being made which can create serious problems for the business.

Assessment activity 13.2   *Maths*

2B.P4 | 2A.P5 | 2B.M2 | 2B.D2

Tilly and Oscar have been making cake pops for four months. The business did well at Halloween and Christmas and they hired temporary staff and bought a more reliable van. January, however, is quiet and they have less cash so they ask you for advice. In particular, Tilly wants to know if she can buy a new oven in March, costing £2000.

Tilly and Oscar have given you their predicted sales revenues and payments for the next twelve months, together with Tilly's notes. These are shown below.

Tilly's notes: Our opening balance in January was £1000. We expect to be busy at Easter and supplying children's parties during the summer, and will hire temporary staff again then. I also intend to advertise more in March and May.

Use this data to prepare an accurate annual cash flow forecast for them, including an evaluation of this method to show Tilly and Oscar how they can use this tool to manage their finances. Attach an explanation of the implications of regular and irregular inflows and outflows for their business. Identify the main issues they need to consider and suggest appropriate actions they could take.

Item	Jan £	Feb £	Mar £	Apr £	May £	Jun £	Jul £	Aug £	Sept £	Oct £	Nov £	Dec £
Sales income	700	900	1200	2000	1600	3000	3100	3200	1500	1800	2800	3500
Expenditure	1400	1400	1600	1400	1500	2000	2000	2000	1400	2200	2000	2000

Tip

Include in your evaluation any limitations of cash flow forecasting that Tilly and Oscar should note.

The use of budgets in business

Introduction

Many people budget in their private life to make sure that they can always pay their bills and do not get into debt. They also try to save on a regular basis. Do you?

The purpose of budgets in business

In Unit 2 you learned that a budget is a list of items on which the business plans to spend money, and the amounts to be spent on each item. After a period of time (normally a month), the amount of money spent on each item is calculated and any differences between planned and actual expenditure are investigated. There are several reasons why businesses have budgets.

A forecasting tool

Budgets show planned future expenditure. The process of producing the plans forces the manager(s) to think ahead even if there are short-term problems.

Resource planning

Resources are items needed by a business to fulfil its purpose, for example a hospital needs a building, equipment and medical staff. Preparing a budget may highlight situations where extra resources may be needed. For example, if a hospital planned to extend its A&E department, it might need an additional building as well as more staff and equipment.

To control resources

As well as planning how to use resources, a budgetary system checks on how resources are being used. This is why the budget system is called **budgetary control**.

To motivate staff to achieve performance targets

Ideally managers will contribute towards setting their own budget and then explain this to their staff. They should also discuss the **performance targets,** which are the levels of achievement that are necessary to earn enough revenue to support the planned levels of expenditure. The main targets usually relate to sales (how much we must sell) and production (how many goods we must make). The aim is to motivate staff to achieve the targets.

What type of resources does a hospital need?

Types of business budgets and their differences

Whereas the owner of a small business is personally responsible for the overall budget, this is not possible in a large organisation. Medium and large businesses normally have several departments or divisions. Each is run by a manager who is responsible for their own budget. Ultimately all of the separate budgets in a business will be combined into a **master budget** which covers the whole business. This system ensures that all managers are working together towards the same overall plan.

The main differences between the budgets relates to the categories of expenditure that are controlled.

Sales

This is normally the starting point of the budget process because the planned sales dictate the level of activity for the other budgets. For example, in a manufacturing organisation, the production department knows how many items it must produce and the purchasing department knows how many components or raw materials will be needed to achieve the sales target.

In all organisations, the sales department must forecast its target sales for each month. In a service organisation or retail business, this means forecasting the expected number of customers and the average value of sales to each one. Several factors must be considered when preparing this budget as shown in Figure 13.4.

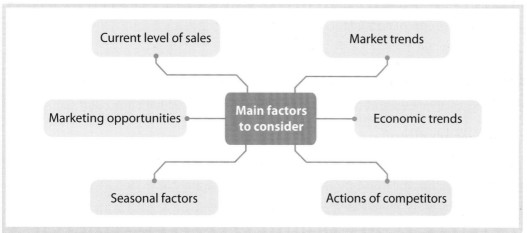

Figure 13.4 Factors to consider when preparing a budget

The main items in the sales budget are projected sales figures and expenditure on specialist sales staff and marketing activities, for example advertising, promotions and attending exhibitions. The sales budget is unique because it is the only departmental budget which budgets for income as well as expenditure.

Production

This is often the largest budget in terms of the total money which is planned to be spent. It can include labour costs, raw materials and/or other components, energy (gas and electricity), maintenance of equipment and storage of stock.

The main factor which decides the size of the production budget is the quantity of products forecast to be sold in the sales budget.

Key term

Master budget – this comprises all the departmental budgets brought together for the whole business.

Discussion point

A critical factor in preparing the sales budget is the price(s) at which the product(s) will be offered. As a group, discuss the benefits and drawbacks of setting a low price against setting a high one.

Did you know?

Wise businesses keep stock levels to a minimum to reduce the space needed and the amount of money tied up in stock. They prefer to use suppliers who can provide a fast delivery service.

Purchases (materials)

The type of items purchased will depend on the type of business, so a manufacturer buys raw materials and components, whereas a retailer buys finished goods for resale.

Production tells the purchasing department which items are needed and the required timing of deliveries. The main issues with the purchasing budget are quantity and price of the goods. If prices are rising, the purchasing department may need to find alternative, cheaper sources of supply.

Labour

Labour is required by all departments and is often identified in a separate budget because pay rates are usually the same throughout the business. For example, an administrator in marketing will be paid the same as one in purchasing, and sales staff in Bolton will be paid the same as those in Brighton. In these cases, wage levels are controlled centrally and are not under the control of individual department heads.

Another factor affecting the wage bill is overtime or temporary staff hired at busy periods. Overtime is normally paid at a higher rate and can be costly.

Overheads

Some types of cost cannot be easily allocated to a particular budget. These include the salaries for senior managers, cleaning, heating, security, building maintenance and business rates. Sometimes, these costs are allocated between departmental budgets on the basis of size of floor area.

Cash

This is almost identical to cash flow monitoring because in this budget the amount of expected cash inflows and outflows is forecast to predict a final bank balance.

Capital expenditure

Capital expenditure is money spent on large durable items such as machinery, vehicles and buildings. Capital budgets are normally set separately from departmental budgets and individual items are judged on value for money.

Profit and loss

As you learned in Unit 2, a profit and loss account is an official document produced by businesses each year. However, businesses often produce unofficial profit and loss accounts at other times to see what it would look like – and take corrective action if necessary. The first one can be produced from the master budget.

Activity	Knowing the numbers

Understanding how much is forecast to be earned and spent is vital for all businesses – but this is often the reason why *Dragons' Den* candidates fail! In groups, look at two or three applicants on YouTube and assess how good they are at 'knowing the numbers' before you read the WorkSpace that follows.

Did you know?

The total labour cost for a business is sometimes called 'the payroll'. McDonald's employs 85,000 people in the UK and over one million worldwide, so needs to keep a tight rein on its payroll bill.

WorkSpace

▶ Shelagh Brownlow

Chartered Accountant and Business Advisor, Brownlow's Accountants

As a qualified Chartered Accountant and partner in a large business consultancy firm, the last thing Shelagh Brownlow expected was to have financial difficulties when she ran her own business. But that's exactly what happened. In 2002, she bought out the accountancy section of the company, and with 12 staff, set up her own firm, specialising in business accounts and payroll. Technology was evolving rapidly, which did not suit some older workers. Three payroll specialists left in quick succession and replacing them proved difficult. Some payroll clients were lost which affected revenue and created financial difficulties. In 2006, she was relieved to let a larger practice take over the operation. She decided to start again on a smaller scale and to use her experience to help other small businesses. Today she specialises in helping business start-ups and trouble-shooting SMEs which get into financial difficulties.

Shelagh is kept very busy! Unfortunately many people go into business being frightened of the figures, perhaps because they hated maths at school. They don't understand what the numbers mean and rely on a book-keeper to look at their accounts every few months to give them feedback. This historic information does not help a business which is struggling to survive. When cash is short, some people use their credit cards to prop up the business, but this is expensive and doesn't solve the problem as credit cards still need to be repaid every month. Most don't budget and tie up too much money in stock or fail to chase debtors for outstanding payments. Shelagh says that anyone running a business must understand and know the important numbers and review their costs regularly. They should also transfer some money to a business savings account each week to provide a cushion for unexpected financial emergencies.

Shelagh also gives advice to young people who plan to go into business. She tells them to remember three things: firstly, that cash flow is critical – without cash the business cannot survive; secondly, to understand your expenses, review them regularly and budget to keep them under control; thirdly, to know your personal breakeven point – by this she means how much money you need to earn to live on. If the business then provides this income, you know you can survive!

Think about it

1. How has Shelagh's own experiences helped her to advise small businesses?

2. Why are some business people frightened by business finances?

3. Identify three mistakes commonly made by people running a business.

4. What do you think are the 'important numbers' that Shelagh refers to?

5. How does understanding cash flow, budgeting and your personal breakeven point help you to run your own business?

Controlling budgets

Budgetary control

Budgetary control is a management system used in business to control costs.

The system used to produce and maintain budgets begins several weeks before the actual start of the budget year. Normally one or more meetings are held for each department where the departmental head, who is the **budget holder**, discusses with their manager what should be included in the next year's budget. They will discuss the outcome of last year's budget and the forecast sales figures for the following year. They will also discuss any known changes, such as an agreed pay rise for all staff or the fact that more efficient equipment has now been installed.

The best budget is one that has been negotiated, not imposed, and that the budget holder believes to be tough but achievable.

Table 13.3 shows how the budget system works.

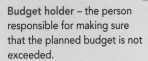

Key term

Budget holder – the person responsible for making sure that the planned budget is not exceeded.

Did you know?

The budgeted spending of the UK government in 2013 was forecast to be £676 billion.

Did you know?

Some people think that referring back to the last year's budget as a starting point builds in systematic errors, so it is better to start from scratch. This is known as zero-based budgeting.

Table 13.3 The budget system

Progress	Activity
Stage 1	There is a review of how things have worked out with the previous/current budget. This gives a guide on the items to be included in this next budget.
Stage 2	Planned activity levels, e.g. level of sales for the year to come, are now used to determine planned budget figures. The budget is set.
Stage 3	The budget period commences. The budget holder must base decisions on budget figures, e.g. how much overtime to allow.
Stage 4	Feedback is given to the budget holder at regular intervals (e.g. monthly), who can then take corrective action if problems are occurring.
Stage 5	At the end of the budget year, final information on the overall budget performance is available. This forms the basis of next year's budget.

How budgetary control is used in businesses

An important use of budgetary control is to identify overspends and underspends so that appropriate action can be taken. The aim is to identify problems and correct them quickly before they escalate, especially in the case of overspends. If these are widespread across the business, it could wipe out any profit the business is making over the year.

Underspends are not as risky and the budget allowance for this item will probably be reduced in the next budget.

The benefits of budgetary control for a business

There are several advantages for a business operating a budgetary control system as shown in Figure 13.5.

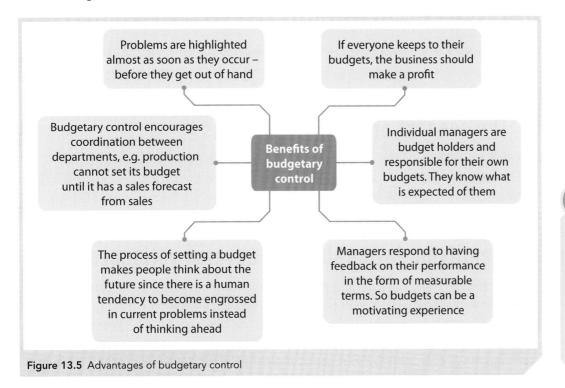

Problems are highlighted almost as soon as they occur – before they get out of hand

If everyone keeps to their budgets, the business should make a profit

Budgetary control encourages coordination between departments, e.g. production cannot set its budget until it has a sales forecast from sales

Benefits of budgetary control

Individual managers are budget holders and responsible for their own budgets. They know what is expected of them

The process of setting a budget makes people think about the future since there is a human tendency to become engrossed in current problems instead of thinking ahead

Managers respond to having feedback on their performance in the form of measurable terms. So budgets can be a motivating experience

Figure 13.5 Advantages of budgetary control

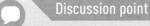 **Discussion point**

Some budget holders argue that there is no point trying to keep spending low, because they will simply have a reduced budget next year. The answer is therefore to 'spend up' the budget to prove you need it! If you ran a medium-sized business, would you agree with this statement?

Why is this type of spending bad for a business?

Using variance analysis to inform business decisions

The concept of variance

Variances occur when the actual performance is different from the budgeted figure. These are identified by measuring the actual performance against the budgeted plans by checking on records.

Key terms

Variance – occurs when there is a difference between a planned budgeted figure and the actual measured result.

Favourable variance – this shows an underspend, i.e. less has been spent than planned.

Adverse variance – this shows an overspend, i.e. more has been spent than planned.

The concept of variance analysis

Identifying a variance is only the first step. The next is to determine why financial performance was not as expected. This means analysing the variance to assess whether it is favourable or not, how serious it is and why it occurred. If necessary, appropriate action must then be taken.

Identifying favourable and adverse variances

A variance is found by measuring actual performance. For example, if a production department making plastic toys is budgeted to spend £44,000 on plastic granules each month and records show that only £40,000 has been spent, the variance is 44 – 40 = £4,000. This is a **favourable variance** because less money has been spent than planned. If £51,000 had been spent, the variance is 44 – 51 = –£7,000. This is an **adverse variance** because more has been spent than planned.

Activity — Understanding a budget report

Here is an example of a production budget report. Read this carefully and make sure that you understand how the variance amounts are produced.

Item	Budget allocation (£)	Actual result (£)	Variance (£)
Materials	50,000	45,000	+5,000
Labour	200,000	220,000	–20,000
Electricity	11,000	10,000	+1,000
Total	261,000	275,000	–14,000

The cause and significance of variances

All variances must be identified and investigated. The aim is to correct the situation, particularly if the variance is adverse. High adverse variances are particularly serious because money is being lost and the reason for the variance must be found. Some variances will be under the control of managers, but others will not, such as rises in fuel prices or utility bills.

Budget items where variance figures are small (positive or negative) will probably be ignored. If a variance is continuously positive, action may not be taken until the next budget is set, when the figure for this item will probably be reduced.

Remember

Large adverse variances are very significant because they mean higher expenditure which will reduce or eliminate profit.

How variances affect business decisions

All businesses aim to keep adverse variances to a minimum. Therefore, the cause of the variance is critical, for example:

- Poor workmanship or faulty equipment may have resulted in rejected items which have to be scrapped. In this case, more training is required and/or equipment needs to be repaired or replaced.
- If raw material or stock prices are rising, alternative suppliers may be found or different types of materials or brands of stock purchased.
- If business expenses are increasing, greater controls may be enforced. For example, business travel may be by budget airline and mileage allowances may be reduced.

If the cause of a large adverse variance cannot be corrected at departmental level, it will be brought to the attention of senior managers who may have to agree to an amendment to the budget, replace the budget holder or reduce the forecast profit.

Assessment activity 13.3
2C.P6 | 2C.P7 | 2C.P8 | 2C.M3 | 2C.D3

You have been asked to give a presentation at a business seminar on the importance and use of budgets to business. In preparation, carry out the following activities. Your presentation needs to consider the variances in Tilly's budget report and evaluate the influence of these on the financial decisions that she and Oscar will have to make.

1 Arrange to talk to the budget holders of two contrasting businesses to find out how they use budgetary control. One could be a small business, such as a local shop or hairdresser, and one much larger. This could be your school or college, or a medium or large business in your area. Find out the process they follow, the type of problems they have faced and how budgetary control has helped them to solve these.

2 Assess the budget report prepared by Tilly and Oscar for their cake pops business which is shown

below. Identify favourable and adverse variances and make notes about how these could affect their business and the actions they should take as a result.

Tilly's notes

Labour cost includes temporary staff hired when we are very busy. We spent more on diesel for the van because prices went up.

3 Prepare your presentation. Include a description of the purpose of specific budgets in your chosen businesses and then explain and compare the budgetary control systems they use. Either using data from your selected businesses, or the data provided by Tilly and Oscar, identify favourable and adverse variances in the budget, and evaluate the influence of these on the financial decisions that are made by a business.

Tilly's Budget Report for August

Item	Budgeted expenditure (£)	Actual expenditure (£)	Variance (£)
Cake mix	125	175	−50
Icing	375	300	75
Melted chocolate	500	400	100
Sticks	120	120	0
Labour	750	1000	−250
Fuel for van	100	150	−50
Electricity/gas	100	100	0
Total	2070	2245	−175

Introduction

Today most businesses carry out many of their operations online. Even if they do not have a website, they send emails, exchange information and buy raw materials or consumables online. Many use social media to promote their products and to recruit new staff.

The majority of businesses have their own website. This may simply provide basic information or be a complex, dynamic website with which users can interact. Planning an online presence, including the design and features of the website, means considering the issues and risks involved, as well as the benefits to be gained.

In this unit, you will investigate these aspects and design a website to meet the needs of a business that wants to have an online presence.

Assessment: This unit will be assessed through a series of assignments set by your teacher/tutor.

Learning aims

In this unit you will:

A explore business activity online

B understand the issues relating to doing business online

C investigate the uses and features of websites

D design a website to meet the needs of a business.

> I am really interested in online business and the opportunities it can offer. I want to be able to create a website and understand online marketing. There are so many new developments, such as using social networking sites to promote a business and mobile sites, so this unit will help me to find out more.
>
> Michael, *15-year-old Business student*

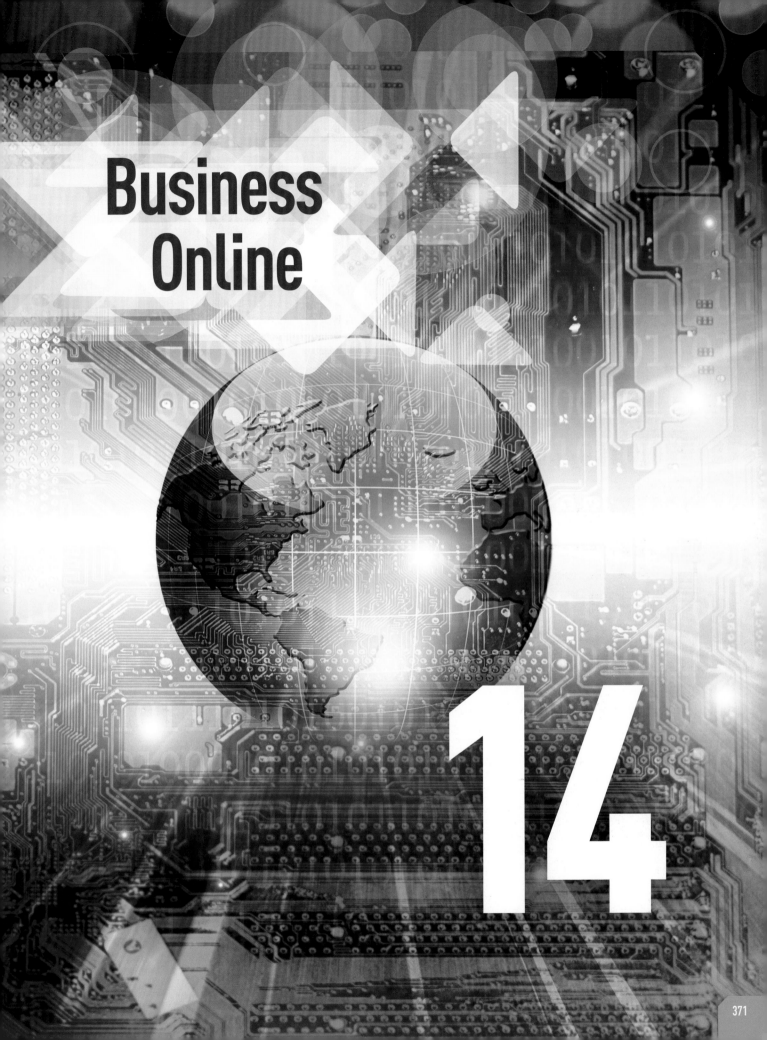

Business Online

14

BTEC
Assessment Zone

This table shows you what you must do in order to achieve a **Pass**, **Merit** or **Distinction** grade, and where you can find activities in this book to help you.

Assessment criteria			
Level 1	**Level 2 Pass**	**Level 2 Merit**	**Level 2 Distinction**
Learning aim A: Explore business activity online			
1A.1 Identify the purpose and features of the online activity of three businesses	**2A.P1** Describe the purpose and features of the online activity of two contrasting businesses **See Assessment activity 14.1, page 381**	**2A.M1** Compare the ways in which two contrasting businesses conduct their online business activities **See Assessment activity 14.1, page 381**	**2A.D1** Assess, using examples, how the current online business environment impacts on the achievement of business aims **See Assessment activity 14.1, page 381**
1A.2 Outline how two businesses have amended their online business activities in line with changes in the online business environment	**2A.P2** Explain how two contrasting businesses have amended their online business activities in line with changes in the online business environment **Assessment activity 14.1, page 381**		
Level 1	**Level 2 Pass**	**Level 2 Merit**	**Level 2 Distinction**
Learning aim B: Understand the issues relating to doing business online			
1B.3 Maths Identify factors a selected business needs to consider when deciding to operate online, including planning, implementation, staffing, finance and distribution	**2B.P3** Maths Describe the factors a selected business needs to consider when deciding to operate online, including planning, implementation, staffing, finance and distribution **See Assessment activity 14.2, page 389**	**2B.M2** Maths Assess ways in which a selected business could deal with the operational risks associated with an online presence **See Assessment activity 14.2, page 389**	**2B.D2** Maths Evaluate the suitability of having an online presence for a selected business **See Assessment activity 14.2, page 389**
1B.4 Maths Outline the operational risks involved in establishing an online presence for a selected business	**2B.P4** Explain the operational risks involved in developing an online presence for a selected business **See Assessment activity 14.2, page 389**		
Level 1	**Level 2 Pass**	**Level 2 Merit**	**Level 2 Distinction**
Learning aim C: Investigate the uses and features of websites			
1C.5 Identify the uses and features of the websites of two businesses	**2C.P5** Describe the uses and features of the websites of two contrasting businesses **See Assessment activity 14.3, page 397**	**2C.M3** Compare the uses and features of the websites of two contrasting businesses in terms of presentation, usability and accessibility **See Assessment activity 14.3, page 397**	**2C.D3** Evaluate how the features of a selected business website improve the user experience **See Assessment activity 14.3, page 397**

Level 1	Level 2 Pass	Level 2 Merit	Level 2 Distinction
Learning Aim D: Design a website to meet the needs of a business			
1D.6 English Plan the design of a website with a minimum of four and a maximum of eight interlinked pages in response to the needs of a selected business	**2D.P6** English Plan the design of a website with a maximum of eight interlinked pages that meets the needs of a selected business **See Assessment activity 14.4, page 405**	**2D.M4** Explain how the plan for the design of a website meets the needs of a selected business **See Assessment activity 17.4, page 405**	**2D.D4** Present, using feedback gathered, recommendations for changes or improvements to the functionality, accessibility and usability of the website created **See Assessment activity 14.4, page 405**
1D.7 English Create a website independently, with a minimum of four and a maximum of eight interlinked pages in response to the needs of a selected business	**2D.P7** English Create a website independently, with a maximum of eight interlinked pages that meets the needs of a selected business **See Assessment activity 14.4, page 405**		
1D.8 Demonstrate the functionality, accessibility and usability of the website created	**2D.P8** Demonstrate how the functionality, accessibility and usability of the website created meets the needs of a selected business **See Assessment activity 14.4, page 405**	**2D.M5** Assess, using feedback from others, the suitability of the website created in meeting the needs of the business and the customers **See Assessment activity 14.4, page 405**	

Maths / Opportunity to practise mathematical skills   English / Opportunity to practise English skills

How you will be assessed

The unit will be assessed by a series of internally assessed tasks. These will enable you to demonstrate that you understand the purposes of having an online presence, the activities carried out online and the issues businesses must consider. You will compare websites and identify their uses and features. You will design, build and test a website for a business client and review the feedback.

Your assessment may be in the form of:

- a booklet or leaflet or information sheet which describes the purposes and features of doing business online and the impact of changes in the current online environment on the achievement of business aims.
- a display that identifies and explains the operational risks
- a report that summarises the features of different websites and relates these to the user experience.
- a presentation which features a website you have created to meet the needs of a business client
- observation sheets and witness testimony from your teacher/tutor.

Online business activity

Getting started

It is forecast that by 2016, 50 per cent of the world's population will be using the internet, over one trillion devices will be internet connected and web transactions will be worth over £2.7 trillion. If this is true, can any business survive without an online presence?

Activity

Identifying online activities

Add a new category, 'social and entertainment', and suggest five sites that would go into it.

Discussion point

In 2012, Barclays launched Pingit, an app which enables you to pay money to a contact in your phone address book quickly and easily. Is this the future, or are there some snags? Research PingIt and discuss your thoughts.

Introduction

In 2012 more than 52 million people in Britain used the internet for a range of services.

Range of online business activities

Business organisations, both large and small, aim to meet all the needs of online users by carrying out many different activities, as shown below.

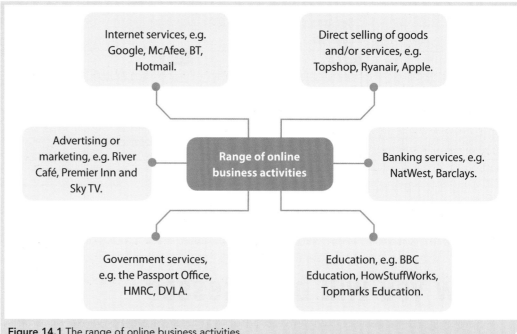

Figure 14.1 The range of online business activities.

- **Internet services** provide internet connections, browser software, security and information. They include Internet Service Providers (ISPs), search engines, security software providers and email providers.
- **Direct selling of goods and/or services**. This includes providers of films, music, clothing, food and beauty products as well as holiday companies, cinemas, ticket agencies and airlines.
- **Banking services** are offered by all UK banks. Customers can carry out most transactions online apart from paying in and withdrawing cash.
- **Education** is available on many sites, for example training courses. Information on courses of study is provided online by educational establishments as well as UCAS.
- **Government services** are accessed through the Gov.UK portal which provides information on many topics from student loans to driving tests.
- **Advertising and marketing**. Many businesses use their website to showcase their products or services such as restaurants, hotels and Sky TV.

Types of online presence

The best online presence for a business depends upon several factors:

- **The size and scale of the business**. A large business will have more resources to invest in its website. One that operates nationally or globally will aim to appeal to a greater range of customers than a local business, such as a hair salon.
- **The sector the business is in**, for example:
  - **Public sector organisations**, such as government departments and NHS hospitals, have websites that highlight their services.
  - **Privately owned** businesses will aim to promote their brand and products to increase profits.
  - **Not-for-profit organisations**, such as voluntary and charitable organisations promote their cause online to increase donations.

Types of activity

The type of activity depends upon the supplier and target customer.

- **Business to Business (B2B)** is when one business deals with another, e.g. H. Samuel buying watches from Rotary or Seiko.
- **Business to Consumer (B2C)** is when businesses sell to customers, such as H. Samuel offering Rotary watches on its website.
- **Consumer to Consumer (C2C)** concerns two individuals, for example, personal comments posted on forums and private sales through Gumtree or on eBay.

Complementing offline activities

Some businesses use their website to complement their offline activities. Argos lets customers 'click and collect' from their local store. Other examples include newspapers with online editions; cinemas and train companies offering online booking services, and entertainment websites, such as Sky and the BBC.

Activity   Researching top 100 websites

Download the latest top 100 website list from IMRG or Hitwise. Work out which businesses on the list complement their offline activities and in what way. Find these websites by going to www.pearsonhotlinks.co.uk and searching for this title.

Types of website

- **Passive presence.** Often called 'brochureware', this basic website provides information about products or a service and contains a few linked and illustrated pages. There may be a photograph of the staff and products, a price list, details of opening hours, customer reviews and contact details.
- **Interactive presence.** In addition to providing information, this enables customers to interact, for example by sending an email, using a Call Me button or through web chat. It may invite online transactions or offer an online service, such as a banking website.
- **Interactive customisation.** This enables users to customise products online. At Moonpig you can design your own greeting card and on digital image processing sites like Bonusprint you can build your own photo album.

Activity

Identifying benefits for a local radio

Carrying out research, suggest three benefits of a local radio station having its own website.

?   Did you know?

Multichannel marketing is when a business provides several ways for a customer to buy goods, for example online, in a store, over the phone and by catalogue. Research shows that customers buy more from these businesses.

Activity

Researching 'click and mortar' businesses

Businesses with a high street and online presence are sometimes called 'bricks and clicks' or 'click and mortar' organisations. In groups, identify five examples. Then suggest three advantages of only operating online, like Amazon or Moonpig.

Doing business online

Introduction

You are opening a small retail outlet. Why would it be useful to operate online and what benefits would you gain?

Purpose of doing business online

The purpose of operating online will be linked to the type of business and its main operations and aims. These may include:

- Promoting and/or providing goods or services
- Providing customers with easy access to information.

Achievement of business aims and objectives

Online operations must be designed to help the business achieve its aims and objectives. These may include:

- **Profit maximisation** by increasing sales and revenue
- **Market growth** by offering goods and services on a global scale
- **Increasing market share** by selling more than their competitors.

It is important that a business is clear about what it wants to achieve and can also identify its target customers, because these factors will influence both its online activities and the features on the website.

Activity   Identifying aims and objectives

Check out the main Pixar website, and then check out one of its film websites, e.g. Monsters University. Identify the aims and objectives of each one.

Access these websites through www.pearsonhotlinks.co.uk.

Provision of effective communication

Operating online increases the number of methods a business can use to communicate with consumers.

- **Bulletins and email newsletters** can be sent regularly to customers who have 'opted in' to receive them to give information on sales, promotions and other events.
- **Forums** enable businesses to read the views of groups of consumers and then respond to these. Forums for specific communities – such as Shetlink which connects people living in the Shetland Islands – provide information on forthcoming events and issues of interest.
- **Mass communication** is far cheaper by digital means than standard methods such as TV, outdoor or press advertising. Social media, particularly Facebook and Twitter, can be used to communicate directly with potential customers to promote new products and events.

- **A distribution list** is a contacts list which includes home and email addresses and mobile numbers as well as other data. Large businesses – such as Tesco – have massive email distribution lists taken from their customer databases. Small businesses can benefit either by renting a list or paying to be included in an email newsletter sent to a large group.

The customer interface

This relates to methods by which the customer and business can contact each other. Traditional methods of letters, telephone calls or visits are now not the only methods.

- **Indirect contact** with customers is easier for online businesses which can provide FAQs pages and pop-up screens to answer queries. Customers also carry out many operations themselves – from checking the status of their accounts to printing bank statements and checking out the goods they buy. This reduces the number of 'customer facing' staff required by a business.

- **Online customer service** must be excellent to impress customers. This should include keeping the customer informed about the transaction – such as when an item has shipped; providing full contact details, answering email enquiries promptly, asking for feedback and taking immediate action if customers are unhappy.

> **?** **Did you know?**
>
> UserVoice is software that helps businesses to collect and analyse customer feedback and support customers better. Check out the benefits for businesses on their website. You can access the website by going to www.pearsonhotlinks.co.uk and searching for this title.

> **Activity** Complaining online
>
> Identify at least five methods an unhappy customer could use to complain about a company online, then suggest the possible outcomes. Then read the customer case studies at Get Satisfaction and identify how at least two businesses have improved their customer satisfaction rates. Access the website at www.pearsonhotlinks.com

- **One-to-one relationships** are possible for customers who can email customer service or click a Live Chat button to talk to someone.

- **Mass customisation** – sometimes called **personalisation** – relates to information tailored to suit each user. For example, BBC weather can be personalised to your own area, cinema chains like ODEON can provide information on films showing in your own area and Amazon promotes products to you based on your previous purchases.

Identify three benefits of personalising content on a cinema website.

CONTINUED ▶▶

Relationship marketing

This focuses on the importance of retaining customers and rewarding loyalty, rather than simply attracting new ones. This makes good sense for many reasons – it saves money, loyal or 'repeat' customers will promote the business to their friends and are a regular source of revenue. Research by Adobe Marketing has shown that 41% of a website's revenue typically comes from 8% of visitors. Online rewards to repeat customers can include personalised emails with vouchers, discounts or other incentives, invitations to special events and priority service.

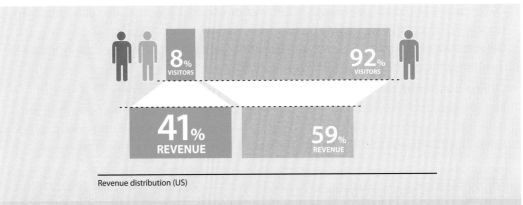

Revenue distribution (US)

Figure 14.2 41% of revenue typically comes from 8% of visitors (Source: Adobe digital index report – The ROI from Marketing to Existing Outline Customers, 2012)

Advantages and disadvantages of having an online presence

Table 14.1 Some of the advantages and disadvantages of having an online presence

Advantages	Disadvantages
It reaches a global audience on a 24/7 basis.	The business is more visible and must respond promptly to enquiries and emails.
It provides up-to-date information and offers to attract customers very cost-effectively.	It takes time to develop expertise and maintain an effective online presence.
It increases brand/business awareness.	Problems, e.g. outdated information or a slow website, can mean loss of business.
It enables the smallest business to compete with larger competitors.	The lack of price competitiveness is soon obvious to customers.
It provides background information about the business and contact details.	It is important to promote an online presence so that customers know about it.
It can provide customer services, technical support or recruitment online.	There are costs involved in setting up and maintaining an online presence and ensuring security for payments.
It can use links/social networking to promote the business and obtain customer feedback.	A sudden increase in demand may mean more staff or investment are needed for packing and delivery.

How businesses operate online

Whilst the main way of operating online is to have a website, many businesses use other methods too:

- Instead of a website, they may have a listing on Yell.com or Google Places and receive and answer enquiries by email.
- They can share files using Google Documents or OfficeZilla and use an online calendar to plan, share and collaborate with other people.
- They can track competitors through Google Alerts and promote the business on Facebook, Google+, Twitter or through uploading videos to YouTube.
- They can recruit new staff using LinkedIn (the professional social networking site), and get updates on matters of interest by RSS feed.
- They can hold video conferences and talk to customers on Skype.
- They can write a blog and sell goods on eBay or through another online shopping site, such as notonthehighstreet.com.

? Did you know?

Many large businesses today have **two** websites – a desktop site and a mobile site which looks good on a smartphone. They may also have an app to promote other services they offer.

Activity   Investigating Dropbox and Pinterest

Marty writes travel reviews and is often away on business. His wife, Sarah, is an interior designer. Investigate Dropbox for Marty and Pinterest for Sarah. Identify **two** benefits of using each site.

Market presence

An online business has the potential to have a greater market presence than an offline one for the following reasons.

- **24-hour visibility** occurs because websites never close. Information can be provided or orders received at any time and automatically acknowledged.
- **A global presence** enables customers anywhere in the world to find out about the businesses, which can greatly increase its promotional and trading opportunities.

What benefits do newspapers like the Financial Times gain from having an online presence?

Just checking   ✔

1. What is the difference between B2B, B2C and C2C?
2. State two benefits of relationship marketing.
3. Identify two advantages and two disadvantages of having a website.
4. In addition to having a website, suggest four other ways a business may operate online.

? Did you know?

A greater market presence has put pressure on most online retailers to keep their prices competitive.

Researching trends and changes in the online business environment

What social media sites do you use every day – and why?

Introduction

By 2015, it is predicted that mobile shopping will account for $305 billion in sales worldwide, 23% of global ecommerce turnover (Source: ABI Research). How do you think this increase will affect businesses?

Changes in media format including the growth of social media

Media formats relate to the different ways in which information is communicated, e.g. letters, newspapers and CDs. Today these formats are declining in use in favour of email, online news bulletins and music downloads. Once people used the internet mainly to find information on websites and email. Now they can do far more – and communicate with other people direct through social media sites.

The growth of social media has increased dramatically since Facebook launched in 2004. In 2012 Mark Zuckerberg announced they had achieved 1 billion users. Twitter users now number over 140 million. Other popular sites included LinkedIn, Google+ and Spotify.

The impact of growth of social media on online business activity

Social media enables businesses to use sites like Facebook and Twitter to engage with customers. This is far cheaper than traditional advertising, but many businesses struggle to do this well.

Even if you use Facebook and Twitter regularly, you need new skills to promote a business effectively, such as how to create an effective brand page on Facebook and use promoted tweets on Twitter. You should also know the limitations of social media. Generally, it is better for promoting brands and encouraging repeat purchases than promoting complex professional services.

Changes in technology

Technological changes affect people's behaviour and how they access online information.

- **Smartphones** are a popular way to access the internet. Websites configured for desktops are too cluttered for a mobile so businesses need a mobile site too.
- **Tablet** sales have also increased, with Apple's iPad the market leader. Desktop websites work on tablets, but are not ideal. A tablet friendly site allows zooming and doesn't use Flash.
- **WiFi availability** through hotspots enables people to go online in many places – such as in coffee shops and on trains.
- **Mobile apps** enable businesses to offer rapid access to specific services for customers, from weather reports to checking bank balances.

Check how your favourite sites look on a mobile at Think with Google and then find out the best tablet websites at the mediaspacesolutions blog. To access the website for these, visit Pearson hotlinks, and search for this title.

Online advertising

Methods of advertising online include:

- **Web banners** on sites, which promote an item by displaying the information across the screen.
- **Sponsorship** which enables sites to include advertorials, where they provide information about a sponsor's product.

- **Google Adwords** which enables short text adverts to appear at the top and side of a search screen displaying the results for a related phrase. This is charged on a 'pay per click' system, so the advertiser only pays if someone clicks on the advert.

Activity   Identifying different adverts

Using Google, search for 'celebrity magazines'. Check if any sponsored adverts appear. Choose 3 or 4 of the options, e.g. Now, OK and Glamour, and identify which content is sponsored, which is advertising and which is editorial (written by the magazine).

Effect of the current online business environment on the achievement of business aims

Facebook and Google are both trying to encourage businesses to advertise on their mobile sites. Unless businesses adapt their online activities to match changes in consumer behaviour and technological developments they are likely to have problems. They may see sales and profits fall and lose market share to competitors who do respond more positively.

Assessment activity 14.1   2A.P1 | 2A.P2 | 2A.M1 | 2A.D1

You have been asked to produce a leaflet on business aims and the online business environment. As a focus for your investigations, identify two contrasting businesses and investigate the purpose and features of their online activities. Research trends and changes that apply to both businesses and investigate how each business has responded to changes in the online business environment.

Highlight the differences and similarities as you compare the online activities of your businesses. Finally, identify the business aims they want to achieve and assess the extent to which the current online business environment impacts on the achievement of these. Give examples to support your judgement.

Tips

- You will find this task easier if your contrasting businesses are quite different, e.g. one very large, one small; one a 'clicks and bricks' organisation, one a purely online business.
- Assess how the online activities of the business affects the achievement of its aims and whether failure to adopt these are having a negative impact.

Did you know?

The Internet Advertising Bureau (IAB) is the trade association for online and mobile advertising. Find out more at their website. Visit Pearson hotlinks to access their website.

Did you know?

Research by marketing agency Somo in 2012 identified that only 57% of UK online retailers had a mobile website and most don't have an app!

Activity

Research trends yourself

Divide into four groups. Group 1 should research Facebook trends and advertising for business, group 2 on Twitter for business, group 3 should use ThinkwithGoogle. com/insights to find out about future trends, group 4 should research IAB and online advertising. Summarise your findings in a brief presentation.

Planning and implementation

Getting started

Do you think that all businesses should have some online presence, or are there still some businesses where this isn't suitable or even helpful?

Introduction

Any business that wants to operate successfully online must plan this carefully. There are various factors they must consider.

Suitability of the business as an online operation

There is no point in operating online unless there are benefits. If the business provides a personal service, the first step is identifying which activities can be offered online and which cannot, for example, hairdressers and beauty salons can offer an online appointment system and doctors can offer a repeat prescription service online. Photographers can use an online presence to showcase and sell their work online.

Activity — Identifying online and offline activities

Identify which of the following business activities can operate online and which can only operate offline: a takeaway; a vet; an interior designer; a restaurant; an estate agent. Then suggest **two** businesses which cannot benefit from operating online.

Why some businesses do not operate online

Some businesses choose not to operate online. For example, David is a decorator who works hard and has many loyal customers. His objections to an online presence include:

- The cost of buying software and hardware, such as a laptop.
- The time involved in maintaining the website and keeping it up to date.
- The lack of a personal touch with customers. To assess and cost a job, David needs to visit the customer to see what is needed.

Deciding on a domain name

All websites have a **domain name**, which is normally the same as the business name, for example, www.asda.com. Ideally the name will be short and easy to remember and spell. Many UK businesses own the name ending with .com or .co.uk to make sure as many customers as possible find their site. A name must be officially registered before it can be used. It is then leased to the owner for a specified period, after which time the owner can choose to renew it or not.

Set-up

A website can be created in-house or outsourced to an external agency.

- **In-house** – a basic website can be created through an online website builder such as BT and 1&1. However, more advanced technical and design skills are required to produce a complex website.
- **Outsource** – a professional agency will advise on all aspects of a website, including security. If the business wants to build and promote a recognisable brand image, it is usually worth paying a professional.

Key term

Domain name – the unique name that identifies a website.

Find out if you could register your own name followed by .co.uk by using the WHOIS query box at the Nominet website (for .com, go to the Internic website). Then find out about the services offered to small businesses by companies such as Volusion and check their charges.

Coping with the additional work

If the number of customer enquiries or sales increases, so too will the amount of work. More staff may be needed to respond to requests promptly, check orders and pack and distribute goods. If the owner personally creates the goods, the number of orders could exceed their ability to cope. Operating online means that a business's products and services are available 24 hours a day, seven days a week, which may have an impact on working hours.

Technical and design skills

Creating and maintaining any business website requires technical and design skills. These may include programming and design skills, knowledge of database technology and familiarity with different web servers and platforms to:

- plan the structure and design the site to reflect the business image and allow for future development needs
- ensure the site is accessible to disabled users which is a legal requirement under the Disability Discrimination Act
- include security features, such as encrypted pages and protection against hackers.

Changing and updating

The website must be kept up to date, accurate and relevant to the customer. Over time the needs of the business and its customers may change, so the website should be regularly reviewed to ensure it meets the needs of its users.

Relationship marketing

You read about relationship marketing in the previous section. So far as your website is concerned you can attract repeat visits by customers by giving them a more personal experience. For example, on the Amazon website customers see recently viewed items and a selection they may like to view. This helps to attract repeat business.

Relationships with other businesses

Setting up online is likely to involve collaboration with other supporting businesses:

- **Financial service providers** – these provide a merchant service to receive payments and advise on other types of payment services.
- **Distribution and delivery service** – customers expect goods to be delivered promptly and in good condition, which may require specialist packing and the completion of customs forms.

Why can a surge in orders create problems?

Operational risks

Introduction

All businesses must know the risks of running an online operation and take steps to prevent problems.

Payment security

Online customers must be able to pay for the goods they buy, usually by credit card, debit card or PayPal.

Many small traders use PayPal because it is well known, secure, easy to use and trades in different currencies. Most businesses offer the alternatives of paying by credit or debit card. To do this they need to have an internet merchant account such as WorldPay which checks and verifies the card is valid.

Why should order forms prevent obvious customer errors?

Customer errors

Customers may order goods in error if the ordering process is complicated or unclear. To prevent this, all order forms should be designed to automatically check for errors by querying unexpected entries (such as very large quantities) and blank areas.

The returns policy should be clearly stated and observe the legal rights of customers.

Protecting the data of customers

All businesses have a responsibility to abide by the requirements of **the Data Protection Act 1998**. This requires that the data kept by businesses must be accurate, secure, not kept longer than necessary and customer information cannot be disclosed to other people.

Updating the website

Websites need updating regularly to ensure the information they provide is accurate, for example, product descriptions and prices. Stock levels should be accurate to save customers the frustration of ordering out-of-stock items. Updating the website is an opportunity to maintain customer interest by including new promotions or features.

Language problems

Large global companies often operate websites in several languages. Smaller firms cannot do this so must take account of the needs of non-English speaking customers. Many words and phrases will have different meanings outside the UK, especially slang or colloquial expressions which should be avoided. If the text is relatively short and clear, the user can translate it online using tools such as Google Translate.

Did you know?

You can tell a site is encrypted by the locked padlock symbol and 'https' on the address line.

Activity

Investigating CNP fraud

A common form of online crime is CNP fraud. Go to the Card Watch website and research a definition of CNP fraud. To access the website, visit Pearson hotlinks, and search for this title.

Discussion point

A major issue for online business is basket abandonment – when a customer starts to buy and then leaves the site. Amazon reminds registered customers they have done this, in case it is a mistake. What makes people abandon a website while purchasing, and what can businesses do about it? Share your ideas as a group.

Did you know?

A Sky box in the UK is a device for receiving television transmissions, whereas in the Caribbean it is a method of importing goods from America!

Legislation and regulations

Online customers are protected by consumer legislation, such as the Sale of Goods Act and the Supply of Goods and Services Act. In addition, they have the following further protection:

- **The Distance Selling Regulations** give online buyers the right to cancel many goods or services up to seven days after the goods are received or the service is ordered.
- **The Company (Trading Disclosures) Regulations** states that all businesses operating a website must provide full details about themselves to customers.

Link

This topic links with *Unit 4: Principles of Customer Service* and *Unit 12: Introducing Law and Consumer Rights.*

Activity   Privacy online

Concerns about online privacy have resulted in Facebook facial recognition being banned in Germany and suspended in the EU and Google street view being outlawed in the Czech Republic and Greece. In 2012 there was also the EU Cookie law. Research this to find out what it is and how it affected businesses.

Vulnerability to hostile attack

All online businesses can be vulnerable to cybercrime. Firewall protection and anti-virus/spyware software is essential and the ISP which hosts the site will also advise on website security.

Financial fraud aims to deprive customers or businesses of money that is rightfully theirs, such as by the creation of a spoof site or phishing email which requests a customer's personal details or bank account information. A keylogger is a virus that copies and transmits the user's keystrokes, including log-in details to their bank account.

Hardware and software failures

A technical fault can temporarily take a business's website offline, resulting in the loss of sales. Other problems can include hardware malfunction or corrupted software. This can result in loss of critical data, which can also occur in an emergency such as fire or flood.

To protect against such disasters, most businesses have back-up servers and systems in place to ensure data can be restored quickly.

Why do toys have such strict safety standards?

Global regulations

Goods must be labelled and packaged to conform to the requirements of the country where they are sold.

- Health and safety means there may be specific regulations that apply to certain products. Toys, for example, have strict safety standards, from the type of paint used to the length of cord on pull-along items.
- Labelling issues relate to many products. The country of origin must always be clearly stated and the seller's name.
- Standards vary around the world – for electrical goods, medicines, pesticides, etc.
- Unfamiliar trading conditions can deter many businesses from exporting their goods. Fortunately, the British Chambers of Commerce, Business Link and the Institute for Export amongst others provide helpful advice.

Did you know?

BSI stands for the British Standards Institute. It advises British producers on laws, regulations and standards that might affect their products and services.

Staffing

Introduction

Developing an online presence may mean staff are concerned about how they might be affected.

Impact on staff

The decision to launch an online operation may mean that some staff will worry that their job may become redundant. Others will be concerned about changes to their job description and the duties they undertake, or fear that they may not have the necessary skills to cope.

Use of call centres

Many large businesses have call centres to answer customer queries and provide customer support, for example, Marks & Spencer and Tesco. Staff have access to the customer and product databases and can see relevant information on screen during the call.

Imagine you work for a call centre for a clothing company. What sort of queries do you think you will receive?

Continuity of service

Service breakdowns and system failures put pressure on staff as they may be unable to do their own jobs if there is a major problem, and may also have to deal with calls from anxious customers. Most online businesses aim to provide a continuous 24-hour operation for their customers.

Loss of personal contact

Many customers – and staff – feel they have less personal contact with an online operation. Customers can place orders online, email for information or contact the call centre, but the system can fail because there is less personal help and advice. FAQ sheets will provide general information, but do not enable customers to discuss personal issues with someone they know.

Familiarity with technology

Staff must be trained to work effectively with new technology. Any new recruits should already have experience with the technology being used.

Finance

Introduction

All websites cost money to set up and maintain. A large, interactive website can be expensive, yet predicting financial benefits is difficult. No business can afford an expensive online presence that brings few benefits.

Many businesses negotiate a loan with their bank to help with set-up costs.

Initial set-up costs

These will depend on whether the developments are being outsourced and the scale of the operation. Costs are likely to include the additional hardware requirements (for example, computers, servers, etc.) and software requirements including the operating system, applications programmes (for example, Microsoft Office®), web authoring software and graphics packages. There will also be the cost of the domain name(s) and the initial charge made by the ISP for hosting the site.

Fixed and running costs

These costs are likely to include the ongoing internet connection charges, the cost of the annual anti-virus software subscription, electricity charges, packaging materials and postage/distribution costs.

Increased interest

Problems can occur if there is a sudden increase in interest which the site cannot handle. It may crash or run slowly, which is annoying, and may mean loss of potential customers. Orders cannot be met if there is insufficient stock to meet customer demand.

Did you know?

Even large websites struggle with massive surges of interest. Ticketmaster can struggle when very popular tickets come on sale and Glastonbury is renowned for this. If the site crashes mid-transaction, fans may be unsure whether their purchase is successful or not.

Activity   Researching website costs

The cost of going online and setting up a business website can vary hugely depending upon whether you do it yourself or employ a professional. Even then, fees can vary a lot and in some cases you may be charged every time you want to make changes to the content. Divide into four groups and research different options and services in your area. Then compare your findings and vote for the best one.

Just checking

1 List four initial set-up costs for an online business.
2 Suggest three possible effects on staff of starting an online operation.
3 Identify four additional concerns for a business which wants to trade globally from its website.

Distribution

Introduction

Fulfilling orders can create difficulties, particularly if they are being sent to remote places overseas or if the business sells certain types of goods.

Fulfilling customer orders

Customer orders must be fulfilled accurately and promptly. The aim is to get the goods to the right person promptly and in the right condition. Doing this consistently will help the company to gain a reputation for reliability. This means that the business must be able to deliver to customers overseas and in remote parts of the UK.

Benefits to customers

The ideal online purchase will result in a customer receiving goods quickly, at the time and place of their choosing. If they have also saved money by buying online rather than in store and know that unsuitable items can be easily returned at no charge, there is little reason not to buy.

Activity Assessing delivery services

Shutl offers an express delivery service for online retailers and Collect+ provides a parcel drop-off and collection service through corner shops and convenience stores. Investigate both and identify the benefits they offer customers.

Scale of business

A business that sells only within the UK should have few problems. Those that distribute goods globally have other concerns including:

- special documents to comply with shipping regulations
- special labelling or packaging for perishable or hazardous goods
- choosing the best method of transport based on the type of goods and the destination
- insurance in case goods are damaged or lost in transit.

Special types of goods

Some types of goods need special attention:

- Fragile goods must be packed carefully with protective material and clearly labelled.
- Perishable goods must be delivered promptly. They are often transported in special vehicles, such as refrigerated lorries.
- Hazardous goods usually need special paperwork, such as a Dangerous Goods Note.

What are the risks involved in selling fresh flowers online?

Ease of distribution

Online businesses that provide a service have fewer problems with distribution because nothing has to be physically moved. An insurance quotation can be emailed to any destination, flight bookings can be completed in seconds with the reservation being held on the airline database, hotel rooms can be confirmed by email immediately.

Activity Comparing distribution companies

In groups, identify the training given by the British International Freight Association (BIFA). Then investigate the services of distribution companies such as DHL, FedEx and UPS by visiting their websites. Which website do you find the easiest to use and why?

Just checking

1 Identify four kinds of planning or implementation issues a new online business may face.

2 What type of start up and running costs would be involved with an online operation?

3 What precautions need to be taken to ensure that goods are distributed promptly?

Assessment activity 14.2 *Maths*   2B.P3 | 2B.P4 | 2B.M2 | 2B.D2

For this activity, you can either use the business that you chose for Assessment activity 14.1, or you can choose a different one. Prepare an information sheet which illustrates the issues and considerations related to doing business online, using your selected business as the focus.

1 Start by identifying and describing the factors that your selected business needs to consider when deciding to operate online, in particular those related to planning, implementation, staffing, finance and distribution.

2 Assess the operational risks involved for that business in developing an online presence before assessing how your selected business could deal with those risks.

3 Conclude by using evidence to evaluate whether your selected business would benefit from an online presence, and, if so, your recommendations on the activities it should carry out.

Tip

Provide a conclusion about whether the business should have an online presence.

Link

For this assessment activity, you could select your own proposed enterprise that you are planning for *Unit 1*.

Using a website to operate a business online

Introduction

All websites are created for a reason and many have more than one use. These uses should be complementary, for example providing information about the business and selling goods. It can be confusing for users if the website tries to achieve too many different purposes.

Why businesses use websites

A business can use its website and its online presence in several ways.

- **For commerce:** the primary purpose for many businesses is to encourage customer transactions. Examples include retail shops, banks, ticket agencies and travel firms.

- **To present information:** businesses can use their website to advertise products and job vacancies, provide information about the company and its employees and include features on new products or promotions. They can ask customers to sign up to receive newsletters and offers.

- **To store information:** the website can be used to **archive** old information, such as past press releases that may be helpful to anyone researching the business. **Cloud storage** enables computer files and data to be held on remote servers, rather than on the business system, and are accessible from anywhere in the world.

- **To download information:** offering downloads means that large data files are available on the website, for example menus on a restaurant website. Media files are useful to promote products and present news broadcasts. On a car manufacturer's website you may watch a short video clip about a car and download a brochure too.

Identify two other types of businesses that make brochures available online.

- **Customer browsing and real-time information:** all websites should be structured so that it is easy for customers to browse. Some provide information in 'real time', such as airlines and airports, which show when planes have arrived or departed. Share prices and news bulletins are also often provided in 'real time'.
- **To collect feedback:** customer feedback enables businesses to evaluate their products and services. Most retailers follow up online transactions by asking customers to review their purchase and experience.

Activity   Researching Survey Monkey

Survey Monkey enables small businesses to compose and issue questionnaires easily to customers. To access the website go to www.pearsonhotlinks.co.uk and search for this title. Then consider the advantages of having a Survey Monkey blog.

- **To improve efficiency of operations:** a website improves efficiency if it obtains information that enables the business to respond better to customer needs. A restaurant offering online bookings knows how many customers are expected, can allocate appropriate time slots and is ready to greet guests on arrival.
- **To communicate:** many businesses share content with social networking sites, such as Facebook, to improve communications. Anyone with internet access can hold meetings, video or audio conferences using sites and apps such as Skype or join.me.
- **For media sharing:** photographs and video clips of new product launches and positive customer reviews can be posted on YouTube or on the business website.

> **?**   **Did you know?**
>
> Offering an online booking service improves operational efficiency for cinemas because fewer people need to queue for tickets on arrival.

Activity   Investigating Comic Relief

Investigate the Comic Relief website to see how it communicates its message and how it offers you the opportunity to share information with other people.

- **As a source of education:** websites such as Comic Relief and Amnesty International aim to educate people about their cause. On the Citizen's Advice Bureau website you can click through to an online information portal. Many academic institutions and educational establishments provide online library facilities. Online learning courses and assessment materials are available on other sites, including the BBC.
- **To provide interactive features:** these encourage a deeper level of engagement with the customer. The features are shown in Figure 14.3.

CONTINUED ▶▶

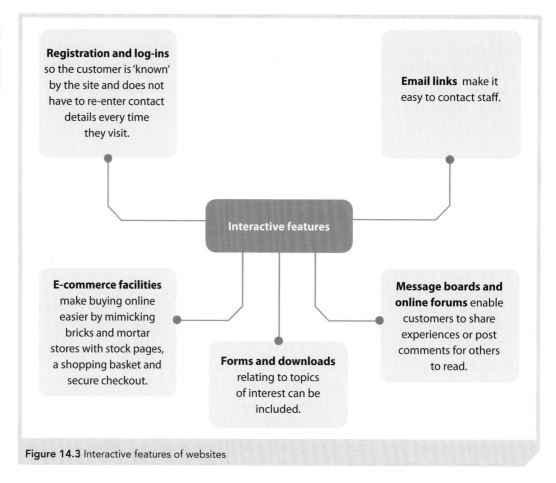

Figure 14.3 Interactive features of websites

- **To enable global trading/commerce:** a website means that the business is open to receive enquiries or orders 24 hours a day, 7 days a week. Time zones and national holidays are irrelevant.

Discussion point

Discuss the benefits international businesses gain by having specific websites in different countries (e.g. amazon.co.uk and amazon.com for the US.

Activity   Investigating Mumsnet

1 Mumsnet is an important website because it is said to represent the views of millions of parents. How does it gather this information? Find out by assessing the features on the website.

2 Do you think Mumsnet meets the needs of fathers? If not, suggest what features you would include on a comparable site for them.

WorkSpace

▶ Caroline Boardwell Reid

Managing Director, Croft Mill Ltd

Croft Mill started as a mail order fabric business. Until 2008, it was run by Caroline's father. When he retired, the business closed and all that remained was a database of past customers. Today it is a thriving enterprise, attracting more customers every year. How has this been achieved and by whom? The answer is simply that Caroline took over and converted Croft Mill into an online operation.

How do you make a successful business from a list of old customers? Caroline did it by finding premises, buying stock and borrowing her husband's old computer. She searched for funding and found that a local Regeneration Fund was helping businesses that wanted to create a website.

Caroline chose a professional company to help her. She was attracted to them because they offered her the opportunity to manage and update the content herself, although she pays a monthly fee for their services. She says one of her problems is finding the time to be creative, to upload new images and keep in regular contact with her customers.

Today Caroline fulfils orders from around the world, including America, Australia, Sweden and Denmark. When there has been a sudden increase in demand – especially after a new catalogue has been launched – all the family and several friends have been able to help out. A big challenge is postage rates. Since fabric can be heavy, it is difficult to quote accurate prices online as it depends upon the type of fabric ordered and the destination.

In the future, Caroline wants to use social media to further market the business. She wants to develop her blog to include more than just news articles. She is also considering creating a mobile site for use on smartphones.

Caroline says that a website developer must be able to offer advice on the features that would appeal to their client's customers. In Caroline's case, the website includes superb pictures of fabric to tempt impulse buyers. She also knows that technology and the needs of a business are always changing. These provide new opportunities for anyone who operates their business online.

Think about it

1 What is the main purpose of Caroline's website?

2 Identify **two** ways in which a professional website developer can help a new online business.

3 Suggest **two** reasons why Croft Mill has been successful.

4 Identify **three** challenges that Caroline faces running an online business.

5 Go to the Croft Mill website. To access the website go to www.pearsonhotlinks.co.uk and search for this title. Assess the features of the Croft Mill website and identify three ways in which these features have been designed to appeal to customers.

Types and features of business websites

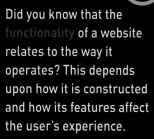

Getting started ➡

Did you know that the functionality of a website relates to the way it operates? This depends upon how it is constructed and how its features affect the user's experience.

Types of websites

All websites comprise a collection of web pages that are linked together and hosted on a web server. However, their complexity can vary considerably from very simple to extremely sophisticated.

- **A static website**, often called a brochureware site, is the simplest type because the information is passive. The pages are pre-prepared and coded in HTML with text and graphics so that information is shown in a format similar to a brochure. These sites are often used by businesses such as florists, caterers and small restaurants.

- **A dynamic website** responds to the user, by gathering information the user provides, and by updating the content from a related database. For example, Google creates pages 'on the fly' depending on the search term entered by the user, the BBC website uploads news reports, and Rightmove specialises in houses for sale. The content is changed or customised frequently and automatically by either the business or the customer.

Activity | Exploring dynamic websites

Explore dynamic websites that identify relevant content, such as StumbleUpon or Reddit.

Key term 🔒

Functionality – refers to the way the website operates, or functions.

Platforms and compatibility

Users access websites in different ways, using a range of computers and browsers. Any website should be designed to operate effectively and look good regardless of the platform used. The main variations are:

Did you know? ❓

- As smartphone screens are small, the web pages have to be much smaller, but the buttons must be large as people are using touch screens.
- One of the most commonly used action buttons is the Facebook 'Like' button.
- An ecommerce website is a dynamic website which can also process financial transactions.

- the operating system, for example, PC Windows, Mac OSX or iOS

- the browser used, and whether this is Internet Explorer (IE), Google Chrome, Firefox, Safari or Opera

- the hardware – whether the site is being viewed on a PC, tablet or smartphone.

How can apps like ShopSavvy and Sccope help you find the best deals on the high street?

Construction features

Some functions and features on a website improve the user experience, such as navigation bars and the speed a page loads. Others include:

- **hyperlinks** which connect relevant items, pages (and websites) together
- **action buttons** for the customer to take action, such as submit an order or sign up for a newsletter
- **hot spots** which are used on a graphic or text to activate a function, such as showing a picture or an additional menu
- **templates** which provide a basic layout and look for a webpage. On some web authoring programs, a wizard will help you to select colours, text style and background images
- **forms** which are used to obtain customer information. They should be kept short and simple.

Interactive features

These may include a link to the business email address and forms for customers to register, make an enquiry or log in.

Under the Disability Discrimination Act, it is a legal requirement for all websites to be accessible to all users. For example, images can be coded so that blind users can 'read' them with a screenreader program and text can be converted to speech. You also need to offer resizable text and ensure all your text is clearly readable (dark text on a light background) for anyone who is partially sighted. It also means thinking about the needs of deaf users if you include a video or audio file.

Aesthetics

This refers to the appeal of the website, both visually and audibly.

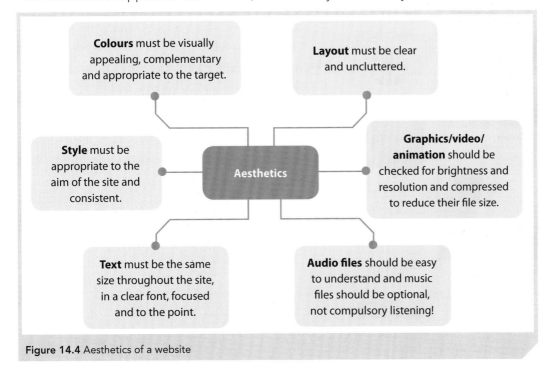

Figure 14.4 Aesthetics of a website

💬 Discussion point

According to the experts, you have between 5 and 20 seconds to impress a new user before they click off your site – and teenagers are the most impatient of all! Is this true? What puts you off immediately? Compare your ideas.

Activity

Thinking about website accessibility

Anyone who is colour blind appreciates links showing as underscored when they point on them. Can you think why?

User experience of websites

Introduction

Website users are very fickle. On average, 35 per cent of users 'bounce' off a website. This means they leave without going further than the first page they visit. The aim is to lower the **bounce rate** as much as possible.

How features improve user experience

What features are attractive to users? Obviously the content must be relevant and interesting, easy to read and appealing. The needs of the customers must also be met. You only have seconds to prove this!

Methods to improve **usability** include:

- Ensuring that the content on each page is clearly and attractively laid out and the information is appropriate and appealing to users.

- Feedback forms so that customers can post their views. Many sites include a pop-up questionnaire to ask customers their opinion of a website.

- Dynamic interactions mean that customers can be categorised by their responses into different types, for example user type A, B or C. This information then generates a specific type of automated response targeted at that person's preferences.

- Style sheets (called cascading style sheets or CSS) help to keep the same look and feel throughout the website. This is because the instructions that control how the website looks are stored in a separate file. To change something like the text colour means making one change in this file rather than making changes repeatedly for different pages.

- Making the site more interactive by embedding digital assets such as videos, pdf files, photographs and sound files. The user can click on these to obtain more information, such as watching a model displaying clothes or downloading an information booklet.

What features on the John Lewis website make it attractive to users?

Activity   Assessing websites

1 Divide into groups. The 'do' groups should investigate award-winning websites and the 'don't' groups awful websites. You can do this by looking at websites that list good and bad websites.

2 Both groups should make a list of the features that make different websites good or bad.

3 Both groups should get together to compose a class list of the top five 'do's' and 'don'ts' that should be observed by all website designers to improve the user experience.

Assessment activity 14.3   2C.P5 | 2C.M3 | 2C.D3

Your group is considering offering its services as website developers. You have received enquiries from the following businesses:

- A local DJ, Jake Butler, who provides a mobile disco for weddings and parties
- Petra Martin who has started her own business – Petra's Party Cakes
- Ashraf Saddique, who runs a successful car valeting business
- Fatima and Jocelyn, who have started a jewellery-making business called Rings 'n' Things.

Select **one** of these businesses, or another business client, as agreed with your teacher/tutor. This client may be a member of your group who, to achieve Unit 1, plans to start an online business. Prepare a report for your client in which you focus on identifying the uses and features of business websites and how these improve the user experience. You need to be able to select which features would be most appropriate for your client. Do this by identifying two existing, contrasting businesses that both have websites. One of these should be in the same line of work as your business client; the other should be a different business website that provides ideas for other features.

Review the two types of business you have chosen and consider their business needs. Take a look at both of their websites and, in your report, describe the uses and features of these sites and how they relate back to their needs. Spend some time viewing the websites and make notes about their presentation, usability and accessibility. Compare the two websites and think about which you would likely return to, Consider your choice and describe in your report how you think the uses and feature of your chosen website helped you come to your decision.

Conclude your report by looking at your findings and provide appropriate advice to your client.

Tip

Features you should evaluate include the website navigation, interactivity and relationship marketing aspects, such as registering on the site and contact details.

Design a website to meet a client brief

Getting started

What should a website for a solicitor, a vet and a tea room in a tourist area look like? Can you think of some immediate differences?

Introduction

Producing a website for a specific business is different from producing a hobby site for yourself. You need to identify the main purpose of the website, the target customer and how the website needs to look and feel to meet their needs.

Planning the design of a website to meet a business need

Your client is the owner of the business. Their 'brief' is the list of requirements they have. Some clients may have very specific ideas, while others will not. It is up to you to consider the main reason the site will exist and the priorities of the business. Then choose the website layout, structure, design, content and features which would work best and present these to your client before you start work.

To start you should decide:

- what pages you will need
- how your pages will link together
- what they will look like.

Many designers start by creating a **storyboard** which gives a visual image of the site. This shows how the content is grouped together and the links between the pages. This can also be shown by a **site map** which summarises and groups the content in hierarchical form.

Did you know?

The 'three clicks rule' says you should be able to complete any action on a website within three clicks, for example, go back to the home page or get to the action page containing the order form.

Key terms

Storyboard – a graphic representation of the site and how each page links.

Site map – shows the content of the site hierarchically, with links to each section.

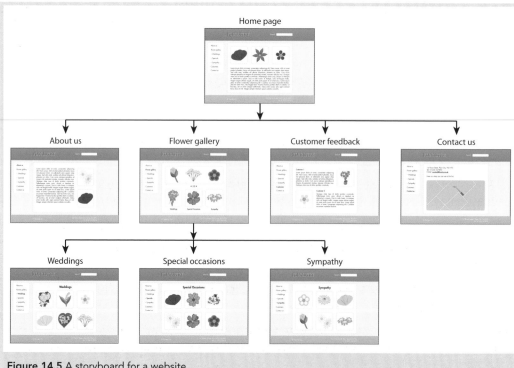

Figure 14.5 A storyboard for a website

Each item listed will be a link that the visitor can use to find that information quickly. The proposed design can be illustrated on sample pages that show:

- the header at the top of each page, which includes the business name and logo
- a footer at the bottom, which may include additional links
- a navigation bar – which is usually across the top of the page, or down the left-hand side (or both on a large site)
- a search box at the top right
- prominent business contact details.

Activity — Investigating site maps and storyboards

Check out the site map on the Croft Mill website to see how it has been constructed. Then look at other examples of website storyboards on Google Images, and site maps at other sites you use regularly.

Website software tools and techniques

Your website pages will be a mixture of several elements, including text, graphics and forms. Below are the main tools or techniques.

- **Text** has two aspects – how it looks and how it reads. It must be clear and large enough to be read easily. All headings must be consistent. Explanations should be short, using simple vocabulary – and no jargon! Every word must be spelled correctly, it must be grammatical and all your apostrophes must be in the right place. Never over-crowd a page with too much text – it will put people off.

- **Tables** are used to present data in an easy-to-read format. For example:

Delivery charges	
Under 10 miles	£2
11 – 50 miles	£10
Over 50 miles	£15

- **Forms** ask the visitor to enter information into different fields or to select different options.
  - **A text field** is a box into which any type of information can be entered, such as a name, email address or telephone number. Each box may only hold a single line of text.
  - **A text area** allows the user to leave a comment because the space to complete is larger.
  - **Buttons** enable the user to carry out an action, such as 'submit' the form.
  - **Radio buttons** enable the user to click on one preference between two or more options.
  - **Check boxes** enable the user to 'check' (click on) boxes they agree with. More than one preference can be chosen.

- **Frames** are one way to divide up your webpage into sections, for example, so that the navigation bar or menu stays in view even though the main content will scroll. Frames can make printing more difficult and your website less accessible. For these reasons, most web developers prefer to use style sheets.

CONTINUED ▶▶

- **Navigation** includes all the aspects that users need to find their way around the site.
  - **Menus** are usually along the top of a webpage or down the left-hand side. Keep menus short. It is better to have sub-sections than to put people off with too many options.
  - **Hyperlinks** take users somewhere else. An internal link will take the user to another section of the website. External links go to websites the user may find interesting.
  - **Anchors** are used to take a user to somewhere specific on a page, such as to the top or to a particular item. The first anchor is placed in the hyperlink itself and a second named anchor is placed in the destination position.
- **Interactive components** encourage the user to become involved with the site and find out more.

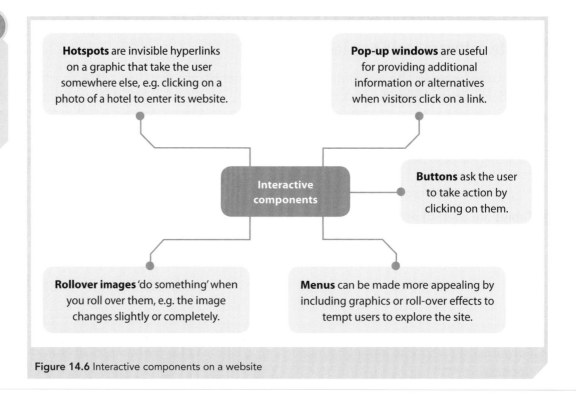

Hotspots are invisible hyperlinks on a graphic that take the user somewhere else, e.g. clicking on a photo of a hotel to enter its website.

Pop-up windows are useful for providing additional information or alternatives when visitors click on a link.

Interactive components

Buttons ask the user to take action by clicking on them.

Rollover images 'do something' when you roll over them, e.g. the image changes slightly or completely.

Menus can be made more appealing by including graphics or roll-over effects to tempt users to explore the site.

Figure 14.6 Interactive components on a website

- **Colour schemes, styles and templates** determine the look of your site. They must be consistent and pleasing to the eye.
  - **Cascading style sheets** control how your webpages will look.
  - **Page layout** relates to where you position the various elements on the page, such as the text, graphics, links, forms and other assets.
  - **Text wrapping** enables you to put text alongside an image rather than underneath it. You can choose the left or right side.
  - **Background colours** can be anything you like, but the lighter they are, the easier it is to read dark text.

- **Embedded multimedia/digital asset content** refers to graphics, sound, music, videos and animations you want to include on the site. HTML recognises the type of file from its extension.
  - Graphics can be photographs: .jpg or drawings: .gif or .png.
  - Sound files include .midi, .wav and .mp3.
  - Video files include .avi, .wmv, .mov and .mp4.

  Although the files are 'embedded' in the HTML code, they are not actually placed there. Instead a 'tag' points to the file that must be used. For example, an 'img' tag points to an image file. You will practise this in the next section.

- **Simple client-side scripts** refers to the code that is stored on the user's (client's) computer, rather than that on the server that hosts the site. If you interact with the site and something happens very quickly, such as a pop-up window, this is controlled by code stored on your computer, usually JavaScript. JavaScript allows you to make a website more dynamic, for example letting the user drag icons or move text.

Activity	Creating a pop-up window

JavaScript is usually embedded in HTML. Below is some HTML/JavaScript that will pop up a window showing a name. See if you can distinguish between the HTML code and JavaScript. Copy it into a browser and see what happens – and change the name, too, if you like!

```
<html>
<head>
<script type="text/javascript">
function show_popup()
{
alert("Ben Obi-Wan Kenobi");
}
</script>
</head>
<body>
<input type="button" onclick="show_popup()" value="And today's name
is..." />
</body>
</html>
```

- **Other languages:** although you do not need to know coding to use most web authoring packages, it is usually far more enjoyable and satisfactory to learn the basics.
  - **HTML** stands for Hypertext Markup Language. It is the foundation of the web. Mark up tags tell the web browser how to display each page.
  - **DHTML** is Dynamic HTML and is used to create interactive and animated website features.

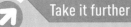

Take it further

If you want to learn how to code, or to practise at your own pace, there are many good tutorial sites online. To access the website go to www. pearsonhotlinks.co.uk and search for this title. Then on this site you can learn HTML, CSS, JavaScript and more, and test any code you write quickly and easily.

CONTINUED ▶▶

Accessibility features

These features will make your website more accessible to users with a disability. They include

- **Alt** (alternative) tags which provide an explanation for an image that cannot be viewed for some reason, for example <img alt="The Golden Gate Bridge in San Francisco" />
- **Zoom** features enable users to magnify parts (or all) of the website to see it more clearly. Most browsers now support zooming, but this will enlarge everything on the page, not just the text. Coding the text size to be 'relative' rather than 'absolute' allows it to be changed by the user.
- **Text-to-speech** coding enables anyone with a visual impairment to hear the text, rather than have to read it.

Browser compatibility

A website must look good in all browsers. Unfortunately for developers, there are not only several different browsers available but different versions, too. Since each browser renders a page differently and not all browsers support every type of file (for example, a .wav sound file won't work on Google Chrome), you need to test your site to see how it works on different browsers and make any corrections required.

Exporting and compressing digital assets

You export a file when you change it from one type to another, usually so that it can be used by a different program. Compressing a file means making it smaller so that it takes up less memory and downloads much more quickly.

Some digital files are automatically compressed, such as .mp3 files. Others are not. Graphics or video files may be very large and will need compressing before they are included in a website.

Images should be checked for brightness and many are better if they are cropped or resized. Close-ups are better or simple photos with a clear focus. If you tick 'aspect ratio', the image stays in proportion as it is resized. Image resolution refers to their quality, and image-editing software can usually save images optimised for the web. A useful starting value is 640 **pixels** across for a large image and 320 for a small one, but you should adapt this to best fit your design.

What are the benefits of resizing photographs for a website?

The code below uses an 'img' tag to point to a .jpg file. Read the explanation and then decide what alternative text you would include on a favourite photograph of yours.

```
<img src="imagefile.jpg" alt="Alternative text..." height="75"
width="100" />
< - Open the tag,
img - The HTML image tag specifier.
src="imagefile.jpg" - A path to the jpeg, gif or png file to display.
alt="Alternative text..." - Text displayed in place of the graphic
when image files can't be shown (for whatever reason).
height="75" - Display the image 75 pixels high.
width="100" - And 100 pixels wide.
/> - Close the tag.
```

Suitable file names for web pages

Each page of your site should have an individual URL, for example, www.mysite/home and www.mysite/aboutus. This allows you to identify your pages quickly and easily in your web folders. Also, if a user lands on any page of the site from a search engine, they can use the URL to see where they are.

Website hosting

Once your website has been checked, the files are uploaded to a web server. This is a computer that is constantly connected to the Internet. Large businesses may have their own local server, but small firms will use a web hosting company. Files are uploaded using a File Transfer Protocol (FTP) program. This is part of some web authoring packages, such as Dreamweaver.

A web-hosting company will host many different websites on its servers, each of which will have an individual domain name. Many hosting services offer a wide range of services to clients including obtaining/registering domain names, website-building software and security features.

Testing the website

All your pages should be checked before they are uploaded, but some problems may only be obvious when your site goes 'live'. Then you should check that:

- your website functions properly, for example all links and action buttons work properly, and any interactive components or embedded assets do what they should.
- each page looks good and is of high quality – headings and spacing are consistent, there is no inaccurate information or wordy text, the colours are pleasing and everything is clear and easy to read.
- the website is user-friendly. 'Usability' refers to the ability of users to interact with the website and find their way around easily and quickly.

 Did you know?

It can be useful to check the site using a tablet device to see how it would look to customers accessing it on an iPad.

Ensuring that a client brief is met

Feedback from others

This is vital because by now you will be so familiar with your website that you may not spot any flaws or problems. Show the website to several people who represent your target customer and ask for feedback. Find out if the site achieves its purpose and inspires users to take action. If they have problems or don't understand your navigation, you need to know!

Next demonstrate the site to your client. Ideally, they will have been involved in key stages of the development so the finished product will not come as a complete surprise (or a shock!).

How can an online focus group help to give feedback on a proposed website?

Activity   Devising a website checklist

1 In small groups, devise a checklist for observers to complete as they assess your website. The aspects to include are: resolution; effectiveness; content; presentation; navigation; usability; accessibility; performance and purpose.

2 Add any additional aspects you think are important and a method of scoring feedback for each one.

3 Compare your forms and adopt the best one.

Assessing the suitability of the website

The aim of obtaining feedback is not to collect compliments but to check that the site achieves its purpose of creating and keeping interest in the business or its products. You also want to know if users are inspired to take action as a result. Ideally the scoring system in your checklist will enable you to quickly identify common issues that reviewers identified. You must also note important revisions requested by your client.

The importance of revising website designs

The final stage is to make the necessary revisions to your design to ensure that your client brief is fully met and all agreed changes and improvements have been made. Remember that all websites are a work in progress! They constantly need updating and amending to meet the ongoing needs of the business and its customers and how they access and respond to online information.

Remember

It can help to reread your client brief regularly, so that you keep focused on the needs of the business.

Just checking

1 Why is it useful to prepare a storyboard before designing a website?

2 Explain why digital assets may need to be compressed to be used on a website.

3 What is meant by 'functionality' and how can you test this?

4 Why is it important to get feedback from other people, including your business client?

Assessment activity 14.4   *English*   2D.P6   2D.P7   2D.P8   2D.M4   2D.M5   2D.D4

Your business client has asked you to prepare a website that will incorporate the features that you identified in assessment activity 14.3. Your teacher/tutor will provide you with the full client brief.

1 First, plan the design of your website. This should have a maximum of eight interlinked pages that will meet the needs of the business. Prepare a storyboard and site map to illustrate your design. Arrange a first meeting with your teacher/tutor, who will represent your client, to present your ideas. Explain your design and say how this will meet the needs of the business.

2 Create the website. You must do this on your own. Then arrange a second meeting with your teacher/tutor and demonstrate how the functionality, accessibility and usability of your website will also meet the needs of the business.

3 Test the website and arrange for others to use it. Obtain feedback, then assess how well the website will meet the needs of the business and its customers. Then meet with your teacher/tutor and present your recommendations for changes or improvements to your website, based on the feedback you have obtained.

Tip

Remember that you do not actually need to make changes to the website. You do need to demonstrate that you have obtained feedback and identified the areas where improvements or changes are required.

Introduction

When you go shopping, what influences the purchases that you make? Most retail outlets are carefully designed to provide subtle hints to customers about what to buy and to guide them through their shopping trip, exposing them to promotions and special offers as many times as possible. It is the job of visual merchandisers to create these layouts.

Visual merchandising is an important role in retail outlets. By planning how stores are laid out and organising displays that will draw in customers, visual merchandisers can channel them past special offer stock, and encourage them to buy the most profitable items in store.

In this unit, you will learn about the tools and techniques that visual merchandisers use to entice customers into your store and encourage them to buy different products.

Assessment: This unit will be assessed through a series of assignments set by your teacher/tutor.

Learning aims

In this unit you will:

A understand the responsibilities of visual merchandisers in retail businesses

B understand the principles of visual merchandising

C apply visual merchandising techniques.

> I want to get a job that gives me an opportunity to be creative. I love fashion, and being a part-time merchandiser in a clothing boutique allows me to spend my working days planning outfits for mannequins. I love it when I help to build a window display that stops customers in their tracks!
>
> Melissa, *15-year-old BTEC student*

Visual Merchandising in Retail Business

17

This table shows you what you must do in order to achieve a **Pass**, **Merit** or **Distinction** grade, and where you can find activities in this book to help you.

Assessment criteria			
Level 1	**Level 2 Pass**	**Level 2 Merit**	**Level 2 Distinction**
Learning aim A: Understand the responsibilities of visual merchandisers in retail businesses			
1A.1 Identify the activities of visual merchandisers in two retail businesses	**2A.P1** Describe using relevant examples from research, the activities of visual merchandisers in two retail businesses operating in different sub-sectors **See Assessment activity 17.1, page 415**	**2A.M1** Analyse how the size and sub-sector of two selected retail businesses affect the responsibilities of visual merchandisers **See Assessment activity 17.1, page 415**	**2A.D1** Critically evaluate the impact on business success of the activities and responsibilities of a visual merchandiser in a selected retail business **See Assessment activity 17.1, page 415**
1A.2 Outline the responsibilities of visual merchandisers across retailers of different size	**2A.P2** Explain using relevant examples from research, how the responsibilities of visual merchandisers vary across specific retailers of different size **See Assessment activity 17.1, page 415**		
Learning aim B: Understand the principles of visual merchandising			
1B.3 Outline the techniques used by visual merchandisers in two retail businesses	**2B.P3** Explain using relevant examples from research, the techniques used by visual merchandisers in two retail businesses operating in different sub-sectors **See Assessment activity 17.2, page 421**	**2B.M2** Explain the benefits of the effective use of visual merchandising techniques and tools to retail businesses operating in different sub sectors, including their customers and suppliers **See Assessment activity 17.2, page 421**	**2B.D2** Compare the effectiveness of the techniques and tools used by visual merchandisers in two retail businesses operating in different sub-sectors **See Assessment activity 17.2, page 421**
1B.4 Identify the tools used by visual merchandisers in two retail businesses	**2B.P4** Describe using relevant examples from research, the tools used by visual merchandisers in two retail businesses operating in different sub-sectors **See Assessment activity 17.2, page 421**		

Level 1	Level 2 Pass	Level 2 Merit	Level 2 Distinction
Learning Aim C: Apply visual merchandising techniques			
1C.5 Maths Plan a positive retail environment	**2C.P5** Maths Plan a detailed, positive retail environment using appropriate annotations **See Assessment activity 17.3, page 428**	**2C.M3** Use feedback to analyse the effectiveness of the positive retail environment plan and the product display design **See Assessment activity 17.3, page 428**	**2C.D3** Justify suggested improvements to the positive retail environment plan and the product display design in response to feedback **See Assessment activity 17.3, page 428**
1C.6 Maths Create a product display design for use within a positive retail environment	**2C.P6** Maths Create a realistic and appropriate product display design for use within a positive retail environment **See Assessment activity 17.3, page 428**		
1C.7 Outline how the positive retail environment plan and the product display design meet the given design brief	**2C.P7** Explain how the positive retail environment plan and the product display design meet the given design brief **See Assessment activity 17.3, page 428**		
1C.8 Gather feedback on the positive retail environment plan and the product display design	**2C.P8** Gather feedback on the effectiveness of the positive retail environment plan and the product display design **See Assessment activity 17.3, page 428**		

Maths Opportunity to practise mathematical skills

How you will be assessed

This unit will be assessed by a series of internally assessed tasks. The tasks will be based on retail businesses in your local area.

Your tasks might be based on a scenario where you are developing a careers guide to promote the work of visual merchandisers, or you might produce a report for a local business, explaining how they can improve standards of merchandising in their store.

Your assessment could be in the form of:

- a leaflet about the work of visual merchandisers
- a presentation on the techniques and tools used by visual merchandisers
- a plan for the layout of a store and a window display
- a report on how you could change your store plan in response to feedback from customers.

Visual merchandising activities

Introduction

Visual merchandising techniques focus as creating displays that attract attention.

Working alone or in a team

In larger retailers, it might be necessary to work in a team to plan and build displays or lay out stores. Smaller retailers might have a single visual merchandiser who works alone to produce plans which are then executed by store staff.

Designing floor plans and displays

The placement of shelving and displays can influence customers' opinions. Clever layout plans will guide customers past special offer stock and/or more expensive lines.

Designing window displays

Special displays, highlighting the best products available, can be used to attract customers to a new seasonal range or offer.

Drawing design plans

Plans can be quickly constructed using pen, paper and rulers. This might be suitable for a small retailer which cannot afford expensive software and does not need to share plans across a number of branches.

A **planogram** is a chart showing how a display should be laid out. This will specify how many items should be displayed and how they must be positioned. It is possible to use specialist software to construct a planogram. This can be expensive and is often used by bigger retailers who need to provide the same display to a number of stores.

Following a design brief

Managers or senior merchandisers draw up a set of instructions or **design brief** for how they want merchandising and customer service staff to lay out stores. This means that layouts are consistent in every branch.

Assembling and dismantling displays

Displays often have to change overnight. When product ranges change, shelves might have to be positioned at different heights. New lighting might need to be installed, sometimes new walls have to be built or old ones demolished.

Using props and lighting

Displays involve more than just products. Carefully selected **props** make a display more interesting. Christmas displays often involve empty boxes which have been gift wrapped. The key is to choose props that customers will not confuse with the products on sale.

Lighting is important. It can create a sense of drama or can be used to highlight a specific product.

Using space and lighting

Is it better to fill a space with as many products as possible or to focus on a smaller range of your best items? Sometimes less is more, for example, high-end retailers often use space to make their products look more valuable. Other retailers use large blocks of identical products to create impact, or stock vast amounts of products to sell them at a low price.

When you are next shopping look at a display and think about what factors the shop staff have considered when assembling it.

Activity   Investigating space and lighting

Identify one high-end shop and one bargain shop in your area. Compare how these shops use space, lighting and window displays. How do you think these affect customers' expectations of the shops?

Dressing mannequins and using posters

Clothing stores use **mannequins** to combine different products into an outfit. This helps customers to see themselves wearing those items and encourages them to buy. Posters can attract attention from across a shop floor, helping to bring customers to look at a display.

Making prices visible

One of the main reasons that potential customers decide not to make a purchase is that they do not immediately know the price. Some products must be displayed with a sell-by date or country of origin by law. Ensuring that space is provided for this information is an important part of the visual merchandiser's job.

 Key term

Mannequin – a model of a person on which clothes can be displayed.

Just checking

1   What is a planogram used for?

2   Explain one advantage of careful layout planning.

3   How can props and lighting be used to influence customers?

4   Describe three ways of using mannequins in a retail outlet other than displaying clothes.

5   Why is it important to make sure that customers can see the price of goods when you build a display?

How size and sub-sector affect visual merchandisers

The effect of size

The number of staff working on visual merchandising varies according to the size of the business. The larger a business is, the more likely it is to hire specialised staff such as merchandisers. A micro business might not be able to afford to employ staff to specialise in this area, instead relying on the skills of shop staff or the owner. As retailers grow into small and medium enterprises, they might employ staff from their head office to specialise in this role.

Large businesses might have a large team of visual merchandisers who work regionally or nationally, travelling from store to store. Large national department stores, such as Debenhams, have teams of merchandising staff in each store working from plans provided by senior merchandisers at their head office. Global brands, such as Apple, often provide detailed merchandising instructions to their stores in different countries to ensure a consistent brand image.

Activity   Researching visual merchandising services

Visit Retail Merchandising Services (RMS) and read about the merchandising services that they provide to retailers. What are the advantages and disadvantages for small retailers of employing visual merchandisers permanently rather than hiring experts when they need them? To access the website for this, visit Pearson hotlinks. You can access this by going to www.pearsonhotlinks.co.uk and searching for this title.

The effect of sub-sectors

Different retail sub-sectors take different approaches to visual merchandising. This is often dictated by the type of products that they sell.

Retailers in each sub-sector have their own unique requirements for storing goods.

- **Automotive** – goods, such as cars, take up a lot of space and cannot be moved easily or quickly.
- **Clothing** – clothing often requires hanging rails and shelving. Store layouts vary. Low-cost retailers use **gridiron layouts** where stock is displayed in rows. Upmarket outlets use a **boutique layout** where stock is laid out on tables.

Why do many clothing stores prefer to use a boutique, rather than gridiron, layout?

- **DIY** – safety is a concern in these stores as there are many heavy and dangerous products. Merchandisers must consider safety and inform customers about uses and dangers of products.
- **Electrical** – these retailers often use a closed-sell approach, shutting high-value products in cases and using dummy models on the shop floor.
- **Food and grocery** – foods and groceries are normally divided into three categories: chilled, frozen and ambient. Each has its own storage requirements. Chilled food requires fridges operating at 5 degrees, frozen food requires freezers at −18 degrees.
- **Footwear** – retailers like Matalan use a 'pile them high' approach. Mid-market companies, such as Office, use a boutique layout with sections for different brands.
- **Homewares** – this can include large items such as furniture, high-value items, such as art prints, and dangerous items, such as knives. Stores like Ikea group homeware products together based on different rooms in a house.
- **Music and video** – these items are often small and of high value, creating security problems for retailers.
- **Non-specialised stores** – these often use a combination of merchandising techniques depending on the type of products they sell.
- **Personal care** – high-value goods, such as razors, must be stored securely. Many items are small and attractive to thieves.
- **Second-hand stores** – these stores sell a wide range of goods, so visual merchandising must be based around what the store has in stock at the time or themes, such as Mother's Day.

? Did you know?

Some manufacturing companies employ freelance merchandisers to visit retail stores and manage displays, working from planograms provided by senior merchandisers. Some manufacturers, for example Schwartz (which makes spices), send their own merchandisers into retail stores to ensure that their stock is displayed to their specifications. This is especially useful to smaller firms.

What factors would you have to consider if you wanted a display of fruit to look attractive?

Just checking

1. Why might visual merchandising be more difficult for a small retail business?
2. Explain how a multi-national company plans and implements its visual merchandising.
3. Compare and contrast the features of visual merchandising in three different retail sub-sectors.

Responsibilities of visual merchandisers

Introduction

The responsibilities of visual merchandisers vary depending on the size of the business and the retail sub-sector it operates in.

 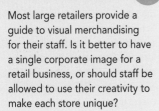
Giving feedback

Visual merchandisers provide vital information to the stakeholders of a business.

- **Head office** provides feedback from customers and requests for expensive props.
- **Buying teams** know which products sell well and what issues with packaging or product quality the business may have.
- **Members of the visual merchandising team** provide ideas for props and creative ideas for displays.
- **The departmental manager** advises on upcoming changes in displays.

Discussing client briefs

Freelance visual merchandisers review design briefs with their clients. It is important to confirm that the ideas in the brief are realistic. Cost is also important. Expensive lighting and props might reduce the profit that can be made.

Sourcing props

Retailers of different sizes face different challenges in sourcing props. National chains have to buy large enough quantities to use in every store. Smaller retailers have more freedom to choose props, but a smaller budget to buy them with.

Research

It is important to understand the local market. Researching customer **demographics** and regional attributes will tell you about your customers. For example, supermarkets such as Tesco display Diwali goods in areas with a large Hindu community.

Visual merchandising packs

In chains, head office visual merchandising staff create packs of planograms and point-of-sale (**POS**) materials. These are branded promotional items, such as posters, that can be displayed in store. The planogram includes guidelines on how to use props, to ensure consistency of appearance in all stores.

Liaising with staff

Visual merchandisers should liaise with sales staff and arrange coaching on how goods should be displayed for shop floor teams. Merchandisers can help staff to improve their ability to build displays and lay out a store.

Consistent brand image

The layout of a store and the image of the company must complement each other or customers may get the wrong impression of the business.

Working within a budget

Building elaborate displays can be expensive, but spending a lot on props reduces your profits. An important part of a design brief is the cost of a display.

Customer buying patterns

When they build a display, merchandisers need to understand different factors that customers consider when they make a purchase. These are shown in Figure 17.1.

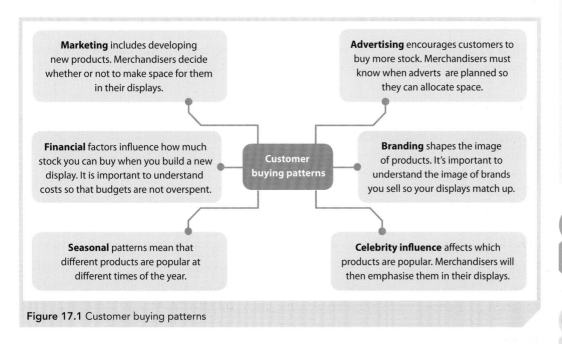

Marketing includes developing new products. Merchandisers decide whether or not to make space for them in their displays.

Advertising encourages customers to buy more stock. Merchandisers must know when adverts are planned so they can allocate space.

Financial factors influence how much stock you can buy when you build a new display. It is important to understand costs so that budgets are not overspent.

Customer buying patterns

Branding shapes the image of products. It's important to understand the image of brands you sell so your displays match up.

Seasonal patterns mean that different products are popular at different times of the year.

Celebrity influence affects which products are popular. Merchandisers will then emphasise them in their displays.

Figure 17.1 Customer buying patterns

 Link

This topic links to *Unit 2: Finance for Business.*

? **Did you know?**

Merchandisers must use colours and POS material that fit the company's brand image.

Assessment activity 17.1

2A.P1 | 2A.P2 | 2A.M1 | 2A.D1

Ken Hicks is the owner of a fashionable clothes store who wants to attract more customers and increase sales. He would like to learn more about visual merchandising and has hired you as a subject expert to advise him. He asks you to research two companies that you think are good at visual merchandising. Your evaluation of how the activities and responsibilities of a visual merchandiser impact on business success will help Ken make a decision. The retail businesses should be different sizes (i.e. one small and one large) and operate in different retail sub-sectors. Focus on at least three different activities that the visual merchandiser completes.

Use your research to prepare a presentation that uses examples to describe the various activities of visual merchandisers operating in your selected retail businesses. Look at how the size and sub-sector of retailers affects the responsibilities of a visual merchandiser. Analyse the differences between these responsibilities within the different retailers. Give examples from your chosen businesses.

Visual merchandising techniques

Introduction

Visual merchandising is about encouraging customers to buy products. Retail outlets are carefully designed according to how shoppers think when they are browsing, and there are a number of techniques used to maximise sales.

Psychological techniques

Merchandising staff use their knowledge of how the human mind works to build displays and create an environment in store that encourages people to buy.

- **How to appeal to customer senses:** Knowing how to stimulate customers will help merchandisers to create more effective displays.

Table 17.1 Ways to appeal to customers' senses

Sense	Example
Sight	Bold colours attract the eye to a display. Stock in colourful packaging is often 'blocked' to create a visual impact.
Touch	Customers are often encouraged to handle mobile phones to feel how light they are. Soft fabrics, such as wool, appeal to clothes shoppers.
Smell	Pleasant smells, such as fresh food or flowers, create a sense of freshness in store.
Taste	Providing food tasters encourages people to crave more. This is especially effective when tied to a special offer.
Hearing	Fast or slow music can be used to create different environments.

- **Discounts:** Special offers, such as 50 per cent off, encourage people to look at a display. This boosts sales of the discounted stock as well as complementary products.
- **Time limitations:** Highlighting when an offer ends encourages customers to make a purchase. If people think something will only be available for a short time, they will make an effort to visit your store.
- **Music:** The type of music playing influences how customers behave. Faster music keeps people moving quickly, slower music encourages people to take their time and browse.
- **Minimalist versus 'pile them high' displays: Minimalist** displays create an impression of exclusivity in premium retailers. '**Pile them high**' displays are better suited to discount retailers.

Display techniques

The type of display technique used by a retailer depends on the goods that they sell and the ambience they wish to create in store.

- **Open sell displays** – products are displayed on shelves or rails. Customers are free to handle goods as much as they like. This is more commonly used for lower value items.
- **Closed sell displays** – goods are displayed in cabinets or clear counters. This is often used by businesses like Tatty Devine or Storm which sell high value items, such as jewellery or watches. Customers cannot handle goods themselves; they need to ask staff to show them the items.
- **Themed displays** – these can be used for holidays, such as Easter, events, such as the World Cup, or for seasonal events, such as strawberries in summer.

Visual techniques

Sales staff can influence customers through a range of visual techniques. These may include:

- **Demonstration areas:** Having a space in store where staff can display products being used helps customers understand how complex goods such as tools work. This also works for toy stores and home goods in department stores.
- **Trials:** When a customer can 'try before they buy', they can be persuaded to buy items such as computers or cameras.
- **Sampling:** This is especially popular with products such as food or make up. Giving customers a small amount of a product helps them to see how much they like it.
- **Placement of add-ons:** Products, such as smartphones, often have items, such as cases, located nearby. This tempts customers to make an extra purchase.

What skills do demonstrators need to encourage customers to buy the product?

> **? Did you know?**
>
> Bakeries are often located at the rear of a retail outlet, so that the smell of bread spreads throughout the store, making customers hungry and encouraging them to make a purchase.

> **? Did you know?**
>
> Supreme, a skateboard store in Los Angeles, has a half pipe on their shop floor which allows staff to demonstrate and customers to try out skateboards, generating excitement in the store.

> **Activity**   Considering trials and sampling
>
> Car salesmen often take customers for a test drive so they can test a car. This helps customers to imagine themselves driving the car and to try out its features. Suggest **five** other situations where retailers could use samples or trials. For each, give **two** reasons why this encourages customers to buy.

Visual merchandising tools

Getting started

Where would you start if you were asked to build an eye-catching display? To change windows and rearrange shelving, you need to have a range of equipment to allow you to customise props and adapt the environment in your store.

Display props and working tools

Visual merchandisers work with a range of different tools. These allow them to change the structure of a retail outlet to fit their planograms and are illustrated in Figure 17.2. Their display props include:

- **Mannequins** – to show how clothing or jewellery can be combined.
- **Display units** – often provided by manufacturers, such as cardboard stands to hold DVDs of a recent film.

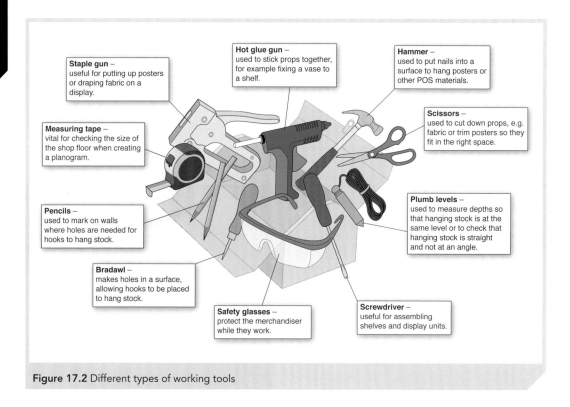

Staple gun – useful for putting up posters or draping fabric on a display.

Hot glue gun – used to stick props together, for example fixing a vase to a shelf.

Hammer – used to put nails into a surface to hang posters or other POS materials.

Measuring tape – vital for checking the size of the shop floor when creating a planogram.

Scissors – used to cut down props, e.g. fabric or trim posters so they fit in the right space.

Pencils – used to mark on walls where holes are needed for hooks to hang stock.

Plumb levels – used to measure depths so that hanging stock is at the same level or to check that hanging stock is straight and not at an angle.

Bradawl – makes holes in a surface, allowing hooks to be placed to hang stock.

Safety glasses – protect the merchandiser while they work.

Screwdriver – useful for assembling shelves and display units.

Figure 17.2 Different types of working tools

When merchandisers use these tools they must also consider other factors that will affect the success of a display. These factors include the following.

General corporate tidiness

Retail businesses often set standards of corporate tidiness so standards are consistently high across a chain. Staff often start and finish their day by vacuuming and dusting, and must make sure they work within health and safety guidelines.

Appropriate POS materials

Signs are normally approved at a business's head office for use throughout the organisation. These are known as corporate-approved signs. They are normally used by chains. Smaller stores might use a computer and a printer or a local print shop to create signs. Most stores avoid handwritten signs as they can look scruffy.

Creation of ambience

- **Targeted specialised lighting from spotlights:** This helps to highlight selected products or specific areas in store. Creative use of shadows can also create an appropriate mood in different parts of a store.
- **Floor lighting by fluorescents:** Lighting goods from below can create a glowing effect that draws customers' attention to specific products.
- **Varied floor coverings:** Using different surfaces, such as wood or coloured vinyl sheets, identifies different areas in a shop, helping customers to know where they are, and contributes to the feel of the store.
- **Use of mirrors:** This creates the illusion of space and light, making a small store seem bigger or making a small amount of stock look larger.

Importance and use of colour

Colours must be selected carefully. They should fit the brand image of the retailer and be appropriate to their products.

Display planning tools

Design drawings: Merchandisers in small stores might sketch their design ideas by hand.

Computer software: Large retailers can afford software that creates planograms. Merchandisers enter space measurements and details of their stock and a plan is generated instantly.

Planograms: These are diagrams showing the organisation of products in a display or on shelving. These can be drawn by hand or on a computer.

Give three reasons to explain why it so important that retailers plan their displays.

Activity Thinking about planograms

Look at examples of computer-generated planograms on the Shelf Logic website. To access the website for this, visit Pearson hotlinks. You can access this by going to www.pearsonhotlinks.co.uk and searching for this title. What advantages do computer-generated planograms have over hand-drawn planograms?

Effectiveness of displays

Retail businesses should identify what works well and how improvements can be made to make more effective displays. Merchandisers can measure their success by checking two key performance indicators – how many customers browse their store (**footfall**) and revenue received from purchases.

 Key term

Footfall – the number of people who walk into a store.

Just checking

1 Identify five tools used to construct a window display for a department store.

2 Why is tidiness important as well as good visual merchandising?

3 What factors would you consider if you were designing a POS display for a small shop?

Using visual merchandising techniques and tools successfully

Think about which displays capture your attention when you are out shopping.

Benefits of successful visual merchandising

If it is done well, good visual merchandising can bring a number of benefits to different groups.

Retail businesses

- **Increased customer traffic** – an attractive window display will increase footfall. Well-planned layouts will encourage customers to look at the whole store, not just certain aisles or displays.
- **Increased profitability** – good displays and an appropriate store layout will increase the amount of money that customers spend and cost less than an advertising campaign.

Customers

- **Improves accessibility to categories of goods** – if the layout of the store is logical, customers will find it easier to get to the goods that they need.
- **Improves self selection** – if a store is well planned, it is easier for shoppers to find what they want. This means that customers can spend as much – or as little – time as they want looking at goods in the store.
- **Informs on fashion and trends** – good merchandising promotes the latest trends and fashions, informing customers about new developments. Retailers, such as H&M, put clothes together on rails or mannequins, helping customers to see how to combine items. Technology stores, such as PC World, have displays that tell customers about new developments.

Suppliers

- **Increased sales** – goods displays encourage customers to buy products, which means that orders from retailers increase. This is why many suppliers help retailers by providing POS materials and props for merchandisers to use in their displays and layouts.
- **Improved marketing of their products** – featuring a brand on an aisle end or in a window can increase public awareness of that product. Choosing the right store is important – it must be relevant to your target market.

Activity Investigating POS materials

Visit the Cardworks website and read about the different types of point of sale material that they produce. To access the website for this, visit Pearson hotlinks. You can access this by going to www.pearsonhotlinks.co.uk and searching for this title. Name **ten** retailers, operating in different sub-sectors, and suggest how each retailer could use **two** different types of POS material.

Just checking

1 What is visual merchandising?

2 Describe five factors that can influence the work of a visual merchandiser.

3 Why is branding important when preparing a visual merchandising plan?

Assessment activity 17.2   2B.P3 | 2B.P4 | 2B.M2 | 2B.D2

Ken Hicks finds your presentation very helpful, and he is interested in hiring a visual merchandiser for his clothing retail business. Before he makes a final decision, he wants to find out more about visual merchandising and how it could benefit his business. Ken asks you to produce a booklet based on the two businesses featured in your presentation.

- Before you start writing your booklet you should research the techniques and tools used by visual merchandisers across different sub-sectors. Pick two retail businesses in different sub-sectors and use examples from these to compare the effectiveness of the techniques and tools for each of your selected retail businesses.

- Research the benefits of successful visual merchandising techniques for both of your businesses. So that Ken can understand these benefits explain them in your booklet, including how they benefit both customers and suppliers as well as the business.

Imagine you have to dress a mannequin in clothes that you own. Which would you pick to attract a customer?

Apply visual merchandising techniques

Supporting design ideas

The range of products/goods to be used in a display

Merchandisers must decide whether to promote a single item or a range of different goods. Focusing on one product can have more of an impact. The more items in a display, the less attention you draw to each one.

The type of props that will enhance products

Stores like Laura Ashley use a wide range of goods in a display, from chairs to candles. Since the store sells all these goods, there is no need to source props. Retailers that stock a limited range such as Calvin Klein must decide what to add to a display of clothes and mannequins to make it more interesting.

Any time constraints

Displays might be planned months in advance, but merchandisers might need to set them up overnight. Fashion stores, such as Zara, reflect new lines every week.

The use of appropriate support merchandise

Complementary products can enhance a display. If you are selling clothes, you might add shoes and jewellery to help customers accessorise their outfit.

Themes, activities, events, seasons

Displays and store layouts often benefit from specific links – such as Christmas, Mother's Day or Easter, and events, such as the World Cup are good opportunities to highlight new stock.

Signage, colour, styling and composition

These must match your products. Colours should fit brands, signage should use appropriate fonts. All of the elements should be assembled into a coherent image.

The direction of any lighting to be used

You may want to illuminate stock to highlight it, or use shadows to create an atmospheric environment. This will depend on your brand image.

Planning a positive retail environment

A **positive retail environment** entices customers into the store and encourages them to buy products. This is important for as there is a link between the retail environment and the number of sales made by the business. To design a positive retail environment, visual merchandisers should consider the following features.

Layout

- **A gridiron layout** is how stores such as supermarkets are laid out. Aisles are organised at right angles to one another in a repetitive pattern. Shelves are normally up to 10 foot high.
- **An open or free-flow layout** has stock placed in islands and clusters, allowing customers to move freely between them. There are no high shelves, providing clear **sightlines** throughout the store.
- **A boutique layout** is where products are organised into groups according to the brand. Products are displayed in a minimalist way on tables with clear sightlines throughout the store.

Activity	Considering floor layouts

Sketch a floor layout for a supermarket. Consider the type of goods sold, such as food and clothes. Label your diagram to explain which type of layout you have selected, and why.

Location of stock

This must be carefully thought out. Positioning at eye level helps customers notice goods. Aisle ends are normally the best space for special offers. Availability of space must be carefully considered, as every square inch of shelving is an opportunity to earn money. Space should only be allocated to goods that customers are interested in.

Displays should make sense and have some link with adjacent stock. For example, if a shelf contains pasta sauce, it makes sense for the next shelf to house pasta.

Customer traffic flow

The layout of your store will determine how customers move through it. The entrance to your store sets the tone for this.

Table 17.2 Types of store entrance

Flat	A solid wall, often glass. Fashion retailers often use this to make the shop floor part of a window display.
Recess	Doors are set back into a display window, allowing customers to see displays as they enter.
Open	This is inviting as there is no barrier between the street and the store.
Automatic doors	Can be inviting to customers, making the store more accessible to the elderly or disabled.
Multi-level outlets	Can combine different types of entrance, giving different departments their own identity.

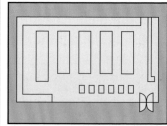

Gridiron

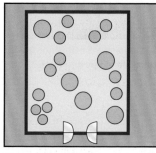

Open or free flow

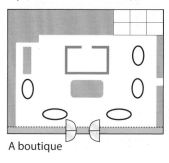

A boutique

Figure 17.3 The three styles of store layouts

 Key term

Sightline – an imaginary line from a person's eye across a shop to different areas or objects.

CONTINUED ▸▸

Visit a local retailer and conduct a survey. Look for examples of how they display new goods, the type of goods they double up on and the type of goods that are placed by the door. Discuss your findings as a group and suggest **three** ways that the retailer could improve the positioning of their goods.

Planning a positive retail environment

Position of fixtures

- Shelves at a 90 degree angle are useful for products with attractive packaging, such as ready meals or DVDs.
- Shelves at a 60 degree angle are used for products of an unusual shape so customers can see different surfaces at once.
- Shelves at a 45 degree angle are useful for stock, such as fresh fruit in punnets, allowing customers a clear view into containers.

Product positioning effects

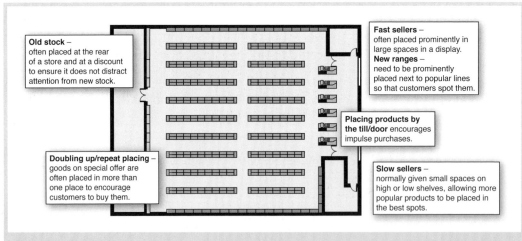

Figure 17.4 The layout of a store is specially designed to ensure customers are attracted to new stock

Product presentation

The type of presentation will depend on your products.

Table 17.3 Types of product presentation	
Hanging	Can be used for clothes and packaged goods. Allows customers to see the product at its full size.
Folding garments	Retailers such as Uniqlo create powerful effects by placing large amounts of products in the same colour in large blocks.
Boxed	Products in boxes can be stacked efficiently into shelves with little wasted space.
Pyramid	Free-standing stacks of boxes or tins, e.g. soft drinks, are a popular floor feature, giving height and colour to a display of ordinary goods.

Did you know?

Shelf edge labels (the price tickets placed next to products on a shelf) contain information for shelf stackers. Look closely and you will see information, such as the barcode number (EAN) and the number of facings that should be displayed.

Key terms

Facings – how many packages of the same product are placed next to each other on a shelf. More facings are given to popular products.

Accessibility

- **Height of shelves/fixtures:** Will your customers be able to reach your stock? What stock will be at eye level to promote higher sales?
- **Position of products:** Goods should be positioned logically in groups of similar products so customers can find them easily.
- **Direction of customer flow:** Will customers move clockwise or anticlockwise in the store? They should progress past key displays, such as sales promotions.
- **Sales desk/checkout position:** Will this be at the exit of your store or on a back wall? There should be a clear sightline to the till so customers know where to pay, or till points should be clearly indicated by overhead signs.
- **Exit location:** Can browsing customers easily leave the store? Making the exit hard to access can deter shoplifters, but honest customers might find this frustrating.
- **Effect of the transition zone:** The entrance allows customers to acclimatise to the shop. This is a good place to put special offers and signage to different areas.

> **Discussion point**
>
> Should goods aimed at children be positioned on the top shelf (so they are easily found by parents), or on the bottom shelf (so they are easily found by children)?

Common factors that influence customers

There are many factors that influence customer buying patterns and trends (see Table 17.4).

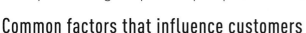

Table 17.4 Factors that influence customer buying patterns and trends

Factor	How this affects customer buying patterns and trends.
Marketing	As companies research customer needs and develop new products, merchandisers need to be aware of trends so that they can keep the ranges up to date.
Advertising	This can lead to increases in demand from customers. This means that merchandisers need to allocate more space to these products.
Branding	The retail environment needs to reflect the brand. For example, Toys R Us decorates the store aisles in the style of different toys, e.g. Barbie pink aisles.
Celebrity influence	The 'Kate Effect' has shaped British clothing retail. When Kate Middleton wears an outfit, retailers stocking a similar product sell large numbers.
Seasonal	Retailers change their store at different times of the year. Hearts and flower themes are appropriate for Valentine's Day, deck chairs and beach balls for the summer.
Financial	The cost of displays and layouts is important. The cost of buying stock, props and POS must be balanced against the potential to generate revenue and profit.

Improving the effectiveness of planograms

Feedback enables businesses to identify what works well and improve things that do not work. Customers might complain if they cannot find a product. Clients may provide feedback to freelance visual merchandisers about the effectiveness of their displays.

> **Activity**   Creating a display for an event
>
> In a group, identify different seasons and events that retailers can use to develop visual merchandising displays. In small groups, pick **one** event and decide what kind of display you would create for a shop of your choosing. Present your ideas to your fellow learners.

Designing a product display

Realistic product display designs

Good visual merchandisers always try to remember a number of key points:

Types of display

Retailers use different types of display depending on the type of goods they sell:

- **Small window display** – within a store, it is often possible to create display windows to highlight specific products or promotions.
- **Internal store display** – this is like a window display, but in an open area, for example a table or podium on the shop floor.
- **Shelf display** – this is a common type of display used in gridiron layouts in a store. The height must be planned carefully so that customers have clear sightlines.
- **Free standing display** – this can allow retailers to have extra selling space alongside their existing fixtures. Merchandising units provided by suppliers are particularly useful for this type of display.

Location and positioning of the display

Clearance stock is often positioned at the rear of the store, while new lines are given greater prominence near entrances or on aisle ends where customers will notice them.

- **Positioning of props** must be considered carefully. Their use should draw attention to the products you want to sell, but not divert attention away from them.
- **Space availability** – the amount of space in your store needs to be carefully planned. Adequate square footage needs to be allocated for each type of display.
- **Links with other stock** must be highlighted to customers. They should know where to find the products in your display.

Links to existing planograms

Your display should mirror existing plans to avoid confusing customers. If stock moves, you should add signs to help your customers find its new location.

Products to be displayed and the shape of the display

Symmetrical display – creates strong, attractive blocks of colour but products need to be in similarly shaped packaging.

Pyramid display – goods need to be in solid packaging and, though they have a strong visual impact, they are time-consuming to build.

Asymmetrical display – more suitable if you have a wider range of products of different shapes and sizes.

Table 17.5 The use and positioning of props

Prop	Use	Positioning
Stands	To display stock	On shelves, free standing on shop floors
Lighting	To emphasise items or create a mood	Above, below or behind stock, depending on the desired effect
POS material	To communicate product details and prices to customers	Next to products on shelves, adjacent to a display
Backdrops	To create a theme for a display or reinforce brand image	Behind a fixture or a display
Mannequins	To display stock, such as clothes, or to complement homewares	In window displays, against shop walls, on podiums on shop floors
Ceiling	To suspend stock or POS signs	Higher or lower ceilings can be added to different areas in a store to create different atmospheres
Wall coverings	To create a theme or promote a brand	Either on a single 'feature wall' for emphasis, or on every wall in a store to create a brand image throughout

Use of signage, themes and colours

Signs are used to guide customers to different departments in larger retailers or to identify till locations.

Themes can create a distinctive environment in one department or across a whole store.

Colours linked to brands, fashions or seasons influence customers' perceptions.

Appropriate ways of informing customers about products

Signs and POS material are normally professionally produced and consistent with the brand image of retailers. Most stores avoid handwritten signs as they can look scruffy.

Effective use of visual techniques

Many visual merchandisers take pictures of their work to help them learn from their mistakes. This also helps them to keep a record of good ideas so that they can use them again in the future.

? Did you know?

Many stores now use neon, plasma screen or LED displays instead of paper or card signs.

Activity   Designing a sign

Design a sign that would be suitable for a display of branded goods in a national retail chain. Label your signage to highlight how and why you have used colours, images and typefaces. Explain why your choices are suitable.

CONTIN'

Use of any corporate/manufacturers' policies

Retailers often use colour schemes to match those of a brand and logos are prominently displayed. Positioning of goods should fit brand image, for example, not next to competing products. Manufacturers might insist their own POS material is used.

Complementary merchandise placement

This can increase revenue by highlighting other goods to customers. For example, DIY stores keep brushes next to paint.

Health and safety considerations

Heavy goods might be kept on lower shelves. Some goods, such as fireworks, have special storage requirements and must be kept locked away. Displays must be safe, so goods do not fall on customers, and walkways must be left clear.

Ethical and cultural considerations of target customers

Customers' opinions influence merchandising. Keeping 'impulse buys', such as sweets, by tills is seen as unethical pressure on parents with children. Products, such as 'lads' mags', are displayed in obscured packaging to avoid offending customers. Cultural considerations must also be taken into account, such as clearly separating halal products.

Feedback from others

Customers can tell you what made them make purchases. Clients can feed back on how well a display matched brand image. This can be used to improve the effectiveness of product display designs.

Assessment activity 17.3   *Maths*   2C.P5 | 2C.P6 | 2C.P7 | 2C.P8 | 2C.M3 | 2C.D3

Ken Hicks wants you to carry out more research. He plans to expand his clothing store with a range of designer clothes for both men and women. Ken asks you to plan the layout of this new area and to produce a plan for a display of the new line. Consider how the new area fits with the space around it and ensure that it visually appeals to consumers. Be prepared to justify your plan in response to peer feedback.

- On your own, review the above design brief and plan a detailed positive retail environment for Ken's new clothes line. Label the different features of your plan.

- Once you have planned how the new area should appear, create a realistic and appropriate design for the display of the new clothing line. Ensure that you refer back to the design brief. Explain why you have selected each feature in your plan and the display design, including any psychological techniques that you have used.

- In a group, assess each other's display and store environment plans. Gather feedback on how well each works. Using this feedback, review your plans. Evaluate the effectiveness of your plans in response to the feedback and suggest improvements that would make them more effective.

Tip

Make sure that you use some of the feedback that you have gathered to justify your recommendations. You might choose to produce an action plan that shows how you think each piece of feedback could be addressed.

WorkSpace

▶ Carrie and Tim Morris

Joint owners of Booka bookshop

Tim and Carrie Morris opened Booka in 2009. They employ five members of staff who help to serve customers, replenish stock and assist with the cleaning of the store.

Careful research helps Tim and Carrie decide which books to stock. Sales records show which titles have been successful in the past, and conversations with representatives from publishers help them to decide which titles might succeed in the future.

Promotional tables provide prominent displays of books that have had good reviews or have recently been made into a television programme. Placing this table at the front of the shop encourages people to stop and browse. Tables placed next to the till are an important source of impulse buys.

The store is laid out carefully so that there is a natural 'flow' from section to section. This helps customers move through the shop and browse. Clear sightlines throughout the store mean that promotional displays near the front door are visible from the café area on the back wall.

Window displays are very important at Booka. Changing the displays regularly helps create a feeling of vibrancy in the shop. Thoughtful combinations of window art and carefully selected props make the shop stand out on the high street. Pictures of the windows are posted on social media sites, such as Twitter. This caught the eye of an American author, who was so pleased with the way Booka promoted her book that she agreed to make a personal appearance in store.

You can find out more about Booka on their website. Access this through Pearson hotlinks.

Think about it

The owners of Booka focus on creating a positive retail environment. Visit Booka's website to see photographs of the store. Then answer these questions.

1 Which visual merchandising techniques are used in Booka?

2 How does the use of these techniques benefit Booka's customers?

3 Why is research important when deciding which books to stock?

4 What does the term 'positive retail environment' mean?

5 To what extent do you think Booka provides a positive retail environment for its customers?

Glossary

A

Active listening – when you make an effort to hear not only the words someone is saying, but to understand the complete message that is being sent.

Adverse variance – this shows an overspend, i.e. more has been spent than planned.

Advertising budget – the amount of money that you make available to spend on adverts.

Agenda – a list of items to be discussed at a meeting.

Appraisal – the process by which a manager examines and evaluates an employee's work.

Archive – to place in long term storage.

Assets – items that a business buys that normally last a long time, such as a van or a computer.

Assets – items the business owns or money it is owed.

Audit – an official check on actions taken and financial claims made by a business.

Augmented product – the core product plus additional benefits or services.

B

B2B market – a business to business market in which one company sells products to another.

B2C market – a business to consumer market in which companies sell products directly to the public.

Bail – allowing an accused person to retain their freedom until the trial, often under certain conditions.

Body language – the messages communicated through facial expressions, gestures and posture.

Bounce rate – the percentage of visitors who leave a website after viewing only one page.

Boutique layout – where stock is laid out on tables in a minimalist style with clear sightlines throughout the store.

Breach of contract – fail to comply with one or more terms of a contract.

Breakeven point – the point where income and expenditure are equal.

Brownfield land – abandoned industrial or commercial land that can be used for new developments.

Budget holder – the person responsible for making sure that the planned budget is not exceeded.

Budgetary control – the process of checking what is actually happening, comparing this with the plan and taking action if things are not correct.

Budgeting – planning future expenditure and revenue targets with the aim of ensuring a profit is made.

Burden of proof – the responsibility to prove the defendant committed the crime.

Business context – the business situation that applies and which must be taken into consideration when the communication is selected and written.

Business format – the way a business is legally owned and operated.

C

Capital – money spent by the business on items which should last a long time (assets).

Carbon footprint – the amount of greenhouse gas that a business releases into the atmosphere as a result of its activities.

Cash balance – the amount of money forecast to be in the bank account after the net cash flow figure has been added or subtracted from the existing bank balance.

Cash inflows – the amounts of money entering a business's bank account.

Cash outflows – the amounts of money leaving a business's bank account.

Chain of production – the steps taken to turn raw materials into a finished product.

Chairperson – the leader of a meeting.

Cloud storage – a means of storing data remotely, rather than on the business computers or servers.

Code of practice – a set of guidelines that set standards of service customers can expect.

Collective responsibility – the entire group is responsible for the actions of any member of the group.

Compensation – payment of money to someone who has suffered a loss.

Competitive advantage – the advantage gained by offering more superior goods or services than competitors.

Consistent (customer service) – providing the same service over and over again to a high standard every time.

Consumables – goods that are used and replaced regularly, such as soap or toothpaste.

Consumer – a private individual who buys and uses goods and services.

Contribution – the selling price minus the variable cost of a product. This is the contribution the product makes to the fixed or overhead costs.

Coordinate – work together in an organised and complementary way so that everyone can do their job more easily and efficiently.

Core product – the basic product designed to meet user needs.

Corporate objectives – the actions necessary to achieve the aims set by the business.

Cost of sales – the cost of producing a product.

Credit trading – a business agreement that payment can be made some time after the event.

Cross-selling – suggesting a related product to a customer to increase the overall sale, for example a hairspray to go with a haircut.

Customer – an individual who makes a purchase from a business to use themselves or to give to others.

Customer profile – the main features of a particular group of customers.

Customer relationship management (CRM) – obtaining data on customers and using this to improve customer relationships and encourage customer loyalty.

D

Debtors (or trade receivables) – people who owe money to the business for goods or services they have received. Trade payables are traders to whom the business owes money because they have supplied goods or services.

Delegate – to assign work to someone within the team.

Demographics – the characteristics of an audience, usually including age, gender, pay, etc.

Design brief – a document which sets out specific details of how a display must look.

Desk research – the research of secondary data by studying reports or journals and checking facts and figures online.

Differentiate – make your business noticeably different from your competitors.

Direct distribution – selling your product direct to the market yourself.

Distribution channels – the route that a product or service takes to get to the market, e.g. manufacturer to wholesaler to retailer.

Dividends – amounts of money paid to people who have bought shares in a business.

Domain name – the unique name that identifies a website.

E

Economy – the system by which a country's money and goods are produced and used.

Efficiency – being competent and making the best use of resources, such as time or money.

Elasticity of demand – the degree to which demand (and sales) increases as prices fall, and vice versa.

Entrepreneur – someone who starts up a new business in order to make a profit, often in a way that involves financial risks (our word 'enterprise' comes from this French word).

EPOS – stands for 'electronic point of sale'. These are computer systems that record transactions and process payments.

Ergonomic – designed to enable people to work safely and productively.

Exchange rates – the value of an individual currency against other currencies.

Exclusion clause – a term which attempts to limit or restrict the liability of the supplier or limit the rights of the consumer.

Expenditure – money that a business spends.

Extension strategy – a plan to revive sales by adapting a product or launching in new markets.

External customers – outside businesses and individuals who want to make a purchase.

F

Face-to-face customer service – when the customer receives service in front of a member of staff.

Facings – how many packages of the same product are placed next to each other on a shelf. More facings are given to popular products.

Fairtrade – products which pay a fair wage to the producer.

Favourable variance – this shows an underspend, i.e. less has been spent than planned.

Financial year – the trading period over which a business collects information for their annual income statement (for example, a business might have a financial year that starts on 1 May and ends on 30 April).

Fixed costs (or indirect costs) – expenditure on items which does not change with the number of items sold or produced.

Floating – launching a public limited company on the Stock Exchange.

Footer – the bottom section of a document.

Footfall – the number of people who walk into a store.

Freelance – a person with specialist skills who works independently. They can be hired for a short period of time when their skills are needed.

Front-line customer service staff – those people who are a customer's first point of contact with the business.

Functionality – refers to the way the website operates, or functions.

G

Gap in the market – when a customer need is not currently met by existing products or services.

Greenbelt land – an area which is protected from building and development to allow people in cities access to open space and natural environments.

Gridiron layout – where stock is displayed in rows, normally at 90 degree angles to one another.

Gross profit – the money made from selling a product (the sales revenue) after the cost of producing that product (cost of sales) has been deducted.

H

Hard copy – the term used for a paper copy of a document.

Header – the top section of a document.

Hot group – a group of highly motivated employees who work together on a project that is above and beyond their normal duties.

I

Income – money which is paid into a business.

Integrity – the quality of being honest and having strong moral principles.

Interest rates – the cost of borrowing money.

Internal customers – colleagues who work in the same organisation and need you to do something.

Interpersonal skills – being able to speak to customers and read their body language.

J

Job description – a statement that lists the main elements of a job and the tasks done by the job holder.

K

Key performance indicator – a way of measuring how well a retail business or a retail employee is performing.

L

Legislation – relates to the laws of the land which everyone must obey.

Liabilities – amounts of money which a business owes.

Limited liability – the owners are only responsible for debts up to the amount they have invested in the business.

Loss – occurs when expenditure is more than revenue.

M

Mannequin – a model of a person on which clothes can be displayed.

Manufacturer – a business which transforms raw materials into finished goods, ready to be sold.

Margin of safety – the amount by which sales would have to fall to reach the breakeven point.

Market – the customers for a particular product or service.

Market research – finding out customer views and opinions.

Market segment – a section of the market with common characteristics.

Market share – the percentage of the total sales of a product accounted for by one company.

Marketing mix – the combination of product, price, place and promotion. This is often referred to as the 4 Ps.

Marketing plan – the document which sets out the marketing activities necessary to achieve the business aims.

Mass market – all the consumers in one market.

Master budget – this comprises all the departmental budgets brought together for the whole business.

Medium – how you choose to advertise to your target market.

Meeting brief – a summary of the main requirements for a meeting.

Message – what you want to tell your customers.

Microbusiness – a business which has fewer than ten staff.

Minimalist – these displays use space to create an open and high-value atmosphere. These are most commonly used by jewellery or high-end fashion stores.

Minutes – the official record of the discussions and decisions taken at the meeting.

N

Net cash flow – the difference between the cash inflow and outflow figures over a particular time period.

Net profit – the money made from selling a product after all costs (expenditure) have been deducted from the gross profit.

Niche market – a small group of customers for a specialised item.

Non-verbal communication – the process of communication through body language, facial expressions, gestures, eye contact and tone of voice.

O

Operating costs (or running costs) – money spent on a regular basis to keep a business running.

Organisational procedures – step-by-step instructions issued to staff to ensure consistent standards.

Outsource – hire an outside firm to do a task, such as distributing goods or installing an ICT system.

Overdraft – this occurs if a business pays more out of its bank account than it has in credit. The bank may allow this but will make an extra charge.

Overheads – the everyday running costs of the business.

P

Perception – what a customer or consumer thinks about something.

Performance targets – levels of achievement, for example in sales and production.

Person specification – linked to the job description, it states the skills and abilities needed to do the job effectively.

Personal audit – a summary of your knowledge, skills, attributes and interests.

Pile them high – these displays are used by retailers that sell items at a low price.

Pitch – the proposal made by a salesperson to sell their products to a potential customer.

Pixel – the smallest part of a digital image. It is a tiny square that is easily seen if you increase the size of the image. The more squares it contains, the higher its resolution.

Planogram – a diagram showing how stock and shelving should be laid out in a display.

Policy – the general direction which the business wants to move in.

POS – point-of-sale materials, such as posters and branded shelf-edge labels, can be used in store as part of displays.

Positive retail environment – a retail store which is well laid out and creates an enjoyable shopping experience for its customers, while using merchandising techniques to maximise sales and profits.

Pricing strategies – alternative methods of deciding the best price to charge.

Product portfolio – the range of products produced by a business.

Productivity – the amount of output produced by a person or industry.

Profit – occurs when revenue is more than expenditure.

Prop – object which is used in a display to complement stock and create visually stimulating displays.

Q

Quorum – the minimum number of people who must be present at a formal meeting to allow official decisions to be made.

R

Regulations – these interpret the law and state simply what people have to do to abide by the law.

Remand – keeping someone in custody.

Remedy – the method used to put things right if you are wronged in law.

Remote customer service – when a business offers customer service by telephone or online.

Reserves – money that has been saved from previous profitable years.

Retail sector – the section of the national economy made up of retail businesses.

Retailer – a business which sells goods directly to the public.

S

Sales environment – the place where sales are made.

Saturated market – a market which is full of similar products which now have little value to consumers.

Segment – to identify and divide customers into groups sharing certain characteristics.

Service deliverer – a member of staff who delivers customer service.

Service specification statement – issued by an organisation giving details of the level of service to be expected.

Share capital – the amount of money invested in the business by the shareholders.

Sightline – an imaginary line from a person's eye across a shop to different areas or objects.

Site map – shows the content of the site hierarchically, with links to each section.

Situational analysis – when a business looks at its own position in the market and assesses how it could be affected by trends and developments.

SMEs – stands for 'small and medium enterprises'.

Social enterprise – a business which uses its profits or surplus to fulfil social objectives, such as helping others.

Specific performance – an order by the court to take a certain action.

Start-up costs – the amount of money spent setting up a business before it starts trading.

Stock take – the stock in a retail outlet is counted to ensure that records are up to date.

Storyboard – a graphic representation of the site and how each page links.

Strategy – how the business intends to achieve its objectives.

Sub-sector – a specific category of products or services offered by a retailer.

Supervisor – the person who works above you and who gives you instructions. You are his or her 'subordinate'.

Supply chain – the stages that goods pass through between the producer that makes them and the retailer that sells them.

T

Target customer – the customer that a business aims to supply.

Target market – the section of the market the business aims to supply.

Team leader – the individual who has overall responsibility for the team and its goals.

Team roles – the parts or roles individuals take on in a team. Each part has a particular skill and way of behaving, and people in the team can take on one or more roles.

Total costs – the total amount of money spent running a business over a certain period of time (e.g. a month).

U

Unique Selling Point (USP) – a special feature of a product (or service) that makes it easy to promote and sell.

Unlimited liability – the owners are personally responsible for all debts, even if this means selling personal possessions.

Up-selling – promoting a more profitable alternative to increase the value of the sale.

Usability – having a website that is easy for visitors to use.

V

Value for money – belief that the price paid is fair.

Variable costs (or direct costs) – costs which vary according to the number of items sold or produced.

Variance – occurs when there is a difference between a planned budgeted figure and the actual measured result.

Verbal communication – what you say and how you say it.

Visual merchandising – the display of products (within the shop and in the window) and the layout of the shop floor.

W

'What if approach' – a way in which managers plan for the future. They look beyond the current situation to consider what might be the result if they make certain changes.

Wholesaler – a business which sells large quantities of goods to other businesses.

Wholesaler – a company which sells goods in bulk to retail businesses.

Word of mouth reputation – customers tell their friends, family and colleagues about their experiences with an organisation.

Working capital (or net current assets) – money the business can raise quickly which is calculated by deducting current liabilities (all current debts owed by the business) from current assets (all money owed to the business at the current time).

Index